Date label overleaf →

Propaganda and Democracy is the first comprehensive study on the relationship of propaganda to participatory democracy in the United States during the twentieth century. The muckrakers were the first critics to question whether the standard practices of communication industries, such as advertising and public relations, undermined the ability of citizens to gather enough reliable information in order to participate meaningfully in society. The communication industry has countered that propaganda merely circulates socially useful information in an efficient manner and, further, that propaganda is harmless to democracy because of competition and professional codes. Agreeing that propaganda is neutral, quantitative social scientists justify their own efforts to render persuasion more effective through experimental and survey research. Still others argue whether citizens can intelligently discuss anything without a formal education in critical analysis. This study critically examines these various schools of thought in an effort to determine and understand the contribution and effects of propaganda in a democratic society.

PROPAGANDA AND DEMOCRACY

University of Chester
Warrington Campus
LIBRARY

Telephone: 01925 534284

**This book is to be returned on or before the last date stamped below.
Overdue charges will be incurred by the late return of books.**

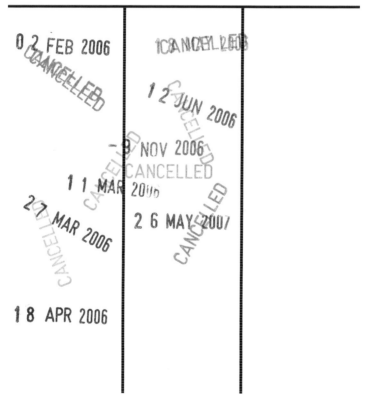

Cambridge Studies in the History of Mass Communications

General Editors

Kenneth R. M. Short, *University of Houston*
Garth Jowett, *University of Houston*

Cambridge Studies in the History of Mass Communications includes books that examine the communications processes and communications systems within social, cultural, and political contexts. Inclusive of empirical, effects-based research, works in this series proceed from the basis that the histories of various media are important means to understanding their role and function in society. The history of a medium – its pattern of introduction, diffusion, acceptance, and effects – varies in each society, interacting with and, in turn, shaping its culture. Moreover, each society reacts differently to the introduction of a medium, and regulatory policies are shaped by both political and cultural forces. The detailed study of various communications forms and the complex message systems is now understood to be the key to unraveling the evolution of modern society and its culture.

Other Books in the Series

PROPAGANDA AND DEMOCRACY

The American Experience of Media and Mass Persuasion

J. Michael Sproule
San Jose State University

CAMBRIDGE
UNIVERSITY PRESS

CAMBRIDGE UNIVERSITY PRESS
Cambridge, New York, Melbourne, Madrid, Cape Town, Singapore, São Paulo

Cambridge University Press
The Edinburgh Building, Cambridge CB2 2RU, UK

Published in the United States of America by Cambridge University Press, New York

www.cambridge.org
Information on this title: www.cambridge.org/9780521470223

First published 1997
This digitally printed first paperback version 2005

A catalogue record for this publication is available from the British Library

Library of Congress Cataloguing in Publication data
Sproule, J. Michael, 1949–
Propaganda and democracy : the American experience of media and
mass persuasion / J. Michael Sproule
p.   cm.
Includes index.
ISBN 0-521-47022-6 (hardback)
1. Propaganda – United States – History – 20th century.   2. Mass
media – Political aspects – United States.   3. Government and the
press – United States – History – 20th century.   I. Title.
HM263.S648   1997
302.23´0973 – dc20   96–3044
                                                               CIP

ISBN-13 978-0-521-47022-3 hardback
ISBN-10 0-521-47022-6 hardback

ISBN-13 978-0-521-02200-2 paperback
ISBN-10 0-521-02200-2 paperback

To Alfred McClung Lee and Elizabeth Briant Lee

CONTENTS

Illustrations follow page 164

ACKNOWLEDGMENTS

I first became interested in the topic of this book when, as an undergraduate student entirely innocent of the term *propaganda*, I was puzzled by the ability of perfectly absurd ideas to garner enthusiastic support. A history major adrift on a large Midwestern campus during the "years of hope, days of rage" (to borrow Todd Gitlin's phrase), I gravitated to the debate team and, as often happens, to associated study in speech communication.

Browsing about the curriculum, I discovered that works on rhetoric, more than anything else I had encountered, salved my curiosity about why and how ideas circulated with consequences. My first mentor in this regard was James L. Golden, whose work amply demonstrated that rhetorical study and contemporary politics made for an interesting mix. Later, in a seminar on international broadcasting, Walter B. Emery encouraged my explorations into matters of propaganda. In the course of researching this subject, I came across a number of intriguing publications from something called the Institute for Propaganda Analysis (IPA). I filed these away for later reference.

After several years of publishing small studies on facets of rhetorical theory and practice, I was casting about for a larger project. Returning to my notes on the IPA, I resolved that if I received a summer stipend from the National Endowment for the Humanities (NEH), I would set up to begin work on an article about the Institute. That first small grant from the NEH allowed me to make my early, tentative contacts with the people and the publications of the IPA. After thoroughly (I thought) preparing to interview Alfred McClung Lee, I discovered in my first ten minutes with Al that he could, without intending to overwhelm me, name several score of people and ideas that I never had heard of – but that were absolutely essential for my research. For the next dozen years, the Lees, Al and Betty, extended to me every possible help and encouragement.

My study would have been smothered had not the NEH rewarded

my tentative formulations with a fellowship that permitted me a year of full-time research in 1983–1984. Much to my consternation, the fellowship period did not permit me even to sense clearly what might be the final parameters of the study. In the years that followed, it proved serendipitous that other responsibilities kept me from devoting all my energies to a topic that frequently seemed, despite a furious pace of reading, to have no discernible end point. Indiana University Southeast and the NEH intervened with travel grants that allowed me to complete my documentary research and interviews. Librarians and staff members at more than a dozen documentary centers named hereafter extended to me great courtesy and invaluable help. San Jose State University contributed two grants to permit transcriptions of my many, lengthy interview tapes. Three irrepressible undergraduate communication majors – Mozhgan Novbakhtian, James Nichols, and Vanessa Greenwood – helped me to complete most of the final research for the book when they became propaganda-citation detectives as part of their senior seminars.

When at this time no more fellowship money seemed in the offing, my wife, Betty, generously agreed for me to take an unpaid professional leave to complete the first draft of this book. With the encouragement of Garth Jowett, this manuscript secured for me a publishing relationship with Cambridge University Press, whose editor, Beatrice Rehl, gently but firmly pressed me to shape a 1,000-page typescript into a more manageable form. Reviews by Victoria O'Donnell and Christopher Simpson supplied cogent guidance. A sabbatical awarded by San Jose State gave me the time to complete a final draft and to tie up many other time-consuming details relating to the work.

No list of persons who helpfully nudged me along would be complete without recognition of my colleagues in Indiana and in California. Conversations with and comments from these good persons have steered me in many a useful direction. Family members, most immediately Betty, John, and Kevin, have tolerated my lengthy preoccupation with screen and keyboard, and for their forbearance, I am grateful. My parents, John and Katherine, have given me lifelong support.

I thank the Speech Communication Association for permission to include in Chapter 1 material from my article in the *Free Speech Yearbook* 24 (1985).

CHAPTER 1

PROLOGUE: DISCOVERING PROPAGANDA

For opponents of U.S. entry into the Great War, popular pacifist sentiment was at a low ebb in the summer of 1918. In late 1914, one could still attract a following by announcing formation of a group to fight increases in U.S. military spending, as when Oswald Garrison Villard, pacifist editor, founded the League to Limit Armaments. But by 1918, most of Villard's erstwhile followers had long seen the new light on the Great War. Among those now sounding the war tocsin were such former champions of the League as Nicholas Murray Butler, president of Columbia University, and the Reverend Newell Dwight Hillis of Plymouth Church, Brooklyn. Backing their new convictions with action, Butler was busy firing Columbia professors for pacifist expressions, and Hillis had become a sought-after speaker at Liberty Bond rallies on account of his repertoire of German war atrocity stories.[1]

Eugene V. Debs still opposed the war. This socialist union organizer and four-time presidential candidate traveled to Canton, Ohio, in June 1918 to protest the jailing of fellow socialists for opposing U.S. participation in the Great War. Debs aimed to rally the socialists, some of whom now favored fighting for Bolshevik Russia, into standing by their earlier antiwar convictions. For his part, the old activist held fast to the April 1917 declaration of the Socialist Party that had characterized the war as a capitalist scheme to salvage U.S. loans to the Allies through the blood of the working class.

Addressing the crowd from a platform placed so that the three jailed socialists could see him, Debs spoke of the irony of free speech suppressed by a nation allegedly fighting for democracy. He charged that the Russian Bolsheviks had found in the Czarist archives evidence of secret Allied treaties "showing that the purpose of the Allies is exactly the same as the purpose of the central powers – plunder." Debs defended unionists and praised their defiance of Wall Street in contrast to the compliance of the preachers: "When Wall Street says 'war,' every pulpit in the land yells 'war.'" Predicting that capitalism in the United

1

States would undergo the kind of crisis that had brought about the Bolshevik seizure of power in Russia, Debs preached continued resistance to capitalism's world war. "They want our eyes focused on the junkers of Berlin so we'll not see those in our own country," he contended. Declaring solidarity of sentiment with those imprisoned, Debs affirmed, "I'd rather be a free soul in jail than a coward on the street."[2]

Debs might have been more careful about what he wished for. By challenging the nation's reigning sentiments, by speaking against ideas put forth by America's first institutionally coordinated program of national propaganda, Debs soon would earn the right to conduct his final (fifth) run for the presidency from behind bars. Until many months after the Armistice, few would mourn his fate.

Debs v. The United States

June 16, 1918, was a risky time for Debs's antiwar rhetoric. By summer 1918, popular enthusiasm for war was the official order of the hour in America. The discursive atmosphere of the nation at large was reflected in patriotic storm clouds hovering over Debs in Northern Ohio. The commissioner of Cleveland, Ohio's, playground system was in the process of organizing a summer program of military regimen for children. Youngsters were trained to make replicas of rifles and bayonets for use in drills under direction of a military instructor. The loyalty of Frank B. Willis, former Ohio governor, was under attack as a result of the revelation that, in 1915, he had written a letter opposing shipments of U.S. arms to Britain and France. For those caught up in the mindset of 1918, such a peacetime expression bordered on treason. Stories appearing in Cleveland's *Plain Dealer* newspaper reported ten- and twenty-year sentences to "so-called conscientious objectors." Feature stories in the paper included a number of lurid tales, among them how the sinking of the passenger liner *Lusitania* in 1915 had been part of a plot involving the German ambassador to the United States.[3]

Eugene Debs was not unaware of the risks he ran in addressing the Ohio Socialist Party convention audience on the topic of war. Active as a speaker during the preceding weeks, Debs had been anticipating arrest for some time. As he looked down from his Canton platform, Debs could not have overlooked the presence of various federal agents, local police, and American Protective League operatives interspersed in the crowd of 1,200. Possibly he observed that many listeners, neatly attired in coat and vest, eagerly were scribbling down what he said to the throng gathered in Nimisilla Park. It would prove the case that the recollections of one energetic note jotter, Clyde R. Miller, would have significant impact on Debs's itinerary and place of residence for the next few years.

Miller, reporter for the *Plain Dealer,* was the product of a central Ohio family characterized by its deep Methodist faith and traditional Republican politics. Miller was typical of the idealistic young men and women of the era who found themselves pulled along in the shifting currents of sentiment both for war and peace. Counting himself among those who "resented the invasion of Belgium and France by the Germans," Miller nevertheless came under the spell of Woodrow Wilson's policy of American neutrality. Casting aside his "congenital" preferences for the Republican Party, Miller voted for Wilson and for neutrality in 1916. Within months, however, Miller ardently supported American entry into the Great War.

Backing his new pro-war convictions with action, Miller tried to enlist in the Canadian armed forces some weeks in advance of the U.S. declaration of war, failing only because of his poor eyesight. After America's decision for war in April 1917, Miller similarly was rejected by the three branches of the U.S. armed forces. He continued working as a reporter but remained, as he later recalled, "eager to do what I could to win the war." Assigned to the federal beat, Miller found it possible to make patriotic contributions to victory through stories boosting the U.S. district attorney and the regional office of the Justice Department's Investigation Bureau. "There were many front-page stories to write about spy-hunts, about saboteurs in munitions factories, about persons guilty of treasonable utterances, about worthless slackers who sought to evade selective service." Miller even accompanied members of the American Protective League, the patriotic group loosely affiliated with the Justice Department, on their raids of homes in the ethnic working-class neighborhoods of Cleveland. As did many others at the time, he condoned such lawlessness as worthy enthusiasm in support of a holy cause. Miller's goal as reporter was to help the war effort by fanning the emotions of war, promoting the righteous fears and hates that made the conflict so compelling to Americans formerly accustomed to disinterest in European intrigues and military operations.

Responding to a call by his city editor to cover the Canton meeting of the Ohio socialists, Miller set out with explicit instructions to report Debs's position on the war. Accordingly, Miller sought out the renowned socialist in Canton's Courtland Hotel somewhat before the scheduled address. Miller questioned Debs about his views on the fight for democracy. Miller later recalled that "from his eyes, his look, his manner I had the feeling that he was the kind of man my dear old Methodist aunt would call Christlike, and yet he said things which I thought were horrible." Debs told Miller of his disgust at the idea of American and German youth extinguishing each other's lives so that the rich and powerful in both lands might enjoy continued prosperity. Dismissing pro-war arguments as efforts to take in vain the names of God and country, Debs affirmed his intention to "do all I can to oppose this war, to oppose our young men going over to fight in this war." Miller was struck by the contrast between Debs's inspiring personal charisma and the traitorous heresy he espoused.[4]

Later in the day, Miller was among those in the audience as Debs addressed the Ohio socialists. Miller wired to the *Plain Dealer* enough about Debs's speech and the preceding interview to fill two or three front-page columns. Soon after sending the story, the thought came to Miller that Debs's utterances clearly violated the Espionage Act. Miller placed a long-distance call to E. S. Wertz, the U.S. district attorney, to inquire about the possibility of prosecution.

> After I had sent in the main story, I called up the District Attorney, whom I knew well enough to call by his first name, and said, "Ed, this is what happened. Are you going to let this fellow get away with it?" Said the District Attorney: "No man is too big to violate the Espionage Act. I will ask for his indictment." And so I phoned that in. It made a nice Page One box. The story was given a big play. The Press Services picked it up; it became Page One all over the country.[5]

Although officials in the Department of Justice in Washington cautioned against prosecuting Debs for his remarks at Canton, Wertz, now quoted nationally as likely to ask for an indictment, proceeded to put the case to a grand jury. Within two weeks, Debs was under arrest on charges of sedition.

It was apparent at the time of Debs's arrest that his case would be a matter of national significance in determining the potency of the Espionage Act as a weapon against wartime dissenters. Debs came to be charged with ten violations of the Espionage Act of 1917, as amended in 1918, including making false statements to interfere with the operation of U.S. military forces, promoting the success of enemies of the United States, attempting to cause insubordination of military forces, attempting to obstruct recruiting, speaking disloyally about the government, making statements calculated to bring the government and its symbols and agencies into disrepute, encouraging resistance to the government, and opposing the cause of the United States. Although the government initially had thrown the book at Debs, only four of the ten charges were presented to the jury, those regarding incitement of insubordination, obstructing recruitment, encouraging resistance, and opposing the cause of the United States.[6]

Pressed by allegations that their client's remarks at Canton were treasonable, Debs's attorneys sought to characterize the Nimisilla Park address as exercise of the Constitutional freedom to discuss the war's general aims and objects. In this connection, Clyde Miller took the stand as a star witness for the prosecution. Attorneys for the government questioned Miller about his hotel-lobby interview with Debs and employed this testimony to establish the defendant's attitude at the time of his address. Miller specifically contributed to the government's effort to enter into the record certain statements from the 1917 antiwar Declaration of the Socialist Party. This declaration had used inflammatory language to characterize the war as capitalist "trickery and treachery" against the working classes and, further, encouraged socialists to use demonstrations, petitions, and persuasion to oppose legislation that would conscript the citizenry and censor the rights of free speech. Miller had ascertained during his interview with Debs that the socialist leader supported this statement of policy by his party.[7]

Critical to Debs's case was the judicial construction of the Espionage Act. Unfortunately for Debs, as for others tried at the time, the presiding judge allowed the law to be interpreted broadly, such that Debs could be convicted on three counts of promoting insubordination, obstructing recruiting, and encouraging resistance even though his Canton address did not specifically incite the listeners to any of these particular acts. Debs was sentenced to ten years in prison by U.S. District Judge D. C. Westenhaver, who characterized Debs's address as "anarchy pure and simple" in that it might have the effect of making citizens less eager for enlistment and for other wartime services to their country. Hopes that Debs's conviction might be reversed upon appeal were dashed by the U.S. Supreme Court when Justice Oliver Wendell Holmes affirmed the propriety of convicting Debs for treason on the basis of the "reasonably probable effect" of his words to obstruct the war effort. According to Holmes, Debs's treasonous intent was proved, not only by the words of the Canton speech itself, but also by his stated opposition to the war as shown both in remarks (to Miller) before the speech as well as in his own statement to the jury.[8]

As Debs and Miller walked together from the Cleveland courtroom, the old socialist put his arm around the young reporter and told Miller not to feel badly for what he had done. Debs remarked that Miller had testified honestly about the interview and speech, and he reflected that the two of them had honestly come to different conclusions about the facts of the war. Debs added: "Perhaps in twenty years you will think differently about this matter; perhaps in twenty years I too might think differently, because neither of us knows all the facts."[9]

As it turned out, only a few months were to pass before one of the two changed his opinion about the war. Soon after the trial of Debs, Miller took service in France with the Education Corps of the American Expeditionary Force. His observations and conversations abroad convinced Miller that "Debs had been more right than wrong about the war." Upon his return to the United States, Miller labored to secure a pardon for Debs, speaking to such fellow Ohioans as Secretary of War Newton D. Baker and Senator Warren G. Harding. Much later, in 1937, Miller founded the Institute for Propaganda Analysis to consummate his atonement for having helped to prosecute and, in effect, to persecute Debs for the exercise of critical free speech. Miller's institute, as will be shown, became a focal center in the effort to sort out the relationship of free speech and social survival, of democracy and propaganda.

Miller's discovery of a forest of propaganda within the tall trees of wartime public opinion was representative of how, in the aftermath of the Great War, many Americans took a new look at the agencies of mass communication. This revolution in opinion, however, does not explain why skepticism about the war's origins and ideological trimmings carried so little weight in 1917–1918 among writers, teachers, preachers, and other intellectuals. The explanation lies in the wartime work of the literati who were deeply implicated in the era's rampant opinion control. What set leading Americans against Debs was a propagandized climate of opinion that, until after the Armistice, was seldom recognized as such even by alert commentators.

Wartime Persuasions

A simplistic mindset on the Great War began to work its way into American public opinion within days of the first cannon shots on the Western Front. The British Navy immediately cut Germany's cable links to the United States, forcing American newspapers to rely on reports filtered through censorship in London. In July 1914, 30 percent of the front-page news from Europe originated in German sources as contrasted to 4 percent during the first half of August. The tendency for war news to be filtered through London and Paris was most pronounced during the first weeks of belligerency and also during the *Lusitania* crisis of May 1915, the two periods when European hostilities commanded maximum front-page treatment in American papers.[10]

Indirect control of war news through cable censorship and courting of American correspondents was accompanied by direct efforts to win over the sympathy of Americans. Britain's attempt at positive promotion was organized by Sir Gilbert Parker, a Canadian novelist, who set up an official, though secret, propaganda bureau in the United States. Beginning with names drawn from *Who's Who in America*, Parker's group developed a mailing list of some 200,000 U.S. opinion leaders. Parker's bureau sent out to this selected group round after round of pamphlets, interviews, and speeches articulating Britain's official view that the Great War was simply a matter of stemming German aggression and atrocities. The British materials usually arrived with a friendly letter from Parker or a note from a source known to the recipient. The publications themselves contained no indication that they were prepared and sent out as part of an official government publicity campaign. Parker also sent English newspapers to 360 U.S. papers, provided films of the war, sent volumes of documents on the war to U.S. colleges and libraries, and, as Parker put it, "advised and stimulated" many Americans to write favorably of Britain's cause. Parker's organization kept up correspondence with prominent Americans of every profession and kept liaison with Anglophilic organizations and groups.[11]

Early installments of English propaganda had carried allegations of German atrocities; however, it was the Bryce Report that became most significant in helping these inflammatory tales to win a respectful hearing in the United States. Sensing the advantage of making German atrocities a centerpiece of Allied war communications, the British government appointed a committee, headed by Lord James Bryce, former British ambassador to the United States, to investigate charges of German horror in Belgium. Bryce's report, based on more than a thousand depositions taken from Belgian refugees, possessed considerable credibility not only because of its status as an official government document but also since the report itself took pains to argue for the validity of the accounts given by the refugees. In the United States, the Bryce Report carried additional prestige owing to its appearance under the editorship of a familiar friend whose book, *The American Commonwealth*, was a widely used college textbook on government.[12]

The sixty-one pages of the *Report of the Committee on Alleged German Outrages* were organized both geographically, according to region, and topically, according to the type of atrocity. The atrocities were further divided into offenses against civilians (e.g., attacks on women and children) and those against combatants (e.g., killing of prisoners). The depositions themselves, presented in a 296-page documentary appendix, were organized geographically and were followed by other evidences of German horror, including both excerpts from diaries purportedly taken from German soldiers and official proclamations by German occupation authorities.

Will Irwin, American muckraker and U.S. war correspondent, had no illusions about the harshness of German conduct in Belgium; but he nevertheless identified the "two tricks" on which the Bryce Report was based. First, there was no cross-examination of witnesses; second, "consciously or unconsciously the commission took advantage of a small immorality common among story-tellers – the human impulse to make yourself the hero or the eyewitness of an interesting episode which you have picked up in conversation or in your reading."[13] From my own close examination of thirty of the depositions, nineteen appeared to be essentially hearsay renderings. Furthermore, five alleged firsthand reports contained glaring internal improbabilities as when one respondent described events allegedly taking place inside a house observed from a distance outside. Of the six apparently credible depositions, four are highly sketchy as to the details of what happened. Yet, despite the internal weaknesses of the Bryce document (and regardless of its having been discredited by the 1930s), its effect on American public opinion in 1915 was significant. Proof positive seemingly was at hand to sustain the Allied claim that theirs was a contest of good versus evil.

German officials and pro-German Americans established a competing propaganda cabinet to coordinate a program similar to that of the British, although smaller. The German effort, "always logical, but never psychological," tended, more than Britain's, toward lawyerly technicalities.[14] Further, unlike the British, who carefully kept propaganda work separate from secret intelligence operations, many of Berlin's operatives worked on propaganda by day and participated by moonlight in efforts to foment strikes or to sabotage American plants producing war materiel for the Allies. Pro-Ally agents in the German camp leaked incriminating documents about Berlin's machinations to the American press, thereby alarming the Wilson administration. When U.S. Treasury agents gained possession of a cache of receipts documenting Berlin's disbursements for propaganda and sabotage, Secretary William G. McAdoo forwarded the information to Frank Cobb, whose New York *World* exposed the secret German campaign in four days of front-page unmasking. Among the *World*'s revelations was that *The Fatherland*, George S. Viereck's Germanophilic publication, regularly requested and received subsidies and that the Kaiser's agents had intrigued not only to gain control of newspapers and news services but also to stimulate lecturers and authors who favored the Central Powers. Covert German efforts to buy war supplies similarly were laid bare, as was the endeavor of Capt. Franz Von Papen, German military attaché, to foment strikes in munitions plants.[15]

The dark shadow of "The German Propaganda" prompted fears that led to a change in the popular understanding of the term *propaganda* itself. Before the war, propaganda, if it had any meaning for an ordinary American, signified chiefly the spreading of self-interested opinions through publicity. Under the influence of anti-German exposés, however, the term by 1915 had begun to take on more sinister connotations of manipulations and half-truths secretly sowed by society's avowed enemies. Britain's more extensive covert propaganda operation would be exempt from censorious treatment until after the Armistice.

Fears of German subversion only added to the sentiment that America should enter the fray. Interventionism already was on the move on account of the preparedness movement, popular in the business community and nominally headed by former president Theodore Roosevelt, and because of the defection of many formerly pacifistic intellectuals to the League to Enforce Peace, a group promoting peace through victory. By 1916, such major progressives as John Dewey, James T. Shotwell, and Walter Lippmann also had made their decisions in favor of participation in the war.[16]

Although slower than the advocates of preparedness to embrace war, adherents of the progressive movement took up the cause with a greater discursive fervor. Dewey and Lippmann preached the thesis that U.S. participation in the war provided the chance to enact democratic reforms on a worldwide scale. A few skeptics, such as Randolph Bourne, scorned Dewey's conversion to the idea of "Rough Riders" sowing reform. Bourne contended that the warrior intellectuals were making themselves mere instruments of military agencies without demanding that the war's so-called reformist purposes be specified in advance.[17] A few other leaders of socialist or progressive opinion supported Bourne's protests of the martial spirit, notably Gene Debs and Senator Robert La Follette; but theirs were isolated eddies in a great river of opinion moving in the direction of participation in the European war.

When Woodrow Wilson threw down the gauntlet in April 1917, the nation's business and intellectual communities were ready to follow. But what of the masses? Policy-makers were horrified by mail addressed to Wilson's new Committee on Public Information (CPI) begging for clarification of why the United States had entered the war. The sight of letters piled two to three feet high in the CPI's office gave impetus to a broadening of the committee's mission from that of coordination to that of promotion. Chaired by George Creel, progressive journalist,

Wilsonian, and minor prewar muckraker, the CPI evangelized for a uniform national opinion keyed to Wilson's new view of the war as Right versus Wrong conducted to spread democracy around the globe. Even when Americans spontaneously began to support the declaration of war, the CPI's campaign continued apace, helping to impart a manic quality to wartime public opinion.[18]

The most high-toned of the CPI's programs was its pamphlet campaign, directed by Guy Stanton Ford, University of Minnesota professor of history, and assisted by academic historians working with James T. Shotwell's National Board for Historical Service. Creel, Ford, and Shotwell defended vehemently the historical accuracy of the CPI's pamphleteering, for instance, by emphasizing how they successfully had resisted pressures from Newell Dwight Hillis and others to use undocumented atrocity stories. More striking, in retrospect, is how scholarship compromised itself when devoted to promoting a national cause. For example, in *Conquest and Kultur,* CPI historians showered the reader with chauvinistic quotations plucked here and there from sundry German writers. This mélange was cited as proof of an enormous pan-Germanist plot to annex vast territories, including portions of Argentina and the United States, to the Kaiser's empire.[19]

Fifty million pamphlets distributed by Creel's committee represented only one source by which wartime public opinion took on antic vehemence. Other of the CPI's programs gave even more visceral exaggeration of the danger posed variously by Germany and by Debs-style pacifist expression. Under Creel's ministrations, Wilson's war pervasively enveloped American citizens at every venue in their personal lives. For those traveling to work, there were trolley posters illustrating all manner of ways that the ordinary citizen personally could help win the war. Poster art, prepared by the CPI's Division of Pictorial Publicity, sparked many a campaign for the Treasury Department, War Department, Department of Agriculture, and Red Cross. Displayed in locales urban and rural, posters supplied some of the most evocative and best-remembered propagandas of the war in accordance with the belief of Division-chief Charles Dana Gibson (of Gibson Girl fame) that wartime art needed to "appeal to the heart." If Guy Ford had proscribed the use of the term *Hun* in CPI pamphlets, this scruple did not extend to Gibson's artists. One image created by J. Allen St. John for the Treasury Department showed a handprint in blood red with accompanying text: "The Hun – his Mark / Blot it Out / with / Liberty Bonds." Others sounded the call to "Beat back the HUN with LIBERTY BONDS" or simply to "HALT THE HUN!"[20]

The Treasury Department's imperative to stoke enthusiasm for bond sales gave vent not only to the ardor of artists but also to the hard-sell tendencies of many a Liberty Loan speaker. Oswald Villard recalled the appeals for cash to "stamp out" the Germans who were "the snakes of the human race." The Rev. Newell Dwight Hillis, most prominent of these speakers, believed that atrocity stories were "vital to the success of the second and all subsequent Liberty Loans." After tours of Belgium and France, Hillis vouched for the complete accuracy of such tales as the "soldier's token," a military talisman said to prompt frightful behavior by picturing the Emperor standing between God and judgment of the common soldier. The popular atrocity tales of bond rallies became so annoying to Wilson that the president wrote George Creel to inquire whether or not the Rev. Hillis could be controlled.[21]

As a result of the Creel committee's liaison with the commercial movie studios, leading directors such as D. W. Griffith and major producers such as Carl Laemmle helped rally the new medium of film to Wilson's cause. Griffith's tour de force wartime picture was *Hearts of the World*, built around scenes of dissolute German troops molesting property and persons in an occupied French village. Laemmle's *The Kaiser, The Beast of Berlin*, a movie whose title renders superfluous its producer's admission that the picture was "a conscious form of propaganda," similarly prompted excited responses from wartime patrons.[22]

Moviedom not only underwrote the war effort with a visual product but also established the context for an innovative marriage between traditional oratory and the entertainment industry. By late spring 1917, the Four Minute Men, 75,000 CPI-sponsored local speakers, were mounting the stages of America's movie palaces in a program of oratory orchestrated from Washington. Admonished to speak no longer than four minutes, Creel's hometown declaimers stood up during intermission time to address their captive audiences on more than forty scheduled themes beginning with conscription (May 12–21, 1917) and including the Liberty Loans, the income tax, the Red Cross, and food conservation. The program reached an estimated cumulative audience of 400 million. Although appeals to fact more than to hate and fear were emphasized in bulletins prepared for the Four Minute Men, observations of Creel's orators suggested that actual practice deviated considerably from the published ideal. From a tour of the West, Solomon Clark, professor of public speaking at the University of Chicago, found that Creel's minions repeatedly invoked images of the Hun, the *Lusitania*, and the rape of Belgian women.[23]

The urge for national service, and attendant self-promotion, was palpable not merely among would-be orators but also within the ranks of the nation's educators who found many occasions to serve Creel's great engine of persuasion. For public school teachers, the *National School Service* bulletin came regularly to explain how the schools might further national cohesion by detailing citizenship obligations. The National Board for Historical Service (NBHS), Shotwell's consortium, not only helped with the CPI's pamphlets but also took over *History Teachers Magazine*, a resource for high-school instructors. While under the control of the NBHS, the magazine stoked the martial mood, for instance, by encouraging teachers to emphasize that Germany presently enslaved ten times more people than had labored in servitude in the old American South.[24]

The impulse to teach history as a warrant for current political policy found expression not only in the high schools but also gained sway in the War Issues courses that appeared on many college campuses as part of the Student Army Training Corps program. At Stanford University, War Issues lectures reduced the Great War's origins to, generally, "The German Ideal of World Domination" (lecture 8) and, immediately, a nefarious German-Austrian plan (lecture 10). Although patriotic historical teaching of this kind proved embarrassing in the postwar years, it served the immediate purpose of boosting the self-esteem of faculty members who no longer saw themselves as useless ivory-tower pedants.[25]

America's writers and preachers also heeded the call to arms. Booth Tarkington, Samuel Hopkins Adams, and others entered service with the CPI's Division of Syndicated Features. Even Upton Sinclair, the socialist muckraker, sent an early draft of *Jimmie Higgins,* an in-process novel, for approval by Creel and other officials. Preachers, for their part, adroitly shifted from pacifism to a theology of holy war in which missionary metaphors abounded as did images of redemption by sword. An estimated 40 percent of the nation's clergy actively rendered war-related services such as blessing the spy-hunting societies, preaching against slackers, speaking up for enlistment, and standing aside as their congregations heaped condemnation upon conscientious objectors.[26]

Shedding congenital skepticism, America's journalists followed the lead of teachers, writers, and preachers by acquiescing in Creel's managed-news framework that forbade the press from roaming through federal agencies, buttonholing whomever was available. Only after the war did Washington correspondents chafe visibly under a press-office system that Creel, in characteristic hyperbole, had described as operating "without the slightest trace of color or bias, either in the selection of news or the manner in which it was presented." Creel's news office also prepared "a weekly digest of the official war news" that went to some 12,000 newspapers in galley form, ready for printing.[27]

Creel also knew the value of the soft-news side of journalism, and the CPI's Division of Syndicated Features turned to Booth Tarkington, Wallace Irwin, and other literati. One striking CPI feature, "The Daily German Lie," became the pet project of Harvey O'Higgins, CPI associate director. His releases asked newspapers to help expose "Official Frightfulness on the Field of Battle" and "Organized Lying in the Field of Propaganda." Representative was a release of August 1, 1918, that mentioned and denied six rumors that the Creel agency attributed to pro-Germans. Among the lies supposedly being spread by enemy agents and sympathizers was that Washington hypocritically preached conservation but diverted grain to brewers and distillers.[28] In the spirit of the moment, O'Higgins apparently felt no qualms about failing to provide evidence that the stories sprang from anything more sinister than normal human credulity.

Advertisers, music publishers, and war correspondents rounded out the ranks of America's communicationists answering the call to the colors. The CPI's Advertising Division, assisted by leaders in the profession, secured donations of advertising space from various patrons who paid for placement of a standard CPI ad to which they could add a brief line recognizing their donorship. One of the pictorials most frequently requested by donors was "Spies and Lies," a publicity piece that catered to the era's propaganda paranoia. The nation's popular songwriters and music publishers similarly enlisted in furthering a manic martial spirit. Irving Berlin's "Let's All Be Americans Now" likened Wilson's war to earlier calls to the sword by Washington, Lincoln, and Grant. "America Here's My Boy" supplied a musical rejoinder to the antiwar classic of 1915, "I Didn't Raise My Boy to Be a Soldier."[29]

Stoking wartime opinion from the front lines were American correspondents such as Irving Cobb and Heywood Broun, who did their part by validating a romantic and glorious view of trench warfare. Although Cobb once referred obliquely to mechanized combat as "massacre," he softened the character of modern war by portraying the boys of the Rainbow Division advancing "like schoolboys on a lark," radiating "great pride in having been chosen for the job." Cobb described those men who had been passed over for the attack as "crying like babies" and begging to be included. For his part, correspondent Heywood Broun enthused over France's "positive genius for warfare" in contrast to America's unfortunate lack of a "fighting tradition." He regaled readers with such stories as that of a "large fat cook" who pleaded for the chance to cross into German lines to retrieve a souvenir helmet and trenchcoat for his girl back home. Only after the Armistice did George Seldes and three other American war correspondents rebel against their self-imposed restraint, taking an oath "to tell the truth about the war."[30]

Although unrepentant radicals such as Gene Debs were willing to sound a discouraging note, most Americans were in the mold of Clyde Miller, embracing official dogma with genuine conviction. The result was a widespread, informal, neighborly pressure for conformity. Just as opinion leaders and intellectuals willingly leant their talents to molding a uniform pro-war opinion, ordinary citizens sought out opportunities to work as quasi-official agitators. The American Protective League, largest of the private loyalty-enforcing groups, numbered 350,000 members and gained semiofficial status and relative immunity to follow up reports of disloyalty too minor for action by the Justice Department. Loyalty societies not only conducted their own "investigations" and anti-slacker raids but also distributed their own pamphlet literature. In *The Conscientious Objector* (issue Number 33 of the National Security League's "Patriotism Through Education Series"), George Herbert Mead, University of Chicago sociologist, contributed an earnest, albeit equivocal, rationalization of the persecutions of the period. With more of a tone of duty than passion, Mead explained that the conscientious objector must realize that his act "renders martyrdom almost inevitable, when his country is involved in a war."[31]

It was well for Mead to accommodate himself directly, if not enthusiastically, to the wartime spirit because naysayers found even reliable old friends little disposed to provide them comfort. Oswald Villard's "refusal to believe those stories of the Belgian children with their hands cut off stamped me clearly as a traitorous pro-German." When Charles A. Beard (a war supporter) resigned from Columbia in protest of faculty firings, the resulting publicity imperiled the sale of his books. Macmillan, Beard's publisher, urgently contacted Guy Stanton Ford, who obligingly "gave Beard a little assignment" so that Macmillan could put out a testimonial "that Beard was working with the American government." Across the land, an expurgation mentality ensued such that German was branded a "barbarian tongue" at Ohio State University and enrollments dropped from 2,291 in 1914 to 149 in 1917. At the same time that Villard was being asked to resign as president of the Philharmonic Society, one of the organization's directors was leading a "vigorous fight to prevent the playing of any German music during the war." No name was more anathematized than that of Senator Robert La Follette in view of his opposition to the preparedness movement, his insistence that the *Lusitania* carried munitions, his support of neutrality up to 1917, and his opposition to conscription. Shunned by his fellow senators, La Follette was expelled from clubs while, at the University of Wisconsin, his effigy was publicly burned.[32]

On occasion, Creel lamented the "noise, attack, and hysteria" stirred up by the superpatriotic societies, and Guy Ford recommended to Creel that the CPI set up a unit to deal with charges that, like those against Beard, stemmed from "absurd misunderstandings." Wilson likemind-edly confided to Creel that "the opposition to teaching German in our schools is childish." These concerns of Wilson and his opinion engineers must have flowed partly from their inability to fine-tune the vectors of vitriol that, in many cases, were propelled by motivations beyond that of national service. Creel and Ford believed that competing textbook salespeople were responsible for much of the paranoia about hidden pro-Germanism in American history books, which, for instance, often spoke highly of German municipal government. Similarly, the vehemence of Newell Dwight Hillis may have originated in his earlier pacifism and his repertoire of prewar lectures that included one praising "The New Germany." Attacks by established Christian denominations on the smaller pacifistic sects were obviously self-serving as well as "patriotic." Economist Scott Nearing believed that college boards of trustees used the war crisis as a convenient opportunity to purge faculty members long viewed as radicals or troublemakers.[33]

So deeply was accusation embedded in the mood of the moment, however, that even the Armistice could not bring expurgation to an end. Despite the CPI's almost immediate disbanding, campaigns against the so-called anti-Americanism of dissidents continued, not only in Congressional hearings on German propaganda but also when revulsion toward symbols of Germany was transferred to the Bolsheviks. This strange transmutation by which Commissar replaced Kaiser as the target of national ire eventually became known as the great postwar Red Scare. The panic reached its high point in late 1919 and early 1920.

As with anti-German manias, fears about Reds foreign and domestic sprang from official and unofficial sources. Half-truths ran rampant in news about the situation in Russia because Western correspondents, prohibited from entering the Soviet Union, "hung about the borders to transmit as truth the rumors and inventions of royalist refugees." Washington helped to metamorphose alarms about Red Russia into fears about domestic revolution. The U.S. Senate, which earlier had authorized an investigation of German propaganda, now empowered Senator Lee Overman's committee to scrutinize "any efforts being made to propagate in this country the principles of any party exercising or claiming to exercise authority in Russia," especially with regard to overthrowing the U.S. government, destroying property, or promoting the "general cessation of industry." In the absence of a discernible civil uprising, anticommunist patrioteers played up news stories about the handful of anarchist bombings, one of which devastated the front of Attorney General A. Mitchell Palmer's house. To minds conditioned by wartime fears of conspiracy and propaganda, strikes in basic industries signaled more than labor's weariness with preachments toward pure production and, instead, proved that the Red Revolution was on.[34]

"It's All Propaganda, Anyway"

The Red Scare sustained the conformity, fear, and hate that represented the darker side of the wartime climate of opinion, while, on the other hand, little in the postwar period reinforced the uplifting and communitarian currents of the Wilsonian vision. The term *propaganda* became more prevalent in an atmosphere that Philip Gibbs, English reporter, described as "lethargy and exhaustion of emotion in the United States." In this climate, the odium of propaganda became attached not only to German and Bolshevik machinations but also to the exhortations and strivings of the late Committee on Public Information. By 1923, Ernest M. Hopkins, president of Dartmouth, observed that his businessmen friends labeled as propaganda the stacks of pamphlets, books, and speeches accumulating on their desks. By the late 1930s, the phrase "it's all propaganda, anyway" had become a national refrain.[35]

Changes in how Americans understood propaganda began when the official view of the war, and those who promoted it, fell into disrepute. American disillusionment with the propagandas of the Great War began in Europe, where the sentiment spread among American troops that atrocity stories had been false concoctions and that the Germans had behaved no worse than any other combatants. War correspondent George Seldes became so skeptical about atrocity tales that he actually was shocked when, at the postwar Leipzig trials, he encountered several documented instances of German soldiers shooting Allied prisoners and U-boats shelling survivors. *Nation* magazine, which earlier had accepted the official interpretation that Germany started the Great War, now (August 1919) agreed that the Russian archives proved that the Allies shared responsibility.[36]

Nation's conversion illustrated how many opinion leaders became willing to tell a different tale now that the troops were out of harm's way. No longer compromised by the CPI and by War Issues courses, historians looked for enlightenment from the flood of formerly secret European war documents. Leading progressive war supporters such as John Dewey, Walter Lippmann, Charles Beard, and Carl Becker expressed outrage at the punitive peace terms being discussed in Paris. In Philip Gibbs's widely circulated books, this premier English war correspondent expressed regret at having helped to put across a distorted view of the war. Gibbs now laid bare the horror and high casualties of front-line combat, the complaints of soldiers about their leadership, the British Army's despair in 1915–1916, and occasional outright blunders by British staff officers. Speaking for ordinary soldiers rather than on behalf of the official leadership, Gibbs wrote of the anger of the Tommies at home-front propaganda that emphasized atrocities and sanitized the experience of war. Gibbs observed the hollow falsity of atrocity stories, and he pointed out the contradiction posed by Britain's propaganda of saving little Belgium and her simultaneous crushing of independence efforts in Ireland.[37]

In contrast to the growing mood to debunk the late war, some figures in the American opinion-making machinery continued to defend, even celebrate, their work. Postwar reminiscences by George Creel touted the CPI's campaign as a "simple, straightforward presentation of facts" whereby the bureau "carried to every corner of the civilized globe the full message of America's idealism, unselfishness, and indomitable purpose." In view of the CPI's educational mission, Creel enthused, "we did not call it propaganda" because "that word, in German hands, had come to be associated with deceit and corruption." In like manner, Charles Merriam, CPI commissioner for Italy and Chicago professor of political science, proudly apprised his academic colleagues of the inside dope about America's weapon of psychological publicity. Not only had the CPI propped up Italian morale by driving home the message that THE YANKS ARE COMING, but, according to Merriam, the organization had been able to counter the enemy's guile without resort to "lies, misstatements, half truths, or exaggerations."[38]

Other of Creel's former servitors added to the burgeoning insider's celebratory literature about opinion engineering. Even before the guns fell silent on the Western Front, William D'Arcy enthused to his colleagues in advertising that "the past year's work" had shown advertising to be "a forearm and standard-bearer of war for human rights." The resulting record was a "proud page in advertising's history." Edward Bernays of the CPI's foreign press bureau was of similar opinion, believing that the Creel committee's record had rehabilitated the very term *propaganda*, which earlier "the German Propaganda" had given "a pejorative meaning." Therefore, Bernays felt no compunctions about associating his own incipient profession of public relations with the word *propaganda*.[39]

Spokespersons for two of the war's smaller mind-managing enterprises paid similar tribute to their departments' erstwhile work. Most significant of the CPI's collateral allies had been the U.S. Army's psychological warfare unit headed by Captain Heber Blankenhorn, a former pacifist and labor-oriented newspaper journalist. In a postwar book, Blankenhorn reported on the work of his crack staff that had included language experts as well as journalists Walter Lippmann and Charles Merz. Blankenhorn's group interrogated POWs to elicit angles for undermining enemy morale. The psychological warfare unit's pièce de résistance was a leaflet postcard, ostensibly for use by captured Germans, that tantalized the enemy by offhandedly listing the lavish rations made available to POWs by the American Expeditionary Forces.[40]

The domestic wing of military mind managing emerged when Robert M. Yerkes, president of the American Psychological Association, took on the task of persuading the U.S. Army to employ intelligence tests for the fair and effective classification of its conscripts. By early 1918, psychological workers were administering intelligence rating scales to some 200,000 men per month and marking the results on a continuum ranging from "A" to "E." In the immediate postwar period, America's psychologists were in a mood to celebrate their profession's services during the war and to leverage aggressively their new image of practicality. In 1921, a large group of psychologists formed the Psychological Corporation, which drew upon the example of the army's recent massive intelligence-testing program.[41]

Despite congratulatory retrospectives by the war's key mind managers, the excessively optimistic and frequently self-serving nature of American publicity was becoming apparent such that a few former propagandists expressed misgivings about their work. Both Walter Lippmann, whiz-kid journalist and erstwhile army psychological warrior, and Will Irwin, muckraker and former director of the CPI's Foreign Section, raised troubling questions about how their recent activities might be squared with traditional democratic thinking. In a review of Creel's somewhat boastful postwar book, Lippmann argued that the CPI could not escape the label of propagandist simply by having avoided outright corruption and deceit. The committee had not offered absolutely honest news but rather purveyed "news and argument which put America in the best possible light and sustained the fighting morale." Lippmann found it revealing that the CPI was considered unfit for continued service in peacetime.[42]

In columns published in the *Atlantic Monthly* of November and December 1919, and later laid out in book form, Lippmann set out a comprehensive view of the problems that propaganda posed for modern Western society. Because leaders now viewed public opinion as decisive, Lippmann believed, "the basic problem of democracy" was to protect news – the source of public opinion – from the taint of propaganda. No modern society lacking the wherewithal to detect lies could call itself free. Offering professionalization as the solution, Lippmann suggested an official bureau to broker disputes about the accuracy of news coverage. The corollary would be to introduce into journalism the research-bureau model under which news could be harnessed to "objective criteria" instead of "gossip and intuitions."[43]

Will Irwin echoed Lippmann's meditations about propaganda and democracy in a less philosophical treatment of the new "Age of Lies." Although convinced that the CPI's overseas dispatches were "nearer the truth than any of the others," Irwin's journalistic conscience made him recognize that "we never told the whole truth – not by any manner of means. We told that part which served our national purpose." Worse yet, Irwin maintained, the success of wartime opinion manipulation insured its continuance. Now propagandists were flooding into Paris to serve up half-truths and outright falsehoods about the Versailles conference.[44]

While erstwhile opinion engineers variously expressed pride or concern, other commentators who had abstained from government service also began to take up the implications of what symbolic orchestration portended for postwar America. John Dewey sounded an early warning that propaganda might constitute a social problem for the postwar world. Dewey predicted that although the wartime censorship and prosecutions of free speech would lapse, agency managers would not forget "the possibilities of guidance of the news upon which the formation of public opinion depends." Observing that not just the Germans had practiced propaganda, Dewey, as with Irwin, pointed to contemporary efforts at "feeding the people with just those things and only those things which the authorities believe that it is good for them to know." An early case study by Charles Beard gave tangible punch to Dewey's cautionary note. Beard reported on the contents of a Syllabus of the World War issued to high-school principals in New York City. Noting that the syllabus advocated peacetime universal military service, Beard cautioned that if this kind of curriculum became the norm, American schools would become "institutions for propaganda" instead of "places where conflicting views of future policy are to be fairly considered."[45]

The idea of propaganda analysis, first broached by major progressive intellectuals, struck an immediate responsive chord with American writers and educators. Robert Herrick, novelist and faculty member at the University of Chicago, complained that the Entente still leveraged control of the Atlantic cables to guide American public opinion, in this case against Russia. Editorialist Frank Crane observed a host of contemporary propagandas by the Irish and the Bolsheviks as well as by those unfriendly to Mexico and Japan. Edward Lowry gave readers of the *Saturday Evening Post* a perspective on how publicity bureaus in Washington functioned. He cited the manufacture of publicity by the U.S. Chamber of Commerce, by farmers, by labor, and by the suffragists who, he added, kept "perhaps the most elaborate and aggressive propaganda shop in town."[46]

The burgeoning antipropaganda literature emphasized the institutional infiltration of self-serving ideology into news. Former army propaganda officers Lippmann and Merz studied one thousand articles on Russia appearing in the *New York Times* between March 1917 and March 1920 which they compared to the actual turn of events. They concluded that, "the news as a whole is dominated by the hopes of the men who composed the news organization." For instance, news reports in the *Times* held out the hope the anti-Red generals would defeat Lenin's forces long after conditions and events had proved otherwise. Similarly comprehensive was Heber Blankenhorn's study of the propaganda employed by the steel industry during the 1919 strike. Working now for the Interchurch World Movement, a group of religious reformers, Blankenhorn concluded that the 1919 strike had been properly conducted and that radicals had been kept at arm's length by strike leaders. In contrast, Blankenhorn's group found that the steel industry had defeated the strike by invoking the false charge of Bolshevism, a deception aided by biased press coverage and "the silence of both press and pulpit on the actual question of justice involved." In particular, Pittsburgh newspapers had acted as the voice of the steel industry, ignoring grievances, falsely intimating that the strike was Bolshevik in origin, playing up adverse comment on the strike, failing to speak up for the free-speech rights of labor, and generally prejudicing public opinion throughout the nation.[47]

At the same time that popular writers diffused the idea of propaganda as democracy's enemy, America's academicians were beginning to develop a theory and a pedagogy for analyzing contemporary propaganda. Raymond Dodge of Wesleyan University and later of Yale worked out a psychology of social influence based on the idea that propaganda's tendency "to hide both its nature and its intention" made it distinct both from education and from advertising. Dodge also characterized propaganda as relying upon an "emotional logic" such as when antipathy was transferred from one object to another. Dodge, however, was gratified that people seemed able to resist persuasion and to become inured to an overused appeal. Everett Dean Martin, director of the Cooper Union Forum, also believed that certain internal resistances to propaganda might usefully be strengthened. Citing excesses such as the conviction of Debs and the "propaganda of the crowd" leveraged to instill hatred of Germany, Martin warned that a continuation of the wartime precedents could bring tyranny. As a safeguard to democracy, Martin advocated the "liberating of our own thinking" through a new program of antipropaganda education.[48]

The postwar discovery of propaganda by Lippmann, Irwin, Dewey, and Beard, and the assimilation of propaganda analysis by other writers and educators, marked the birth of an intellectual movement that became, by the 1930s, a popular social force. The progressives' notion of propaganda as a sometimes popular but always covert and institutionally promoted threat to intelligent public opinion has remained a prominent strain in American social thought. However, Americans never have embraced fully the progressive movement's favored definition of *propaganda*. Alternate views of the term have been put forth by practitioners such as Creel and Merriam and, as will be seen, by scientists, by teachers of critical thinking, and by polemicists. These other perspectives complicate the mission of progressives to expose propaganda as a danger to participatory democracy. The result is a wide-ranging, unsettled, and characteristically American colloquy on the meaning of propaganda for democracy.

CHAPTER 2

THE PROGRESSIVE
PROPAGANDA CRITICS

The Committee on Public Information perfectly illustrated the fault
lines between progressivism's dual dedication to efficiency and to democracy. While the pragmatic "win the war" spirit reigned unchal-
lenged, those who worked to perfect Creel's great engine of mass persuasion rarely paused to ponder whether they were enhancing the
prospects for democratic life of their fellow citizens. Although practitioners George Creel, Charles Merriam, and Edward L. Bernays remained confident after the war that mass persuasion was consonant
with good government, their former cohorts Walter Lippmann and Will
Irwin had become convinced that opinion control was antithetical to
free choice regardless of its seeming indispensability in moving a great
modern republic to decisive action. These repentant warrior progressives helped to set into motion, during the 1920s and 1930s, a major
socio-intellectual movement against propaganda. However, the Great
War actually was not progressivism's first encounter with what Bernays
later would call "the engineering of consent."[1]

Muckrakers and Mass Persuasion

Although the Great War popularized the term *propaganda* and made
coordinated social influence a matter of general public interest, it was
the turn-of-the-century muckrakers who laid the foundations for the
progressive criticism of mass persuasion. One tangent of early popular
muckraking directed specific attention to how powerful institutions
used media and behind-the-scenes press agentry (i.e., public relations)
to gain leverage over public opinion. Ray Stannard Baker, whose specialties included labor and race relations, was among the first of the
muckrakers to probe the relation of new-style publicity practices to
traditional democratic life.

Between November 1905 and April 1906, Baker published a series
of five articles on dubious business practices of the railroads. The first

four essays represented a standard exposé of such commercial dirty-dealing as excessive rates for most shippers and secret rebates to a powerful few such as Rockefeller and Armour. The final installment of Baker's series, however, took an innovative turn and focused explicitly on the ability of railroad corporations to corrupt public opinion itself through hired press agents. Baker's article on "How Railroads Make Public Opinion" helped to set in motion a small but important tangent of muckraking that considered whether promoters, grafters, and pressure artists might carry their corruptions beyond the nation's key institutions by infusing them directly into the public mind.

Baker's study of railroad press relations began with his report that industry executives recognized that "the fountainhead of public information is the newspaper." Baker detailed how the presidents of the Southern, the Erie, and the Delaware & Hudson lines had formed a combination to finance a publicity campaign against a railroad regulation bill passed by the House and pending in the Senate. According to Baker, this triumvirate hired a Boston publicity firm to coordinate a behind-the-scenes campaign designed to influence news coverage of the regulatory fight. Publicity agents offered editors prepared news-style articles that incorporated much material favorable to the railroads, and the agents kept close track of which papers opened themselves to the handouts. The press agents also found which were the leading industrial and commercial enterprises in the various target cities so that when an editor proved unfriendly, railroad representatives might prevail upon local business concerns to contact the editor in support of the carriers.

Although finding no evidence that bribery was involved, Baker doubted whether the railroads' publicity campaign was innocent in the eyes of Liberty. He questioned whether railroad press agents could rightly liken themselves to lawyers for their client before the jury of public opinion. In contrast to the courtroom, the publicity campaign proceeded in secret and, unlike the public relations firms, "the people are unorganized." Baker further argued that the material in the railroad-produced news stories provided a soft foundation for hard-headed thinking on railroad regulation. For instance, the railroads used questionable comparisons between their rates and those prevailing in Europe. Beyond this, railroad representatives skewed Congressional testimony by paying the expenses of certain witnesses who purported to represent the small businessperson. The carriers similarly manipulated a conference held by shippers in Chicago. Baker wondered whether so much effort toward the "'sanitation' of public opinion" did not create a dismal climate for free exercise of the ballot.[2]

As working journalists, muckrakers such as Baker had a sixth sense for recognizing that publicity might become a weapon of antiprogressive forces and be used to dilute the reform spirit that was gathering momentum during the first Roosevelt presidency. A subtle sign that sophisticated American readers were beginning to assimilate the idea of organized publicity was the appearance of stories casting news manipulation in a light vein. George Jean Nathan, later to gain fame as a drama critic, wrote about how the Spanish court boosted the matrimonial prospects of young King Alfonso by engaging photographers to show "the slight monarch in various athletic poses"; similarly, the German Kaiser used family photographs to seem lovable. In "Confessions of a Literary Press Agent" (1906), an anonymous former newspaperman revealed how he encouraged an author's friends to write letters that made the book seem controversial and how he sometimes cloaked the name or gender of the author. In a three-part series on the "Autobiography of a Theatrical Press-Agent" (1913), another anonymous practitioner explained how he boosted a traveling musical comedy by staging jewel robberies, beauty contests, and milkbaths. When the troupe arrived in Georgia, the agent put out a story that the ingenue was the great-granddaughter of General Sherman; later, near the Gulf of Mexico, he staged a photograph of her catching what was in reality the carcass of an already-dead and partially embalmed whale.[3]

By 1910, when Will Irwin undertook his assignment to muckrake the newspaper business, a considerable number of Americans were beginning to understand that currents of public thought might be fanned by the opinion engineers. Irwin's ability to trace links between outside interests, newspaper content, and public opinion made his fifteen-part series for *Collier's* (January–July 1911) a cornerstone in the foundation of postwar propaganda consciousness. The tone of Irwin's work was synoptic, often scholarly, and sociologist Robert Park soon termed the collection "the only adequate account that has ever been written of the American newspaper."

Irwin began by describing the shift of power in favor of news and away from editorials, a transition that came about when cheaper, popular papers began to draw large audiences through sensationalism. Irwin explained how a newspaper's directing hand determined the line taken on large social and political questions whereas, in smaller matters, the sensibilities of an individual writer might prevail. Influencing the editor were a variety of overt or subtle pressures from the outside, chief among them advertising. While the old system of direct subsidies to newspapers from political parties and businesses had atrophied, Irwin observed the lingering tendency of editors not to offend their leading advertisers on the basis of the principle that "modern business demands mutual favors." He further observed the more sinister influence on a newspaper's tone coming from the tendency of editors and publishers to associate chiefly with the wealthy in society and thus to assimilate upper-class views. Rejecting calls to ban advertising or to establish endowed newspapers, Irwin hoped that the professionalization of journalists would overcome abuses in the news.[4]

Immediate reaction to Irwin's series among opinion leaders was almost uniformly favorable, although William Randolph Hearst initiated a libel suit. Furthermore, Irwin clearly had worried the grafters such that, when word got out about his incipient serial, Irwin was flattered at the offer of a $5,000 bribe to drop his researches. Although Irwin muckraked specific instances of press corruption in Cincinnati and Pittsburgh, his overall attitude was one of optimism. He concluded that the market system tended to weed out papers that accepted subsidies or otherwise adopted a servile attitude toward advertisers.[5]

Before the muckraking boom ran its course, Creel and Lippmann, relatively unknown writers before the Great War, had added to the literature of works about manipulative press relations. Two years before he internationalized press-control practices for Wilson, George Creel muckraked the charitable foundations for acquiescing in publicity practices. Creel's immediate target was a grant by the Rockefeller Foundation for a study of the causes of industrial unrest. Creel maintained that "the receipt of donations from men whose activities are assailed by public opinion" invariably compromised the good judgment of recipients who would probably transmute some of "Rockefeller's attitude in the Colorado strike" to the study of labor–management relations. Walter Lippmann, more given to the philosophical essay than the exposé, nevertheless helped to spread the word about self-serving institutional publicity when he contributed an article criticizing the campaign by industry against the minimum wage.[6]

One immediate political result of early media muckraking was the Post Office Appropriation Act of 1912, which mandated not only full disclosure of a newspaper's or magazine's ownership but also required labeling of all material published for payment as an "advertisement." The muckraking approach to publicity entered the hustings when Robert La Follette, in a speech to the U.S. Senate, described "an organized conspiracy to control, to compel, to intimidate, and coerce the judgment of the Interstate Commerce Commission." La Follette railed against a "manufactured" chain reaction of pro-railroad opinion whereby letters to Congress had been prompted by news stories that, in turn, had been stimulated by mail circulars and a year-long outpouring by publicity bureaus.

La Follette's condemnation of press agentry as "un-American" shows how ten years' worth of press muckraking had begun to make modernized American boosterism seem less than completely benign.[7] Yet a decade of exposing the communication industry failed fully to bring home to ordinary Americans a sense that new methods of publicity might pose dangers for democracy. One signifier of the shallow roots of the antipropaganda campaign of the muckrakers was the speed with which Irwin, Creel, and others embraced the go-getting promotional spirit when Wilson offered them the opportunity to direct a mass campaign aimed at spreading progressive democracy around the world. Further, for ordinary Americans, the antipublicity crusade of the early muckrakers lacked an immediate referent in people's experiences. In contrast, after the Great War, progressive propaganda critics could draw upon memories of wartime hyperpatriotism and paranoia and could point to the CPI's all-encompassing promotional hyperbole. Between the *Lusitania*'s sinking in 1915 and the Armistice in 1918, Americans had implicated themselves in attitudes and actions that were sometimes embarrassing or painful to recall.

Another reason that the first wave of antipropaganda muckraking failed to catch the public's fancy was that turn-of-the-century opinion leaders were ill prepared to assimilate lessons about mass manipulation. The early articles on press chicanery were addressed to a reading public that had been socialized to regard public opinion as the outcome of a town-meeting–like process of thoughtful deliberation and to view communication as a technical process for the transfer of information.

The Influence of Rationalism

The audience of opinion leaders available to Baker, Irwin, and other early muckrakers proved, for two reasons, to be less conscious than post–Great War Americans of the vulnerability of public opinion and of the prevalence of self-serving communication. For one thing, late nineteenth-century treatments of public opinion glossed over how newspaper coverage and press agentry had established a mediated form of social influence that supplanted the old direct persuasion of pamphlets and oratory witnessed by de Tocqueville in the 1830s. Also, after 1870, American opinion leaders were likely to have been trained in a mechanical, step-by-step process of written composition that was focused on technical rules for the transfer of information. In contrast, the pre–Civil War curriculum of oratory, rhetoric, and recitation had called upon students to directly experience self-interested persuasion backed by strategic rhetorical posturing.

James Bryce's monumental survey of American political culture, a widely used textbook in the late nineteenth century, is representative of how the nostalgic town-meeting view of directly formed public opinion remained influential even at a time when journalists and press agents were emerging as gate keepers in public communication. Lord Bryce, British ambassador to the United States, believed that public opinion was more powerful in America than in any other democratic country and that it functioned independently as the ultimate source of power both for president and legislator. Bryce did not regard publicity as in any way compromising the "boundless faith in free inquiry and full discussion" held by Americans. He portrayed a rational process of winnowing out ideas in which all "notions, phrases and projects" got an audition and were assessed by the large number of citizens who actively discussed political events.

Lord Bryce recognized the power of the press implicit in people's considerable appetite for news, especially sensationalized reports, but he was confident that Americans were too independent and shrewd to be taken in by newspapers. Nor was Bryce worried about any tainting of public opinion by governmental corruption, believing that although city officials might misuse their offices for personal economic gain, the press generally worked against urban machine politics. Further, while Bryce conceded that the slave-holding class had enjoyed a stranglehold on Southern opinion before the Civil War, he presented contemporary public opinion in America as something not greatly influenced by class differences.[8]

If optimism about public opinion made it difficult to recognize media-originated manipulation, the shift in the academic curriculum from argumentative oratory to informative composition had a similar effect by conveying an impression that public communication chiefly was a technical transfer of information. The professor of rhetoric had been a familiar figure in the small American college of the early nineteenth century, where the theory and practice of rhetoric was integrated into a classical curriculum. At Harvard, the president himself was charged with the responsibility of delivering the weekly lecture in rhetoric. Students often translated Cicero and the works of other orators and rhetoricians as part of their studies of language and ethics. In addition, students typically were required to participate several times a year in the weekly public program of forensic disputations (debates) or declamations of memorized speeches. College catalogues prescribed that students read from leading English textbooks of rhetoric and, after the 1830s, a number of similar works authored by Americans. Examinations typically were not written; instead, students were tested by a method of recitation whereby they defended a position against questions. It was common for seniors to present original public orations at commencement time or during exam periods. Apart from the formal instruction, oratorical and debating societies were important centers of campus life. Indiana University, for instance, saw stiff competition for oratorical honors when fraternities took up construction of a contest oration as a house project.[9]

Whether oriented to a classical political rhetoric of speechmaking (as reflected in Aristotle's *Rhetoric* and Cicero's *De Oratore*) or to newer rhetorical doctrines that synthesized oral and written expression and grounded communication on a theory of the mind, the curricular practices of pre–Civil War rhetorical education emphasized the speaker as a deliberative proponent in a welter of competing social positions.[10] No matter how learned or florid the productions of America's early boy orators might have been, their need to adapt remarks to lay audiences caused them to rely upon an assumed practical wisdom that the citizen needed to make judgments. Oratory's worldview was that of making real a plausible social knowledge for the purpose of building coalitions of belief that might lead to action.

In the years after the Civil War, the emphasis on the citizen-orator's role in public life gave way to a new brand of rhetorical education that better accommodated itself to the needs of an industrial society. The larger scope and magnitude of private enterprise required managers who were able to bring order and efficiency to an administrative-technical apparatus. The shift in academe after 1870 away from oral rhetoric to a technical, written composition accorded well with economic trends toward efficiently organized production, on the one hand, and personal advancement in the corporate structure, on the other.[11] Paralleling the rise of large-scale governmental and entrepreneurial organizations was the emergence of the modern university. Enrollments now were likely to be numbered in the several hundreds (later, in the thousands), and curricula were influenced by the vast increase in available scientific knowledge. To accommodate the new students and new knowledge, colleges replaced a stipulated curriculum and oral recitation with the elective system of courses and with written examinations. Increasing specialization was managed by organizing colleges into separate departments, and national professional societies emerged in various divisions of the natural and social sciences.

Traditional rhetorical instruction found itself at a disadvantage in the academic climate of the late 1800s. Rhetoric's claims to create a socially useful practical wisdom for the citizen fell on deaf ears during a time when America's business increasingly seemed to be business and when science appeared to provide authenticated knowledge on a hitherto undreamed-of scale.[12] The tendency to see rhetoric as merely the communication of previously discovered knowledge (a theoretical condition already present in the new rhetorics of the late 1700s) became manifest in new-style composition courses that were organized to expedite the acquisition of technical competence in writing. More a field than a discipline, rhetoric no longer imbued the curriculum in the new age of specialization. Further, in its truncated form as English composition, rhetoric found itself an unhappy stepchild in newly established departments of English that increasingly focused on the aesthetics of literary communication in novels and poetry. Where rhetorical instruction once had organized itself around argumentation and persuasion, now its goal was to transmit information. Pedagogy accordingly centered on mechanical techniques of using appropriate words and producing efficient sentences, paragraphs, and compositions. Typical was how Adams Sherman Hill of Harvard modernized Richard Whately's *Elements of Rhetoric*. For Whately, argumentation (to produce conviction) and persuasion (to induce the will) were the central considerations of the rhetorical art. In contrast, the first 238 pages of Hill's book took the student up to the level of the paragraph, and Hill placed Whately's concepts of argument and persuasion at the very end, subordinate to prior treatments of description, narration, and exposition.[13]

The dedication of English compositionists to informative description was part of a process by which the idea of a self-promoting speaker gave way to an image of human cogs efficiently exchanging information in an administrative-technical society. Reinforcing the view of communication as objective, automatic response to the environment was the tendency to romanticize the idealized, independent, small-town citizen who experienced conditions directly and integrated implicitly all relevant aspects of economic, social, and political life. Although industrial urbanizing trends were changing the ways in which people carried out their work and social lives, theories of public opinion and of public communication painted a picture of the rational, self-sufficient American not at all vulnerable to propagandized communication.[14]

The Eclipse of Rationalism

The transition from suasive "rhetoric" to technologized "composition" marked a conscious shift away from concern with symbolic manipulation. (This semantic shift presaged the turn to objectivity in the 1940s signaled by the replacement of the term *propaganda* by *communication*.) As appreciation waned after 1870 among opinion leaders for the inherently self-serving nature of social interaction, it is not surprising that the outputs of the early muckrakers would be viewed as astounding. Muckraking articles circa 1906 read today as rather unremarkable descriptions of venality, promotionalism, and self-advancement by persons and groups. In contrast, the pious democratic faith existing in 1900 made these works appear shocking, almost unbelievable. However, even as the muckrakers were framing their first indictments of government and business, social and political theories were divesting themselves of undiluted faith in reason. Antirationalistic views of the public mind and of public communication began to emerge in the decades before the Great War. At first influential only among the avant-garde, these views, when underscored and focused by memories of the late war, enabled postwar progressive propaganda critics to gain a wider public acceptance for their exposés.

By the dawn of the twentieth century, a number of writers were challenging the assumption that logic and discussion – more than human nature and interest – were the organizing principles of society. When Americans began to take Ph.D.s in European universities, they encountered French and German writings on collective behavior that presented a more cynical and pessimistic view of social interaction. By the time of the muckrakers, Gustave Le Bon, for instance, was winning some attention from in-the-know literati in the United States for his theory that "the unconscious action of crowds" had replaced the "conscious activity of individuals."

Le Bon agreed with Bryce as to the increasing power of public opinion in modern society, but the Frenchman parted company with the Britisher on the matter of whether this development favored an intelligent democratic life. Le Bon believed that the crowd's very sense of its own power caused it to yield to instinct. Further, a "psychological crowd" (i.e., mass opinion on a general or specific subject) represented a collective mind formed largely by unconscious thoughts. Because crowds were impressed only by images, they made up their minds on the basis of superficial impressions and tended to accept or reject ideas as a whole. Mass opinion was the product of a simple reasoning by association and by sentiment even when the members of a crowd were highly educated. Le Bon found crowds to be highly suggestible and, because they thought only in images, inhospitable to discussion or nuance. Favoring exaggerations, crowds were apt to regard mere suspicion and rumor as positive proof. Crowds lacked responsibility and tended to abruptly impose a judgment rather than derive it through discussion.[15]

European writings on collective behavior had a significant impact on sociologists in the *fin de siècle* United States, although American writers initially gave a more optimistic face to European formulations. Charles H. Cooley, a leading American sociologist, believed that Europeans such as Le Bon had exaggerated the extent to which impulsive crowds and irresponsible leaders were characteristic of public opinion in a democracy. Cooley was convinced that the masses and their sentiments contributed positively to society because ordinary people were more in touch with the human condition than were the privileged few and because the masses also lacked the "tendency to isolation and spiritual impoverishment" that accompanied great wealth. In like manner, sociologist Robert Park was careful to differentiate between the unreflective crowd, so graphically portrayed by Le Bon, and a discursive public more consistent with earlier American notions of society. In Park's view, a crowd-type sentiment did prevail at the time when people first became aware of an issue; but soon the higher-level formulation of public opinion emerged from "discussion among individuals who assume opposing positions." Believing that newspapers functioned chiefly to control collective attention, however, Park worried that the opinions formed by news were in the realm of "unreflective perception."[16]

If the psychology of the crowd made human foibles more central to American political theory, Freudian psychology and the political philosophy of Graham Wallas, an English social activist and writer, further nudged the nation's opinion leaders away from the old rationalism. Freud had a significant indirect impact on theories of public opinion because his work suggested that individual participants in society's discussions were not as cogent as Park, Cooley, and even Le Bon had surmised. Walter Lippmann, for his part, believed that social science might see a major breakthrough if crowd psychology were combined with Freud's theories of the repression of primal impulses toward aggression and the erotic. Lippmann and other prewar political thinkers also were influenced greatly by Wallas, who developed a theory that "the empirical art of politics consists largely in the creation of opinion by the deliberate exploitation of subconscious non-rational inference."[17]

America's social commentators at first only tentatively appropriated European works on the irrational, but by the 1920s, the views of Le Bon, Freud, and Wallas seemed quite attuned to recently experienced political action. Unvarnished treatments of crowd psychology could be found in textbooks by Harvard's William MacDougall and Cooper Union's Everett Dean Martin, the latter of whom explicitly linked "the crowd and its propaganda." Response to the new evidences of society's irrationality varied from that of Norman Angell, who made human folly central to his political theory, to that of Charles Merriam, who resisted the connection but acknowledged that democracy was on trial in an era of economic and social concentration. William Albig and Max Lerner probably spoke for most when they concurred that, in recent time, social history and social theory had joined to impair permanently the traditional faith of Americans in reasoned public opinion.[18]

Perhaps the clearest sign that the rising specter of unreason would make a place for propaganda in leading-edge social thought was Lord Bryce's postwar political survey. In contrast to Bryce's earlier benign treatment of publicity's impact on public opinion, his 1921 book evidenced a conversion experience. Bryce now saw obstacles to the public's articulating its will, not only because newspaper reports might be misleading or colored but also because of "artificially created and factitious opinion." Bryce believed that the art of propaganda had "attained a development which enables its practitioners by skillfully and sedulously supplying false or one-sided statements of fact to beguile and mislead." He wrote of how self-interested operators might capture an agency of government or how business groups might stimulate a "press propaganda" not only with pamphlets and books but also by using subservient newspapers and magazines.[19]

By assimilating theoretical and practical lessons about human nature, American writers in the fields of sociology and political science were beginning to revolutionize the idea of social influence. However, this theoretical metamorphosis moved only slowly into the practical communication fields of journalism and speech. Founded at the behest of state press associations, journalism schools raised standards of reporting and, by aggressively pursuing Irwin's professionalizing ideal, helped to produce reservoirs of journalistic independence. But by emphasizing practical and technical studies, and later by linking professionalism to the ideal of objectivity, the J-School's curriculum left little room for the historical analysis and critical theorizing needed to reveal the era's high-population publics. Although speech faculty were beginning to sever connection with print-oriented and aesthetically inclined departments of English, they kept to a relatively narrow notion of social influence in their courses in public speaking, drama, and debate. In fact, many teachers of public speaking boasted that they were abandoning old-fashioned political oratory in favor of teaching a plain-spoken style to society's would-be managers. Not until the 1940s and 1950s did the fields of journalism and speech begin to make major contributions to the wider issues of social influence and propaganda.[20]

If academe did not immediately embrace European doubts about whether public opinion (considered collectively or individually) was rational, the transformation was under way even before the Guns of August. When tempered by the experience of the Great War, European influences helped to lay an intellectual foundation in America upon which could be built a postwar propaganda consciousness.

The Juggernaut of Big Communication

The World War, the muckrakers, and the science of the irrational were not the only considerations impelling progressives to examine how well the old symbols of democracy might be stretched to cover the new practices of the mind managers. The growth and consolidation of the communication industry during the 1920s convinced progressives that postwar normalcy would include wartime publicity practices and institutionalized symbolic orchestration. The looming juggernaut of postwar Big Communication shouted to the nation with radio and gestured with the projected images of film. Controlling the enterprise was an interconnected nexus of professionals in advertising, market research, and public relations.

The alliance forged between the medium of radio and the profession of advertising epitomized postwar Big Communication. Although radio's total contribution to the advertising boom of the 1920s was modest, the marriage of radio and advertising fostered the impression that Big Communication had arrived to become an equal of big business, big government, and big urban centers. Radio exuded an aura of energy and scope. Between 1920 and 1924, broadcasting accelerated from a handful of stations to 600 licenses granted; during the same interim, the number of radio sets in use rose from approximately 60,000 to 3 million. To this, advertising's union of professionalism and science added an impression of special knowledge and power. The Great War facilitated burgeoning trends toward professionalism in the advertising field, which already (between 1914 and 1917) had seen the founding of the Associated Advertising Clubs of the World, the American Association of Advertising Agencies, and the Association of National Advertisers. At the same time, academicians offered to harness science to the horse sense of professional practitioners. For instance, Walter Dill Scott, director of Northwestern University's psychological laboratory, showed how ads were impacted by such psychological principles as attention, perception, apperception, the association of ideas, suggestion, and mental imagery. Radio's verve and advertising's desire to view buyers as a bundle of deep-seated drives contributed to the image of small consumers at the mercy of Big Communication.[21]

If radio and advertising established the public face of Big Communication, market and audience research provided the edifice of mass persuasion with eyes and ears. By 1918, when Archibald Crossley was commissioned to establish a survey unit for a Philadelphia advertising firm, market research departments already existed in a few ad agencies such as the George Batten Company of New York. Market researchers found that simply amassing facts and figures did not impress often-skeptical clients; therefore, these researchers, like the copy writers of thirty years before, assimilated methods from social scientists. For instance, psychologist Rensis Likert measured the sales influence of particular radio programs by combining an estimate of the size of the audience with sampling to find out how many listeners actually purchased the product. One of sociologist Paul Lazarsfeld's first publications in the United States demonstrated the importance of phrasing and interpreting questions in assessing consumer decisions.[22]

Market research to flesh out the features of the radio audience was an inevitable consequence of broadcasting's mercantile tilt because radio people had no direct contact with the twinkling glimmers of their uncounted but presumably vast listening audience. Some of the earliest audience research was simply to ascertain signal strength or to determine whether local stations actually were airing network commercials. Program ratings soon became the broadcast industry's chief source of self-identity, however, when Archibald Crossley established a telephone survey in 1929 and later when operators at C. E. Hooper Inc. called and questioned listeners during broadcasts.[23]

Collaboration between Paul Lazarsfeld's Office of Radio Research at Princeton University (later at Columbia) and Frank Stanton's CBS research department perhaps revealed most clearly the impulse to build the greatest possible listenership at each point in the radio schedule. The Office conducted research into advertising effects, psychological factors of selling, the sales impact of particular shows, the characteristics of persons tuning in programs, and which features of a program produced the most gratifications for listeners. A notable outcome of ever more ardent pursuit of this last objective was the Lazarsfeld–Stanton Program Analyzer. The Analyzer allowed respondents to give ten reactions per minute by pressing a green button (indicating the respondent liked the content), a red one (dislike), or no button (indifference). By tabulating what percentage of the audience pressed which buttons when, the data showed those portions of a program generating the most interest.[24] As broadcasters used research to secure the largest number of listeners for their advertisers, considerations of audience size and quality gained ever greater sway as the ultimate measure of successful Big Communication.

With society's powerful business leaders more "word-conscious" than ever, public relations also played its part in producing Big Communication's postwar publicity boom. Although practitioners of public relations owed much to prior-day civic boosting, political spectacle, circus promotionalism, and theatrical press agentry, the Creel committee had alerted publicity workers and business managers alike to the true power of a completely organized system of "intellectual and emotional bombardment." To his amazement, Edward L. Bernays had observed the CPI's ability to penetrate into the huts of Italian peasants where one was likely to find "a picture of the Virgin Mary, and next to it was a picture of Woodrow Wilson." "And that intrigued me," recalled Bernays, "because it indicated the validity of what we'd been doing."[25] In the months after the Armistice, Bernays and other alumni of the CPI fanned out to do publicity work for government agencies, industry, and various social and political factions.

Bernays's approach enlarged upon existing practices of publicity which, as exemplified by Ivy Lee's work for the Rockefellers, chiefly had amounted to finding what seemed the most winsome response to an immediate problem and sending this communication directly to news editors. Bernays typically avoided contacting news people directly as when he promoted the long-term sale of pianos by persuading leading architects to put music rooms in their plans and "by organizing an exhibition of period music rooms designed by well known decorators who themselves exert an influence on the buying groups." Although progressive critics regarded Bernays's covert string pulling as manipulative, Bernays saw himself as "an applied social scientist" who ferreted out "the adjustments and maladjustments" between a client and the client's target audiences. The peripatetic Bernays turned to engineers to promote the idea of good ventilation in cars and to the medical profession to promote consumption of bacon and bananas. While he preferred long-term, behind-the-scenes work, Bernays also implemented short-term, dramatic "high-spotting" as when he organized the nationwide celebration of Light's Golden Jubilee. This event not only commemorated Edison's discovery of the incandescent lamp but also helped the electric power industry to minimize unfavorable publicity resulting from an ongoing investigation by the Federal Trade Commission.[26]

The contributions of cinema to Big Communication's juggernaut were more ambiguous than those of radio, advertising, market research, and public relations, even though the film industry raised the specter of unlimited image projection. Suggestions of film's potential power included not only the enormous weekly audience, which by the mid-1920s had reached 50 million, but also the ability of Hollywood's dramas and comedies to create national idols such as Rudolph Valentino. On the other hand, film's connection to the communication industry was limited by aesthetic considerations. The effort required to translate a written scenario or script into cinematic image kept considerations of artistry and creativity more in the forefront than was the case with the more routinized productions of radio and the more prosaic renderings of advertising. The studio system never regarded its audience as fully amenable to the kind of product that advertising agencies were foisting on radio, where achieving the smallest possible variation in a comedy or drama series was seen as the way to stabilized audiences and profits.[27]

If the relatively refined medium of cinema offered fewer opportunities for professionals in advertising, market research, and public relations, the film medium represented the most direct vehicle available before television to diffuse images of people and of social practices. Apparent to conservative moralists and to progressive critics alike was that American films circumvented many teachings of the church and strictures of the home. Hollywood's preoccupation with the fast life of the fashionable produced films in which nearly three-fourths of plots revolved around sex, love, or crime. During this era of Prohibition, three of every four movies showed characters, usually the hero or heroine, drinking liquor and using tobacco. In addition, by the 1930s, radio-style publicity practices were finding niches in the preparation of films. The advertising departments of film companies experimented with ostensibly informative movie shorts that showed, and therefore plugged, specific products. Audience research, common in broadcasting, also made some headway in Hollywood when Nelson Rockefeller insisted that RKO bring on pollster George Gallup as an adviser. Gallup's work for RKO, and later Disney and MGM, included testing story ideas, possible casts, and various options for promoting a film. Among the pollster's findings was that titles that sounded educational were the kiss of death for a film.[28]

With American business increasingly sold on the value of Big Communication, it was not long until the nexus moved toward the political realm. By 1928, communication practitioners were advising political orators to shorten formal addresses from the customary one and one-half hours to a snappier thirty minutes. The marketing approach altered not only the length of political speaking but also its tone and style as when Bruce Barton, the advertising guru, advised Herbert Hoover to speak briefly, simply, and in a more emotionally expressive manner. Barton also helped to make speaking secondary to publicity practices when he counseled Hoover to emphasize his humanity with fishing trips and when Barton arranged for famous entertainers to state their political endorsements. By 1948, the GOP National Committee formally hired Batton, Barton, Durstine, and Osborn. In 1952, when three advertising and research firms handled Eisenhower's bid for the presidency, the public face of the campaign increasingly was conveyed by panels and documentaries instead of by political speeches.[29]

Postmodern Americans perhaps take as a given the intriguing, if not always reassuring, alliances between the symbol-spewing channels – radio/TV and film – and the symbol-managing professions of advertising, market research, and public relations; however, Big Communication prompted considerable soul searching after the Great War. Clearly, town meetings and small-town intimacy no longer characterized either the messages available in America's urban centers or the methods of public-opinion formation unfolding there. As a result, a literature emerged that tested Big Communication by standards of democracy drawn from the progressive movement. Progressives tended to believe that the mind managers gave institutions and interest groups a new ability to secure action before the public could formulate and articulate its will. Operating on assumptions already laid out by the muckrakers, progressive propaganda critics of the inter–world-war period worried about cooptation of public opinion through ideological gatekeeping in media channels, through massive orchestration of symbols, and through covert ideological diffusion in society's communication channels.

Progressive Propaganda Critics

One of the ironies of World War I was that the muckrakers failed truly to alarm Americans about propaganda until they themselves created the more powerful beast against which they might crusade. The CPI's success in muckraking the Kaiser abroad and the "Kaiserite" at home created a popular audience for the question of whether mass persuasion was inherently an obstacle to mass democracy. Retrospectives on the war-era persuasions by Lippmann and Irwin and alarm bells rung by Dewey and Beard only had whetted popular and academic curiosity about propaganda. Writers and scholars alike found a ready acceptance for new efforts to integrate propaganda into social thought and into social studies. The result was a body of literature generally known during the 1920s and 1930s as *propaganda analysis.*

Critics returning to the muckraker's theme of tainted news produced the largest portion of postwar inquiries into gatekeeping, symbol orchestration, and covert infiltration of ideas. Lippmann and Irwin continued as leaders in press criticism, although others, such as war correspondent George Seldes, became renowned for studies of propaganda in news. Lippmann's major postwar contribution to propaganda critique, *Public Opinion* (1922), projected the problem of propaganda less onto professional journalists, as had his earlier works, and more on the situation of little people caught up in what Graham Wallas, Lippmann's mentor, had termed "The Great Society."[30] Lippmann was interested in how people during the war had constructed fictional and ephemeral pictures in their heads about Allied leaders and nations because the real political world was out of their reach. Public opinion, therefore, was susceptible to becoming a symbolic "pseudo-environment" created by the mind and placed between itself and the real world.

Although recognizing the role of Creel's committee in quickly diffusing "a fairly uniform set of ideas to all the people of a nation," Lippmann in 1922 was more interested in how modern propaganda gained leverage not only from human nature but also from the conditions of giant cities. Urban life made it difficult to have intimate contact with people and events; citizens necessarily filled in their picture of the world with stereotypes. Moreover, the very words used by journalists evoked potentially distorting mental images. Even more superficial "pictures in the head" resulted from photos and movies, as when D. W. Griffith's *Birth of a Nation* diffused a false history of the Ku Klux Klan. Lippmann recounted experimental evidence that stereotypes prevented most people from accurately describing a public event seen with their own eyes.

Lippmann granted that the Jeffersonian view of the wise voter, who enjoyed direct access to fact, accurately had portrayed the simpler conditions of "the isolated rural township." In contrast, agency administrators now presided over a "vast collection of bureaus and their agents" giving them an advantage over confused legislators, who typically understood few of the bills they voted on, and even more perplexed citizens. Because of new modes of propaganda, governments now had resources for "the manufacture of consent." Efforts by progressives to restore public control over the minutia of politics had been unsuccessful despite hopeful experiments with the initiative, referendum, and direct primary.

Lippmann saw the essential weakness of democratic theory as its silence on the matter of how reality was to be made known to the public. To render citizens resistant to propaganda and stereotype, Lippmann recommended establishment of independent intelligence bureaus in government. Turning to infant social science, Lippmann also looked hopefully to public conferences organized around a Socratic dialogue of experts. In Lippmann's ideal discursive environment, expert researchers in government would enjoy lifetime tenure as well as the guarantee of a full and unfettered power to investigate. Granting that no institution was perfect, Lippmann nevertheless contended that his bureaus would help people to "overcome the central difficulty of self-government, the difficulty of dealing with an unseen reality." With the information and opinion provided by research bureaus, voters finally would be able to overcome their stereotypes. Despite his pessimism about the public's mental weaknesses, a strain of thought that became more pronounced in his later books, Lippmann's *Public Opinion* generally was read as a breakthrough in democratic theory and remains as one of the most comprehensive statements of certain features of the progressive view of propaganda.[31]

As with Lippmann, Will Irwin continued as an active press critic in the postwar years. In his most developed statement of the problem, *Propaganda in the News* (1936), Irwin surveyed not only the work of Ivy Lee and other early press wizards but also the opposing struggle of muckrakers to expose tainted news. He chronicled highpoints of German and British war propaganda partly to reinforce his alarm that most European governments had continued their powerful press bureaus in the postwar period. Irwin not only commented on familiar progressive bugbears such as the Ku Klux Klan and the prohibitionist groups; he also examined the infiltration of systematic propaganda into mainstream politics and government. Irwin, who had admired President Herbert Hoover since both were students at Stanford, exposed the campaign of the Democrats to bring down Hoover. In Irwin's account, multimillionaire John J. Raskob, who had been outraged by attacks on Al Smith's Catholic faith during the presidential election of 1928, bankrolled the Democrats in a public relations effort to unseat the victorious Hoover. Conceding that the Depression more than clever propaganda had defeated his Stanford friend, Irwin nevertheless claimed that Raskob's revenge marked the first application of a new method of background propaganda in politics. After Franklin Roosevelt took power, Irwin added, the triumph of governmental publicity was assured when each of the many new federal agencies established its own press office.

Because he retained faith in professionalism, Irwin was not as pessimistic as Lippmann about the ability of press people to detect and expose propaganda. Irwin believed that important news invariably would be printed sooner or later. Although he conceded that commercialism worked against a free press, Irwin emphasized that editors and publishers could not prosper if they acted in ways that cost them a good reputation both with readers and staff. Irwin believed, further, that the muckrakers had permanently changed journalism by alerting news people to the value of longer analytic stories of the kind that now frequently appeared in the Sunday editions if nowhere else.[32] ·

George Seldes, the most influential of the second generation of press critics, was much impressed by Irwin's early series on journalism and by Upton Sinclair's personal account of newspapers as enemies of reformers. After his stint as an American war correspondent in France, Seldes was posted by Robert McCormick's *Chicago Tribune* to Berlin, Moscow, Rome, and elsewhere. Seldes resigned from the *Tribune* in 1929 when his stories about Mexico were suppressed by his editor, and the now-out-of-work correspondent wrote *You Can't Print That!*, a reflection on the role of the postwar foreign correspondent. As told by Seldes, American reporters abroad faced a reign of propaganda, whereby government officials rewarded friendly reporters and threw the others out, and correspondents experienced pressures by their own newspapers to keep friendly relations with foreign officials or to send cables confirming the newspaper's prejudices (e.g., for or against the League of Nations). Seldes attributed the wide influence of *You Can't Print That!* to its focus on overseas conditions and relative silence on domestic press corruption.

In *Freedom of the Press* (1935), Seldes shifted attention from propaganda in the European dictatorships to domestic American obstacles to a freely formed public opinion. Seldes agreed with Lippmann that "the crisis of democracy is a crisis in journalism." Accordingly, he focused on forces arrayed against a free press including "advertising, big business, propaganda, social ambitions, human weaknesses, lack of economic security, [and] its resultant atmosphere of fear." Seldes was refining what would become his stock in trade: culling examples of abuses from official investigations and reports. He identified instances where advertising had corrupted news as when Chicago papers protected tourism by suppressing news of amoebic dysentery in hotels. Turning to public relations, Seldes reported the Congressional investigation of Ivy Lee and Carl Byoir, who had given public relations advice to Nazi officials about how to improve Germany's image in the United States. Seldes muckraked specific outlets, accusing the Associated Press of transmitting baseless speculations of American oil interests about a communist threat in Mexico. He complained that the *New York Times* had failed to curb its pro-fascist correspondent in Rome.

Despite evidences of journalism's frequent adulteration by propaganda, Seldes, as with Irwin, was buoyed by progressivism's characteristic faith in professionalism. He singled out particular newspapers for praise, such as the *Toledo News-Bee*, which had fought against propaganda favoring private utilities. Seldes was most impressed with the formation of the Newspaper Guild in fall 1933 under the leadership of columnist Heywood Broun. Seldes doted on the Guild, reporting the progress of the fledgling group that, in a matter of weeks, had enrolled 2,500 members despite publishers' hints at retaliation. Seldes believed that the Guild, which attracted 8,000 members relatively quickly, consummated the professionalization of reporters by publishing a code of ethical practices that, on the one hand, endorsed confidentiality of sources and, on the other, condemned suppression of news, sensationalism, and the injection of prejudices.

Perhaps the best known of Seldes's works of the 1930s was his *Lords of the Press* (1938), which laid out the careers of Roy Howard (of the Scripps-Howard chain), Robert McCormick, Harry Chandler of the *Los Angeles Times*, William Randolph Hearst, and other of the opinionated and sometimes feudally minded owners of the great newspaper chains. In Seldes's estimation, the press lords not only puffed up news that furthered their personal economic interests in cattle and oil but also frequently put newspapers in the service of redbaiting and antilabor policies. In treating the Squire of San Simeon, Seldes related how William Randolph Hearst's persistent redbaiting of educators and virulent opposition to the New Deal finally had prompted a widespread boycott of the "Hearst propaganda machine."[33]

Books by Lippmann, Irwin, and Seldes showed that criticism of propaganda in news had attained a certain stature. Even more prevalent, however, were the large number of articles that related inside dope about how modern journalism could be adulterated. The *New Republic* published a series of self-confessional articles by representatives of various professions of Big Communication. An anonymous publicity person told of puffing up a nondescript businessman with ghostwritten articles and speeches and promoting this Babbitt's daughter in the society columns. Writing from Iowa, an editor explained how devotees of Babbittry and the Klan made it impossible to dampen panic that the Pope was on the verge of taking over the local schools. Nor was the *New Republic* the only publication opening itself to antipropaganda exposé. Elsewhere journalists gave the inside dope about public relations, for instance, estimating that 42 of 64 items of local news printed in an unnamed New York newspaper had been "rewritten or pasted up from material sent in by press agents." The new-style public relations work of Bernays came in for special attention from time to time as when John Flynn explored "The Science of Ballyhoo" practiced by Creel's erstwhile employee. Flynn wondered whether hiring doctors to make studies, employing professors to make surveys, and setting up various commissions did not make consumers of the news "utterly disorganized and helpless."[34]

If, as Irwin had hypothesized in 1919, the postwar years were an "age of lies," it followed that even photojournalism could be vulnerable to adulteration via publicity. George Jean Nathan, drama and art critic, complained about journalism's ever more promiscuous use of pictures, reckoning that the old audience of yellow journalism, no longer fooled by words, still believed that pictures could not lie. Nathan pointed out that photos could be staged, doctored, or even simply recaptioned as when the "Battle of Manila Bay" became "Navy Goes After Rum Fleet." A similar article in *Nation* revealed instances of news people staging photographs of grieving children and observed the tendency of editors to receive photos of unknown origins from syndicates and publicity agents.[35]

Criticism of news manipulation expanded upon themes already laid down in the era of muckraking and therefore easily became the chief line of progressive propaganda critique in the 1920s and 1930s. However, the war years had both broadened and deepened awareness of symbolic connivance such that American opinion leaders were ready for a propaganda analysis of education, entertainment, religion, and government-agency action. Second in significance to the propaganda analysis of news was the effort to expose how one-sided special interest propaganda might subvert education's promise to develop a thinking individual.

As with the propaganda of news, retrospectives about the Great War set the context for concern about postwar propaganda in education. Two articles in H. L. Mencken's *American Mercury* reminded college professors of their embarrassingly eager and uncritical enlistment in the campaign to build a national consensus against Germany during the late war. Charles Angoff painted a sorry picture of educators stooping to all manner of chauvinistic distortions as when Josiah Royce, Harvard philosopher, branded Germany as an "enemy of the human race" and one chemistry professor argued vehemently, if unconvincingly, that Germany had made no real contributions to that field. In another installment of *American Mercury*'s review of intellectuals and the war, C. H. Grattan took historians to task for having "swallowed the official theory of the causes and nature of the war that came from Lord Northcliffe" (Britain's propaganda chief). He contrasted Albert B. Hart's 1914 book on the war, which discussed how Russia's mobilization and Austria's ultimatum to Serbia had created a dilemma for Germany, with a 1917 article by Hart that presented Germany as single-handedly plotting the war as a first step toward world conquest. Unfortunately for the historians, Grattan observed, Germany sued for peace before the demand for biased war handbooks could reach its full potential in classes conducted by the Student Army Training Corps.[36]

More than retrospectives on the war years, revelations about the propaganda campaign of the National Electric Light Association (NELA) alerted educators to the continuing danger of propaganda in the schools. Rumors about the NELA's behind-the-scenes propaganda campaign to enlist educators against publicly owned power plants led to calls for a Congressional investigation. Opponents of the inquiry succeeded in shifting it to the less public venue of the Federal Trade Commission, which in 1928 commenced hearings; however, the resulting disclosures caused educators to wonder about whether outside funding inherently brought propaganda. Columbia's Edwin Seligman, who investigated the NELA disclosures for the American Association of University Professors, acknowledged that the utility industry had supplied "large sums of money" in the form of stipends, study grants, and travel expenses to universities, colleges, and research institutes not only for studies of electric power but also for lectures and preparation of textbooks. While Seligman found few full-time faculty members to be culpable, he recommended that universities balance carefully the need of teachers for relevant contact with industry (particularly faculty in business and economics) with the principle that professors should function as independent seekers of truth. Seligman's specific recommendations for colleges included avoiding grants that required periodic renewals, refusing outside money for research on questions of public policy, and disclosing all outside support.[37]

"The propagandist is knocking at the school door. In some instances he has already been admitted." This warning prefaced a survey of exhibits, films, book covers, pamphlets, study materials for teachers, free services, lectures, projects, fund drives, and student contests that was conducted by the Committee on Propaganda in the Schools of the National Education Association (NEA). The NEA's committee attributed the influx of outside materials to the example of the late CPI, which had alerted interest groups to the possibility of molding public opinion through the curriculum. The report recommended that educators protect captive audiences of young students from outside material having partisan or commercial intentions. In the years following the NEA report, educators demonstrated their awareness of the danger posed by pamphlets and prize contests that beckoned the nation's children for various partisan purposes.[38]

Exposés of covert manipulation in journalism and education were complemented by muckraking studies of how entertainment fare and religious preachments might provide cover for propaganda. Educators complained about movie shorts that covertly touted products, as when one film about cosmetics displayed a particular brand's label for seventy-eight seconds; also prompting concern were films that promoted political causes such as prohibition or food drives. Given that movies now penetrated "every sizeable hamlet in the country," critics of entertainment propaganda further questioned the social attitudes being projected by cinema. Harold Larrabee observed the tendency of American films to make the poor appear noble and the rich villainous and to associate crime with liquor and foreigners.

Most of the debate about the content of the movies, however, focused on moral standards diffused in film. This general cultural critique of sex, crime, and vulgarity in the movies linked propaganda analysis to a larger cultural revolt of the rural and the religiously inclined against Hollywood-manufactured images of urban Babylon. The Payne Fund studies, conducted by such rising stars of American social science as Herbert Blumer, Edgar Dale, and Louis Thurstone, are the best examples of research on the movies' moral impact on children and youth. Dale discovered that only 9 percent of leading movie characters emphasized socially productive goals over personal ones; this statistic had particular interest value for propaganda critics who worried about which ideologies received the greatest play in public communication.[39]

If propaganda hid behind the graven images of mass entertainment, propaganda critics reckoned that the truths of religious preaching and teaching were equally vulnerable to adulteration. H. L. Mencken's series on idiocy in the late war included reminders by historian Granville Hicks of Reverend Newell Dwight Hillis's atrocity stories and Billy Sunday's lurid prayer in the U.S. House of Representatives that beseeched God to smite the vile, bloodthirsty Germans. *Preachers Present Arms,* by sociologist Ray Abrams, became the bible for religiously minded people determined not to render carelessly unto Caesar. Abrams showed how Washington's turn to war eviscerated the previously powerful strain of pacifism in American churches by motivating church people not only to work in recruitment, bond sales, and food conservation but also to circulate atrocity tales and root out pacifist clergy (about half of whom were forced from their pulpits). The most powerful exposé of postwar religious propaganda was Heber Blankenhorn's study for the Interchurch World Movement of the connivance between the steel industry and Pittsburgh-area preachers to undermine unions and retain the 12-hour workday.[40]

In addition to exposing efforts to coopt journalists, educators, movie makers, and clergy, the postwar propaganda critics spoke to the danger that, despite the demise of the CPI, agencies of the federal government continued to spend the people's money to tell the people what to believe. Some postwar critiques of propaganda in government sprang from fears that the memory of (superficially) unified wartime opinion would tempt federal administrators to revive Creel-style institutional persuasion. Walter Millis described how Herbert Hoover tried, and failed, to use World War I's rah-rah style of press relations to rally support during the Depression. According to Millis, Hoover was misled by the ease with which he used a "high-pressure propaganda drive" to further his policies as wartime commandant of the nation's food supply. A technocratic outsider to Washington, Hoover did not realize that the war's propaganda owed much of its quick and comfortable success to the lack of a viable political opposition and to yearnings for national unity.[41]

Chastened by the Great War, progressive propaganda critics were particularly alert for signs that a new propaganda for war festered under federal auspices. Charles Beard found the public bewildered by the clash of propagandas in which peace proponents organized banquets and exhibits to promote goodwill among nations, and the Navy League (a group "founded mainly by armament-profit makers") poured forth thunder in pamphlets and news stories. George Seldes weighed into the debate with warnings that military men aimed to paint pacifists as dupes of the Japanese. Finding the public confused by competing propagandas of air power versus sea power, Seldes argued that Truth already had been the first casualty even in advance of any hostilities. Citizens needed information from research rather than propaganda from weapons advocates. Robert Wohlforth, a labor expert, wrote disapprovingly of the War Department's citizenship courses that had enrolled some 260,000 young men at high schools, colleges, and training camps. Wohlforth found military instructors outfitting students with an ideological clothing of complacency stuffed "with the sawdust of reactionary platitudes, tin-whistle ideals and big business morality."[42]

The idea that propaganda was an infallible sign of war made the opinion leaders attentive to otherwise arcane historical studies of America's decision to join the Allies. A prominent theme in revisionist interpretations of World War I was the idea that propaganda, more than German brutality or a rational calculus of interests, had brought America to war. Walter Millis's *Road To War* (1935) was particularly influential in alerting Americans to the fact that covert influence was a vector of Britain's war effort from the very beginning. Millis, however, eschewed a strictly Machiavellian view of propaganda, noting that Allied persuasions had benefited from the desire of many American opinion leaders to act upon their "passionate and vocal sympathies to the Allied cause." Britain's propaganda operation in America had been "self-financing," because "our public clamored for the books, articles and motion-picture films which conveyed it." Nevertheless, the totality of Millis's argument made it appear that Americans had been deviously duped by Parker's publicity ploys, leaks from Britain's secret agents, the era's harping on atrocity stories, and the lure of loans and munitions contracts.[43]

Apprehensions about propaganda as precursor to war resonated among opinion leaders during the inter–world-war period. Zechariah Chafee, Harvard's expert on freedom of speech, warned that advocates for war preparedness were benefiting from the eagerness of newspapers to print attacks on peace societies. Journalist Quincy Howe contributed an influential, like-minded exposé arguing that a network of Anglophilic organizations had gained sway over academicians, politicians, and newspaper publishers such that American public opinion almost unconsciously deferred to British foreign policy. The title of Howe's work said it all: in the coming European crisis, *England Expects Every American to Do His Duty.* Senator Gerald Nye made a similar point in his April 1939 speech on "Propaganda in the Next War." Believing that "the greatest danger to our peace in America is propaganda," Nye speculated that propagandists already had fostered the view that if another war broke out in Europe "our participation [is] inevitable, inescapable."[44]

The most startling warning that institutions might boom up a new war came in the form of H. C. Engelbrecht's and F. C. Hanighen's thesis that arms merchants were an important, and hitherto unrecognized, cog in the engine of war. These authors reviewed how weapons marketers manipulated the British press into calling for a naval buildup in 1909 and had used press leaks to angle for sales in Latin America. Arms manufacturers worked against disarmament as when American shipbuilding and steel companies prepared publicity to oppose arms-reduction conferences and, instead, boost a naval buildup. The "merchants-of-death" thesis marked the decade's most tangible confluence of progressivism, revisionism, and isolationism, setting in motion U.S. Senate hearings conducted by Gerald Nye. Nye's investigation helped move Congress to enact a series of neutrality laws designed to control the export of U.S. materiel and capital to warring nations.[45]

Two decades' worth of popular articles and books on propaganda embedded deeply into general public consciousness the progressive view of propaganda as a social problem for democracy. By 1939, Americans saw self-serving propaganda as arguably the major cause of World War I.[46] Ordinary people increasingly understood that civics textbooks greatly had understated the role of pressure-group communications in politics and society. Beneath complaints that "it's all propaganda," lay many dozens of exposés of self-seeking verbal gymnastics by professional patriots, by trade associations, by social-movement leaders, and by all manner of news manipulators such as the oil men and politicians who wanted to scare up an American occupation of Mexico.[47] Although the popular critique of mass persuasion was neither coordinated nor entirely consistent, the movement to expose propaganda's threat to democracy exhibited characteristic progressive contours. Propaganda critics viewed manipulation as the key problem of modern social influence, believing that citizens were fully capable of making self-government work once they learned about those institutions and groups laboring to coopt the channels of public communication. Progressive writers saw themselves as a necessary part of a movement to energize democratic life by educating America's political and economic consumers to detect manipulation not only in news but also in other important agencies of social communication.

Academic Critics

From the first, propaganda analysis was a popular paradigm. Journalists and intellectuals alike found a ready audience for works outlining the new contours of democracy in the environment of Big Communication. Academic students of propaganda, however, had interests closer to home than merely publicizing manipulation and promoting democratic reforms. The era's concern about propaganda beckoned scholars both to integrate propaganda concepts into their theories of society and to configure the curriculum to empower students against massive image building and subtle ideological cooptation.

As historians had been foremost among those scholars working for the CPI, so were they among the first to discover how propaganda might inform their discipline's work. In an address at the 1921 joint convention of the American and Mississippi Valley historical societies, F. H. Hodder recommended that members of his audience "review our American history for the purpose of inquiring to what extent propaganda may have been used as a source and may have become a part of it, as it is written." As an example, Hodder cited how historians reproduced the promotional work of patriot leaders who successfully had transformed a "street brawl between common soldiers and town roughs" into the Boston Massacre.[48]

Not only did historians view propaganda as a concept helping to clarify their source materials, but they assimilated into their research subsidiary concepts of public opinion, news sensations, censorship, news control, and the power of officials to orchestrate perception. Historians were particularly interested in propagandas associated with wars, not only the genocidal conflict of 1914–1918, but also those stretching back to the English Civil War. Later, when conditions in Europe began to point to another outbreak of mechanized killing, academic studies of the Great War's propaganda won considerable attention from general-interest readers of historical works.[49]

However common was the term *propaganda* in inter–world-war historical studies, this master term and its subsidiary concepts probably went more deeply into the field of political science given the aspirations to theory of this evolving department of social study. An early study examined Spain's propaganda of "racial and cultural solidarity" with Latin Americans, a theme that became more successful when Spain dropped ambitions for colonial reconquest and after she was defeated in 1898 by the United States. Following this lead, many political scientists also turned to case studies of atrocity propaganda, the Anti-Saloon League, business and ethnic groups in politics, and party publicity bureaus. Harold Stoke gave a new perspective to conservative complaints about the New Deal when he wrote of "the continued absorption by the executive of a larger degree of legislative initiative and power." Propaganda, Stoke added, was an inevitable instrument when, in a political system characterized by executive initiative, an administration sought popular consent.[50]

While some political scientists pursued case-study inquiries into propaganda, an equally characteristic response by others was to theorize on links between propaganda and public opinion. Leading political scholars of public opinion included Peter Odegard, Harwood Childs, and Harold D. Lasswell. Odegard's *The American Public Mind* (1930) took cognizance of a great number of influences shaping public opinion, including church, family, schools, newspapers, and various publicity and propaganda channels and tactics. Childs of Princeton University became a leading researcher of pressure groups, cooperating with Edward Bernays on a bibliography on public opinion and later debating Bernays on whether competition was enough to protect the public from propagandists. As long as courses on the public mind carried the title "Public Opinion *and Propaganda*," Childs's legacy remained in force.[51]

No single name is more associated with the politics of propaganda than that of Harold D. Lasswell, political theorist of the University of Chicago and later Yale. Lasswell's work best synthesized the societal, psychological, symbolic, and methodological tentacles of the free-floating conglomeration that was academic propaganda study. Lasswell's prominence in propaganda theory dated from his Ph.D. dissertation on world war persuasions that had been published in book form in 1927. This historical-critical study of symbolism seemed to place him at the driving center of the social and intellectual movement to study mass persuasion. However, Lasswell's work (as with that of Lippmann) would diverge noticeably from mainstream progressive critique in later years when (as will be seen) he allied himself with practitioners and new-style symbol scientists.[52]

If Lasswell was the political scientist most associated with the study of propaganda, Leonard Doob of Yale became the leading expert on the psychology of the phenomenon. Doob did graduate work in psychology and sociology in Germany in the early 1930s and began work there on a Ph.D. study of news propaganda, which later he completed at Harvard. Extensively rewritten, Doob's analysis of the mental and social dimensions of mass persuasion appeared in 1935 as *Propaganda: Its Psychology and Technique,* a book widely used by students in American colleges and universities before World War II. Doob set out the mental context of propaganda by discussing motivation, attitudes, stereotypes, personality, and values. While noting that propaganda was not automatically successful, Doob observed that people were susceptible to suggestion, especially from prestigious sources, and thus the symbols of propaganda might arouse and recombine preexisting attitudes. Propaganda sometimes resulted from the explicit intentions of a persuader but also could be unintentional as when educators indirectly transmitted the social heritage of a culture. Doob concluded with a survey of such leading propagandists as Ivy Lee, Edward Bernays, and the Communist Party, and he explored newspaper, radio, movies, and other channels. Overall, Doob's book represented an effort to illuminate the process by which propaganda changed attitudes with a view toward helping to induce some resistance to the phenomenon.[53]

Sociologists, as with psychologists, saw propaganda both as supplying a useful cornucopia of concepts and as providing a focal point for analysis of social interaction. Frederick Lumley's general sociological survey featured propaganda as a means of social control related to, but distinct from, education. William Albig's text on public opinion described propagandized messages and coopted communication channels as a major influence on the public mind. In individual articles, sociologists worked to define propaganda, as when Lumley offered the idea that propaganda not only fed people packaged conclusions but also exaggerated and concealed selfish interests. Other sociologists distinguished between propaganda and education, between group and individual appeals, and between censorship and propaganda. Case studies, such as S. H. Foster's analysis of war news in American papers, were less characteristic of sociological research (compared to that of history and political science).[54]

Academic sociology's interest in propaganda was expressed not only in chapters and articles but also in book-length treatments of the subject by Frederick Lumley, Ray Abrams, and Alfred McClung Lee. Lumley's *The Propaganda Menace* (1933) articulated well the expansion of propaganda analysis from prewar studies of news control to the postwar assaying of manipulation in schools, churches, and other apparatuses of social exchange. As in Doob's book, Lumley's brought out examples of concealed and self-serving promotions by superpatriots, capitalists, politicians, educators, and preachers. However, unlike psychologist Doob, sociologist Lumley presented propaganda – "promotion which is veiled" – as inherently evil because such covert machinations "cast suspicions on all communicational activities." In contrast, Doob believed that a science of propaganda should avoid ethical contrasts between the true or false and the good or bad. Nevertheless, the two agreed that a liberal education would help people who were submerged in biased symbolism to swim up toward the fresh air of intelligent reflection. Lumley also accepted Doob's premise that a number of factors limited propaganda's power.[55]

Studies by sociologists Abrams and Lee gave detailed treatments of how religion and news functioned respectively to channel thought and action. Abrams's study of propaganda and the preachers, described earlier, entered the popular literature; nevertheless, consistent with the academic temper of the times, this University of Pennsylvania sociologist worked to cast a scientific patina on his evocative data. At the book's end, Abrams positioned himself (somewhat too self-consciously) as having worked "from the point of view of the social scientist, who, eliminating moral praise and blame, endeavors to study all social phenomena as objectively as the chemist views the reaction of two elements placed together in a test tube in the laboratory." Alfred Lee's exhaustive sociology of journalism not only provided a social history of newspapers since colonial times but also conveyed a remarkably systematic and synthetic understanding of Big Communication as a whole. The index of Lee's *The Daily Newspaper in America* laid out a who's who of American social influence and a what's what of pertinent agencies and organizations.[56]

Concepts of propaganda seemed a good match for the disillusionment and ballyhoo of the Jazz Age together with the skepticism and longing for change that characterized the era of the Depression. In this milieu, seemingly every scholarly field harbored at least a few academicians interested in how Big Communication worked. Economists wrote of propaganda's employment in promoting tariff and monetary policies. Zechariah Chafee surveyed legal obstacles to peacetime free speech, for instance, explaining how *The Great Dictator*, Charlie Chaplin's spoof of Hitler, might be edited or banned. Propaganda's arrival as a significant theoretical construct seemingly was assured when the Social Science Research Council (SSRC), a consortium that connected disciplines to outside grantors, approved a bibliographic project headed by Harold Lasswell. However, as will be seen, Lasswell's heterogeneous collection of cultural critiques, quantitative experiments, and historical-critical case studies proved tenable only because growing fissures between the humanities and the quantitative social sciences were relatively unobtrusive in 1931 when the project was initiated.[57]

Although academic social scientists were leaders in propaganda studies, minor contributions to the literature could be found in a number of applied fields as well. In journalism, where social criticism lurked in the estimated 10 percent of courses devoted to the field's background, Ralph Casey and O. W. Riegel mounted notable forays into American and English political publicity bureaus and into the worldwide rise of radio and news propaganda. Because the field of speech was founded to revitalize the smaller persuasions of oratory more than to uncover the institutional vectors of public opinion, writers there chiefly applied propaganda to public speaking and debate. However, one could find in speech journals an occasional piece that might probe the large-scale dissemination of symbols either through speechmaking or in drama. Although the litterateurs who dominated the field of English had little interest in prosaic propaganda, the field's compositionists and semanticists did endeavor to add to the understanding of social influence.[58]

During the 1930s, therefore, American educators in many theoretical and applied fields contributed an important praxis of democracy when they assimilated the progressive propaganda paradigm into their scholarship and teaching. The result was to transform *propaganda* and *propaganda analysis* into terms not only having great currency among ordinary Americans but also carrying great theoretical significance for intellectuals and academicians. Before the Great War, *propaganda* was an amorphous term that, if it had any referent at all, conjured up images of Papists actively working against Protestants. The notion of "The German Propaganda," prevalent after exposure of the Kaiser's campaign of subversion, first connected propaganda to contemporary politics. The process by which propaganda came to denote self-interested social influence generally, rather than merely deceit by outsiders, was completed by postwar retrospectives on the Allied and CPI persuasions. Now society had a meaningful single label for the undemocratic, underhanded publicity that first had provoked the muckrakers. By the mid-1930s, the concept of propaganda encompassed not only covert manipulation of news and control of government bureaus but also included self-interested messages insinuated into a variety of ostensibly neutral civic channels, particularly education, entertainment, and religion. Basic to almost all definitions of propaganda was a concern that, through covert orchestration, people might be influenced by biased symbols without realizing that they had been herded into the propagandist's corral.

Central to the progressive conception of propaganda was the idea that education represented the best hope for reconciling new modes of mass persuasion with traditional American democracy. The move to reform society by educating people about social influence assumed that the public was sufficiently intelligent for modern politics but lacking in accurate information about institutions and groups. Taking the progressive view that society was dynamic and competitive, propaganda critics worked to unravel various alliances between powerful institutions and the channels and technologies of mass communication. Viewing propaganda as a new tool of social competition that posed dangers for democracy, their writings were intended to alert the public so that citizens would assume their proper roles in the Great Society.

Although propaganda critics succeeded in accomplishing their goal of making ordinary citizens more wary about communication, their work produced various counterpressures. Critical aspersions cast upon Big Communication energized practitioners such as Ivy Lee, Edward Bernays, and George Gallup to produce an opposing literature defending the democratic legitimacy of their professions. Further, propaganda critics irritated conservative political leaders who, as things turned out, did far more than merely respond with a counterbibliography of books and articles. Academe also saw a reaction against progressive propaganda critique when social scientists such as Lasswell began to align more with the originators of symbols than with the consumers of them. Another and particularly ironic reaction against propaganda analysis began after 1940, when progressives, wanting to rally the nation against fascism, began to resent the inherently self-reflexive practice of criticizing the purposes of those who prepared communication.

CHAPTER 3

DIFFERENT LESSONS I:
MANAGED DEMOCRACY

For most intellectuals of progressive inclination, the chief moral of the Great War was its demonstration that the modern public was vulnerable to dubious contrivances promoted by political leaders and institutional managers. However, maintenance of vital democratic participation never was progressivism's only benchmark for the good society. Efficient pursuit of social progress and securing unity by overcoming factions were two further progressive tenets standing ready to undergird an optimistic view that democracy could be reconciled to new techniques for guiding the public. Notwithstanding propaganda's theoretical dangers to free public choice, the promotions of the Creel committee and the army's successes with psychological leaflets and intelligence testing together testified to the mobilizing benefits of mind engineering. If the war no longer seemed an unalloyed good, could the warrior progressives be faulted for helping to execute a decision that, however imperfect, was sanctioned by long debate culminating in a legislative vote? Was there not positive value in the work of the opinion managers to enhance food conservation and tax compliance while at the same time helping to maintain unity of purpose against domestic naysayers and foreign saboteurs?

These questions portended challenges to the progressive critique of antidemocratic tendencies in social influence. Although critics were producing the largest body of literature on propaganda's relationship to democracy, a number of important writers during the period between the world wars began to articulate different lessons learned about mass persuasion. Among these alternate points of view, the two most influential in America's professional and intellectual circles were the *practitioner vantage point* and the *scientific perspective*. Both of these challenges to progressive propaganda analysis gave more optimistic readings of what Big Communication meant for America and how the nation should regard and handle the communication industry. They muddied the allure of progressivism's democratic ideal (informed citizen participation in social competition) by emphasizing progressivism's other goals of efficiency and social harmony.

The Practitioners Respond

Given the rise of a promotional culture and of consolidations in the communication industry, the mind engineers of public relations, market research, and advertising had a stake in laying out a practitioner position on social influence. Able to quickly discern solutions for the image problems of clients, practitioners who spoke up publicly for their craft were able with equal skill to frame defenses that drew on the American go-getting tradition of boosterism. The focus of propaganda critics on the macrosocial level had predisposed these analysts to view orchestrated social influence as not only culturally powerful but also inherently damaging to free choice. In contrast, professional persuaders knew from experience that success came against odds and that institutions frequently had meritorious, if not unimpeachable, motives. Yet the controversy about whether propaganda was culturally powerful (according to the progressive critics) or diluted through audience reception (the practitioner position) was only part of a broader dispute between these camps: the democratic morality of mass persuasion. As a result of the muckrakers, the practitioners had been on the spot to defend their communicative crafts since before the war. Ivy L. Lee, the public relations counsel, long had been recognized as an important practitioner spokesperson.

Ivy Lee's promotional work for the Red Cross had permitted this founder of public relations only a relatively peripheral role in the Great War's persuasions. However, during the decades before his death in 1934, Lee was a sought-after representative of the practitioner or professional view of propaganda. Since 1906, when he issued a public announcement of his promotional principles, Lee had been aware of the value of speaking to the general public about his craft in addition to privately counseling his clients. In this "Declaration of Principles," Lee emphasized to editors that his bureau always would do its work "in the open," that the material sent out would be accurate, and that he would welcome requests for further details.[1]

Lee's first principle of publicity was action, "giving the best possible service." He told corporations to adopt "an attitude of citizenship rather than a merely selfish relation to the community at large." Railroad executives, for instance, should make clear that they wanted to avoid accidents more on humanitarian grounds than to save money. Lee emphasized the proactive dimension of winning a good reputation, advising executives to maintain a candid relationship with newspapers and to speak directly in the idiom of the people rather than in the language of lawyers. He spoke up with warnings that publicity was not "a sort of umbrella to protect you against a rain of an unpleasant public opinion."

Lee's philosophy of communication was based on an extreme version of intellectual democracy. Lee defended corporate advocacy on the basis that facts and truths could not be considered self-evident. "All I can do is to give you *my interpretation of the facts*," he emphasized. From this precept, Lee deduced an ethics of publicity: *"The essential evil of propaganda is failure to disclose the source of information."* It followed that the cure for propaganda was embedded in the professional practices of editors who, Lee emphasized, should exercise their right to know the source of the information that they printed as news. In a session following an address to the American Association of Teachers of Journalism, Lee was pressed on the matter of ethical publicity. Lee granted the point that "complex, modern life" increased the dependence of editors on publicists in various spheres of society and, further, that "in the person of the modern publicity man, we have someone who is marshaling the evidence for his side." Lee, however, countered with claims that, as a reporter, he would welcome this welter and would promptly "go to work to develop my story in my own way." Lee summarized his own ethic of communication as never sending out "a statement of fact which I knew absolutely was a deliberate lie." Lee added that he would be willing to purvey opinions with which he disagreed but, in such a case, exclusively under the name of the corporation.[2]

Offended only by deliberate lies in factual matters that could be determined absolutely, Lee's publicity practices were articulated in terms that placed extreme faith in the morality of institutional leaders, the competence of journalists, and the discerning power of readers. Starting from the positions that truth was relative and propaganda necessary, Lee's emphasis on open connections between persuader and journalist placed the ethics of mass communication solely in the realm of professional codes and practices. Such a sanguine view of mass persuasion perhaps blinded this otherwise sensitive courtier of the crowd to the risk entailed by recoiling from only concealed sources and baldfaced lies (elements of what U.S. Army psychological warfare experts later would term *black propaganda*). In fact, Lee's Pollyannaish willingness to adjust nearly any idea to nearly any public ultimately drew him into the final embarrassment of his career when he blundered into functioning as an indirect adviser to Hitler's government.

By the 1930s, Lee had become greatly interested in the role that communication might play in bringing about greater cooperation among nations in an era when "guns still speak the only international language." Lee's recommendations for communication as a bridge to world understanding carried the aura of Machiavellian amorality, however, as when he offered that Japan could win greater sympathy for her occupation of Manchuria by openly distributing pictures of improvements in orderliness, education, and economic development.[3] Moreover, Lee placed himself in jeopardy when the German chemical trust retained him to help improve the image of Germany in the United States. The House Un-American Activities Committee (HUAC), then under the control of liberals John McCormack and Samuel Dickstein, was taking testimony about the work of public relations professionals for foreign accounts.

Most of HUAC's heat in executive session was absorbed by the public relations partners Carl Byoir, Carl Dickey, and Vincent Lancaster. Dickey, for instance, admitted that his firm had worked to minimize the impact on tourism of Hitler's anti-Semitic policies. Although Dickey said his firm had not tried to promote Hitler's government, he acknowledged sending out a publication on church–state separation in Germany prepared by the Friends of New Germany, a Nazi-controlled organization. For his part, Lee denied having distributed any propaganda materials whatsoever on the basis that there was no publicity capable of making Americans accept Nazi Germany's treatment of the Jews. On the other hand, Lee acknowledged meeting with cabinet-level officials in Germany, apparently including Joseph Goebbels. Lee soon suffered the fate of his fame when his testimony was released to the press during HUAC's public hearings. Newspaper headlines seized on the idea of a famous public relations practitioner serving as adviser to the Nazis, a trauma that may have contributed to Lee's death five months later of a brain tumor.[4]

Lee's humiliation might also have doomed the defense of public relations' democratic ethics but for the continuing work of the ubiquitous Edward L. Bernays. Since the early 1920s, Bernays had become the most active intercessor for professionalized public relations in a program that included publishing books and articles, giving lectures, participating in programs and debates, and sending out thousands of copies of *Contact,* his own in-house publication. The following description of Bernays's charming and disarming manner was as true in May 1984, when I visited this founder of public relations in his Cambridge, Massachusetts, home, as when John Flynn wrote it for the *Atlantic* of May 1932:

Small of stature, careless in his dress, not always even newly shaved, he resembles rather a diminutive, absent-minded professor than the alert business man. What is more, he is utterly without posture when he talks about his profession. He offers no hypocritical explanations about the purposes behind his campaigns; he considers them quite proper and important to business, and defends them on purely pragmatical grounds. He discusses his art, his business, his methods, and himself with complete objectiveness and with a frankness which is engaging in one who, accustomed to talking with important business men about their affairs, might be expected to take refuge behind a screen of reserve and pretense.[5]

Certain it is that only a man of Bernays's vocational zeal could have optimistically appropriated the term *propaganda* for the title of his 1928 book or, that same year, would have unashamedly employed *manipulating* as the active title word of an essay published in a sociological journal. Neither of these terms bothered Bernays because he saw his work, during and after the war, as a straightforward response to democracy's need for a wide diffusion of symbols.[6]

Bernays's two influential early books illustrate his view of how the lion of publicity and the lamb of free choice might dwell in democracy's peaceful garden. In *Crystallizing Public Opinion* (1923), Bernays developed his two-way–street notion of publicity whereby the public relations counselor "interprets the client to the public, which he is enabled to do in part because he interprets the public to his client." Recognizing the origins of his craft in "the circus advance-man" and in "the semi-journalist promoter of small-part actresses," Bernays believed, nevertheless, that the modern public relations specialist played an indispensable democratic role by permitting action based on the "truths by which society lives" that were "born of compromises among conflicting desires and of interpretation by many minds." Public relations people accomplished this by working in the middle range between the public's lack of mental independence and full information, on the one hand, and people's tendency to stubbornly hold to fixed views, on the other. One tactic for such reconciliation was to capture attention by creating newsworthy events.

As with Lee, Bernays espoused a democratic relativism that left it to the practitioner to identify the difference between propaganda and education. "The advocacy of what we believe in is education. The advocacy of what we don't believe in is propaganda." Bernays recognized that the mediator's role given to practitioners implied obligations to society as well as to client. However, Bernays believed it was possible to center ethics in the person of the persuader, who "must never accept a retainer or assume a position which puts his duty to the groups he represents above his duty to his standards of integrity." Bernays described the chief social value of public relations as its opposition to suppression of minority views. In fact, dissident ideas gained the most from wide publicity since otherwise they could never overcome established conceptions.[7]

In *Propaganda* (1928), Bernays continued his defense of special pleading as intrinsic to democracy. The only alternative to open competition through propaganda was to turn over the governance of society to committees of elders who would "choose our rulers [and] dictate our conduct, private and public." Instead, propaganda energized the modern society by helping institutions to cope with people's tendency to bond into groups and defer to group leaders. Savvy practitioners did not subscribe to the old mechanistic view that words were automatic stimuli producing consistent reactions. Instead, communication professionals understood their role as that of creating circumstances whereby, for instance, a home-design exhibit or a school contest might influence the habits of those who identified with decorators or educators.

In *Propaganda*, Bernays nevertheless evidenced an increased sensitivity to the ethical dilemmas of public relations counsels who, as lawyers for a client's position, also took on some of the prerogatives of judge and jury. Corresponding was Bernays's more comprehensive ethical code whereby the practitioner would reject the dishonest client, the fraudulent product, and the antisocial cause. Bernays emphasized that the best propaganda was organized around the continuous promotion of socially sound aims, and he touted its value for educators raising funds for the schools and for the NAACP working against lynching. In the final analysis, Bernays emphasized a benign quality of propaganda resulting from its inevitability ("propaganda in some form will always be used where leaders need to appeal to their constituencies") and from its dependence upon a persuader having "something to say which the public, consciously or unconsciously, wants to hear."[8]

Bernays sought out every possible venue to promote his gospel of propaganda as mass-mediated democracy's last, best hope. In popular articles, he emphasized how propagandists could not succeed unless they adjusted their policies to the needs and interests of the public. In a 1938 debate with Ferdinand Lundberg, the socialist muckraker, Bernays maintained that "everybody in America is free to use propaganda"; hence, propaganda was "the voice of the people in the democracy of today." In a speech given as part of a radio broadcast on NBC's "America's Town Meeting of the Air," Bernays emphasized that propaganda not only provided an alternative to force but also made the unfamiliar views of minorities available to citizens. Turning to academe, Bernays worked to win a place for honest propagandizing in higher education; at New York University, he undertook what certainly was one of the first courses to be offered under the title of "public relations."[9]

The Audience as Target

Bernays may have been right that propaganda was inevitable in a society where democracy required linking many minds through communication. However, it was indisputable that many of those who controlled this connecting of minds regarded the audience as something like a target. Basing their optimism on the work of army psychological testing to sort out democracy's human capital, postwar psychologists boasted of how their field could boost labor efficiency and industrial output. Others emphasized the utility of scientific principles in probing the characteristics of consumers, fleshing out the stages of a buying decision, and testing the efficiency of advertising.[10] Clearly, psychological testing and consumer research allowed institutions more efficiently to target the minds of modern people; but what was the impact of this science of audience analysis on democratic life? Chief among those attempting to reconcile marketplace technocracy and citizen participation was George Gallup, who promoted polling as a resource for boosting the efficiency of democracy. Gallup became the major spokesperson of business-oriented researchers who defended their work as magnifying the voice of consumers and voters thereby contributing not only to institutional competence but also to intelligent mass participation.

Given his undergraduate major in applied psychology and his work with the University of Iowa's college paper, Gallup embarked early upon the synthesis that eventually would make his name synonymous with scientific polling. Gardner Cowles, Jr., publisher of the Des Moines *Register and Tribune,* picked up the expenses attendant to Gallup's early research on readers' level of interest in various departments of the newspaper. One nugget that Gallup relayed to Cowles was the discovery that readers had an almost insatiable appetite for pictures; this spurred Cowles to develop *Look,* a magazine of photojournalism. Gallup soon turned to polling, which better married his interests in politics, journalism, and survey methods. In 1932, Gallup did some crude sample-based postcard polling to test the name recognition of his mother-in-law, Ola Bradcock Miller, who was running for Iowa Secretary of State. Soon thereafter, he formed the American Institute of Public Opinion (AIPO) and began to sell political surveys to newspapers.[11]

Gallup was not alone in perfecting the techniques of random-sample polling for political and commercial buyers; but he far exceeded Elmo

Roper, Archibald Crossley, and other early pollsters in publicly defending and promoting the craft. In *The Pulse of Democracy* (1940), Gallup and his Canadian colleague, Saul Rae, presented political polling as the very substance of a thoroughly modern democracy. In their view, polling was a natural response to the basic problem of American politics: "Shall the common people be free to express their basic needs and purposes, or shall they be dominated by a small ruling clique?" Democracy, Gallup and Rae maintained, implied more than mere voting. "It is a process of constant thought and action on the part of the citizen." They believed, further, that mass media upset the old balance between persuaders and public by giving elites more channels to monopolize the conversation with less-informed ordinary people. Maintenance of the American political system required "building machinery for directly approaching the mass of the people and hearing what they have to say." What was needed was a means to find out how people were reacting to events and propaganda during the interims between elections. Here polling was just the tool to sustain America's democratic faith by more efficiently ascertaining common opinions and thereby bridging the gap between citizens and their leaders.

In evangelizing for a polling-based democracy, Gallup and Rae argued that surveys, more than elections, provided a specific indication of opinion on actual issues. In this view, polls were a more reliable measure of opinion than newspapers, which reflected the babel of many voices. Further, because polls were less likely to be captured by "a small but powerful pressure group parading as a majority," these tallies were superior as a channel for free expression to public meetings and letter writing. Nor did the American tradition of voluntary associations suffice as a substitute for polling because these private bodies were, in Gallup's and Rae's estimation, self-interested pressure groups. As proof of polling's plebiscitary capabilities, Gallup and Rae cited survey data that showed most people in opposition to Franklin Roosevelt's plan to enlarge the Supreme Court. These data, the pollsters emphasized, gave an important perspective to FDR's significant – but ambiguous – electoral mandate of the previous fall.

Not only did Gallup and Rae present polls as a means for trimming the sails of society's elected leaders; they saw opinion surveys as indicating the actual – usually limited – strength of pressure groups. Gallup and Rae pointed to data showing only 3.8 percent of the public favoring the Townsend Plan of $200-per-month pensions despite the clamor of the Townsend Clubs, which had caused many Congressmen to turn "political somersaults." In another case, they credited polling as causing union leaders to distance themselves from sit-down strikes, a tactic that only a minority of those polled found agreeable. Gallup and Rae pointed to polls showing that the majority in Louisiana was not fooled by Huey Long's political machine and believed that state elections were dishonest. The two pollsters further argued that one of the greatest services to democracy of scientific nose counting was to provide hard data about attitudes on foreign policy. Where politicians in 1914–1916 had conjectured about opinions on the war in Europe, now Gallup's organization provided charts showing that sentiment had shifted in favor of U.S. aid to the Allies.

Conscious of the implications of polling's great power, Gallup and Rae took pains to deny that mechanized attitude tallies empowered a new technocratic elite at the expense of traditional representative democracy. Gallup and Rae attributed much of the criticism of polls to fears of a tyranny of the majority that had been articulated since the time of Alexis de Tocqueville. Instead, polls served as antidote for "mobocracy" and demagoguery because, by accurately reflecting public sentiment, polls invariably exposed the pretensions of self-appointed local Caesars. No wonder that politicians and interest-group leaders, who desired that "polls should do their propaganda for them," became outraged when their shallow support was exposed. Gallup and Rae summarized four reasons why the polling performed by the American Institute of Public Opinion posed no political risks. First, the AIPO was financed by a "multipartisan group of over one hundred newspapers." Second, polls could be and were checked against election results. Third, skepticism about the polls helped to keep up "an alert and critical attitude toward them." A final safeguard was the "competition between various types of polls and competition between the polls and other guides to public opinion." Gallup and Rae argued that only by freely taking democracy's pulse could the democratic nations best the dictators whose Achilles' heel was their corresponding *in*ability to know the minds of the people.[12]

In a popular primer containing eighty questions and answers about polls, Gallup attempted a catechismal treatment of how polling was a boon to intelligent democratic life. "Almost always the public is ahead of its legislators," he maintained. Gallup offered the example of where polls of spring 1940 showed support for conscription before congressional leaders publicly advocated the measure. Surveys most certainly did not overstate the views of persons uninformed on the issues, Gallup maintained, because survey researchers screened such folk with filler questions and then tabulated these respondents as uncommitted. Nor should citizens be worried about the types of questions asked or about the people who framed them. Questions were selected after consultation with the nation's opinion leaders, and, afterward, "every effort is made, before a question actually appears on the ballot, to eliminate any possible bias."[13]

The notion of efficient democracy through quantitative polling rested upon the same relativistic, majoritarian assumptions that sustained public-relations practitioners Lee and Bernays. Gallup and Rae denigrated "rigid standards of absolute value," deducing from this premise that "it is all the more vital to measure the standards which the people set for themselves."[14]

The Measured and Managed Public

Academic social scientists became greatly impressed by the innovations, particularly quantitative ones, that practitioners were employing to measure and guide the public. The impulse of scholars of society to facilitate a managed kind of democracy was amplified not only by the exciting prospect of efficient communication articulated by Gallup, Bernays, and Lee but also by an earlier opinion, found in Le Bon, Wallas, and Freud, that elites might need to save the public from its own frailty. Contributors to the social-scientific perspective on propaganda believed that academe's unique contribution to society might be to measure the public mind with scientific instruments so that people could be fitted by qualified institutional managers to appropriate patterns of thought and action.

The measurement-management school of thought, driven by notions of organizational efficiency and of public irrationality, invited academicians to lay out the process by which Le Bon's psychological crowd emerged around key issues. To this end, a considerable cadre of researchers (most notably Thurstone, Likert, and Lazarsfeld) showed that it was possible to assess people's mental attitudes accurately – and that the endeavor could be quite useful. Political scientists Merriam and Lasswell appropriated the idea of a psychologically measured public to promote a modernized kind of democracy whereby seasoned experts would use data about democracy's human capital to more efficiently manage politics from the top. Other researchers (Mayo, Lewin, and Sherif) carried the measurement impulse into the world of human relations in working groups.

The psychological view of the public gained great credence in academic social science from the successes of social psychologists in creating attitude-scale questionnaires which, when marked by respondents, allowed a mathematical tally of how opinions differed on various social, economic, and political questions. Scales created by psychologists Floyd

Allport and D. A. Hartman had people registering opinions on a number of topics ranging from the League of Nations to President Calvin Coolidge. The data revealed distributions of opinion and also permitted the authors to correlate opinion both with demographic factors such as sex and religion and with such psychological considerations as personality. The researchers found, for instance, that men were more likely than women to register extreme positions on the scales and that persons at either pole tended to be surer of their opinions than those who located themselves in the middle. Attitude scales now began to supply the pins by which the old macroscopic notions of public and crowd could be held down for precise display and dissection.

Work on attitude measurement proceeded apace during the 1920s and 1930s. L. L. Thurstone, an educational psychologist, developed improved methods for tapping distributions of opinion with verbal scales. With E. J. Chave, Thurstone clarified, on both the theoretical and the pragmatic levels, how an expressed verbal opinion (e.g., that entering the Great War had been a mistake) served as a measurable outward sign of mental attitude. Rensis Likert pursued similar lines of inquiry for the Psychological Corporation and later for the Department of Agriculture where, as field research director, he measured responses toward the department's policies. Attitude data of the type gathered by Thurstone and Likert offered, in the view of Erwin Esper, "a disembodied statistical abstraction characterizing a group." Such data permitted the unwieldy notion of a whole discursive public to be replaced with a more manageable construct presenting a "public" as the sum of individual responses recorded on questionnaires.

The scientific tenor of attitude scales led communication researchers to focus on pure effect. It is true that a number of early attitude studies expressed some explicit value judgments as when William Biddle used attitude tests to find how better to teach resistance to propaganda and when Thurstone wrote of the "socially approved effect" on children of a movie exposing high-stakes gambling. However, the critical analysis of effects soon atrophied because the focus on factual results was more in the spirit of scientific work calculated objectively to unravel social processes. Even Thurstone's article on the effect of movies on children's attitudes set as its goal to "ascertain whether the effect of motion pictures on school children can be measured and whether the effects of different kinds of pictures can be predicted." Attitude studies increasingly went in the direction of elucidating the process of persuasion per se. For instance, William Chen discovered that measured attitude change dissipated over time; Henry Wegrocki found less intelligent respondents to be more influenced by propaganda; Douglas Waples and his associates found that readers' predispositions influenced what they selected to read and how they interpreted it.[15]

A particularly influential program of effects research was pursued in the Office of Radio Research (ORR) established by the Rockefeller Foundation under the auspices of Princeton University. Managed by Paul Lazarsfeld, Austrian emigré psychologist, the program was overseen by Hadley Cantril, Princeton psychologist, and Frank Stanton, director of research at CBS. The program was designed by Cantril and Stanton to determine why people listened to radio. Stanton, a psychological researcher who soon became CBS president, was naturally interested in what lured people to programs and to what extent a program and its ads boosted the sales of products. Since his existing surveys already showed who listened, where, when, and to what, Stanton was preoccupied with "the why of listening, that is, the motivational elements." This was clearly a psychological problem in Stanton's estimation, and he looked forward to the results forthcoming from the ORR. "Once the real motivating factors are isolated for various groups or sections of the audience, then educators and advertisers might put their time on the air to more efficient use."[16]

Given the considerable resources poured into the ORR, the Rockefeller Foundation pressed Lazarsfeld for results. Accordingly, Herr Director (Cantril's jesting title for Lazarsfeld) arranged for the group's work to be chronicled in two special issues of the *Journal of Applied Psychology* and in a book. In introducing the first set of journal articles, Lazarsfeld described the ORR's early objective as plumbing the deep recesses of the persuasive process for the benefit of educators, advertisers, entertainers, and opinion molders, all of whom needed to know how messages reached their mark. The particular role of the psychologist was to employ tests and inventories to help "those who want to make radio more effective." In the second set of studies, Lazarsfeld attempted again to systematize miscellaneous articles on the sales influence of programs, on consumer surveys, on panel studies of advertising, and so forth, with the observation that "studies on the effect of radio are moving into the foreground." Lazarsfeld suggested that, conceived in the psychological mold of his studies, a new "discipline of general communications research seems in the making."[17]

In 1939–1940, Lazarsfeld and his research team prepared *Radio and the Printed Page* in a flurry of day-and-night labor with the objective of guaranteeing renewal of the Rockefeller grant. The volume reported studies of various factors associated with radio listening such as the finding that persons of higher socioeconomic status listened to presidential addresses. Other studies were based on asking people what listening to a particular program meant for them and then following up on the perceived gratifications that were mentioned. For instance, quiz programs allowed a listener who was well read but lacked formal educational credentials to enjoy a form of psychological revenge against teachers and persons holding high degrees. Results from further studies of listening behavior included such findings as the slight preference of low-income people for news on radio instead of via the print medium.[18]

For attitude measurement fully to supplant general concepts of the public or crowd, it was necessary for researchers to be able to project the results of their small-scale surveys onto a whole population. As the Lazarsfeld program indicates, the impetus for improved techniques of population sampling and statistical analysis initially came more from marketers than politicians or academic theorists. Radio broadcasters were particularly anxious promoters of sampling research since their ephemeral audience could not be ascertained directly and in full. Lazarsfeld recalled that "soon commercial audience research became a dominant feature of the communications research field, recruiting the aid of academicians in most of the social sciences."[19]

In turn, the attention paid to Lazarsfeld, Gallup, Likert, and others by corporations and government agencies caused universities to be receptive to programs of survey research. In 1939–1940, Lazarsfeld moved the Office of Radio Research to Columbia and renamed it the Bureau of Applied Social Research; Likert and Angus Campbell opened their research shop at the University of Michigan in 1946; and the National Opinion Research Center moved to Chicago in 1947 under the leadership of Clyde Hart. Lazarsfeld recalled that academe showed little interest in sample-based surveys before 1936 but that major universities soon began to see survey research as looming large in social science. Columbia University turned to Lazarsfeld with a competitive objective, expecting that he would train students there in empirical methods as Samuel Stouffer was doing at Chicago.[20]

Lazarsfeld's innovative surveys diffused into the social sciences the idea that the public was less a deliberating whole and more a scattering of individuals whose opinions could be summed and projected. (Gallup's new-style polls had the same impact.) To be sure, Lazarsfeld's study of the 1940 presidential election (reported in 1944) did retain the notion that interpersonal conversation was relevant to opinion formation. However, this six-month study of a panel of 600 citizens ultimately presented the voting decision as more an inevitable outcome of an individual's preexisting socioeconomic status and family history than a thoughtful choice based on society's great conversation. It was easy for new-style students of public opinion to forget Park's distinction between the unreflective crowd and the discursively alert public in the stampede of social scientists to assimilate discoveries about objective determinants of the voting process and to embrace statistical sampling. The conception of the public as an impressionable and irresponsible crowd was predominant in cutting-edge social science even if the term *crowd* itself was considered passé for its inattention to specific measurement. William Albig, sociologist, lamented the turn toward "atheoretical, non-ethical, largely quantitative descriptions of some particular segment of the opinion process," which had replaced "questions of ethics in relation to the formation and effects of public opinion." This implicit psychological denigration of the citizen, Albig believed, promoted a skepticism about democracy itself.[21]

Albig's criticism given in the late 1950s, however, does not reflect the sense of excitement building in the 1920s about the possibility of using psychological measurement to build a new science of politics. The perspective on public opinion provided by attitude measurement and survey data accorded well with an administrative perspective on politics then being developed by political scientist Charles Merriam. Merriam, who had no qualms about the practitioner's role, saw the army's alpha and beta tests as a model of a "more precise political science" oriented to "study of the measurable, comparable, and controllable political reactions." After the war, he called for his discipline to deemphasize macroscopic historical and comparative analysis in favor of the microscopic view of politics afforded by psychology. Guided by science, political scholars would help government to meet the challenge of social change without suffering waste and inefficiency through graft, deadlock, or civil war. Better measurement of social facts and forces would come when, under the tutelage of psychology, scientists provided "definite measurement of elusive elements in human nature hitherto evading understanding and control by scientific methods."[22]

Merriam, however, never was a mere theorist of managed democracy. After his stint with the CPI, Merriam worked on problems of civic education with support from grants by the Laura Spelman Rockefeller Memorial Foundation. Merriam believed that it was vital to build a cohesive and loyal citizenry able to overcome divisive tendencies brought by competing allegiances to region, race, religion, and economic class. He believed that psychiatrists and physiologists could cooperate in an endeavor "to build the citizen from the ground up." Political unity was not something to be left to chance or to uncoordinated effort, but instead would come through appropriate measures implemented by such agencies as the schools, press, political parties, and "the special patriotic organizations."

Merriam's postwar work on civic loyalty turned the idea of propaganda analysis on its head by focusing on the need for some degree of social cohesion and examining how such agencies as schools and such channels as film figured in the process of making citizens. Symbols and psychology played prominent roles in Merriam's review of the process of state building. Expressed through oratory, architecture, and state ritual, symbols trained citizens in how to participate in the civic order. Similarly, Merriam maintained, future work in civic loyalty would need to focus on the psychological adjustments of the people. Merriam's interest in smoothly managed social change was evident not only in his study of civic training but also in his work on propaganda per se. In the 1933 report of the President's Research Committee on Social Trends, Merriam took no position on social control through "new techniques of pressure and propaganda." Instead, he looked ahead to a survey of the matter by the Social Science Research Council. The President's committee as a whole expressed great faith in the SSRC's ability to stimulate "the integration of social knowledge, in the initiative toward social planning on a high level."[23]

Merriam's work to amalgamate psychology and managed politics greatly influenced his later more famous pupil, Harold Lasswell. Chief among the influences on Lasswell's political science were the psychological perspective on politics and the administrative view of social influence – both espoused by his academic adviser, Merriam. Lasswell's intellectual debt to his mentor is apparent not only from the content of his significant early works treating propaganda and the psychological dimensions of politics but also from his occasional autobiographical remarks. Lasswell once described his "interest in political propaganda" as having germinated while he worked with Merriam in the senior man's large-scale project to study comparative civic training around the world. In 1924 and 1925, Lasswell twice visited Europe to study, conduct research for Merriam on German civic education, and visit archives of war propaganda. By the time he finished his Ph.D. study on propaganda symbols, Lasswell had assimilated not only Merriam's interest in symbolic social process and psychology but also in managed social change. This is clear from Lasswell's decision to approach propaganda from the standpoint of techniques that the persuader might select for use. Lasswell later was the person tapped by the SSRC to conduct the survey of propaganda that Merriam had looked forward to in the 1933 Social Trends report.

Although Merriam's influence is the chief explanation of why Lasswell's work on propaganda diverged from mainstream progressive propaganda critique, the younger man's work was cast not only in the mold of his mentor but also in directions set by two further giants of the Chicago School of social science, Mead and Park. Mead was the Chicago School's chief expert on differences between significant symbols and physical signs, and his work influenced how Lasswell formulated his somewhat idiosyncratic research program on propaganda. As Lasswell later recalled, "the choice of propaganda as a topic of study grew out of a wish to examine the place occupied by the symbolic among the nonsymbolic events of war or peace." Lasswell's early definition of propaganda showed the imprint of Mead: "Propaganda is the management of collective attitudes by the manipulation of significant symbols." Lasswell attributed his treatment of the persuader–audience relationship to the influence of Mead's analysis of the self.[24]

Lasswell was as impressed with Robert Park as with Mead, not only picking up Park's crusade for empirical data gathering but also treating propaganda from the standpoint of Park's characteristic attention to the urbanization of America and the consequent massification of social relations. Lasswell's interest in the beneficent administrative use of propaganda flowed partly from his having accepted as inevitable the replacement of small-town primary groups with the more typical secondary urban relations through mass media. Lasswell believed that propaganda was a necessary antidote to the dissolution of "the bonds of personal loyalty and affection which bound a man to his chief." Propaganda technique steered by psychological calculation was the inexorable condition of modern life since "the propagandist who works upon an industrialized people, is dealing with a more tense and mobile population than that which inhabits an agrarian state."[25]

Under the influence of Chicago School social science, Lasswell's work on propaganda became less a handbook for critics wanting to spur grass-roots social change and more a theoretically informed treatise on how to manage the Great Society by means of symbols. Lasswell was the American social scientist most often mentioned in connection with the study of propaganda; so it is a matter of some interest to observe how his approach to the subject originated and evolved. All the more so, since Lasswell's *Propaganda Technique in the World War* (1927) seemed, in many ways, entirely congenial to the purposes of mainstream progressive critique. Lasswell showed how Allied and German propagandists strategically manipulated information and symbols to create a self-serving picture of the war. For those interested in debunking Allied machinations, Lasswell's book provided a cornucopia of information about how the war's supposed good guys preached unrealistic war aims, sophistically distorted war guilt, and salaciously used atrocity tales to justify a Christian war. If, however, the lyrics of Lasswell's book seemed in accord with postwar skepticism, his book ultimately marched to a different melody.

Lasswell's approach was less an exposé and more a realistic empirical exposition and theoretical assessment. As a political realist, Lasswell took as a given that governments had to control the opinions of their people. With the advent of democracy, social control necessarily proceeded through symbols more than by force. "If the mass will be free of chains of iron, it must accept its chains of silver." From this vantage point, propaganda technique could be seen as a matter of efficaciously solidifying the polity as opposed to wantonly manipulating citizens. Observing that "the traditional species of democratic romanticism" had collapsed, Lasswell believed that social scientists should contribute a realistic understanding of how symbols actually worked in the formation of public opinion. The business of the scientist of symbols was "to discover and report, not to philosophize and reform." Accordingly, Lasswell's objection to falsehood and exaggeration was that such tactics might backfire. He did admit, however, that propaganda could be misused by administrative agents for their own personal objectives, for instance, to puff up a current regime or to favor the business interests of wartime leaders.[26]

Lasswell's succeeding works on propaganda enlarged both upon the necessary amorality of symbolic strategizing and upon the idea of the scientist as neutral reporter. In his 1933 article for the *Encyclopaedia of the Social Sciences,* Lasswell reasoned that "propaganda is surely here to stay; the modern world is peculiarly dependent upon it for the coordination of atomized components in times of crisis and for the conduct of large scale 'normal' operations." He predicted that people eventually would abandon their dainty scruples about propaganda and heed the reassurances of practitioners that modern society's deliberations required freely circulating, but clearly self-interested, representations. Lasswell concluded that "propaganda as a mere tool is no more moral or immoral than a pump handle." He further endorsed the practitioner's refrain that "the only effective weapon against propaganda on behalf of one policy seems to be propaganda on behalf of an alternative."

In addition to enlarging upon how propaganda represented a necessary tool of managed democracy, Lasswell pursued during the 1930s his notions of the proper scientific study of social influence. He pointed to efforts then under way to more precisely measure the influence of propaganda with methods ranging from reading the pulse rate of listeners to larger-scale studies of voting behavior. In his own book on war propaganda, Lasswell had been able only to sketch out the general impact of propaganda in weakening enemy morale and in recruiting allies. Later, he expressed embarrassment about being unable to massage the available archival materials into a truly scientific treatment of propaganda's effects. Lasswell became preoccupied with how the scientific method might inform the selection and classification of propaganda content. By the time that he and colleague Dorothy Blumenstock reported findings on communist propaganda in Chicago, Lasswell had greatly refined his methods for the "empirical investigation of symbols" as part of a "new field of scientific activity."[27]

Lasswell and Blumenstock rounded up material about the usual suspects, that is, propaganda as disseminated through publications, slogans, and demonstrations. However, they not only gave these forms of content the customary historical review but also developed various indexes and measures by which data in these categories could be systematically assessed and brought to bear on the question of whether communist propaganda had succeeded or failed. For instance, the authors developed an Attention Index to measure "the number of persons, in proportion to the total population, who during a given period of time focus their attention upon symbols of specified kinds for at least a certain (small) amount of time." As applied to the propaganda channel of mass demonstrations, the index showed that the percentage of Chicagoans participating in communist demonstrations rose from .76 percent in 1930 to a high of 1.69 percent in 1932, declining slightly in 1933 and 1934. In probing the effect of the propaganda, Lasswell and Blumenstock developed specific criteria, such as distinctiveness and adaptiveness, for assessing "tactical skillfulness in managing symbols." These became rubrics for specific measures, for instance, the finding that 40 percent of the symbols used by the Communist Party in its leaflet slogans were of foreign origin – case in point, the "Third International."[28]

Lasswell's work on political propaganda is remembered chiefly for his focus on analyzing content; however, his overall approach to politics was equally oriented to the personality of political leaders. In *Psychopathology and Politics* (1930), Lasswell gave as realistic an account of the symbolic dimensions of politics as did his future colleague in the Yale Law School, Thurman Arnold, although Lasswell gave the subject a more theoretical and clinical slant. "Our thesis is that our faith in logic is misplaced," Lasswell wrote, adding that Freud's technique of free association gave perhaps a more useful handle for grasping how thinking actually worked. After reviewing theories of personality development, Lasswell examined case situations of certain unnamed political agitators and administrators, finding that their actions were highly connected to deep-seated anxieties and motives. "Political prejudices, preferences, and creeds are often formulated in highly rational form, but they are grown in highly irrational ways."

Lasswell's psychological theory of politics culminated in what he called a "politics of prevention," whereby society's key minds would strive to steer the polity with objective scientific findings. According to Lasswell, the problem of modern politics was not the conflict of democracy with autocracy; rather, "our problem is to be ruled by the truth . . . and the discovery of the truth is an object of specialized research." Mere discussion could not prevent the triumph of backward or irrational policies because symbols often served chiefly as foci for irrelevancies and rationalizations. The symbols bandied about in discussion conjured up fictitious values created to mask human interests steeped in narcissism. "Political movements derive their vitality from the displacement of private affects upon public objects." Although public discussion might relieve social strains, it could do little to achieve policies that married what people demanded to what they needed. In fact, Lasswell maintained, research in human personality showed that "the individual is a poor judge of his own interest." A more promising avenue was to make sure that society's administrators and social scientists received an education that was both self-reflective and closely connected to empirical reality.[29]

Lasswell's early career provides the clearest marker of academe's drift away from concerns about a manipulated public to an interest in a public measured and managed. Lasswell's style of propaganda research became the norm in social science because the questions he asked and the approaches he used matched important trends percolating throughout the academy. His focus (and that of Lazarsfeld) on mapping out social process with data was in accord with the desire of social scientists to distance themselves from starry-eyed reformers and speculative philosophers alike. Similarly, the dedication of Lasswell and Lazarsfeld to large-scale quantitative data collection fit the move of grantors, particularly the Rockefeller Foundation and the Carnegie Corporation, to underwrite innovative scientific social research. As before, the term *science* was key; Lasswell and Lazarsfeld's work on a communication-managed society was attractive (as will become clear) because the resulting data accommodated the wish of grantors to serve society without explicitly stoking controversies between reformers and standpatters.

If the instrumental approach to opinion measurement gave a restricted reading of democracy's people, the move at least permitted symbol scientists to be of conspicuous aid in smoothing relationships between institutional managers and their employees and outside publics. Studies of workers and working groups being undertaken in various universities were particularly attuned to explaining how communication, scientifically studied, might render society more smooth-running. At the Harvard Business School, Elton Mayo received a $500,000 grant from the Laura Spelman Rockefeller Memorial to determine what workers actually experienced as they carried on their tasks. The program included tests of physical fatigue by Lawrence J. Henderson and various reflections by Mayo and Fritz Roethlisberger on how Freudian psychology might uncover the psychological preoccupations of people, for instance, the tendency toward false dichotomies such as success–failure or superiority–inferiority. Mayo and Roethlisberger later joined a program of research going on at the Hawthorne plant of Western Electric near Chicago. As described by Roethlisberger, the Hawthorne studies "went roughly through four phases: from an almost exclusive concern with employee productivity, to a concern with employee satisfaction, to a concern with employee motivation, and finally to a growing realization that the productivity, satisfaction, and motivation of workers were all interrelated." One important finding: The workers informally arrived at a norm of what constituted a fair day's work and punished those who deviated in any direction from it.[30]

Contemporaneous with Mayo's research program were various studies of group dynamics less directly linked to the business setting. At the Iowa Child Welfare Research Station, Kurt Lewin and his associates Ronald Lippitt and Ralph White were investigating the impact of group atmosphere. They organized ten-year-old boys into groups that met over several weeks under the leadership of an adult who implemented one of three leadership styles: democratic, autocratic, or laissez faire. In autocratic groups, the adult leader determined all policies and work assignments. In the democratic condition, these decisions were made by the boys themselves with adult advice. The Iowa researchers found that under autocratic leadership a group either exhibited around thirty times more aggressiveness than a democratic group or became characterized by a high degree of apathy. Democratic leaders were much better liked than the autocratic ones. Further research showed that groups developed a characteristic pattern of aggression and that novice members would soon shift to whatever was the now-prevailing pattern after being transferred from another group.[31]

With his work on the development of norms, Muzafer Sherif provided additional evidence that a group developed a shared world view distinct not only from that of its individual members but also from that of other groups. Sherif constructed an experimental situation where individuals and groups were called upon to estimate the perceived movement of light against a dark background that presented no stable structure for comparison. To handle the undefined situation, individuals and groups invariably developed a standard range of estimates and a norm (reference point) within the range. Sherif concluded: "The psychological basis of the established social norms, such as stereotypes, fashions, conventions, customs and values, is the formation of common frames of reference as a product of the contact of individuals." Sherif's psychology of norms provided scientific evidence for the usefulness of various commonly used concepts of group mind or psychological crowd, and he also showed that the phenomenon of group dynamics could be specifically measured.[32]

Viewed in one light, research on group dynamics reaffirmed certain features of democracy. The studies showed that small, deliberating groups actually did influence their members; in Lewin's work, one could find support for the idea that the democratic climate was superior to the authoritarian. But research on the social world of human groupings exhibited even more directly the efficiency dimension of progressivism with its attendant assumption that a well-functioning organization might maximize the welfare of all participants. Viewed from a propaganda-critique point of view, research about employee motivation and group norms carried a sinister aura of academicians helping covertly to coopt workers into management's frame of reference. However much the Hawthorne studies envisioned a more satisfied employee, this research tended to present workers in instrumental terms. Similarly, studies of group norms could be seen as helping managers to find base lines for the purpose of extracting more performance and production. Socialists and labor advocates attacked the work of Lewin and Roethlisberger, arguing that an effort to make workers happier and more productive merely adapted them to their undesirable condition of low power and low control.[33]

If the social-science view of communication favored administrative efficiency, it was not on that account authoritarian. Pioneer social scientists were imbued less with a will to power and more with a technocratic beneficence resulting, in part, from their engineering-mathematical background. Thurstone began his career as an engineering teacher and Roethlisberger as an engineer-practitioner. Lazarsfeld obtained a Ph.D. in math, and his fellow statistician, Stouffer, also was highly trained in that subject. The engineer's quantitative bent of many early expositors of the social-scientific school of propaganda study helped to rein in their left-liberal politics. Lazarsfeld, a socialist from his early days in Austria, retained a leftist orientation to politics throughout his career. The young Roethlisberger avidly read Upton Sinclair and Karl Marx and, although he moved to a humanistic liberalism, was always shocked when his human relations program was "stigmatized as a tool by which management could co-opt the worker to the establishment."[34]

Youthful enthusiasms aside, quantitative researchers were never prime candidates for radicalism because their practicality found them forsaking early socialist flirtations for a benevolent liberalism. Generally, the measurement-oriented scholars reflected the classic American intellectual stance of wanting to see society made both efficient and democratic. Hadley Cantril, Princeton psychologist, is representative of most quantitative scholars of social influence who, while holding their political commitments close to the vest, nevertheless saw themselves clearly in the ranks of reformers loosely attached to the progressive movement.[35] Even if measurement-oriented scholars retained an interest in social reform, the quantitative studies of attitude change, listener gratifications, public opinion, industrial relations, and group dynamics nevertheless tended to draw researchers into the top–down mindset that long had characterized their liberal-minded practitioner predecessors Ivy Lee, Edward Bernays, and George Gallup. Focus on social process and a psychological view of people put the academic scientists of society in a frame of mind to assume that the polis languished chiefly because of inaction on the part of enlightened administrators.

Foundations for Science

The support of granting foundations further increased the attractiveness of ignoring the muckraker's beloved unorganized public and, instead, doing opinion-measurement work for administrators and institutions. The social-science approach to propaganda thrived partly as a byproduct of the decision by leading foundations to support quantitative research in social processes. First among these foundations was the Laura Spelman Rockefeller Memorial. Between 1922 and 1929, the Spelman Memorial provided $20 million of support for the University of Chicago's urban research program, for the Harvard Business School studies of Mayo and Roethlisberger, for Yale University's Institute of Human Relations, and for selected other social science research institutes and endeavors. Also active in supporting social science research during the 1930s was the Carnegie Corporation. Carnegie supported the Social Science Research Council and Harvard's Russian Research Institute but did not contribute extensively to communication research until the 1940s.[36]

The Spelman Memorial later became the social science division of the larger Rockefeller Foundation; however, it was John Marshall, associate director of Rockefeller's humanities division, who became the leading financial angel of communication research. Under the direction of Marshall, Rockefeller money underwrote Douglas Waples's University of Chicago research program on reading and, more important, Lazarsfeld's Office of Radio Research. Marshall subsequently became highly interested in how communication research might serve in the crisis of approaching war. Rockefeller grants subsequently underwrote Lasswell's program, administered by the Library of Congress, to content-analyze propagandas foreign and domestic.[37]

The granting philosophies of the Rockefeller and Carnegie foundations were similar as regarded the emerging social sciences and, moreover, were consistent with what Lasswell and Lazarsfeld wanted to accomplish. Both foundations were interested in the link between science and social knowledge, believing that by supporting new methods of research they might contribute to objective high-level understandings of how society worked. The emphasis, accordingly, was on innovation and objectivity. On the point of innovation, Marshall described his foundation's very role as "to encourage the development of new methods of acquiring knowledge." A number of early Rockefeller grants in the mid-1920s were earmarked to stimulate America's first survey research operations, for instance, at the Institute of Religious Research and at Howard Odum's Institute for Research in Social Science at the University of North Carolina. Lazarsfeld's innovative and somewhat unique statistical research work in Vienna caught the attention of the Rockefeller Foundation's Paris office and led to his receiving a fellowship to study in the United States. Charles Dollard, Carnegie administrator, similarly recalled the eagerness of his organization to support "emerging fields that had to be helped."[38]

The Rockefeller and Carnegie foundations were interested not only in innovative research but also in objective scholarship of the kind least likely to raise eyebrows among foundation trustees and among federal officials who watched over the tax-exempt status of philanthropies. Some foundation trustees simply did not understand social science or associated it with socialism such that the Carnegie staff sometimes had to overcome resistance to grants in the area. However, the businessmen who sat on the Carnegie board did not really fear possible aspersions on capitalism cast by research since, in the words of senior officer Florence Anderson, "research doesn't really undermine much."[39]

"Action programs," of course, were a different story, Anderson noted; but even here the difficulty in making grants was less a matter of internal politics than of external scrutiny. Anderson recalled that grants "in the public affairs field" were always "tricky" because of "I.R.S.

regulations under which you get your tax exemption." The rub was the requirement that "no substantial part of your income can be used to influence legislation." It took little stretch of the imagination to realize that much social research could lead to recommendations for change which, in turn, might imply legislation. For its part, the Rockefeller Foundation also was sensitive to outside criticism about its grants stemming from the time when George Creel and other muckrakers had stigmatized a Rockefeller project to improve industrial relations, branding the effort as a mere prop for the Rockefeller corporations. For this reason, the Spelman Memorial proscribed grants for organizations that promoted "social, economic, or political reform" and to groups "engaged in direct activity for social welfare."[40]

Support from the Rockefeller and Carnegie foundations took prestigious departments at leading universities not only in the direction of innovative and objective research designs for opinion measurement but also toward a managed-reform approach. Research about communication processes, in particular, allowed foundations to indulge simultaneously their interests in social amelioration with their desire to aid society's leading institutions in bolstering stable social adjustments. To promote a non-controversial brand of social improvement, grantors embraced a top–down kind of reformism keyed to efficiency, focused on social stability, and tied to authorized organizations and leaders. Research funded by Rockefeller and Carnegie tended to be of a kind that sharpened the adroitness and acuity of established institutions. For instance, under terms of a ten-year Rockefeller grant, Yale's Institute of Human Relations pursued problems of industrial relations, mental health, and business failures.[41]

The foundation-approved marriage of psychological publics, top–down reform, and research-enhanced social harmony was a powerful synthesis that enabled quantitative social scientists not only to gain points with private-sector institutions and with grantors but also to establish themselves as arguably the only truly scientific students of propaganda. The measurement-for-management approach to propaganda created a congenial context in which social science could differentiate itself from the humanities and therefore coalesce as an academic profession having a recognized venue and a valued set of competencies.

If *management* was the term that rallied social scientists of communication for their outward work with private and public institutions, *science* became the rubric under which quantitative communication research established its intellectual center of mass within academe. Scientific objectivity bespoke an orientation to knowledge that fit the desire of social scientists to differentiate their productive role from that of both academic humanists and grass-roots reformers. Strict adherence to research methods pioneered in the natural sciences seemed the best route for social scientists to highlight the scientific as opposed to the social axis of their title. Academic organizers in various social fields, such as political science's Charles Merriam and sociology's Ernest Burgess (Park's associate), began after the Great War to spread the gospel of a new, quantitative science of society. For the study of human behavior to be taken as scientific, leading-edge researchers believed that they studiously had to avoid making explicit value judgments and contributing specific suggestions for reform. The scientific and political concerns of leading social researchers now flowed along separate vectors. Lazarsfeld put the point most starkly in later (private) criticisms of his younger colleague, C. Wright Mills, for mixing research and politics to the extent that Mills arguably had failed to produce "any decent piece of research." Further, Lazarsfeld believed that neither Mills nor Samuel Stouffer ever had succeeded in reconciling "political interests and technical emphasis."[42]

Preachments about scientific method in social research were part of a process by which the meaning of science itself had been transformed. Formerly understood as an organized body of systematized knowledge based on historical or naturalistic observation, science increasingly became associated with the specific methods of experimentation and statistical analysis that had helped to produce startling advances in the physical and natural realms. A similar methodological metamorphosis seemed necessary if students of society were to appropriate the key scientific principles of process and prediction. This shift in the meaning of science, which began in psychology, eventually extended even to the field of international politics where, in 1931, Columbia's James T. Shotwell argued that "the application of scientific methods to international problems is an essential part of their practical settlement." The older historical approach to world politics, which the nineteenth century had considered quite scientific, now seemed to carry the danger of becoming in Shotwell's words a kind of "glorified journalism."[43]

The scientific-process approach to social influence that imbued the work of Lasswell and Lazarsfeld was, from the standpoint of cutting-edge social researchers, refreshingly distinct from the kind of historical-critical propaganda studies that were pursued by scientifically untrained humanists. Attitude studies and experimentation with task groups permitted scholars to dissect and measure the crowd and the public in ways that the old-time macroscopic theorists could only dream of. The Social Science Research Council became a major influence within academe in diffusing the quantitative, process approach to social science. The Spelman Memorial and the Carnegie Corporation provided millions of grantor dollars to the SSRC, which, in turn, acted as a retailer for foundation largesse, spreading the money among its seven constituent professional societies in anthropology, economics, history, political science, psychology, sociology, and statistics. The SSRC was dominated by persons such as Merriam who were committed both to the new statistical-experimental social science and to establishing social science as a distinct profession.[44]

The Fragmentation of Humanistic Communication Study

Propaganda critique, of course, continued during the time when quantitative communication science was establishing a closely linked nexus of researchers, grantors, and institutions devoted to measuring the public for better management. However, interest in propaganda's connection to democracy suffered from the failure of humanistically inclined social scientists to link high-level theory and research to the problem of citizen participation. Working separately, humanist students of communication produced no theory–praxis synthesis strong enough to compete with the growing measurement-management orientation in social science. The effect was to alienate propaganda critique from allies needed for leveraging scholarship to help reactivate citizen initiative in public communication. The humanistic strain of academic communication study ultimately fractured into several uncoordinated departments: (1) grand theory lacking a critical application (Mead, Parsons, the Frankfurt School, and Dewey); (2) community surveys lacking a critical application (studies of Chicago and Middletown); (3) high-level academic calls to action lacking implementation (Robert Lynd, the Payne Fund); (4) case-study propaganda critiques that were marginalized and lacking in impressive theoretical grounding; and (5) antiquarian and insular applications of rhetoric to politics (in the speech field).

The grand-theory approach in modern social science was exemplified by the work of Le Bon, Wallas, and others who wove together general observations into large-scale conceptions of how society functioned. When high-level theorists of the postwar period, such as George Herbert Mead and Talcott Parsons, continued this abstract treatment of self and society, their olympian vantage point found them silent on the specific connections of propaganda to democracy. Mead's work on the significant symbol and Parsons's framework of social roles and institutional types provided such a high-level notion of social influence that these upper-story conceptions had the effect of distracting both humanists and quantitatively oriented scholars from the question of whether communication in a particular time and place improved or worsened democratic society.

Even where humanistic grand theorists trod near problems of propaganda, their ambiguity was more likely to intrigue measurement-oriented scholars than to inspire a more theoretically grounded propaganda critique. Barrington Moore, a Harvard social scientist who favored the historical approach, found it curious that Samuel Stouffer, the prophet of quantified sociology, and Parsons, the consummate theoretician, behaved as if their divergent approaches were completely compatible. In Moore's wry estimate, his two colleagues in the Department of Social Relations got on so well because they both pursued methods that allowed one to avoid specific historical realities.[45]

The ironic gravitation of grand theory toward quantified measurement, and away from grass-roots propaganda critique, may be observed further in the reception given to the emigré scholars of the Institute for Social Research of Frankfurt – the famous Frankfurt School – upon their arrival in America. The most notable immediate influence of Frankfurt School theorizing on American social-influence research occurred when Paul Lazarsfeld became fascinated with richly complex and theoretically tantalizing ideas resonating in Theodor Adorno's critical work on radio music. Lazarsfeld attempted to integrate Adorno into the communication-measurement studies being pursued in the Office of Radio Research; however, results of this collaboration were not impressive. After recovering from the shock of discovering a whole building full of people conducting studies of likes and dislikes "to benefit the planning departments in the field of the mass media," Adorno contributed four provocative papers, only one of which saw publication under the auspices of the Princeton Radio Project. In the first of this foursome, Adorno treated the intrusion of the commodity market into music, arguing that the result had been a standardization of output, the development of commodity fetishism, and a pronounced regression to infantile listening. Lazarsfeld was incredulous that Adorno felt no compulsion to anchor such broad theoretical brush strokes with quantified data. Adorno's Marxian–Freudian analysis of music was quietly dropped from the radio research project.[46]

Although the Lazarsfeld–Adorno collaboration came to naught, the ORR's director nevertheless wrote of how critical and administrative studies might, in theory at least, be mutually supporting. Believing that the sensibilities of modern intellectuals often became the moral standards of tomorrow, Lazarsfeld argued that administrative researchers should be "more hospitable to criticism," for instance, about "such material as never gets access to the channels of mass communication."

But a participatory politics of communication was far from Lazarsfeld's idealized conception of an interesting or useful research topic. His notion of criticism was less in the direction of dissecting the motives of contemporary persuaders, channels, or institutions and more toward the application of qualitative data to intriguing macrosocial trends. The kind of circumscribed critical scholarship that Lazarsfeld hoped to obtain is illustrated by a content analysis of popular biographies prepared for Lazarsfeld by Leo Lowenthal, another Frankfurt emigré. Lowenthal demonstrated that politicians and businessmen (archetypes of production) had given way as popular heros to "idols of consumption" drawn from sportspeople and entertainers.[47]

If the broad theorizing of the Frankfurt School intrigued leading quantitative social scientists such as Lazarsfeld, propaganda critics were little inclined to undertake the laborious effort required to link Adorno-style reflections to practical problems of institutional manipulation in American social struggle. Alfred Lee, media sociologist and eventual director of the Institute for Propaganda Analysis, attended seminars offered by Adorno and others who, in Lee's words, tried "to appear unique missionaries" despite the backdrop of existing American critical sociology. Lee believed that the attraction of German critical theory was that it allowed American academicians to salve their censorious impulses absent of any clear and specific focus on what was happening in the United States. Another attraction of the German work, Lee recalled, was that its "obscure terminology and more complicated theories" made the emigré scholarship look "more scientifically respectable, academically respectable."[48]

John Dewey's work represented the best hope that grand social theory might give propaganda critique sufficient weight to steal some attention from the measurement-management approach to public communication. Prompted by Lippmann's continued work on public opinion, Dewey had returned to the relationship of propaganda to grassroots, participatory democracy.[49] In *The Public and Its Problems* (1927), he explored how modern publics might better organize themselves consistent with the idea of from-the-bottom-up social change. Dewey described *publics* as originating when groups of people found that they shared an interest in the indirect consequences of social action. For instance, regulations against child labor and various provisions for social insurance came as a result of people's desires to soften the hard edges of socioeconomic circumstance. While small communities were the test tube in which American publics traditionally had been precipitated, these face-to-face entities now had been invaded "by forces so vast, so remote in initiation, so far-reaching in scope and so complexly indirect in operation, that they are, from the standpoint of the members of local social units, unknown." For this reason, even though technology held people together minimally by widely circulating opinions, the public was confused and unable effectively to take up political life.

Dewey argued that America required a new machinery of democracy so that "the inchoate public now extant may function democratically." He embarked upon a search for those "conditions under which the Great Society may become the Great Community." Believing that democracy was "community life itself," Dewey was interested in how communication through symbols produced a mutuality of desire and purpose whereby energies were transformed into shared meanings that provided an alternative to pure force. Dewey believed that people learned community life – democracy – through the give-and-take of communicative action. However, he pointed to the current focus of radio and film on amusements that diverted citizens from political life. Although it would be difficult to reactivate publics through communication and information, Dewey maintained, the alternative approach of rule by experts did not solve democratic dilemmas resulting from the current eclipse of the public. If the masses were indeed "intellectually irredeemable," then their willfulness coupled with their power would act to render them uncontrollable by experts or intellectuals.

Believing that publics could not function without a high level of knowledge about social actions and consequences, Dewey expressed concern that such understandings were currently vested in experts and, as a result, were largely inaccessible to nonspecialists. "There can be no public without full publicity in respect to all consequences which concern it." In Dewey's scheme of a revitalized modern democracy, mere voting was not enough because intelligent choices implied a prior attention to "the improvement of the methods and conditions of debate, discussion and persuasion." Improving discourse was "*the* problem of the public," Dewey maintained. He looked to a day when the places occupied by prejudice and propaganda would be assumed by free inquiry and full publicity. Dewey believed that such a transformation would require providing opportunities for the face-to-face talk that characterized family and neighborhood. Local, neighborly association was Dewey's primary wellspring of the Great Community, although he recognized that occupational and vocational communities also could help to build up people's experience in understanding and regarding one another.

In grounding modern democracy on twin pillars of communicated social knowledge and neighborly mutual appreciation, Dewey came around to the rhetorical world view earlier expressed by Protagoras, the rhetorician of Greek democracy. Unfortunately, while Protagoras and other sophists actually did build democracy by teaching cobblers and tanners to speak in the agora as equals of the aristocrats, Dewey and his sympathizers had little concrete to offer as method to bring about a new democratic utopia. Dewey's disciple, James Harvey Robinson, also rhapsodized on intelligent citizenship, critical education, and wide-ranging discussion about controversial matters – all absent of any program to nurture such practices in specific locales. While Dewey was musing about a discursive utopia, social science's data collectors were busy turning up all sorts of specific insights about people and society that pointed to real utilitarian avenues for administrative action. Ultimately, Dewey's idea of building the intelligent democratic society from the bottom up never propelled a significant academic praxis.[50]

As with the grand theories (American and German), the grant-supported community studies also failed to create a cadre of researchers interested in pursuing localized communication reforms. It is true that wide-ranging social communication was an ideal that figured prominently in both the University of Chicago's program of urban studies and in Robert and Helen Lynd's comprehensive survey of Muncie, Indiana. Further, both programs revealed trends in communication that showed places for reform. However, in both research projects, the concept of social influence remained nearer to grand-theory's pursuit of interesting generalizations than to critical propaganda study's desire to point out local abuses. As with grand theory, community-based studies provided more fodder for measurement-oriented social science than for propaganda critique.

In an overview of the University of Chicago's urban-studies research program, sociologist Robert Park explained that transportation and communication were the primary factors in explaining what he termed the "ecological organization of the city." In the Chicago School's scheme of the city, communication's role was to help regulate the necessary readjustments of competing individuals and groups. In this "state of unstable equilibrium," social mobility meant geographic movement (transportation) but also implied the stimulation of new cognitive awarenesses and ideas through communication. Because newspapers provided a contemporaneous, living record of society's adjustments, Park saw them as crucial in mediating the restless relations of urban residents. He described the city's crowds and publics as highly attuned to "psychological moments," that is, to perceived crucial situations. Cities, therefore, were in "perpetual agitation, swept by every new wind of doctrine, subject to constant alarms." Unfortunately, he believed, up to this point, the flux of the urban environment had been studied only by means of "general observation and almost no systematic methods."

In the urban world described by Park, indirect secondary relations and social control through mass transportation and communication were replacing direct, face-to-face, primary relations of individuals in the community. Harried parents surrendered many of their functions to the schools; churches lost influence to newspapers; and social control, previously achieved through community mores and customs, shifted to positive strictures of law. Further, executive departments of government increased their influence at the expense of legislative bodies whose heyday had been the era of town meetings. In this connection, urban political machines such as Tammany Hall in New York represented efforts to marry the personal style of control found in primary groups with "the formal administrative organization of the city." Archetypes of new-style indirect social control were press agents and advertisers whose appeals targeted "a sentiment and opinion neither local nor personal." Publicity (a secondary public opinion) operated straightaway through newspapers (and current books) and obliquely through research bureaus whose findings were diffused by journalists. Like village gossip, news now served as a general agency of social control notwithstanding the preoccupation of press reports with public officials and the notorious.[51]

Just as Park presented the communication industry as part of the process by which urban people were mobilized, a similar interest in the large cultural impact of mass persuasion could be discerned in the work of the Lynds. In *Middletown* (1929), Robert and Helen Lynd surveyed how life had changed for residents of a moderate-size town between the 1890s and the 1920s. The Lynds' book was organized functionally around occupation, home life, child rearing, leisure, religion, and community activity. The book also highlighted the differing situations of the working class as opposed to the business (owning-managing) class, with much attention paid to how the industrial economy brought difficulties and uncertainties to the contemporary working people of Muncie. Nevertheless, class-oriented language was employed infrequently and in a very moderate tone (the term *class* itself was not to be found in the index).

The Lynds were interested in social changes occurring in Middletown and found that communication played an important role. Newspapers not only buttressed the interests of the business class but also were widely suspected of letting advertising influence editorial comment. The Lynds themselves cited cases where newspapers had misrepresented or withheld information about unsafe products and business matters. They found that brand-name advertising had combined with installment credit to make people more outwardly prosperous but less independent. As with the automobile, new modes of communication had transcended the utilitarian realm to become important pastimes per se. A torrent of periodicals and other publications were available to the reader. The radio and phonograph had widened exposure to music but had lessened the former practice of solo and group singing. The auto and the movies loomed large as influences on morals, the automobile by virtue of its hold on family budgets and its provision of a romantic venue for young people. Indications of cinema's power were its special attractiveness to children (who often watched without their parents), its providing an alternative to direct human contact, and its role in diffusing a worldliness that broke down distinctions between youth and adults. For its part, radio standardized families in the direction of passive listening.[52]

The vast data gathered by the Lynds and the Chicago researchers held out the promise of informing the public of how citizens could become active in the discourse of their localities. However, the community studies of Chicago and Muncie were prepared in a way that made them more suitable for quantitative researchers and authorized institutional leaders than for grass-roots reformers. On a theoretical level, the systematic survey work of the Chicago sociologists and the Lynds previewed certain characteristics of measurement-oriented academic studies of social influence. The Park and Lynd programs both began with the objective of answering a comprehensive set of questions about a region rather than drawing particular lessons from an episode of social struggle in the manner of muckrakers and propaganda critics. Both programs involved team research supported by grants of the Rockefeller foundations. In this they differed from the more opinionated marshaling of facts, the interpretive conclusions, and the lone-wolf condition typical of progressive critics. The emphasis of the Chicago and Muncie studies on social theorizing explains why the then prevalent term of *propaganda* is conspicuously absent.

The methodological as well as the theoretical slant of the community-study researchers similarly proved to be more compatible with measurement-oriented research than propaganda analysis. The Park and Lynd groups explicitly invoked the idea of objectivity as an important aid in collecting data. Park and the Lynds took pains to locate their methods within the scientific framework, and both characterized their work as anthropological and descriptive, even if their evolving, adaptive techniques did not yet share the self-conscious preoccupation of Lasswell and Lazarsfeld in matters of methodology. To the extent

that reform figured in the studies of Chicago and Muncie, the ameliorative impulse was a detached and indirect one in which the scientist
yielded up general information about social problems that others perhaps might act upon. For instance, Park and his colleagues treated
juvenile crime synthetically as part of the unfolding social process. The
Lynds, it should be observed, did complain about conditions faced by
workers. However, sociologist Alfred Lee characterized both Park's and
the Lynds' research as offering a technical recipe for social change under
official auspices. "What they have in common is chiefly a concern with
using their research techniques and theories to shed understanding or to
help people cope with social problems as those problems are defined by
constituted authorities or by responsible voluntary group leaders."[53]

Although the Lynds' comprehensive survey neither attempted nor
prompted a literature devoted to greater citizen participation, Robert
Lynd later produced a notable theoretical call to action that proposed a
program of communication criticism capable of challenging the
measurement-for-management approach of Gallup, Lasswell, and Lazarsfeld. His call to action, and that by the Payne Fund researchers,
represented a third line of humanistic communication inquiry that
might have, but did not, ally itself with antipropaganda critique.

Robert Lynd's *Knowledge for What?* (1939) represented the era's
most powerful vision of an academic, social-scientific praxis of research
and criticism to enhance local participatory democracy. Lynd faulted
both the "scholars" in his field for their remoteness from "immediate
relevancies" and the "technicians" for their tendency to define problems
"too narrowly in terms of the emphases of the institutional environment
of the moment." Lynd was particularly concerned about the "seductive
quality" of empirical work on social processes. In his view, one who
gathered data and charted trends "places oneself inside the going system, accepts temporarily its values and goals." Inevitably, the social
researcher found conditions to be ever changing and, therefore, became
"drawn deeper within the net of assumptions by which the institutions
he is studying profess to operate." Because of the tradition of objectivity
that sheltered them, empiricists frequently became so preoccupied with
describing social change that they never paused to ask the question:
"'Where are our institutions taking us, and where do we want them to
take us?'" In this way, "empiricism can become as much of a blind
alley as can logical speculation."

In casting his criticisms of the newly dominant empirical trend in
social science, Lynd examined not only the work of economists but also
the efforts of advertisers and market researchers. Lynd found polling
and "techniques for the 'management of public opinion'" to be particu-

larly anomalous. These practices certainly constituted new instruments of democracy, Lynd believed; however, he faulted Gallup for treating polling and opinion control without an explicit view of how these techniques functioned in the context of "the pressure forces within American economic and political institutions." Lynd included the question of democracy's survival against propaganda and pressure as one of twelve current social problems that social scientists should investigate. "Can political democracy be built upon economic undemocracy?" Lynd wondered. This query implied a further inquiry into the media of communication. "Can democracy afford to depend so largely as we do upon privately owned media of public information operated for private profit?" Was not such a laissez-faire attitude toward the formation of public opinion dangerous in a world "bristling with dictators wielding all the arts of propaganda" and in a nation where "the 'management of public opinion' for private ends is highly developed"?[54]

Although Lynd fleshed out how social scientists could nudge along the Great Community, his book proved not to be particularly influential in the context of the 1930s. Lazarsfeld expressed interest in Lynd's program, but this attention seemed actually to deflate Lynd's energy for promoting a direct connection between academic inquiry and practical, democratic changes in communication. In their first contacts, Lazarsfeld, the measurer, and Lynd, the praxical visionary, functioned as allies. Lynd was instrumental in bringing Lazarsfeld, along with what became the Bureau of Applied Social Research, to Columbia. "The University would never really have accepted it if it hadn't been for Lynd," Lazarsfeld recalled. Not only had Lynd touted and defended the Austrian emigré around Morningside Heights; he also helped to prevail upon the president of Princeton University to release the radio research project and its lucrative Rockefeller grant. Given the sentiments that Lynd had expressed about research carried on with unstated (but quite clear) pro-managerial value premises, it is difficult to account for his early enthusiasm for Lazarsfeld's bureau. Lynd's work to win the bureau for Columbia appeared to result partly from his guilty conscience for having not lived up to the expectation in the department that he himself would develop a program of quantitative analysis akin to that going on at Chicago.[55]

Not surprisingly, the Lynd–Lazarsfeld alliance failed to prosper. Lynd, almost inexorably, grew critical of the bureau's emphasis on research for business enterprises. Lazarsfeld, who tried to involve his colleague in the work of the bureau, did not understand Lynd's objection to using contract income to underwrite good research and attributed Lynd's disaffection to exaggerated fears about "selling out to the capitalists" and "buying the students off." It seems that Lazarsfeld and Lynd each gave out reminders about the potential limitations of the other's orientation to the field. As an ex-preacher, consummate moralist, and peaceful radical, Lynd increasingly was moved to involve himself in the consumer movement, adult education, and propaganda analysis. However, such efforts toward an active social praxis inevitably made Lynd less productive as an academic writer. Here Lazarsfeld's ability to generate a seemingly limitless stream of books and articles grated on Lynd's sense that he should be building a larger scholarly bibliography and probably reduced Lynd's appetite for making the difficult bridge between academic research and involvement in reform groups. In a plaintive letter to Lazarsfeld, Lynd asked why his colleague did not rest a bit on his considerable laurels instead of "feel[ing] you have to pile on more & more." For his part, Lazarsfeld was sometimes awed and made to feel self-conscious with reference to Lynd's high-toned moral positions. Each seemed destined to catch the conscience of the other.[56]

If Lynd's *Knowledge for What?* showed how a theoretically based call to action might fail to bring fruit, the Payne Fund studies illustrated how a call to action based on measurement also could come to naught in a social-science atmosphere where reform and research rubbed together uncomfortably. The Payne studies were a series of twelve volumes published in the early 1930s with financial support from the newly created Payne Fund philanthropy. From the first, the Payne-financed research program found itself somewhat uncomfortably poised between the scientific and reformist poles of American social science. The founding father of the studies, William Short, envisioned them as supplying the proof that finally would induce the nation's parents to join with leading organizations in a campaign to reform the movie industry. On the other hand, W. W. Charters of Ohio State University, who served as the program's research director, did not expect to attack the movies directly; rather, he planned an open-ended inquiry into what movies might portend for social life.

However much these two purposes were (or were not) in accord, the published volumes implied an intent to nourish a grass-roots effort to clean up the movies. Charters introduced the series with the comment that "from the point of view of children's welfare the commercial movies are an unsavory mess." Among the data that Charters cited to buttress his conclusion were Herbert Blumer's findings that movies greatly affected the emotional life of children. Blumer studied more than 1,500 narrative accounts (60 or so cross-checked by interviews) given by children and adolescents about their experiences with particular movies. He discovered not only that youths acted out movie themes and daydreamed about them but also that one-third of grade-school children reported experiencing nightmares based on films. Blumer concluded that movies dulled moral judgments by exerting a powerful "emotional possession" on impressionable youth in the form of aroused feelings and released impulses accompanied by a fixation on imagery. Edgar Dale's movie-content study gave weight to Blumer's findings by showing that crime was a theme in 27.4 percent of films – accompanied by love (29.6 percent) and sex (15 percent).

Although the Payne studies provided considerable grist to challenge the communication industry, their impact actually was less than might have been expected given the scope and size of the research program. During the 1930s, film makers did reluctantly make cosmetic responses in the direction of censoring sex and violence. However, Blumer himself recalled that the movie studios and the public alike had been "easily able to ignore the Studies." As to the scientific status of the research, a contemporary assessment was given by Samuel Stouffer, then Harvard's leading quantitative social scientist, who approved of criticisms that the Payne researchers had collected anecdotes "which illustrate but do not prove." For quantifiers such as Stouffer, who deprecated the attempt to straddle data collection and reform, the Payne research clearly illustrated the awkwardness of attempting such a synthesis. For instance, in each case where Dale set out findings about movie content, he explicitly provided a rather pat editorial moralism. After finding that only 9 percent of the goals pursued by leading characters were social in nature (as opposed to such individual objectives as love or revenge), Dale opined that this emphasis was "at variance with the views that we are trying to develop in the schools, homes, and churches."[57]

Neither Lynd's theoretically based call to action nor the Payne Fund's data-based invitation to reform won many recruits for bringing together in one program the objectives of researching and reforming American communication practices. Neither Lynd's nor the Payne Fund's calls for a research-reform praxis seemed particularly sophisticated on a theoretical level, nor were they, pragmatically, likely to promote a smooth working relationship with outside institutions and grantors. Both calls to action orbited too distantly from academe's successful measurement-management-theorization axis.

Ultimately, therefore, propaganda critique in academe gained little sustenance from leading-edge humanistic studies of communication in the 1930s. For their part, grand theorists either ignored issues of American participatory democracy (Mead, Parsons), conjectured abstrusely about social communication (the Frankfurt School), or waited upon others to take action (Dewey). The community studies, on their part, pitched their extensive data more in the direction of a richer social theory than toward a set of democratic communication reforms. Similarly, calls for a research-reform synthesis by Robert Lynd and by the Payne Fund investigators offered little guarantee that efforts to link study to direct action would repay, especially given that better opportunities seemed to lie in the directions proposed by Lasswell and Lazarsfeld.

Propaganda critique, of course, was a fourth line of humanistic research offering competition to the quantified science of communication measurement and management. To be sure, academic propaganda analysts could point to a large number of specific inquiries completed by the mid-1930s. Yet the undertaking seemed rather helter-skelter. With many small studies arrayed across numerous social-science fields, propaganda critique's heterogeneity and fragmentation were palpable. Needed was a large-scale theoretical framework and a compelling vocabulary of analysis to integrate the compartmentalized studies and bring them clearly to bear on richly described common problems. Available, instead, were unintegrated studies of institutions (Lee), channels (Lumley), or psychological responses (Doob). With the exception of Lee's study of newspapers, the book-length treatments of propaganda produced in the 1930s (Doob, Lumley, Odegard, and Albig) pursued a tepid, textbook-level of theorizing. The most recognizable single methodological aspect of propaganda critique was common-sense muckraking, a meat-and-potatoes approach unlikely to rivet the attention of anyone in the academy. Notably absent during the era was broad thinking about propaganda and democracy of the kind later produced by Alfred Lee (after the 1950s), Jacques Ellul (in the 1960s), and Terence Qualter (in the 1980s).[58]

Ironically, there was available within the literature of the humanities a conceptual communication framework upon which academic critics might have built a theoretically validated program of directly reinvigorating citizen participation in public debate. Even undergraduate students in the mid-1800s were well acquainted with the classical scholarship in rhetoric. Aristotle's *Rhetoric* and Cicero's *De Oratore,* for instance, laid out a broad range of concepts of communication directly focused on public deliberation in a competitive, democratic setting. However, with the replacement of oratorical rhetoric by mechanical English composition in the late nineteenth century, the theory and practice of rhetoric had become so obscure and antiquarian that it went completely undiscovered in the giant bibliography of propaganda studies prepared by Lasswell et al. for the Social Science Research Council. Although Lasswell's compendium included works on public speaking, the tome reported nothing of the 2,500–year-old philosophy of rhetoric that underlay contemporary speech textbooks. Only by the mid-1940s did Lasswell discover classical rhetoric – too late to have had any influence on the germination of communication research.[59]

To be sure, the classical heritage of rhetoric was well known by humanists in the field of speech. Although these scholars gave both attention and application to concepts of rhetoric, they maintained a rather insular orientation during the 1920s and 1930s that found them chiefly writing short articles to one another in journals of the field. Furthermore, rhetoricians in speech departments tended to focus on the oratorical persuasions of nineteenth-century small-town America or on those contemporary nooks and crannies where face-to-face speaking captured attention. They did not pursue at length the pressing macrosocial problem, examined by Dewey, Lasswell, and the Chicago School, of democracy no longer nourished directly by face-to-face oratory and, instead, dependent upon the secondary symbolic interactions of mass media.[60]

Although the humanistic study of communication was alive during the inter–world-war period, the mission of progressive critique to dilute propaganda with grass-roots discussion and action never drew significant theoretical support from grand theory, from community studies, from calls to action by high-level researchers, or from classical rhetoric. The fragmentation of humanistic communication study prevented the emergence of a research-action nexus oriented to participatory democracy that might have challenged the use of audience measurement to better manage top–down communication.

By 1943, divorce proceedings were well under way between social science's quantitative scholars of communication and the various humanists. A summary of the field of communication science prepared by Irving Janis made it clear that in this divorce, custody of social-influence research likely would be awarded to the academic quantifiers. Janis, a psychologist on duty in Lasswell's wartime content-analysis shop, prepared a roster of approved topics for social-science work on problems of communication. His "seven major classes of variables" included: (1) "communicator's environment" (economy, setting); (2) "personality characteristics of the communicator"; (3) "media of communication" (placement and physical appearance of the signs); (4) "content" (words used); (5) "audience's environment" (time and place); (6) "psychological predispositions" (personality and attitude toward communicator); and (7) "reactions to the communication" (attitude change or voting behavior). These categories were constituted to minimize such archetypal foci of propaganda analysis as the persuader's social purpose, the cooptation of channels by elites, and competing interests of different publics.[61] Janis wrote in a time when conditions created by the new world war already were making the alliance of practitioners and academic quantifiers so appealing that commentators on social influence were wont to forget the old muckraker's theme of manipulation.

CHAPTER 4

DIFFERENT LESSONS II: PROTECTING THE PUBLIC

Out of the disorderly collision of Big Communication and traditional democracy emerged not only alternate conceptions of propaganda but also correspondingly different views of the public. Most commentators of the inter–world-war period granted a presumption to public opinion in the belief that people possessed an innate discursive competence sufficient to function at a minimal level. Progressive critics saw the public as open to being educated about propaganda; both practitioners and communication scientists justified their work on the basis of people's ability to select advantageously from among competing propaganda. However, pessimism about whether democracy's people were up to the tasks of twentieth-century life represented an undercurrent of tantalizing power. Progressive critics acknowledged that clever propagandists could temporarily fool the people; practitioners spoke of the public's ability to spite itself through stubbornness; and communication scientists were attracted to the notion that public life was itself basically irrational. These caveats about participatory democracy drew strength from two further inter–world-war schools of thought about propaganda: the straight-thinking and the polemical perspectives on social influence.

Lippmann and Dewey

Alarmed about wartime obsessions and manic displays, proponents of straight thinking were emboldened to advocate direct intervention as essential for correcting weaknesses in people's modes of thought. Driven by a vision of an irrational citizenry helpless before clever propaganda, straight thinkers developed a theory and pedagogy premised on the idea of cognitive incompetence. They argued that people could not be trusted to think intelligently unless their logical skills were first measured and then meliorated through formal training. Walter Lippmann, the journalist-philosopher, and John Dewey, America's philosopher-laureate, were the two best-known commentators on the public during the 1920s and 1930s, and they became – albeit unintentionally – the spiritual guides for the straight-thinking approach to propaganda.

Lippmann's metamorphosis from a fellow traveler of muckraking to a legitimizer of elitist democracy made him a weather vane for society's evolving conceptions of the public. However, Lippmann's deepening concern about democracy's rank and file was not born of a conversion experience; certain fissures were present from the beginning in how he conceived of his fellow Americans. While the young Lippmann spoke up for outcasts and reformers and worked as a journalist under Lincoln Steffens, this precocious progressive also imbibed newer psychological conceptions of politics from his mentor, Graham Wallas, the English guild socialist, and from his own readings of Freud. Harbingers of Lippmann's distrust of the people and his recourse to administrative steersmanship could be discerned in his two prewar books. In *A Preface to Politics* (1913), Lippmann's juxtaposing of psychoanalysis and politics supported his conclusion that progressives should consider not only the intellectual architecture of their reform measures but also the social intelligence of the people. In *Drift and Mastery* (1914), Lippmann faulted the small-town individualism that seemed to underlie Wilson's progressive program, arguing that the vast scope of modern life required large-scale administrative measures to harness the nation's considerable resources. He further argued that the "distracted soul" and "murky vision" of the people might be a greater obstacle to social progress than the "malicious contrivance of the plutocracy."[1]

Lippmann's direct and sometimes painful immersion in political and psychological opinion control during the war may have diluted and even postponed his inchoate movement toward a paternalistic-administrative conception of mass democracy. As a worker in the army's psychological warfare unit, Lippmann contended with the jealousy of Creel's CPI and his own growing disdain of military organization. He fared little better in the war's political sphere, where he alternated between insider and outsider, eventually losing his place as whiz kid of the Inquiry project that was shepherding Washington's vision of the postwar world. Lippmann experienced firsthand how elites might be confused or spiteful and how they might mismanage their publics. These perceptions suffused his *Liberty and the News* (1920) and his co-authored piece on the wishfully inaccurate reporting of the Russian civil war by the *New York Times*.[2]

Lippmann's early works were reconcilable in varying degrees with the picture of an intelligent discursive democracy struggling to survive in an arid informational atmosphere characterized by a chiefly one-way flow of communication about society. His later works merged the metaphor of the-public-as-cipher to an elitist notion of managed democracy and, therefore, were less entangled with strands of progressive propaganda critique. In *The Phantom Public* (1925), Lippmann extended the analysis, begun in *Public Opinion,* of a public confused by facts, overwhelmed by newspapers, and haunted by symbols. Lippmann presented citizens as consummate outsiders to government, unable to anticipate problems, and arriving late, if at all, to an issue. Nor was the public's civic retardation entirely unfortunate since "when public opinion attempts to govern directly it is either a failure or a tyranny." Lippmann saw people as prone to becoming dupes of organized special interests whenever they tried to deal with the specific merits of issues. The public was best situated as a reserve force to which elites could appeal on those occasions when leaders proved unequal to the task.[3]

Lippmann's writings constituted the most prominent indication of how theoreticians of political society were moving from the old democratic faith expressed by James Bryce to the notion of the irrational and helpless public seen in the works of Le Bon and Wallas. His influential views were significant in setting up the intellectual environment in which the straight-thinking movement grew, although his specific remedies did not focus on education. Never directly an apostle of straight thinking, Lippmann doubted whether either education or more information could better empower democracy's people. His specific reforms looked, on the one hand, to benign social science research, or on the other, to a kind of quasi-propaganda analysis that would help people to detect better the self-interested groups of special pleaders.[4] Nevertheless, in his role as the nation's best-known prophet of civic incompetence, Lippmann functioned as a doting uncle to those lesser-known minions working to improve the political and social reasoning power of Americans.

John Dewey's vision of face-to-face participatory democratic communities stood in diametric opposition to Lippmann's overwhelmed and properly overlooked mass public. However, as his brother public intellectual, Dewey figured in the development of the straight-thinking movement without necessarily having intended to do so. But where proponents of straight thinking drew indirectly on Lippmann's pessimism, they made immediate recourse to Dewey's writings on education and society, even though the old philosopher's support for the new movement at best was ambiguous. Dewey's interest in the intelligent discursive public never was reducible to simple formulas of critical thinking. His energy, as we will observe shortly, was focused on the cultural problem of democracy's survival in an era characterized by propaganda, by the authoritarian organization of schools and industry, and by a rising mechanical view of value-free science. Ironic it is, but Dewey nevertheless became a reference point for the straight-thinking approach to propaganda, a perspective on social influence distinguishable for its relatively pessimistic view of people's intelligence and its somewhat mechanical practices of pedagogy and assessment.

Dewey wrote on making participatory democracy work in schools, in politics, and in the workplace, although his vast outpourings were always tantalizingly abstruse and sometimes hidden in obscure journals. Dewey clearly believed that ordinary people had the intelligence to direct their society; but because he praised the scientific method as an appropriate inductive logic for modern people, and because he offered a five-step framework of reflective thinking, his works on public life could be – and sometimes were – narrowly applied. Dewey advocated neither value-free science, nor government by managers, nor a bare-bones hypothetico-experimental model of thinking.[5] However, his writings on pedagogy, logic, and society sometimes were perceived during the 1920s and 1930s to support both the quantification of thinking and a step-by-step pedagogy to guide students along the straight and narrow path of correct reasoning.

Certain prominent pieces of Dewey's program reinforced trends that, when put together in a synthesis not linked to his own project of democratic reform, supported a circumscribed science of critical thinking. One such piece was Dewey's effort to connect thinking to psychology. Dewey believed that knowing was invariably associated with "diverse functions of affection, appreciation, and practice," a situation that made for many "intimate connections of logical theory with functional psychology."[6] Dewey's tendency to view logic as a mental process connected to psychosocial reality was part of his general move away from the limitations of the older formalistic classical logic. Philosophers such as Morris Cohen and Ernest Nagel resisted Dewey's effort to supplant what they revered as the "autonomous science of the objective though formal conditions of valid inference." They granted that Dewey's psychological process approach to thinking might carry "pedagogical soundness" but argued that "questions of validity are not questions of how we happen to think."[7] Dewey's promotion of a psychological view of logic certainly reinforced a growing notion that reasoning could and should be measured with psychological tests similar to those being developed to assess human intelligence.

Closely related to Dewey's psychologizing of logic was his marrying of inference to the scientific method per se. Dewey had in mind an experimental kind of logic based on his conception of thinking as a process of doubt leading to inquiry. Dewey's pragmatic logic saw science contributing to the doubt–inquiry process by giving useful data. Praising Charles Peirce's notion of the "laboratory habit of mind," Dewey valued scientific inference for replacing a search for settled propositions with a striving for facts. Here scientific results displaced first principles as the starting point for reasoning.[8] In his later work, *Logic: The Theory of Inquiry* (1938), Dewey continued to "develop a theory of logic that is in thorough accord with all the best authenticated methods of attaining knowledge." He emphasized that logical forms should be scrutinized on the basis of whether they did (or did not) lead to productive inquiry, and he favored a dynamic logic with constant connection to practical concerns.[9]

Dewey never presented the methods of science as supplying new categories for formalizing thought, since the steps of scientific method required outside judgments, observations, and applications. Nor did Dewey advocate a scientific reasoning about society that merely borrowed techniques of experiment and statistics without looking at actual social conditions, possible results, and the worthiness of ends.[10] But in a time when scientific method was coming to be seen as the neutral application of cut-and-dried procedures, Dewey's broader applications of science to thought were easy to overlook. Dewey's works on logic presented thinking as a mental process best reformed by the scientific method and provided, therefore, a general warrant for psychologists and educationists who worked during the 1920s to develop a theory and pedagogy of straight thinking.

Dewey's most direct connection to the straight-thinking movement was his pedagogical analysis of certain discernible steps in the process of thinking. In *How We Think* (1910), Dewey provided an attractive five-step outline of how intelligent thought was driven by the psychological need for resolution of difficulty and could profitably model itself on the method of science.

> Upon examination, each instance [of reflective thinking] reveals, more or less clearly, five logically distinct steps: (*i*), a felt difficulty; (*ii*) its location and definition; (*iii*) suggestion of possible solution; (*iv*) development by reasoning of the bearings of the suggestion; (*v*) further observation and experiment leading to its acceptance or rejection; that is, the conclusion of belief or disbelief.

Complementing Dewey's compelling linkage of psychology, logic, and science was his pedagogical argument that better thinking could be taught. Dewey recommended that the teacher guide students in observing, drawing on past knowledge, generalizing, and applying new knowledge. While he remarked on the close resemblance of "the methods of instruction with our own analysis of a complete operation of thinking," Dewey never suggested that reflective thinking should be taught or measured by means of his five-step process. To the contrary, he argued that such an abstracted, logical schema better suited "one who already understands" than "a mind that is learning."[11] Yet, in the glow of Dewey's elegant framework, it was easy to lose sight of this philosopher's cautionary notes that any step could come first. Dewey's pedagogy of reflective thinking invited more restricted readings in the direction of a process-oriented, step-by-step approach to measuring and teaching the art of thought.

Progressives drew great inspiration during the 1920s and 1930s from Lippmann's and Dewey's wide-ranging critical studies of society, science, communication, and knowledge. The voluminous outpourings of these two towering proponents of an intelligent modernism nurtured, on the one hand, the critical tangent of progressivism as when they inspired sociologist Frederick Lumley to theorize about detecting and combatting propaganda.[12] Lippmann and Dewey also informed progressivism's hope for practical administrative efficiency by holding out the promise that science and education might improve the process by which people thought about social issues. Lippmann's phantom public and Dewey's applied psychologic diverged in philosophical grounding and practical recommendations.[13] However, these two currents of interpretation came together in ways that nurtured the literature of the straight-thinking movement. In amalgamated form, Lippmann's and Dewey's ideas fed a view that the weak-minded and dangerously neurotic public could not be trusted to take intelligent political action without formal training, supported by quantitative assessment, in how to think.

Thinking as Science

The ideas of thinking as a science, and of scientific method as a solution for logical dilemmas, were in the air in the first decades of the twentieth century and were as likely to show up in popular commentaries as in textbooks.[14] Of the many works on straight thinking, those by the American sociologist Edwin Clarke and the English psychologist Robert Thouless were most influential. Clarke presented his book as a "handbook on scientific thinking in the social sciences," and he examined the pernicious influences both of personal prejudice based on emotion and social prejudice resulting from imitating prestigious persons. Clarke described the salutary effect of formal logic, scientific method, and

Dewey's reflective thought process, and he further explained how to evaluate sources of information. Here he observed the dishonest influence on thinking of government propaganda during the Great War and of business propaganda in the postwar period.[15]

In a similar effort to separate straight from crooked thinking, Thouless explained that the latter was based on emotional reactions reinforced by certain negative connotations of words. Thouless further described advocates as frequently employing one or more of some thirty-four dishonest tricks of argument, which included diverting discussion to trivial points, begging the question, and creating prestige through unsupported suggestions confidently asserted. Straight thinking, in contrast, was best exemplified by the scientific method in which "the scientist weighs, measures, and calculates without any use of emotional phraseology, guided only by a simple creed of the universality of the law of cause and effect."[16]

As social scientists joined philosophers in drawing the boundaries of straight thinking, the measurement impulse crept into the enterprise to improve the discursive intelligence of the people. Goodwin Watson of Columbia's Teachers College and his student, Edward Glaser, led the movement to develop cognitive assessment scales for critical thinking. Watson, who cited Dewey and Columbia's James Harvey Robinson on the importance of open-minded thinking, believed that precise measures of this characteristic would be indispensable in designing future curricula and methods capable of creating a better world. His tests encompassed six forms variously designed to measure the following tendencies:

(a) to cross out, as distasteful, terms which represent one side or another of religious or economic controversies; (b) to call sincere and competent persons who hold different opinions on religious and economic issues incompetent or insincere; (c) to draw from given evidence conclusions which support one's bias but which are not justified by that evidence; (d) to condemn in a group which is disliked, activities which would be condoned or approved in some other group; (e) to regard arguments, some of which are really strong and others of which are really weak, as all strong if they be in accord with the subject's bias, or all weak if they run counter to that bias; and (f) to attribute to all the people or objects in a group, characteristics which belong to only a portion of that group.

Watson mentioned various successful applications of his tests, for instance, when one charity speaker assessed college audiences and when researchers measured the impact of a course on race relations (which reduced by 30 percent the tendency of students to mark extreme responses). Watson further recommended his tests to social workers, psychoanalysts, and researchers wanting to assess the effectiveness of various types of propaganda material. By documenting apparently inconsistent and weak reasoning, the tests indicated to Watson not only that people needed "a keener analysis of 'facts,' 'evidence,' and 'arguments' " but that reasoning deficiencies were complicated because "different people react with widely different attitudes to the same facts and arguments."[17] Here Watson reflected the growing tendency to view intelligent public action as limited more by people's internal psyches than by inputs of external propaganda. Such an interpretation stood in contrast to progressive propaganda critique, which emphasized putting accurate information into people's hands.

Building on Watson's work, Edward Glaser surveyed various works on straight thinking to develop a somewhat more sophisticated set of six assessment yardsticks. As a further part of his dissertation study, Glaser developed eight lesson units in critical thinking that provided an education in definitions, weighing evidence, the nature of probable inference, deductive and inductive reasoning, logic and the method of science, the scientific attitude, prejudice as a factor in crooked thinking, and propaganda's connection to crooked thinking. Students exposed to these experimental units showed an average gain in critical-thinking scores significantly greater than those registered by control groups. Glaser emphasized that although results of critical-thinking tests were associated with I.Q. scores, the former were more malleable through education than the latter.[18]

Supported by articles and books in the fields of philosophy, social science, and education, straight thinking grew up during the 1930s as an alternative to progressive-style propaganda critique. Initially, the distinctions between the two approaches were not entirely clear. Such ambiguity was evidenced not only by content of instruction but also by the fact that Glaser developed his tests and lesson units in cooperation with the Institute for Propaganda Analysis which, as will become clear hereafter, served as the institutional linchpin of progressive antipropaganda work. Both as rubric and as pedagogy, propaganda analysis began as the more prominent approach; however, certain intellectual and social conditions of the late 1930s and early 1940s caused straight thinking to overwhelm almost completely its formerly dominant partner. The shift may be observed by comparing the 1937 and 1942 yearbooks of the National Council for the Social Studies (NCSS).

The NCSS's yearbook of 1937, *Education Against Propaganda*, advocated a program of study to inform citizens about the communication industry so that they could fulfill their democratic responsibilities to "make intelligent choices between alternatives presented to them by leaders and organizations." The volume began with topical articles: propaganda and social competition (by social scientist Harwood Childs); newspaper concentration and advertising pressures (by Harold Lasswell); financial, political, and social ties of newspapers (by journalism professor Ralph Casey); censorship and propaganda faced by foreign correspondents (by journalist/educator O. W. Riegel); biased images in films (by educational social scientist Edgar Dale); worldwide systems of radio control (by psychologist Hadley Cantril); pressure groups and the schools (by educator Howard K. Beale). Next came reports about educational programs designed to inculcate resistance to propaganda. General methods included inviting representatives of various points of view to address students, conducting Dewey-type reflective discussions, and identifying such propaganda devices as the "we–they" technique. Additional proposals included one by a college social studies teacher who recommended having students read and compare newspapers critically. A historian explained how he taught students to evaluate historical documents for evidence and for bias. High-school teachers contributed tips on researching the communication industry, leading class discussions, comparing newspapers, and discussing certain broadcasts of NBC's "America's Town Meeting of the Air" program.[19]

The propaganda analysis of the NCSS's 1937 volume focused on pollution of public opinion by distortions and biases in the communication media; in contrast, the pedagogy of straight thinking explicated in the 1942 yearbook evidenced little interest in the nexus of self-promoting persuader and wide-ranging media. The newer volume placed relatively more emphasis on emotional states and reasoning fallacies that plagued citizens by impeding correct inference. Where students of 1942 applied critical analysis to actual social questions, the political context was blander and less likely than propaganda analysis to challenge powerful interest groups and the communication industry. For instance, one unit of instruction for high schools invited students to draw conclusions about the growth of Buffalo, New York, and the relative speed of nineteenth-century canal travel. Another unit of critical-thinking study in 1942 directed students to problems of school and community life as illustrated by an assignment to investigate the administration of and student satisfaction with the cafeteria.[20] As will become clear hereafter, the transition from propaganda analysis to straight thinking was facilitated by a belief that the former focus of educators on persuaders and channels had promoted a destructive cynicism not at all appropriate for a nation at war.

Closely allied to the straight-thinking movement was the rising interest in semantics registered during the 1930s. The turn to semantics can be seen as yet another manifestation of the belief that the chief problem of democracy was not the manipulation of citizens but rather their relative inability to work with words. The idea that symbols were somehow a sign of social danger was coincidental with the demise of early nineteenth-century rhetorical study and practice – in which stylistic innuendo and bombast alike were appreciated – and their replacement with science and a mechanical-technical view of social communication.

Even Dewey, no logical positivist, was troubled by the power of nonreferential words to create a pseudoreality. Notwithstanding his concern for community, Dewey harbored little appreciation for the spaciousness of the old rhetoric that Richard Weaver, a rhetorical theorist, believed had sustained nineteenth-century politics. Where Weaver saw democracy strengthened when audiences and orators were bonded culturally by grand abstractions and florid phraseology, twentieth-century proponents of referential language and thinking-for-yourself were likely to see artifice or, worse, deceit.[21] The vituperative expressions of the Great War gave moderns even more reason to distrust words, and popular writers on semantics emerged to explain how language tyrannized its users.

Semantics cropped up in many varieties in the decades after World War I. One of them was the influential referential semantics of C. K. Ogden and I. A. Richards. In *The Meaning of Meaning* (1923), Ogden and Richards offered a science of symbolism that attributed many problems of thought to the popular myth that symbols were directly and naturally connected to the reality that they purported to represent. In contrast, Ogden and Richards presented meaning as an interpretative process bounded by one's psychological and environmental contexts, and they contrasted the representative and emotive functions of words. Widely influential was their semantic triangle consisting of symbol, reference (i.e., thought) and referent (i.e., the thing symbolized), which they used to emphasize the speculative connection between the first and third elements of meaning. Richards later offered the semantic approach as a "new rhetoric" appropriate for modern people wanting to flee the ornaments of rhetorical style but who needed advice on how to overcome the social problem of misunderstanding resulting from language. Here the useless macroscopic wordplay of the old rhetoric could be redeemed in the careful microscopic analysis employed by the new.[22]

Equally if not eventually more influential than Ogden and Richards's referential theory of semantics was the like-minded general semantics movement initiated by Alfred Korzybski. Korzybski's *Science and Sanity* (1933) pursued, sometimes obscurely, such relatively familiar problems as mistaking words for material conditions. But this Polish emigré also contributed greatly to the general semantic worldview, for instance, with his insightful (if not abstruse) analysis of the orders of abstraction that resulted when people connected events, objects, and symbols. Korzybski's work was brought to the intelligent reading public partly through the effort of S. I. Hayakawa, an English professor, whose very accessible books moderated certain obscurantist tendencies in general semantics. In *Language in Action* (1941), Hayakawa began by posing semantics as a solution not only to the public's "verbal superstition" and "primitive linguistic assumptions" but also to the new and "unparalleled semantic influences" that included commercialized media, public relations, and the "propaganda technique of nationalistic madmen." He envisioned a world in which the science of symbols would render problems tractable by keeping people "scientifically aware of the mechanisms of interpretation" so that they could "guard themselves against being driven mad by the welter of words with which they are now faced." Not only did "snarl" and "purr" words (e.g., "reds" and "economic royalists") prematurely close off cooperation, but sensational newspaper reports impeded discussion by omitting the context of a statement.

Turning to Korzybski's slippery slope of abstracting, Hayakawa noted that much historical misery had been caused by high-level abstractions such as "Jew" versus "Christian." Democracy would be better served by a multivalued orientation that realistically perceived the goods and bads of political leaders and positions. Such an orientation was superior to the simple either–or attitude about social questions that impeded the adjustment of conflicting interests. If only citizens could be educated to see behind the orators and advertisers who wanted people to guide themselves with words alone instead of locating meaning in material conditions.[23]

Most semanticists were as apt to attend personal maladjustments as to promote sanity in politics; however, in *The Symbols of Government* (1935), Thurman W. Arnold, Yale law professor and soon-to-be New Deal trustbuster, gave the era's most closely argued political application of word-science. Arnold believed that psychological contradictions running amok in people prevented them from consistently following "any conceivable set of moral or rational principles." Similarly, although institutions felt a need to invoke doctrines and reasons, they adhered only loosely to many conflicting principles, and they used symbols either to camouflage the contradictions or to dominate the public. One of Arnold's prime examples was the Tennessee Valley Authority's employment of symbols to make a government-owned and operated electrical system look consistent with capitalist enterprise. Reformers and scholars understood too little the basic principle (familiar to politicians) that the symbolic manipulation of groups "binds society together" and is required to hold power.

As a legal realist, Arnold believed further that the symbols expressed in law did not guide society as much as they comforted people. As with theology, law tried to set up rational principles to mask contradictions. As an example, he cited the effort to surround New Deal relief efforts with symbols that made the enterprise look like productive employment. Here "the symbolic effect of public works became more important than their practical need." A related instance of where symbolic stratagems masked reality could be seen in the Supreme Court's use of various dodges to avoid ruling on the constitutionality of the National Recovery Act until after the program had lost popularity.

Although Arnold cast his lot with the New Deal reformers, his analogy for government's relation to the public was that of physicians in charge of an insane asylum. Having no reason to argue "the soundness or unsoundness of their ideas," these benevolent administrators aimed "to make the inmates of the asylum as comfortable as possible, regardless of their respective moral deserts." Such an orientation allowed reformers to solve practical social problems without worrying in the abstract about whether their therapies were contradictory, whether the recipients were rational, or whether the cures were permanent. Concluding with a minor nod to the public's intelligence, Arnold believed that citizens were capable of accepting his medical analogy and, thus, could revere the mystic symbols of government without, on their account, "foregoing sensible and practical advantages." Nevertheless, Arnold's semantic realism expressed a higher level of cynicism about words than would be found in works by educational optimists such as Hayakawa and Richards, who hoped to turn the science of symbols into a vehicle for utopia. Rather than seeking to heal the breach between words and reality, Arnold reveled in their separation as something necessary for political institutions to work.[24]

Synthesizing the work of Arnold and other prominent realist students of language was Stuart Chase, the economist and social critic, whose *The Tyranny of Words* (1938) greatly popularized the semantic worldview. By 1936, Chase was digesting various heavy books on the subject and was corresponding with Ogden and Korzybski as he prepared his own foray into the power, danger, and promise of symbols. Reviewing the work of various semantic pioneers, Chase covered such topics as the importance of context in meaning, the dangers of excessive abstracting, and the prevalence of the tendency both to view symbols in magical terms and to assume that the word was the same as the thing. "Endless political and economic difficulties in America have arisen and thriven on bad language," Chase maintained. To prevent purveyors of semantic "blab" such as Hitler from victimizing the public, it was important to teach people to translate words into specific and verifiable meanings. Although members of the public were not stupid, they did lack an adequate method for intelligently deciphering the language used by their leaders. Here Chase heartily endorsed the scientific method and the science of symbols as promising avenues for revolutionizing political life. He was particularly intrigued with Ogden's Basic English, which consisted of 850 words and five grammatical rules that, Chase thought, could become a precise universal language.[25]

Semanticists contributed to straight thinking by enlarging on the idea that language itself was responsible for people's seeming inability to discuss intelligently and systematically matters of politics and society. The more pessimistic of their number focused on the absurdity of abstract principles and the concomitant hopelessness of rational discussion. The more optimistic regarded the public as trainable in the ways of words. Just as mainstream straight thinking looked to science and systems of logical reasoning, semanticists invoked both the larger scientific method and certain microscopic principles of symbolic science.

Devotees of straight thinking and scientific semantics challenged the assumption of progressive critics that elite manipulation was the basic cause of public perversity. The new prophets of dialectical hygiene deduced from contemporary situations of politics and from modern conditions of communication that the irrational public itself threatened democracy. They came to believe that people needed an education in how to reason and to use words even more than in how to recognize manipulation. Common to semanticists and straight thinkers alike was the idea that intelligence could play only a little role in modern politics until the public's patterns of reasoning, listening, and speaking were broken and then recast. They took on the mission to protect the public from itself by diffusing methods of careful mental operation. Theirs was an education in Thinking 101 rather than a project to alert members of an already competent public.

Progressive Polemics

Pessimism about public opinion also imbued persons whose approach to propaganda followed a polemical vector that entailed identifying, and acting directly to neutralize, dangerous communication from political opponents. Although favoring a program of political transformation and/or expurgation rather than scientific thinking, the antipropaganda polemicists shared with the straight thinkers the belief that a gullible public required protection more than information. The object became less to educate the people, à la the muckraking tradition, and more to sound alarm bells such that Americans would support the work of activists to reconstruct national institutions. Polemical propaganda analysis was a critique conducted in an overtly partisan parlance and accompanied by action to purge society's communication channels of opposing ideologues and ideologies.

During the inter–world-war years, the Left produced a larger literature of antipropaganda polemics than did the Right (however, as will be seen, conservative polemicism more than made up for its meager cadres by leveraging the like-minded in business and Congress). Progressive propaganda critique may have lacked support from high-level communication scholarship and from research-supporting grantors, but antipropaganda muckraking found confederates among various polemicists and activists of the progressive (or otherwise nonrevolutionary) Left. Although these leftists exhibited progressivism's moderate and nonviolent style of politics, as well as its emphasis on education, they departed from their muckraker brethren by featuring a fighting vocabulary and by undertaking action projects having a directly political connotation. These writers and operatives corrected what they probably viewed as a weakness of antipropaganda muckraking, namely, its assumption that the public, once alerted, spontaneously would rise up to take action. The propaganda-purging polemicists of the Left seemed to have imbibed more of the era's angst about an unreliable public and so resolved to take protective political action in the name of the people.

The politically active auxiliaries of muckraking not only revealed themselves with a vocabulary that laced critique with calls for fundamental sociocultural change but also worked directly to engineer ideological transformation through education, journalism, consumer organizing, and government agency action. Our treatment of leftward antipropaganda polemicism begins with the more literary contributions, including the realist progressivism of Thurman Arnold, the socialist progressivism epitomized by Upton Sinclair, the cultural-critique progressivism of James Rorty, and the scientific progressivism of those who advocated consumer product testing. Our attention then turns to those progressive polemical allies of the muckrakers who directly labored to engineer social transformations via institutions of education, journalism, and consumerism and via the New Deal.

Thurman Arnold's use of linguistic realism to skewer opponents of the New Deal illustrated how the analysis of social influence could itself become a weapon in sociopolitical struggle. Arnold, a professor anxious to dabble in politics, wrote his provocative *The Folklore of Capitalism* (1937) to take symbolic realism into the thicket of the struggle over the New Deal's agencies and objectives. Arnold framed his semantic analysis of 1930s political battles in terms that continued the symbolic nihilism found in his earlier book. To Arnold, arguments about legal and economic traditions amounted to nothing more than versions of folklore, which had the effect of impeding necessary action. Similarly outmoded was the idea of the Thinking Man who consciously chose governmental systems after intelligent discussion. Instead, Arnold contended, people actually adopted political creeds and policies through faith instead of reason and also as part of a search for prestige and security. As a result, debate followed stereotyped patterns that could only be understood by study of a particular nation's psychology. Reliance on polar terms such as *justice* versus *injustice* was particularly vicious in ruining judgment by channeling reactions into ruts. Ultimately, the practical treatment of a nation's actual needs fell by the wayside as a result of ideological combat waged through opposing abstractions. While granting the "old creed of democracy" was "a useful slogan to stir national pride in a people who had no ruling class," Arnold observed that, today, "everyone recognized the limitations of the average man – and few thought that these limitations disappeared in a group."

The bulk of Arnold's book was devoted to uncovering various Depression-era folk tales that were invoked to defend laissez-faire economics against legislative and regulatory initiatives of the Roosevelt administration. Arnold pointed out, for instance, that industrialists liked to use "the language of personally owned private property" as if such actually applied to the situation of modern people who depended on vast industrial and organizational systems for their goods and transportation. Similarly, the minions of business mythologized corporations as individuals and thereby induced people to associate regulations on capitalists with limitations on the liberties enjoyed by ordinary citizens. Arnold described advocates of free enterprise as also enjoying success in convincing Americans that the extraction of money by advertising and "high-pressure salesmanship" was not at all comparable to the so-called forced confiscation of property by government taxation.[26]

Upton Sinclair was another writer who went beyond exposé to enter the political arena with polemical antipropaganda broadsides. This socialist muckraker developed a veritable one-man literature of self-published antipropaganda pronouncements that argued for purging journalism, religion, education, and the publishing industry of antidem-

ocratic people and practices. He began this series with a semiautobio-
graphical account of how reactionary owners and dishonest norms in
journalism worked against reform. Sinclair's *The Brass Check* (1919)
laid down a broad challenge that "American newspapers as a whole
represent private interests and not public interests." Sinclair's critique
of news propaganda focused more on the capitalist system of ownership
than on particular publicity techniques; hence, he likened journalists to
prisoners of an urban whorehouse who were paid when they redeemed
the customer's brass check. The Pasadena socialist pointed to biased
coverage of the Interstate Commerce Commission's hearings caused by
editors who, beholden to wealthy newspaper owners, skewed coverage
away from reformers and toward the "class-interests" of railroad over-
lords. Sinclair accused the press of consistently ignoring reformers such
as Rose Pastor Stokes, of printing false quotations from unionists such
as Eugene Debs, and of circulating untrue reports about the home life
of socialists or radicals such as Thorstein Veblen and Jack London.
"How comes it," Sinclair wondered, "that the Associated Press makes
all its mistakes one way?" Sinclair proposed the municipal ownership
of newspapers and called for unionization of reporters, most of whom
wanted to be honest but lacked the professional independence to act
honestly.[27]

Sophisticated practitioners of journalism then and now often have
characterized Sinclair's work as not only romantically self-serving in its
tone but also naive in its particulars about journalism. George Seldes,
who greatly admired Sinclair, acknowledged these weaknesses upon
which "boss-serving bootlickers and apologists pounced thankfully."
However, for reporters caught up in the sometimes heavy-handed ideological censorship of the era, Sinclair's work focused anxieties earlier
unleashed by Irwin's 1911 series on the press. *The Brass Check* created
a sensation among news people in the 1920s and significantly influenced
such contributors to press criticism as Seldes and I. F. Stone.[28]

Sinclair continued his anticapitalist propaganda critique with explorations of religion, superpatriotism, higher education, the public schools,
and popular literature. In *The Profits of Religion* (1918), Sinclair described lucre as either preoccupying preachers or putting their pulpits
into the service of the powerful. Sinclair's novelized exposé of patriotism, *100 Percent* (1920), focused on Peter Gudge, an uneducated patent
medicine peddler and religious charlatan whose career as a police spy
and agent provocateur for business reactionaries enabled him to win
the title of "100% American." In *The Goose-Step* (1923) and *The
Goslings* (1924), Sinclair turned his attention to the plutocrats and their
bureaucratic henchmen who had transformed the educational system

into an apologetical apparatus for capitalism. Beginning with the Los Angeles public schools, Sinclair provided snapshots of business groups steering and starving education. Turning to his (almost) alma mater, Columbia University, Sinclair portrayed trustee-capitalists punishing politically nonconformist professors. Venturing into capitalism's wont to transform literature into propaganda, Sinclair's *Mammonart* (1925) ranged through the centuries to reveal how most artists flattered the vanity of the ruling class. In *Money Writes!* (1927), Sinclair faulted publishers, who were under the control of Wall Street, for encouraging American writers to glorify the parasitic lives of the bourgeois class instead of following the lead of Theodore Dreiser, Jack London, and Carl Sandburg who worked against inequality by writing from the perspective of the laboring millions.[29]

Weighing in with a third installment in the leftward antipropaganda polemical literature were the cultural critics represented by James Rorty. In *Our Master's Voice: Advertising* (1934), Rorty, a former advertising copywriter and press publicist, presented his erstwhile professions as vastly important cultural forces that shaped "the economic, social, moral and ethical patterns of the community into serviceable conformity with the profit-making interests of advertisers." Ads not only set up "the acquisitive culture" as a standard but also induced a critical silence about this phenomenon. "The more space a magazine devotes to promoting buying the less space it devotes to instruction, comment or criticism concerning economic or political affairs."

Exploring certain class differences in advertising's courtship of its audience, Rorty found some slight direct or implied criticism of the economic system in periodicals catering to lower and upper classes and less emphasis on advertising's trinity of "fear, sex, and emulation" in the higher-tone magazines such as *Harper's Bazaar*. An overarching problem of advertising's relation to its audience, however, was the profession's ambiguous connection to truth. "Advertising is an exploitation of belief" and, therefore, according to Rorty, it trafficked in "human weakness, fear and credulity." In addition, if print advertising intruded into American culture, radio's confusing clatter of voices was even more blatant in its influence. "Our radio culture is acquisitive, emulative, neurotic and disintegrating."[30]

A fourth important strain of the Left's antipropaganda polemicizing came in the form of a rash of pro-consumer books contributed by social critics and engineers who wanted to spread the word about intelligent consumption. Believing that a program of hit-and-miss exposure would not be sufficient to safeguard the public against wasteful, poorly made, and unsafe products, progressive scientists wanted to root out abuses in the capitalist marketplace by stimulating interest in product testing and consumer cooperatives.

Major works bringing the consumer idea to the general public included *Your Money's Worth* (1927) by Stuart Chase, an economist formerly with the Federal Trade Commission, and F. S. Schlink, an engineer formerly attached to the National Bureau of Standards. Chase and Schlink contrasted how the government purchased materials on the basis of tests and specifications to the situation of the unorganized consumer who had no way of making sure whether an advertised product was effective or even safe. They encouraged citizens to base purchasing on scientific tests rather than meaningless and deceptive ads. They further argued that advertising's miasma of misinformation permitted manufacturers to accrue profits from worthless or actually poisonous cosmetics, foods, and drugs. In *100,000,000 Guinea Pigs* (1933), Schlink and Arthur Kallet, a fellow engineer, carried even further the idea that consumers unknowingly functioned as experimental subjects for a host of useless and often harmful products. These authors attributed the increased incidence of cancer to potassium chlorate found in toothpaste and arsenic sprayed onto vegetables. Moreover, misled by advertising, consumers willingly ate cereals with too much roughage, slathered on face creams containing irritants, and relied on antiseptics that were ineffective against many common germs.

Some consumerist books went beyond progressive calls for consumer organizing, product testing, and greater publicity for research about harmful products. Socialist language frequently intermingled with progressive parlance in consumerist polemics of the 1930s. In *Counterfeit* (1935), Kallet portrayed the profit motive itself as the basic source of economic fraud and suggested changes that went beyond consumer education. Kallet argued that the solution to capitalism's symbolic larceny was "not in legislation but in a fundamental change in our economic system." His proof included cases where fabrics labeled "part wool" contained only 10 percent of the substance, where "fancy" pineapples might not be the highest grade as was implied, where manufacturers charged excessive prices for common materials sold as cures, and where producers skimped to such an extent that, in the case of auto brakes, the product became not only less useful but positively dangerous. Kallet also explored the exaggerated claims, misleading "guarantees," and fraudulent testimonials that plagued consumers.

In *Partners in Plunder* (1935), consumerists J. B. Matthews (then a socialist) and R. E. Shallcross assailed capitalism from an impassioned, if not somewhat muddled, neo-Marxist position. In their view, consumers not only were gypped by fraudulent advertising for often dangerous products (that usually were planned for quick obsolescence), but the whole profit-oriented business system had transformed government, labor unions, newspapers, churches, and schools into agencies working "against the interests of consumer-workers." Matthews and Shallcross characterized the New Deal as the nation's master strikebreaker and blasted liberals for naively paving the way for fascist reactionaries. A disjointed subsequent book by Matthews envisioned a consumer-oriented society that would "enthrone engineering integrity" as an alternative both to capitalism's fraudulent prices and injustices and to the mediocre products of the Soviet workers' state. In arguing for replacement of the market system, rather than Chase and Schlink's solution of better consumer education, the radical consumerists showed a disposition to conceive of ordinary people as pawns of clever business propagandists.[31]

Through the writings of semantic realists, muckraker socialists, cultural critics, and consumer scientists, the antipropaganda political tangent of the progressive movement seemed to agitate for fundamental economic, social, and cultural changes. With the progressive movement now occasionally linked to the verbal barbs of socialism, cultural critique, and consumerism, progressivism as a whole became implicated in the radical challenge to America's status quo then being sounded not only by nonrevolutionary polemicists but also by those who were anxious to throw up street barricades. Although progressivism generally was a middle-class, reformist, education-oriented movement aiming for participatory democracy (and also favorable to efficiency and social harmony), this diffuse crusade now began to take on a political-extremist appearance from the perspective of nervous rightists. Worse yet, from the vantage point of the Right, was that progressive partisans were not merely issuing forth a literature of polemical critique; their minions actively had begun to diffuse challenges to the status quo through institutions and associations of the progressive education movement, the consumer movement, the adult-education movement, the professionalizing trends in journalism, and the New Deal's action agencies.

Big Progressivism

Rightist antipropaganda polemical activity was not prompted as much by fears of Big Communication in the Great Society as by alarm about what might be called Big Progressivism, that is, the movement of action-oriented progressives to infiltrate a message of social-change-through-participatory-democracy into major channels of social management. Big

Progressivism's social-change activism raised the specter of significant transformations in the nation's economy and culture. Progressive critics and activists, with their eyes fixed on capitalism and the communication industry, often did not appreciate their own success in having created a politically relevant nexus consisting of the Progressive Education Association, the Consumers Union, various community forums associated with adult education, the American Newspaper Guild, and such governmental agencies as the Federal Theatre Project. Neither progressive critics nor activists fully recognized that leftward institutional proselytizing inevitably would be treated by rightists as propaganda. What ultimately animated rightist antipropaganda polemicism were the significant gains that politically active progressives had made in American institutions, particularly those supported by tax dollars.

Under the auspices of the Progressive Education Association (PEA), established in 1919, reformers had set as their task to regenerate public schools by dedicating education to the liberation of young minds from regimentation. Teachers challenged passive, rote learning and fidelity to a universal, stipulated curriculum while, at the same time, they employed the psychology of child development to support giving more attention to the pupil than to the curriculum. This educational naturalism emphasized allowing students to express their own interests and to exercise initiative. Closely tied to the child-centered curriculum was the effort to make education relevant to what was going on in the community. Here educators implemented Dewey's ideas of treating the school as a small community and of emphasizing modes of thought that could be used against social problems of all types.

In its narrowest sense, progressive education meant making classrooms democratic and organizing them to meet the needs of children; but this educational movement also carried the wider political connotation of employing the school as a fulcrum for changing society itself. Always implicit and frequently explicit in progressive educational circles was the notion that schools should inculcate a collective spirit designed to replace rugged individualism, and that schools should expose children to progressivism's realistic view of society. A leading exponent of the school-changed society was Harold Rugg of Columbia's Teachers College who believed that the realistic appraisal of the outside community was the culminating objective of public education. By discussing social conditions, Rugg explained, "American youth shall visualize an entirely new world." In Rugg's scheme, youth would be "set at the task of helping to erect a nation-wide planned regime." On the one hand, the new reformist order would intelligently organize enterprise to simultaneously eliminate physical want and implement a ten-hour work week. At the same time, reformers would "redistribute political control among all classes of our people and thus achieve a reconciliation of individual liberty with true social efficiency."[32]

The idea of progressive education as leading edge of a total social transformation was expressed further in the Progressive Education Association's Committee on Economic and Social Problems that counted among its members such luminaries as George Counts, Merle Curti, Sidney Hook, and Goodwin Watson. The committee's 1932 report proclaimed that capitalistic individualism was outmoded and harmful and that, under the auspices of progressive education, youth would remake society along cooperative, collectivist lines. "They [youth] owe nothing to the present economic system except to improve it, they owe nothing to any privileged class except to strip it of its privileges." This report was particularly effective in "brand[ing] the stigma of radicalism on the PEA" as education historian Lawrence Cremin recalled. Although the PEA's sociopolitical visionaries were in the main supporters of the New Deal, Goodwin Watson recalled that his colleagues maintained "cousinly" contacts with socialists, communists, and Trotskyites, often inviting speakers from these groups. Watson was typical in his rejection of "the dictatorial aspect of Communism and their negative approach" combined with a belief that the "profit-making business corporation was hopelessly bogged down in contradictions which would make it impossible for it to continue to function." Watson described the PEA-type radical as not subversive in ways that deserved FBI attention but nevertheless "clearly subversive in a philosophical sense." Valid from an analytic standpoint, such a distinction would not hold good when subjected to the kind of from-the-Right polemical propaganda analysis that soon would be under way.[33]

Consumerist organizations provided a second vector of progressive pro-democracy propaganda activity. The consumer-movement's work in product testing was only one harbinger of transformations in the traditional organization of workplaces and marketplaces that might be in the offing. Already before the turn of the century, middle-class women had organized state consumer leagues in the belief that consumers, manufacturers, and distributors might unite to assure honest products sold at a cost that permitted decent working conditions. Leaders of the National Consumers' League included Newton D. Baker, formerly Wilson's secretary of war, and Jane Addams, social-work reformer.[34]

Equally radical from the standpoint of economic traditionalists was the belief of progressive consumerists that product testing could and should replace advertising. In 1929, Schlink began a Consumer Club to promote both "scientific buying" and do-it-yourself home manufacture.

This modest undertaking was reorganized as Consumers' Research, a product-testing laboratory, when E. C. Lindeman of the New School for Social Research conveyed to Schlink a grant he received from Mrs. Willard Straight, a liberal philanthropist. Unfortunately, Schlink's harsh management style precipitated a labor dispute within Consumers' Research, and the resulting employee strike divided the consumerist leaders of the organization. Kallet sided with the strikers against Schlink (and J. B. Matthews) and established the separate and eventually more successful Consumers Union organization, which similarly emphasized product testing. A particularly untoward effect of this falling out was that Matthews became bitterly anti-union. He soon transformed himself into an ultra-redbaiter, with Kallet and other former friends in the Left among his many targets.[35]

Another line of progressive, consumerist thinking was reflected in the Cooperative League, a group endowed in 1919 by department-store executive Edward A. Filene to educate the nation about credit unions and practices of cooperative buying and selling. With other allies such as Newton Baker, Filene soon broadened the purpose of the Cooperative League, making it more of a progressive educational foundation and renaming it the Twentieth Century Fund. A kindred project of Filene was the Consumer Distribution Corporation, headed in the 1930s by progressive lawyer Percy S. Brown, which functioned to promote retail-buying cooperatives around the nation. The corporation lobbied for lower prices and launched cooperative stores by organizing groups of member-owners in major cities.[36]

The program of a 1938 Inter-Faith Conference on Consumers' Cooperatives shows the involvement of clergy and religious lay leaders in the drive to democratize the marketplace. One of the speakers was Harvard's Kirtley Mather, a prominent Baptist layperson who was then also serving as the secretary of the Consumers Foundation. A prominent academician drawn to the consumers movement was Paul Douglas, University of Chicago economist, who helped to organize the Illinois Consumers and Investors League and who was active in the Roosevelt administration's NRA Consumer's Advisory Board. Douglas spoke up for the idea of consumer cooperatives and, believing that neither manufacturers nor labor looked out for the interests of consumers, favored a U.S. Department of the Consumer. Sociologist Robert Lynd similarly wrote on consumer problems and spoke at conferences on consumer protection.[37]

Adult education was another dimension of progressivism's action program to bring about wide citizen participation in social and economic life. Local adult-education centers, such as that organized in

Boston by Kirtley Mather, Harvard Geology professor, and Dorothy Hewitt, YWCA, gave structure to the somewhat amorphous movement to promote schooling beyond the traditional classroom. The American Association for Adult Education, established in 1926 through a grant of funds by the Carnegie Corporation, gave a national focus to adult-education efforts, which also included university night schools, local continuing-education centers, agricultural extension programs, library and museum classes, the Civilian Conservation Corps, women's clubs, and adult reading groups.[38]

A particularly evocative dimension of adult education was the public forum, oratorical and electronic, that gave voice to debate about controversial views. In 1935, for instance, Kirtley Mather helped to found the Newton Community Forum. He presided over a series of Sunday afternoon gatherings that, beginning with addresses by nationally known speakers, culminated in questions and a general discussion from the floor. In Des Moines, Iowa, school superintendent John W. Studebaker received a large grant from the Carnegie Corporation to underwrite an ambitious system of public forums. The program was set up so that, over a two-week period, the staff would travel successively to ten schools and moderate an open discussion of a controversial public question, with between 15 and 1,500 citizens attending.[39]

Progressives also hit upon the idea of combining public forums with educational radio. Mather, for instance, regularly broadcast a radio program on significant contemporary ideas and problems, and his debut broadcast featured Hadley Cantril, Princeton psychologist, holding forth on the psychology of propaganda. Lyman Bryson of Columbia's Teachers College, who chaired the CBS network's advisory board on adult education, put into place "People's Forum," a small panel discussion (without audience) broadcast from CBS Chairman William Paley's private dining room. Bryson's formula for generating a good discussion was to bring together a celebrity, an expert, and an ordinary citizen and to make sure that the panel included at least one woman. The premier example of the radio forum, however, was George Denny's "America's Town Meeting of the Air" program, hosted by the Town Hall, Inc. in New York and broadcast once per week in the evening by NBC's Blue Network. Beginning in 1935, this program brought together three or four prominent speakers of opposing views whose presentations were followed by questions and discussion from the audience moderated by chairman Denny.[40]

Although the progressive public forum idea seemed a natural outgrowth of traditional American democracy, the approach could be construed as favoring those who issued challenges to existing society and culture. Although the forums emphasized speakers of moderate views, it still was the case that the programs gave wide currency to controversial ideas and to dissident voices that, otherwise, might have lacked a legitimate public platform from which to issue fundamental political and cultural challenges. Among the controversial leftists featured as speakers in radio's "Town Meeting" programs of 1939–1941 were Roger Baldwin of the American Civil Liberties Union, educator Harold Rugg, and Earl Browder, General Secretary of the American Communist Party.

Joining teachers, consumerists, and adult-education leaders in widening the public exposure to social-change agendas were the nation's journalists, who were exhibiting worrisome tendencies toward political and professional independence as abetted by the Roosevelt administration. Not only did individual reporters seem to support the New Deal even more than did the average citizen, but 25 percent of Washington correspondents admitted to serious disagreement with the general editorial philosophy (usually pro-Republican) of their newspapers. Other opportunities for independent initiative in journalism came courtesy of the professional J-Schools, where the ideal of objectivity frequently was invoked, and also through the longer analysis-story format that permitted reporters to explore a whole situation instead of merely relating daily developments. Although more than half of Washington's correspondents recalled having a story buried or killed for policy reasons, new conditions in journalism cast doubt on how long ideological censorship could hold progressive reporting at bay. At this time, the New Deal had spurred journalistic independence by opening the door to collective bargaining, thereby producing the American Newspaper Guild (ANG). The ANG's organ, *The Guild Reporter,* soon was leading crusades against ideological censorship and news suppression.[41]

An even more striking example of how the New Deal seemed anxious to propagandize for progressive-style social change came in the form of the Federal Theatre Project (FTP). Under Federal Theatre's auspices, for example, Sinclair Lewis's novelized vision of fascist revolution in America, *It Can't Happen Here,* gave wide currency to a general stigmatizing of rightists. Lewis wrote in a time when, despite the recent assassination of Huey Long, the American Left was highly fearful about nativist demagoguery. MGM quickly purchased film rights to Lewis's book when the work still was in typescript form, although, by early 1936, the studio announced that it was abandoning the project to fashion a film from the novel. Progressives were concerned about

MGM's not entirely clear but evidently political turnabout, and officials of the WPA Federal Theatre Project offered to take on producing this ominous political thriller. After feverish efforts by Lewis and associates to trim the fiction into a playscript, *It Can't Happen Here* opened simultaneously on October 27, 1936, in over twenty theaters around the United States.

Lewis's play provided an unsettling snapshot of future America played out in miniature in a small New England town where the unholy fascist alliance eventually found itself at bay. Tardy but nevertheless courageous opposition had slowly coalesced, personified by an idealistic college student, a crusading small-town publisher, and a strong, independent-minded, liberal editor, a woman who was the only one to see through the dictator in his early guise as presidential candidate. Many commentators applauded the play's dark insinuations that a fascist America might spring from a liaison of convenience among rightist politicians, myopic business leaders, apolitical professionals, struggling farmers, and shiftless street toughs. Rightists, however, were decidedly displeased by the idea of government sponsoring political theater to stigmatize business and sanctify liberals.[42]

From the Right's point of view, the same annoying polemical tendency shown in Lewis's FTP play could be discerned in American film making. A premier example was *All Quiet on the Western Front* (1930), a movie that captured the antiwar and pacifistic ethos of Erich Maria Remarque's novel of the same title. Remarque's work traced the progression of eager young German recruits from enthusiasm to disillusionment to horror and ultimately to death. This film, in fact, had been produced with a propaganda of pacifism in mind. Carl Laemmle, Sr., president of Universal Pictures, acknowledged to George Viereck that the film was one (of only two) that he had produced with the aim to get across a political point (the other, not surprisingly, was *The Kaiser, The Beast of Berlin*). "Naturally, I do not advertise the fact that my new picture will create hatred of war, but between you and me, I hope and pray that it will."[43]

Progressive propaganda analysis may have lacked allies among the nation's leading humanistic students of communication, but muckraking critique found many a sympathizer among those working in the humbler domains of education. By the middle 1930s, progressive ideals of marketplace and social democracy were being propagated through the schools, through consumer organizations, through adult-education forums, through efforts by progressive journalists to attain independence, and through a cultural challenge (plays, films) that in some cases was abetted by the New Deal.

The Right's Polemical Response

In addition to harboring concerns that a new propaganda of Big Progressivism was in the offing, the Right had another problem. In the 1930s, there simply was not an intellectual cadre capable of arguing for social efficiency and social harmony with the same verve shown by progressives who evangelized for participatory democracy (and associated other leftward transformations). Radio educator Lyman Bryson thought he knew why this situation obtained (a condition, we might note, that would continue until the 1960s). As he put together panels for his "People's Forum" programs, Bryson noticed that conservative speakers were difficult to recruit because, as defenders of the status quo, they tended to "see nothing to be gained by discussing the question, and they know that there's a danger of losing something." Bryson believed that rightists preferred in general to keep a low profile "except when there's a strong left wing, when they feel that they're under attack."[44] (American business ultimately would intervene to pick up the slack.)

Whatever the reason, just a few rightist intellectuals during the 1930s penned significant antipropaganda polemics. One such contribution was Charles Miller's critique of American textbooks on behalf of postwar patriotic societies. Miller complained that British influences were acting to dim the glory of American history by pruning out patriotic stories of the Revolution and the War of 1812 and by emphasizing the Magna Carta over the Declaration of Independence. Turning attention to government agency publicity, Elisha Hanson, counsel to the American Newspaper Publishers Association, argued that "for the first time in their history, the American people have seen their Government turning to propaganda in myriad forms to win their favor and keep their support." Two Washington journalists, writing under the pseudonym of George Michael, fleshed out Hansons's complaints about publicity efforts in the alphabet agencies of the New Deal. They even provided an eight-page list of the New Deal's paid publicity agents.[45]

Once progressive organizing and the New Deal agencies had upped the stakes in the struggle between conservatism and liberalism, however, the Right did not feel able to remain silent. Business organizations such as General Motors and the National Association of Manufacturers promptly substituted for the lack of an antipropaganda strike force among rightist intellectuals. Until 1936, American business leaders had kept a low profile in the New Deal's shadow, suffering in relative silence a succession of high-finance exposés, official intrusions into business practices, frequent calls for public ownership of corporations, criticisms of capitalism's focus on wealth and individualism, and a drumbeat of attacks on advertising (an institution that business leaders viewed as essential for mass marketing).

By 1936–1937, however, business was again finding its voice. Major corporations and trade associations alike began to sell concepts of capitalist enterprise to a public that apparently had been weaned away from the Coolidge-era notion that the business of America was business. Among the first corporations to practice a proactive public relations of business entrepreneurship was General Motors. GM prepared four-color, two-page ads for big-circulation magazines that, under the theme "Who Serves Progress Serves America," did more than promote a particular corporation. By describing the work of GM's labs, these public relations ads made a general pitch for free initiative and competition. GM also targeted specific audiences by preparing films for factories, schools, and community groups. An example was GM's "A Car is Born," a portrayal of how an automobile was built from start to finish. Further, in its Plant City Program, the nation's largest auto maker made friendly contacts with opinion leaders and small-business people in each city serving as home to a GM factory. GM and Ford both sponsored radio symphony programs; Ford's program included sociopolitical commentary by conservative spokesman W. J. Cameron.

Just as major corporations reached for public relations and advertising to promote principles of free enterprise, trade associations also employed publicity practices to political purpose, for instance, to stave off regulatory demands of the New Deal. "The American Family Robinson," a radio program sponsored by the National Association of Manufacturers (NAM), portrayed a family solving its problems with the father figure dispensing traditional wisdom about social trends, labor conditions, and legislation. The U.S. Chamber of Commerce placed advertisements in major periodicals and subscribed over 3,000 billboards in major cities. Public relations mogul Edward Bernays was among those active in helping business to appropriate the communications media and professions as counterweight against the organizing power of progressives. Bernays viewed the various anticapitalistic currents of the mid-1930s as bringing about a turning point for public relations. The inclination of business leaders to circle the wagons helped Bernays's infant profession to gain the ear of business leaders and become a permanent department of corporate operations. Bernays, of course, saw this trend as giving birth to better social adjustments as business increasingly matched its policies against "public interest and public opinion."[46]

American business did not stop with a general defense of private initiative and enterprise but also aimed specific attacks at major critics.

No longer content to play silently the role of scapegoat for the nation's economic and social troubles, business spokespersons paid particular attention to attacks originating in the consumer and progressive education movements. The Advertising Federation of America (AFA) struck out against the consumerists by mailing booklets, sending out speakers, and sponsoring radio talks to defend a profession which the AFA claimed was vital to lowering prices by widening markets. The AFA specifically attacked Harold Rugg of Columbia for leaving the impression in his books that all advertising wickedly coaxed consumption and, worse yet, that most advertising was dishonest. On the national and local levels, advertisers successfully pressured newspapers and magazines not to accept membership solicitation ads from the Consumers Union.[47]

Progressive education also experienced the ire of capitalism's public-relations counteroffensive. Expostulations by progressive educators always had been prone to parody because of their frequently pious tone and jargonistic style. However, spurred by business leaders, critics now fixed upon the political implications of modernist educational publications and curricula. Typical was an article in *Nation's Business* that began with this warning: "Parents who marvel at the growth of such organizations as the 'Young Communist League' should read the school books their own children are studying." An accompanying cartoon showed a bear holding a book emblazoned with the hammer and sickle. This character, personifying the teacher, directed the attention of students to capitalism, personified by a top-hatted pig. The body of the article focused on books by the ubiquitous Harold Rugg, whose texts were characterized as "propaganda in school." A prime example was one of Rugg's guides for the teacher in which the instructor was told to correct students who persisted in affirming the statement that the United States was a land of opportunity.[48]

The business community's most substantial attack on textbooks came when the National Association of Manufacturers commissioned Ralph W. Robey, an assistant professor of banking at Columbia University, to review some 500 schoolbooks. Robey and his staff drew the conclusion that a substantial proportion of the books were un-American in view of their tendency to emphasize failings in America's governmental and economic systems. Firing back for the progressive side, Max Lerner lambasted the NAM for attempting to blacklist authors and texts after having earlier failed to shoehorn business propaganda into these books. Lerner's complaint represented a backhanded compliment to the conservatives' polemical counterattack against the progressive and New Deal proselytizing. In the resulting accusatory climate, adult-education leader

Kirtley Mather found his Newton Community Forum under attack by the city's former mayor, Sinclair Weeks, for having invited Arthur Garfield Hayes of the American Civil Liberties Union (ACLU). Weeks characterized the civil-liberties group as "carrying the banner of communism" and apparently did not trust his fellow citizens to compare Garfield's ideas to those of another speaker, George Sokolsky, the NAM's favorite pro-business commentator.[49]

In a climate where public forums became associated with un-Americanism, granting foundations began to opt out of the effort to empower citizens directly. The Carnegie Corporation tired of underwriting the American Association for Adult Education and, instead, switched support to an adult-education research institute at Columbia. Also in 1941, the Sloan Foundation, which had funded the Institute for Consumer Education at Stephens College (Missouri), withdrew from this enterprise.[50] Even before Pearl Harbor solidified the sense of a national-security emergency, therefore, rightist antipropaganda polemicism had begun to undermine the kind of grass-roots citizen participation hoped for by Dewey and expressed in the nation's many local forums, centers, associations, programs, movements, and channels.

Efforts Left and Right both to circulate ideology and to hamper the other side's propagations showed that a polemical approach to propaganda and antipropaganda now competed in the contest to define propaganda's relationship to democracy. The polemical battles of the inter–world-war years suggested that taking action (variously to sow and to spike propaganda) might be the best alternative when faced with a public that was constantly exposed to seductive expostulations from the enemy's camp. The era's polemical propaganda action also included efforts by Left and Right to capture Congress for the purpose of energizing antipropaganda polemics.

Antipropaganda Polemics from Congress

The anti-spy campaign of the CPI showed that progressives could adopt a conspiratorial outlook and an expurgation mentality and marry the both to institutional action. The postwar Red Scare demonstrated that the Right also could use government institutions to stigmatize opponents. These precedents would play themselves out dramatically during the next two decades in a large number of Congressionally sanctioned antipropaganda investigations. Despite many a head start by the Left, ultimately the Right would fare better.

An early instance of Washington-sanctioned polemicizing against rightist propaganda took place in 1928 when members of the Senate turned the spotlight on the Hearst newspapers. George Seldes and Charles Beard frequently had described the chain as "the cesspool of American journalism," and this view probably marked a consensus among progressives of the inter–world-war period. The train of events that brought Citizen Hearst (publisher William Randolph Hearst) before Congress began in Mexico City. There one Miguel Avila offered to sell George Seldes of the *Chicago Tribune* sensational documents, vouched for by the U.S. Embassy, that purportedly proved that important Americans had been bribed to spread propaganda for Mexico's government. Even though Seldes knew no Spanish, he immediately became wary. "Who would not be suspicious of 'documents' on the letterheads of the Department of Education on which Education was crossed out and Treasury typed in?" Asking around, Seldes learned that the documents contained so many misspellings and grammatical errors as to be obvious forgeries. Nevertheless, the Hearst man in Mexico City paid between $15,000 and $25,000 for Avila's papers, which supposedly carried special codes, and soon Hearst's nineteen newspapers were ablaze with headlines claiming that U.S. senators and others had been bribed by the Mexican government.[51]

A Congressional investigation made short work of the Hearst chain's charges that certain unnamed U.S. senators had accepted $350,000 each from the government of Mexico for the purpose of circulating pro-Mexican propaganda. The first witness was none other than William Randolph Hearst, who artfully backed off from the charges that his journals so recently had resolutely proclaimed. Hearst stated that he personally doubted whether any of the senators actually had accepted any money (and his own handwriting expert later described the various signatures as forged). Robert La Follette and William E. Borah, prominent progressive members of the Senate, each denied under oath (along with Senator J. Thomas Heflin) that they had been contacted or bribed by the Mexicans. After hearing from Avila and other principals of the case, and after consulting various linguists and experts in code decipherment, the special Senate committee came to regard the entire episode as a hoax.[52]

The coming of the New Deal energized the moderate Left's will to use official investigation of propaganda as a leverage point for reform. The isolationist tangent of Midwest progressivism found voice in Senator Gerald Nye's hearings of 1934 on lobbying by munitions makers and by Wall Street during the Great War. Legislation to keep America neutral flowed from the Senate's attention to certain financial arrangements that arguably drew the United States into the World War. Similarly, progressivism's prolabor stance received a boost in 1936 when

Senator Robert M. La Follette, Jr., commenced hearings on the efforts of corporations and business groups to impede labor's exercise of free speech and collective bargaining. La Follette's civil-liberties panel questioned, for instance, representatives of the Associated Farmers of Imperial County (California) about why that group had discussed purchasing machine guns, spying on laborers, and intriguing to bar unions from the county auditorium. Spokespersons for the Associated Farmers defended the first allegation as relating merely to whether the sheriff and National Guard were properly armed and characterized the others as appropriate to ferreting out communists from the migrant labor force.[53]

Another instance of progressivism's antipropaganda polemicizing involved an investigation aimed at reducing the monopoly power of Big Communication. Here Congress probed Hollywood's use of block-booking and blind-selling practices to distribute films. Under these arrangements, the studios required theaters to take all films provided in a block, often not allowing theater managers any more information than an outline of the film stories. Testifying in favor of curtailing block booking were members of the Payne Fund's Motion Picture Research Council (Edwin R. A. Seligman, George F. Zook, and Edgar Dale) and representatives of the Federal Council of Churches. The Payne Fund group criticized Hollywood's focus on crime and antisocial behavior, and the churchmen complained of moviedom's tendency to view the audience chiefly as a source of money. This testimony articulated the underlying philosophy of progressives that better films would come about if local theaters had more say over what they exhibited. In reply, Charles C. Pettijohn, counsel for the Motion Picture Producers, defended existing marketing practices as necessary to place efficiently the industry's large number of films.[54]

Progressivism's investigatory enthusiasm notwithstanding, the Overman committee of the U.S. Senate already in 1919 had raised the possibility that the Right might be more successful in using Congressional investigation as a polemical club against opponents' propaganda apparatuses. In September 1918, a subcommittee of the Senate Judiciary Committee, chaired by Senator Lee S. Overman, began hearings "relating to charges made against the United States Brewers' Association and allied interests" by A. Mitchell Palmer, Custodian of Alien Property. Palmer alleged that German–American leaders not only had undertaken a campaign of propaganda to create a powerful ethnic bloc but also that the German nexus had proved a subversive menace. Charges centered on the political activities of the German–American brewers and also on the subversive work of the Kaiser's Captains Von Papen and Von Rintelin.

Two months after the Armistice, the Senate resolved to augment the mission of the Overman committee, directing that group to "inquire concerning any efforts being made to propagate in this country the principles of any party exercising or claiming to exercise authority in Russia, whether such efforts originate in this country or are incited or financed from abroad." The Overman committee fed the Red Scare that saw a shotgun style of attack against not only communists but also nonrevolutionary socialists and even progressive reformers. The U.S. House got into the act with hearings on "sedition, syndicalism, sabotage, and anarchy." In the resulting atmosphere, legislators introduced bills to prohibit radical newspapers and other feared incitements to revolution. The editors of *Nation* magazine, a high-toned liberal tome, did not know whether to laugh or cry when "we read in a Denver newspaper of the arrest of a foreign-born worker because the police had found in his room a trunkful of incendiary literature – namely, copies of *The Nation,* as we learned from a front-page illustration." Will Irwin noted the unseemly haste of superpatriots and politicians alike to lump their regular political opponents together with the bolsheviks. Strikers became anarchists, socialists became communists, pacifists became the Reddest of the Red – all without much thought and frequently garnished by glaring factual error. Will Irwin termed the phenomenon "Patriotism That Pays," also noting that newspapers contributed to the hullabaloo by emphasizing any possible Red connection to a strike or social disturbance.[55]

Hearings by Congressman Hamilton Fish in 1930 confirmed the political leverage to be gained by using official investigations of feared leftist revolutionaries to tar ordinary progressive political opponents. One group of witnesses at the Fish committee seemed to specialize in associating communists and liberals. Walter S. Steele, a rightist magazine manager, singled out the ACLU for allegedly supporting the violent overthrow of the U.S. government. In a similar vein, H. Ralph Burton, attorney for the Daughters of the American Revolution (DAR), contended that 15,000 American teachers were trained communists and that the party had 2 million sympathizers. Burton obtained the latter figure by summing the membership of organizations, such as those of atheists and pacifists, which "in one way or another, advocate the principles of the communists." Although the Fish committee generally gave pedants and patriots free rein for their observations and speculations, Rep. Carl G. Bachmann wondered aloud about Burton's figure of 2 million proto-communists. His own recollection was that the communist candidate for president in 1928 had not received even 15,000 votes.

Over the course of several months, the Fish committee heard dozens of witnesses, including not only academicians, patrioteers, and police officials but also representatives of liberal, labor, and communist organizations. Roger Baldwin of the ACLU defiantly told the congressmen that his organization "is opposed to your committee and its work." Baldwin defended the presence of William Z. Foster on his organization's board, explaining that the ACLU did not throw Foster off simply because he subsequently had joined the Communist Party. For his part, Foster himself later told the committee that socialists were really fascists since they wanted to keep the institutions of capitalism. One interesting contribution of the Fish committee was that of foreshadowing Hollywood's witch hunt of the 1940s and 1950s. Major Frank Pease, president of the Hollywood Technical Directors Association, testified that he was working to prevent "the occurrence of radical propaganda in the films." Pease asserted that there was a considerable effort afoot to insert Soviet propaganda into American movies. He offered the example of Paramount having imported "the leading soviet cinema propagandist and director, a man named [Sergei] Eisenstein."[56]

Congressman Fish had made clear that among his investigatory aims was to "punish people for seditious statements against our government." The focus by Fish's committee on "disloyal" expression encouraged members and witnesses to blur distinctions among communists, anarchists, socialists, unionists, progressives, and other leftists. Trying to equate these groups, Will Irwin explained, was like completely homogenizing Catholics, Baptists, and Mohammedans. Imprecision, however, was the engine of the redbaiting machine. Overeager defenders of private enterprise found the guilt-by-association approach to be a cheap and easy-to-use device. For instance, Rob Roy McGregor, assistant director of the Illinois Committee on Public Utility Information, suggested that the best way to oppose a candidate who favored public ownership of utilities was to abandon "logic or reason" and, instead, "try to pin the Bolshevik idea on my opponent."[57]

Finding their New Deal–oriented colleagues resistant to establishing yet another Overman or Fish committee, rightists in Congress nevertheless were able to attach their polemical objectives to the growing consensus of American opinion leaders that the Depression might unleash subversion by extremists. In 1934, Congressman Samuel Dickstein, a New Deal liberal, prevailed upon the House to establish a committee for the purpose of investigating Nazi and other propaganda activities in the United States. Dickstein's animus was driven by the anti-Semitism of nativist movements together with a belief that the newly Nazified German government was spreading Hitler's racial theories to America. At work by midyear, the McCormack–Dickstein committee established the groundwork for what became known under Martin Dies as the House Un-American Activities Committee (HUAC). As had proved to be the case with the CPI, the success of liberals in establishing the Special Committee on Un-American Activities set in place a machinery that its sponsors would come to regret.

The approach of John McCormack, HUAC chair, to fascist propaganda was too judicious in tone and too specific in focus to make the hearings a usefully lurid weapon of negative publicity. McCormack generally held the proceedings to their stated purpose of exposing native paramilitary groups and efforts by Hitler's and Stalin's governments secretly to sow discord in America. Early witnesses included German nationals and others active in publicity work for the Friends of New Germany organization as well as informants about William Dudley Pelley's Silver Shirts organization. The committee also took testimony from principals of the public relations firm Byoir, Dickey and Lancaster, who were questioned about promotional activities undertaken in connection with the German consulate and various corporations. Balancing the spectrum were representatives of the American Legion, the DAR, the U.S. Army, and academic anticommunists who continued the dialogue begun by Overman and Fish about Red propaganda activities in labor and in the schools. To be sure, McCormack's HUAC hearings did help to rack up points for progressivism. Considerable testimony was taken relating to whether or not General Smedley Butler, USMC (retired), had been recruited by shady rightists to serve as a military dictator. The McCormack–Dickstein hearings also produced headlines discrediting Ivy Lee, the old nemesis of many a progressive propaganda critic.[58]

Although HUAC initially had been chartered as a temporary investigatory body, the committee reemerged due to a confluence of Dickstein's unsatiated appetite for investigating Nazis and the desire of Martin Dies, an anti–New Deal Democrat of Texas, to weigh in against progressivism's allies in labor, in education, and in the New Deal's alphabet agencies. These two unlikely political bedfellows finally prevailed in 1938 when Dickstein (and McCormack) chose to support Dies's proposed HR 282, which provided for an investigation of "the extent, character, and objects of un-American propaganda activities in the United States." As before, HUAC was to focus on "the diffusion within the United States of subversive and un-American propaganda that is instigated from foreign countries or of a domestic origin and attacks the principle of the form of government as guaranteed by our Constitution."

Although progressives earlier had held HUAC's reins, an anti–New

Deal coalition of Northern Republicans and Southern Democrats took charge of investigating anti-American propaganda when Martin Dies of Texas assumed the chairmanship of HUAC. Where John McCormack had employed closed hearings to prevent HUAC from becoming a mere sounding board for the accusations of fanatics, Dies allowed witnesses in public sessions considerable latitude to launch vague and unsupported accusations against various individuals and groups for allegedly pushing along the Trojan Horse of communist infiltration. Although Dies gave obligatory attention to Nazis and to rightist paramilitary groups, he and most members of his committee showed greater enthusiasm for forays against progressives, liberals, and New Dealers. The nature of the committee as a general political weapon of the Right would be most clearly revealed in attacks against the Federal Theatre Project.[59]

Hints that trouble lay ahead for progressives could be discerned in newspaper interviews given by Dies and by J. Parnell Thomas (R., NJ) in advance of the proceedings. These two almost boasted to reporters of their eagerness to expose the "Communistic" plays being produced by that "unparalleled New Deal propaganda machine," the Federal Theatre Project. Although the first day's hearings focused on Nazi subversive organizations, already by the second day, the Dies committee had begun to assume what would be its characteristic configuration. John P. Frey of the American Federation of Labor loosed all sorts of insinuations against the rival Congress of Industrial Organizations and associated the earlier La Follette civil liberties hearings with the communist movement. Walter S. Steele, next to testify after Frey, exceeded the performance he had given eight years previously before the Fish committee by providing a list of some 640 allegedly communistic organizations. A particularly significant early (and persistent) witness was J. B. Matthews. The résumé of this peripatetic ex-socialist revealed many organizational affiliations that had rendered Matthews a pillar of the Popular Front days when communists, terrified by Hitler, had courted the liberals that they formerly had branded as surrogate fascists. Matthews had turned rightward after the bitter strike at Consumers' Research and now busily denounced his former friends on the Left as intensely as earlier he had excoriated capitalism.[60]

The line of inquiry that perhaps most clearly revealed the political appetites and aspirations of Dies and those of his mindset was the investigation of the WPA Federal Theatre Project. HUAC's reception of Hallie Flanagan, National Federal Theatre project director, provided some of the most curious, ironic, and unintentionally humorous moments in the Dies committee's first year of sanctioning diatribe against progressivism's propaganda. Flanagan, Vassar College drama professor, began by describing her federal job as combatting the "un-American inactivity" of talented professionals. Flanagan was closely questioned about her visit to Russia and her work to establish U.S.–Russian faculty exchanges. Rep. Joe Starnes (D., AL) soon focused on the question of whether FTP staff had distributed the *Daily Worker* and various " 'red' pins." Flanagan, in turn, noted rules against political work on federal time. Drifting off again, Starnes quoted from an article Flanagan had written that he characterized as advocating a kind of drama that increased class consciousness. No, Flanagan replied, she merely had been reporting on the phenomenon of workers' theater in the United States. Back on the matter of plays, Flanagan denied that any federal play had propagated communism, although some admittedly were "propaganda for democracy, for better housing." She defended *Power* for giving both sides of the question of whether power plants should be publicly owned.

Apparently tiring of talk centering on plays that he had not read, Starnes returned to Flanagan's article on workers' theater, insisting that the piece proved her support for spreading revolutionary ideology through live drama. Flanagan reiterated her point that she had merely reported on a new development in her field. Discussion then turned to exactly what the FTP's director had meant by her comment that workers' theaters exhibited a "Marlowesque madness" as they sprang up. Starnes put in: "You are quoting from this Marlowe. Is he a Communist?" Flanagan blandly clarified that she was referring to *Christopher Marlowe*. Oblivious to his tenuous position, Starnes forged ahead, persisting in his demand to know exactly who was this Marlowe. Quoth Flanagan: "Put in the record that he was the greatest dramatist in the period of Shakespeare, immediately preceding Shakespeare." As befit a federal administrator testifying before Congress, Flanagan immediately helped Starnes off the hook by agreeing that some ancient Greek playwrights had been criticized for teaching class consciousness. Nevertheless, Starnes's question of whether Marlowe was a communist quickly took a place of honor in the folklore of the Dies committee alongside J. B. Matthews's earlier redbaiting of ten-year-old Shirley Temple.[61]

HUAC under Dies fully revealed the contour of Congressional investigation used as weapon against the propaganda of opponents. The committee maintained some credence by playing off of general fears about Communist Party and Nazi subversion. Certainly, HUAC's investigation of illegal subversion was reasonable as was probing the propriety of the federal government producing plays having political content. But legitimate investigation always took a back seat in Dies's plan for his committee. The urge was quintessentially polemical, to use hyperbole as a lens to magnify the danger of propaganda emanating from one's immediate political opponents.

At this point, it is clear why the progressive propaganda critics failed to establish an alert, grass-roots citizen involvement that would have neutralized Big Communication and other obstacles to intelligent citizen participation after the Great War. Certainly, progressives did enjoy some success in promoting the idea of participatory democracy as weapon against propaganda not only through critical exposés but also through social-service and professional organizations. However, progressivism's project to make Big Communication's targets more skeptical and alert floundered because, by the late 1930s, four alternate ways of looking at social communication had emerged to challenge the view that propaganda was an inherent problem of democracy.

Two of the emerging alternatives to progressive propaganda analysis functioned to undermine the idea that the best response to propaganda was educational, and therefore indirect. Straight thinking and antipropaganda polemicism both argued for direct action by elites to safeguard the public against propaganda on the assumption that people were relatively helpless and needed to be taken in hand. Straight thinkers offered to help Americans develop a discursive etiquette of correct inference and proper application of data to conclusion. Polemicists of both Right and Left wanted to raise alarms such that the unreliable public not only would recoil from the opposition's propaganda but also would give activists leeway to reshape key American institutions. Funded by American business, and institutionalized in HUAC, rightist redbaiters enjoyed relatively more success than progressives in stigmatizing the opposition.

When straight thinking and antipropaganda polemicism were combined with practitioner defenses and the research ideal of quantitative scientists, the lines were drawn in the battle to decide what propaganda meant for democracy. Did propaganda pollute public opinion and disembowel democracy as the progressive critics maintained? Or was propaganda merely a slicker kind of traditional boosterism as the practitioners insisted? Were progressives correct in believing that exposure and education were the best ways to defuse propaganda? Or did the problem require direct political attack and institutional organizing as polemicists argued? If the polemicists were right that the public needed protection more than education, might people perhaps be redeemed through ministrations of the straight thinkers? And what about the offer of symbol scientists to facilitate the work of enlightened policy administrators in government and in the private sphere? These questions played themselves out in struggles connected with the Institute for Propaganda Analysis.

CHAPTER 5

PROPAGANDA ANALYSIS, INCORPORATED

For the general public as well as for most of America's opinion leaders, the lines of thinking that would differentiate five schools of thought on propaganda were not yet clearly demarcated by the middle 1930s. The Institute for Propaganda Analysis (IPA) stood at the center of the struggle waged between 1937 and 1942 to determine what perspective on propaganda would control and institutionalize the public's enhanced awareness of Big Communication. The IPA presented the progressive movement with a widely recognized institutional platform for a democratic, antipropaganda critique; however, the organization's effort to energize opinion leaders eventually stagnated as a result of competition from persons, institutions, and social trends that supported competing perspectives on propaganda.

Founding

The Institute for Propaganda Analysis emerged as a result of a serendipitous encounter of three energetic individuals who represented three tangents of the progressive movement: Kirtley Mather, the adult-education leader; Edward A. Filene, a promoter of consumer cooperatives; and Clyde R. Miller, Debs's old nemesis and post-Armistice convert to antipropaganda journalism. Mather, nationally prominent Harvard geologist and director of the university's summer program, exemplified progressivism's impetus to promote education beyond the traditional classroom. His credo of teaching people "how to think rather than what to think" led Mather to participate both as a Baptist lay leader and as one of the scientists who organized the defense of John T. Scopes during the famous 1925 Monkey Trial.[1] Mather's radio program and work with the Boston Center for Adult Education attracted the attention of Edward A. Filene, a progressive Boston department store owner and liberal philanthropist. Filene asked the Harvard professor to set up a meeting of key leaders in higher education and business to discuss "education for democracy."

On the evening of March 29, 1937, Mather's group met with Filene at the University Club in Boston. Among those in attendance were Alfred Adler, noted psychologist, George Denny of NBC's "Town Meeting of the Air" program, Lyman Bryson, Columbia University adult-education leader, Edward L. Bernays, the public-relations adviser, and Clyde Miller, progressive educator and publicist for Columbia's Teachers College. Filene told the group of his fears that Americans were becoming the victims of propaganda and that they were losing the ability to make sense of the litany of competing charges and claims. He asked the assembled luminaries for suggestions on how Americans could be taught to think, offering to finance the undertaking. Edward Bernays recalled that as each of Filene's guests added another to the list of widely varying solutions, the atmosphere became "smoke-laden and heavy," with Filene beginning "to nod off in little snatches of sleep."

While Bernays left Filene's confab feeling that "nothing had been accomplished," Clyde Miller drew inspiration from the meeting and immediately went to work on a plan to meet the department-store magnate's objectives. Within a week, Miller was cooperating with James Mendenhall of Columbia's experimental Lincoln School to draft a plan for an "institute for the study of education, public opinion and propaganda." At a subsequent meeting in New York City, Filene again listened to a series of presentations from leaders in education and social affairs. Growing tired of the sundry, conflicting plans, Filene eventually turned to Miller: "You there – here is ten thousand dollars for the first year." At a later June 9 conference in Boston with Filene and Percy Brown, secretary of Filene's Good Will Fund (GWF), Miller obtained a commitment for three years' financing of an antipropaganda institute.[2]

Between June and September of 1937, Miller solicited the support of prominent scholars and teachers who eventually agreed, not without some dissent, that their emerging antipropaganda bureau would be called the Institute for Propaganda Analysis, Inc. Reservations about the Institute's name were interesting in that they identified fissures that later would prove troubling to the IPA's critical praxis. For his part, Robert S. Lynd, Columbia sociologist and social critic, believed that "Institute" gave the organization somewhat of a "pompous" appearance and that "Inc." created an undesirable "commercial connotation." Another perspective, articulated by Frank E. Baker, President of Milwaukee State Teachers College, reflected the widening chasm between social critique and scientific measurement in the study of popular attitudes. Baker preferred a title that featured the term *public opinion* rather than *propaganda*.[3]

On the morning of September 23, 1937, at the office of the United States Corporation Company, the Institute for Propaganda Analysis, Inc., was officially constituted with a board of directors consisting of F. Ernest Johnson (progressive educator and activist), Robert S. Lynd, James E. Mendenhall, Clyde R. Miller, and Robert K. Speer (of New York University's faculty of education). Later in the evening, this group, together with James T. Shotwell (Columbia historian), met at the Columbia University Mens Faculty Club and approved additional board members, including Charles A. Beard (the famous historian), Percy S. Brown, Hadley Cantril (Princeton social scientist), Ernest O. Melby (dean of Northwestern University's School of Education), and Shotwell. The directors then elected officers of the corporation, with Cantril to serve as president, Melby as vice-president, Miller as secretary and executive director, and Speer as treasurer. An executive committee was also constituted, consisting of Brown, Mendenhall, Miller, and Speer.[4]

In his capacity as founder and executive director, Miller took up the task of charting a proper course for the fledgling institute that, in September 1937, existed chiefly in the form of papers of incorporation. Robert Lynd recommended that Miller draw upon the classic progressive's view of the conflict between traditional American democracy and the ability of special interests to monopolize the channels of public communication. In Lynd's view, American democracy assumed "(1) that people are rational, (2) that citizens have equal access to 'the facts,' and (3) that . . . they can and do act intelligently in the sifting of issues both public and private." For Lynd, the greatest problem of democracy was the gap between how free public choice was supposed to work and how, in the context of private interests, democracy actually did operate. Lynd recognized that the institute could not change the system fundamentally, but he believed that the IPA could help to equalize the imbalance of persuasive power then in favor of "pressure agencies secretly grinding private axes."[5] Lynd suggested that the IPA become "a Kiplinger service spilling the stuff on current campaigns," such as those undertaken by Edward Bernays.[6]

Lynd's recommendations were consistent with the exposé approach taken by turn-of-the-century reformist writers. For his part, however, Miller favored a format that married muckraking journalism to progressive education. In a letter to members of the Good Will Fund board, Miller laid out his objectives for the early issues of the *Propaganda Analysis* bulletin:

Our December release probably will be given over to tests and antidotes for propaganda, keyed to the seven detection devices mentioned in the November letter. The January letter may be devoted to propaganda and emotion or to propaganda and conflict. There should follow letters appraising propaganda channels – press, school, radio, motion pictures, etc.; also letters setting forth a typical labor union propaganda campaign, a typical anti-union campaign (documenting by Senate committee evidence and other official evidence); letters setting forth a typical commercial product campaign, a typical build-up campaign for a politician; also letters showing how historical background as well as knowledge of simple psychology and sociology is necessary for understanding of many current issues; also letters on aspects of the international situation.[7]

Miller's plan flowed from his belief that the institute's audience would better be able to follow muckraking case studies if the bulletin first outlined methods for detecting propaganda and then showed how the channels of mass communication actually worked.[8] Miller believed that only such a broad counterstroke would be able to deter what he regarded as an impending breakdown of democracy itself.[9] However, the course that Miller charted raised a fundamental question about antipropaganda praxis. Could an organization establish a theory and method of propaganda analysis while, at the same time, exposing specific propagandas domestic and foreign?

Flourishing

The evangelistic tenor of Miller's educational enterprise was clear from the outset when Miller prepared the first issue of the *Propaganda Analysis* bulletin in the form of a press release. Three thousand copies of Miller's "Announcement" issue of October 1937 went out to newspapers, educators, public officials, and opinion leaders. Beginning with a description of the institute, its board, its plans, and its financial arrangements, Miller characterized the enemy as propaganda understood to be the work of special-interest groups to influence public opinion. He argued that an education for democracy would help citizens to comprehend who controlled, and whose biases influenced, "the channels through which opinions and propagandas flow: press, radio, motion pictures, labor unions, business and farm organizations, patriotic societies, churches, schools, and political parties." Miller offered the institute's program as a way to overcome the "chief danger of propaganda," which he believed was its tendency to stimulate unreflective and emotional responses to problems.[10]

The premier issue of *Propaganda Analysis* not only brought wide attention to the institute in the mass media but also initiated a rush of subscriptions to the bulletin.[11] Just a week after the early publicity attending the "Announcement" issue, Miller wrote Lynd that "we are swamped with work."[12] Miller's fledgling office was receiving about 150 letters per day, including about 30 subscriptions.[13] Two weeks into the IPA's public existence, Miller reported a total of 750 subscriptions. He noted that "if promotion continues and if subsequent letters meet with the response evoked by the announcement letter, we should within two or three months obtain more than the total number of subscriptions counted on for the entire first year."[14] Miller's prognostication proved true since during its first six months the institute could boast of 4,527 subscribers.[15] The final total for the first year was 5,900 as opposed to Miller's initial expectation that the institute's subscription list might reach 2,500.[16]

The initial letters received by the IPA revealed considerable enthusiasm for the organization's antipropaganda program. "Your prospectus is admirable," wrote Harry Elmer Barnes, the revisionist historian. John Studebaker, the U.S. Commissioner of Education, commented that "I think you have a real field of service in promoting a more critical analysis of current propagandas." Gordon Allport, Harvard professor of psychology, reported that he showed the first issue of *Propaganda Analysis* to colleagues who "seemed very favorably inclined toward your enterprise." Mark Sullivan, prominent columnist and critic of the New Deal, congratulated the institute for its ambitious program, cautioning (prophetically) that the group had "taken on a task of impossible proportions." He suggested that the IPA might examine the old propaganda ploy of finding "new words for institutions which, under the old names, have become odious to the public." Sullivan's example was the Agriculture Department's recent substitution of "goals" for "quotas" in communications about what farmers were permitted to raise. William M. Leiserson, member of the National Mediation Board in Washington, D.C., recommended that the IPA investigate the effort of railroad publicity agents to prompt newspaper stories calculated to obstruct labor–management negotiations.[17]

Given the era's virtual obsession with propaganda, it is hardly surprising that initial reactions to Miller's institute were so positive. Educators, politicians, New Dealers, opponents of the New Deal – all shared a concern about the ability of special interests to sow anxiety through covert promotionalism or fear through agitation. Responses to the IPA inevitably would become less uniformly positive when the organization developed specific educational materials and tackled actual episodes of propaganda. If the institute's early honeymoon period with opinion leaders and educators was somewhat artificial, two concrete factors nevertheless underlay the IPA's ability to uphold for a time a very broad mandate to combat ignorance of propaganda. First was Clyde Miller's personal genius as a promoter; second was the intriguing educational construct of the seven propaganda devices.

Partial credit for the institute's quick success is due to Miller for his considerable abilities as a promoter. An experienced journalist, Miller had a sixth sense for finding the front-page potential in a story. Associates described Miller as a genial natural salesman who loved to network with people and who was adept at whetting the appetite of journalists to pursue a story further on their own. Members of Miller's staff were quite devoted to him even though he later became increasingly long-winded and tiresome in conversations with intimates. Acquaintances such as Leonard W. Doob, institute board member and Yale psychologist, remembered him fondly years after the IPA's demise. After his wartime stint with the U.S. Army's Education Corps, Miller had honed a specialty as an educational publicist, first with the Cleveland public schools and later at Columbia University. Miller boasted of increasing Columbia's share of space in New York's newspapers from 400 to 5,000 column inches. The result, as *Time* wryly observed, was to make Columbia "the best publicized educational institution (without a football team) in the world."[18]

Miller's work to gain attention from the press and from opinion leaders included sending out some 20,000 flyers about the IPA to members of the Progressive Education Association and the Consumers Union, to the presidents and deans of the nation's colleges, to members of the Methodist Federation and to bishops and ministers, to editors of educational and religious periodicals, and to Columbia's alumni and education students.[19] Such efforts to boost the institute's reputation and subscription list quickly proved vital to the IPA's very survival. The Good Will Fund's commitment to the institute had resulted from the personal interest of Edward Filene, who left the United States on European holiday five weeks after he met with Miller and Brown to formalize the GWF's three-year grant. Unfortunately, Filene died unexpectedly in Paris on September 26, just as the IPA was getting started.[20] Miller's many overtures for outside public support flowed naturally from a realistic assumption that the ardor of Filene's board for propaganda analysis might be less than that of the elderly philanthropist himself. Miller somewhat anxiously kept the Good Will Fund's board posted about the rush of subscriptions and also sent along newspaper and magazine comment as well as highlights of letters from individuals.

Reinforcing Miller's promotional work in producing rapid growth for the IPA was his introduction of the simple but appealing framework of the "seven common propaganda devices." Miller had a flair for packaging concepts in a catchy and synoptic fashion, and he had developed the seven-devices format for his classes at Teachers College. Miller included the devices in earlier publications, and to meet the pressing deadline of the November 1937 bulletin, he condensed what had become for him a familiar schema.[21] Miller introduced the seven devices with the admonition that "we are fooled by propaganda chiefly because we don't recognize it when we see it." To alert readers to propagandistic material, his bulletin laid out seven things that the alert citizen should watch for:

1. *Name-calling* – the propagandist applies such bad names as "fascist" or "communist" to the opponent to stimulate hate and fear.
2. *Glittering generalities* – "the propagandist identifies his program with virtue by use of 'virtue words,' " such as truth, freedom, justice.
3. *Transfer* – "the propagandist carries over the authority, sanction, and prestige of something we respect and revere [often church and nation] to something he would have us accept."
4. *Testimonial* – to bolster an idea or plan by using a statement from someone recognized by the public.
5. *Plain folks* – when members of society's political or social elite court the public by appearing to be just ordinary folks and therefore wise and good.
6. *Card stacking* – the propagandist relies upon half truths, distractions, and omissions, using "under-emphasis and over-emphasis to dodge issues and evade facts."
7. *Bandwagon* – the propagandist works to make us "follow the crowd, to accept the propagandist's program en masse."

There is little doubt that the framework of the seven propaganda devices was instrumental in securing widespread attention to the institute's program. This formula received considerable press treatment both in general circulation publications and in educational newsletters. Reprint requests poured into the institute's office from authors, lecturers, newspapers, ministers, and patriotic groups as well as from educators in the fields of English, psychology, logic, journalism, sociology, and speech. Edgar Dale, Ohio State professor of education and IPA board member, praised Miller for the seven-devices construct, which Dale described as taking "a number of very complicated fallacies in logic and reduc[ing] them to terms that a fourteen year old child can understand." Forty-five years later, Dale recalled that "the quick popularity of the anti-propaganda movement was caused by the fact that there were seven neat, easily understood principles set up."[22]

To be sure, the seven devices were "gimmicks" as Harold Lavine, the IPA's editorial director (1938–1940), later acknowledged. Although many welcomed Miller's construct as something tangible and widely applicable in helping the general public to recognize and combat propaganda, the simplicity of the seven-device formula was not universally popular even in 1937. One of Robert Lynd's more precocious undergraduate students complained that the "How to Detect Propaganda" issue "reads like a high-school freshman's attempt to brief one of Lasswell's books." Lynd forwarded this comment to Miller with the admonition that "I'm uneasy about the question as to whether people will feel they're getting their money's worth from this general sort of material."[23]

If Miller's evangelism, together with his ability to package concepts in a compelling fashion, had secured for the institute a large audience, the question remained whether a one-man editorial operation could sustain a large-scale, long-term praxis of antipropaganda education. The first five issues of *Propaganda Analysis* bore the unmistakable stamp of Miller's lectures at Teachers College but were unsigned to downplay the IPA's short-handed editorial resources. Miller's dilemma was how to prepare timely material promptly and to present it in a fashion that would satisfy the audience of critical opinion leaders that he had been successful in attracting. None of Miller's early articles quite managed the dichotomy.

In "Some ABC's of Propaganda Analysis" (December 1937), Miller used his favored life-history approach to education as a basis to help readers implement their own propaganda analyses. The bulletin's basic position was that "our beliefs and actions mirror the conditioning influences of home and neighborhood, church and school, vocation and political party." It followed that an important part of propaganda analysis was for people to analyze themselves to find out why they believed as they did. Self-analysis would help critics to *"suspend our judgment until we obtain essential facts and implications involved in the propaganda."* Although Miller's self-reflective approach was thought provoking, critical readers might well have regarded the article's subsequent advice as merely a gloss on basic propaganda theory and popular semantics. Miller recommended inquiring about the persuader's purpose, the ends to which the symbolism was directed, and how words influenced audiences toward these ends. Miller asked readers to pay particular attention to emotional words having little precise meaning.[24]

Similarly generalized were the next two issues of *Propaganda Analysis*, both dealing with newspapers.[25] In the former (January 1938), Miller provided a brief introduction to the process of modern journalism including the profit orientation of newspapers and the effort of both governments and special interests to exert pressure. The second issue focusing on journalism began with a three-page introduction in which Miller reviewed the overt pressure exerted by advertisers and also the self-censorship that resulted from editors and publishers taking on the social attitudes of their wealthy associates. This February 1938 number concluded with reprints of two contemporary articles about practices of journalism along with an expanded section of discussion notes. Although this thirteen-page package was the longest issue that the IPA had yet mailed to subscribers, the result remained a very general gloss on what had become familiar themes of propaganda in the news.

Lynd's early warning to Miller about the risks posed by the seven-devices format and other popularized constructs of criticism accurately forecast the kind of complaints that shortly were to ensue in an era that placed an increasing value on social-science rigor. In February 1938, one dissatisfied subscriber, John Callender, wrote that the four pages of "innocuous generalizations" he was receiving monthly failed to provide an intelligent citizen with timely facts about contemporary propagandas commensurate with the subscription price of two dollars. This correspondent contended that the material in the first several bulletins was both untimely and unoriginal, suited, at best, only for "high school children." Callender went on to speculate that the institute operated out of a private home and that an entirely part-time staff dashed off each month's issue about an hour before the deadline. Hadley Cantril, the institute's president, acknowledged that the Callender missive contained "enough truth" that it "hurt." Cantril advised Miller to lighten his burden by selecting qualified individuals to do deeper case studies. Miller replied that the institute lacked the money to do research on a wide range of current controversies.[26]

Vicissitudes of Critical Praxis

If some subscribers found a mere four pages of generalities on propaganda somewhat unrewarding, this problem was endemic to the rapid and ambitious course that Miller had charted for the IPA. Critic Callender had been wrong in his surmise that the institute was a mere cottage operation, because the organization's staff numbered five full-time and three part-time persons by December 1937.[27] However, the haste that Callender inferred from the brevity and breeziness of the early bulletins in fact did reflect the IPA's all-too-real monthly struggle to the last against impending deadlines. Devoting evenings and weekends to the institute's business, Miller was somewhat in the position of a one-man band as he prepared the bulletins, directed office operations, and coordinated promotional efforts – all while maintaining his full-time position at Teachers College.[28] Miller's tenuous position was evident from his pleas to the advisory board for a quick turnaround of drafts. A week before the IPA was formally chartered, Miller was mailing the draft of the first issue of *Propaganda Analysis* for review by the institute's board and requesting comments and suggestions "by return mail, if possible."[29] The next month, Miller again requested immediate responses from board members to a draft of the "How to Detect Propaganda" issue, asking for final comments on the issue just two days before the press deadline.[30]

As the person most in touch with the institute's mail bag, Miller was only too painfully aware that "our subscribers have been yelling for specific analyses."[31] Months earlier, in fact, Miller had expressed his intention to "employ, on a fee basis, the services of highly competent experts whose years of research make their work accurate beyond question."[32] By early fall 1937, Miller had been successful in prevailing upon Edgar Dale to prepare an issue on motion pictures (hopefully "in terms of the seven propaganda devices"), and he was imposing upon IPA president Cantril for an issue on the radio.[33] Although Dale's March 1938 (unsigned) article on "The Movies and Propaganda" represented the first to be written by someone other than Miller, Dale's submission demonstrated that Miller had not solved his editorial dilemmas merely by parceling out the writing chores. Not only did Dale's draft arrive ten weeks after Miller commissioned it, but the piece apparently required considerable revision. Further, while Dale avoided merely rehashing the propaganda devices, his article did not offer much intellectual meat to replace them. Dale's article gave a quite brief and general review of how motion-picture newsreels and feature films made political comment under the guise of respectively informing and entertaining. On the positive side, however, the examples were fresh and current and were accompanied by many sources for further exploration.[34]

Miller's editorial frustrations of early 1938 showed that it would be no small task to institutionalize an antipropaganda praxis predicated on adult education. After expending some effort to enlist Alfred McClung Lee of Yale to prepare the newspaper bulletin(s), Miller finally had to draft these issues himself.[35] Later, when Miller received a commissioned draft of "Propaganda Techniques of German Fascism" from Robert A. Brady, a New Deal economist who had written a recent book on *The Spirit and Structure of German Fascism*, the manuscript proved to be less than completely satisfactory. In Miller's view, author Brady had produced a typescript "so charged in places with emotion, that it will require rewriting and much more careful documentation."[36] If

Brady proved overenthusiastic as an antipropaganda muckraker, Hadley Cantril showed ambivalence in answering Miller's request for a release on American broadcasting. As founder of Princeton's radio-research project, Cantril's credentials for the assignment were stellar, and he evidently felt an obligation to help in view of his position as president of the IPA's board. On the other hand, the Princeton psychologist felt pressured by his work and somewhat out of touch with current radio programming. With Miller's permission, therefore, Cantril gave the primary writing chores to James Rorty, a popular author; but disappointment with Rorty's draft led Cantril to arrange for Gordon Allport of Harvard to rewrite the article.[37]

The matter of whose name would be attached to the IPA's first article on radio broadcasting brought to the fore a tension between theory and praxis that later would conspire with other causes to undermine the institute's intellectual and political position. Miller wanted Cantril to sign the essay, but the Princeton psychologist resisted this suggestion, making the case that the institute should follow the pattern of the Consumers Union and not "hide behind *names*." In a personal aside to Miller, Cantril almost pleaded to be released from any implied moral commitment to stand as author of a critical essay on the broadcasting industry because, as a rising star in academic psychology, he feared damage to his professional standing.

> How would it be if I get Allport at Harvard to sign the piece? His feelings are essentially the same as mine and since he is not trying to get another $67,000 out of Rockefeller Foundation for radio research, and since he is not connected with a technical committee working under the F.C.C., we could, by using his name, serve our own purpose, and perhaps get more money from the oil king, so that eventually we would have more material upon which to base the criticism and express our opinion, which I should like to formulate very carefully when our regular project is over.[38]

Cantril's reluctance to appear as author of a critical assessment of broadcasting illustrated the sub rosa but irrepressible conflict between "critical" and "administrative" research that Paul Lazarsfeld would attempt to reconcile in principle if not in practice.[39] Cantril's plea to Miller aptly illustrated the real danger that an administrator who entertained critical impulses might not remain credible as a social scientist in the eyes of granting agencies.

If Cantril, the scientist, blanched at directly undertaking the role of educational muckraker, he nevertheless felt comfortable in promoting from behind the scenes an exposé of modern public relations. Cantril saw potential pay dirt in "a release showing how people like Bernays and Ivy Lee try to identify their wealthy clients with existing and accepted social values." Given that Cantril's note to Miller was written on letterhead stationery of the Office of Radio Research (underwritten by the Rockefeller Foundation), it was alternately altruistic and ironic for Cantril to add that "a good case study of Mellon, Rockefeller or the like might not be amiss." Cantril renewed this suggestion a few months later, when he reminded Miller "don't forget our pal, Bernays, and the American Brewery Association." As Cantril saw it, "the theme could be essentially the role of the public relations counsel and the machinations behind modern high powered propaganda."[40]

Although everybody seemed agreed that an exposé of modern public relations was in order (Lynd had made the same suggestion earlier), the resulting draft article placed Miller in the familiar position of paying for a manuscript that required much reworking. The resulting August 1938 issue of *Propaganda Analysis,* which showed the hand of Miller as editor, provided examples of such familiar publicity ploys as "news" photographs of beauties vacationing at resorts conspicuously mentioned in accompanying captions. Turning to the long-planned roasting of Bernays, the article discussed the self-serving bureaus, foundations, and institutes, notably including Bernays's Temperature Research Foundation, which aimed "to boost the sales of Kelvinator refrigerators, air-conditioning units, and electric stoves." Although this example made for a more intriguing propaganda analysis, Ambrose Doskow, one of the Good Will Fund's attorneys, warned Miller that the mention of specific cases brought a greater potential for controversy. Doskow reminded Miller that to characterize Bernays's Temperature Research Foundation as covert propaganda was problematical because "any statement regarding a particular individual or organization which cannot be supported by proof may subject the Institute to a libel action."[41]

Miller's chief problem in spring 1938 was not potential lawsuits, however, but rather the very immediate lack of a smooth procedure for speeding detailed propaganda analysis to subscribers of the IPA's monthly bulletin. Perhaps wearying of tardy, overeager, or lawsuit-skirting contributors, Miller finally faced the fact that he could not retain operational and editorial control of the institute while simultaneously maintaining his full-time duties at Teachers College. To ease his burdens, Miller already had brought into the office Violet Edwards, one of his graduate-student assistants at Columbia, to prepare the educational notes that were appended to issues of the bulletin. Late in 1938, upon the departure of the IPA's office manager, Charles Seidle, Miller tapped Harold Lavine, journalist and husband of Violet Edwards, to serve as a full-time director of editorial and office operations. During the next two years, a relatively stable organizational triumvirate emerged in which Miller, acting as executive director, not only promoted the IPA to outside groups but also oversaw Lavine's editorial department and Edwards's program of services for schools.

With subscribers clamoring for detailed case studies, Lavine immediately demonstrated that his journalistic experience fit the institute's desire to move from generalities to real, contemporary social action and controversy. A fortuitous offer to Lavine set the IPA onto the behind-the-scenes story of how the A&P stores retained Carl Byoir and Associates, a public relations firm, to derail a proposed federal tax on sales by chains. One of Byoir's employees had experienced a falling out with the firm and, before he quit, stowed away files on the A&P campaign, which his girlfriend, who had known Lavine for years, helped to place at the IPA's disposal. Using the files, Lavine was able to prepare an insider's scoop about an alliance engineered by Byoir whereby A&P and labor unions cooperated against legislation unfavorable to the chains. Where previous IPA bulletins had used briefly developed examples to illustrate propaganda in media, movements, and professions, Lavine's article on A&P provided inside dope on a single episode of orchestrated persuasion.[42]

However successful was the institute's exposé of the A&P campaign, the organization could not expect authoritative files of propaganda materials to descend on its office on a monthly basis. Lacking further providential interventions, Lavine was driven back to the more conventional approach of amassing one- or two-sentence examples to illustrate propaganda in news, education, and other spheres. The April 1939 bulletin on news propaganda fingered the usual suspects, for instance, by using investigations of the Securities and Exchange Commission to expose propaganda by electric power companies.[43] The contrast between the institute's detailed A&P case study and the more removed topical reviews of news propaganda demonstrated the IPA's desperate need for field research. And so the institute mounted a major experiment in editorial pump priming by taking on I. F. Stone, who later became legendary as an investigative journalist, as a full-time external researcher. Stone worked for the IPA during a six-month period beginning in May 1939 and ending shortly before he left to become the Washington editor of *Nation*.[44]

During his months with the institute, Stone traveled to Washington, D.C., and to the West Coast in pursuit of material for a bulletin on the Associated Farmers organization of California's Imperial valley. Stone's unsigned report in *Propaganda Analysis* began with the conflict that ensued when migrant farm workers tried to employ for themselves certain recent laws guaranteeing labor's right to organize. Stone explained how leading California agriculturalists and farm organizations established the Associated Farmers group as a response to the threat of strikes and labor stoppages, and he detailed the contributions made to this body by major corporations. While acknowledging that communist agitators were at work among the migrant farm workers, Stone explained how the Associated Farmers misrepresented farm labor problems as solely the result of Red subversion. "The cry of 'Communism' is their chief propaganda stock-in-trade," wrote Stone, in describing how the industrial farmers battled labor organizers with exaggerated charges. "The faithful reader of the *Associated Farmer* begins to believe that Communism is just around the corner." The result, argued Stone, was that small farmers were willing to act as vigilantes. He cited cases where hundreds of farmers were deputized by county sheriffs to combat labor organizers or strikers. Stone turned to hearings of the National Labor Relations Board to document charges that the Associated Farmers routinely used violence to intimidate its foes.[45]

Supported by an expanded educational section, Stone's issue on the Associated Farmers amounted to sixteen pages of detailed case-study analysis showing that the institute was able to mount significant forays into contemporary propaganda. With relevance, however, would come controversy. The mild tempest precipitated by Stone's piece served as a harbinger of the stressful squabbles that later were to embroil members of the institute's board. Russell G. Smith, Bank of America (BOA) executive vice-president, took exception to a reference in Stone's article about the BOA's alleged influence over California agriculture. Not only did Smith contact Miller in the IPA's office, but he made sure that Grayson N. Kefauver, board member and dean of Stanford's School of Education, knew of his ire. Kefauver was anxious to know how Miller and Lavine would handle the objection of the powerful California bank.[46]

Costs more than controversy, however, ultimately doomed the institute's experimental collaboration with I. F. Stone. Expenses associated with Stone's six-months' work for the institute came to somewhere between $3,500 and $5,500.[47] Although Stone worked on several projects for the IPA, apparently only his study of the Associated Farmers was published in toto (and may have been rewritten by Harold Lavine).[48] The institute clearly lacked the resources to back every issue of the bulletin with thousands of dollars of commissioned research. To the contrary, the IPA's leadership hoped to transform its monthly articles into a positive source of income, notably by using articles exposing extremist anti-Semitic propaganda to lure potential grantors.

Extremists and Extremism

Controversy resulting from the institute's letter on the Associated Farmers was both trivial and transient when set against the eventual reaction to the IPA's work on political extremism. A major impetus behind Filene's original overture to Clyde Miller had been the concern of progressives about radical political groups, particularly those purveying anti-Semitism. Although the institute waited a year to begin its inquiry into the propagandas of hate and fear, the organization made up for its tardiness by devoting five issues of *Propaganda Analysis* during 1939–1940 to the subject in addition to the institute's first book-length study. By giving special attention to nativist fascist groups, the IPA had in mind not only living up to its early implied commitments but also promoting future funding from grantors.

Miller had pinned his fund-raising hopes on convincing major religious organizations that the institute was a valuable resource for defusing the social crises of the period. To this end, Miller invited religious leaders to an all-day conference at the Gramercy Park Hotel on December 13, 1938, to help IPA officials with fund raising. Accepting the call to join with IPA board and staff in discussing the organization's past work and future plans were Richard Rothschild, a representative of major Jewish organizations, the Reverend Leon M. Birkhead, Methodist clergyman and director of the Friends of Democracy, and Mrs. Herbert H. Lehman, a prominent Jewish layperson and wife of New York's governor.[49] An immediate outcome of the parley was the IPA's first foray into domestic extremists. All present agreed that publishing an exegesis of fascist literature would provide a "tangible product" making it easier to secure funds from leaders of religious and pro-tolerance organizations, particularly Jewish groups.[50] After the meeting, the institute's staff began work on such an article with the Reverend Birkhead and an artist. Birkhead contributed his extensive private collection of pamphlets and leaflets produced by domestic nativist groups.

With a powerful punch provided by fourteen provocative illustrations from Birkhead's collection, the January 1, 1939, issue of *Propaganda Analysis* gave a sixteen-page survey of domestic fascist organizations and their hate material. The IPA's exposé emphasized not only the connection between nativist agitators and Nazi Germany but also the extreme anti-Semitic character of their propaganda. The institute's analysis showed that Father Charles Coughlin, the radio orator, had appropriated material from pamphlets circulated by the fascist Fichte Association headquartered in the Third Reich. Further, subscribers learned how the Germans kept up formal contacts with the Knights of the White

Camellia and other domestic fascist organizations. According to the IPA's bulletin, anti-Semitism was basic to the appeal of the American fascists as shown by their effort to portray every national tragedy from the Civil War to World War I as caused by Jews. Making the words *Jew* and *communist* odious was essential to the purpose of the domestic fascists. Having vilified these terms, all that remained was for the agitators to label any opponents as Jewish or communist. According to fascist publications cited by *Propaganda Analysis*, the Pope and FDR were Jews, and the American Federation of Labor and the Democratic Party were controlled by Jews.[51]

The first bulletin on domestic fascist groups, hastily assembled in the IPA's New York office, was only one tangent of the organization's accelerating interest in the machinations of America's rightist extremists. Some weeks previous, the IPA's leadership had arranged for Alfred McClung Lee, journalist and sociologist, and his wife Elizabeth Briant Lee, an anthropologist, to write a book on the radio addresses of Father Charles Coughlin.[52] Coughlin had become a major political figure of the late 1930s, forging his own radio network, buttonholing legislators, publishing pamphlets, and organizing his National Union for Social Justice. After breaking with Franklin Roosevelt in 1936, Coughlin's remaining support came chiefly from the Right, and progressives noticed an increase in anti-Semitic references percolating through his attacks on internationalism and communism. Further, Coughlin's speeches increasingly drew information and interpretations from fascist publications although he criticized Naziism and apparently had no significant direct contact with Germany or Italy.[53] The IPA's leadership agreed that the Lees' book on Coughlin not only would supply a timely exposé but also would aid in transforming passive support from tolerance groups into active financial backing.

Work on the Coughlin book started when, in September 1938, Alfred Lee took a position with Raymond Rich Associates, a New York public relations firm that specialized in promoting academic organizations and liberal causes. The institute quickly arranged for Lee to receive a six-week leave of absence, later extended, to coauthor the book.[54] By early February 1939, Miller and Lavine were circulating the Lees' draft manuscript, entitled *The Fine Art of Rabble-Rousing*, both for editorial revision and as an inducement for commitments by potential contributors. Clearly, fund-raising considerations had contributed not only to the book's breakneck production schedule but also to its stress on anti-Semitic tangents of Coughlin's sermonizing. Rothschild, representing Jewish advocacy and charitable groups, had been kept closely apprised of the draft manuscript, and he was considered a possible source of support for promoting the book.[55] For his part, IPA board member Leonard Doob acknowledged that "Lee's writing sparkles," but Doob wanted Lee to visit Detroit to get a scoop on who was backing the radio priest. Doob, however, despaired that the IPA would pursue such a course because of his impression that "Rothschild wanted to have something appear as quickly as possible."[56] Most conferees at a February meeting agreed that the effort to emphasize Coughlin's animus to Jews had produced a manuscript that, unfortunately, neglected the radio priest's expressions about democracy, economics, and international relations.[57]

Whatever criticisms were raised about the Lees' book in its draft form, the typescript of their exposé became a valuable asset in securing both moral and material support for the institute. Mrs. Lehman wrote Miller that both she and the governor had read the Lees' draft on Coughlin's radio speeches and expected that the book would be "exceedingly effective." The Lehmans also enclosed a contribution of $200.[58] A few days later, Miller received even better news. Frank N. Trager wrote to announce that the American Jewish Committee (AJC) would convey to the institute a sum of $12,500 "toward research work in defense of America against the propaganda attacks of foreign-inspired groups."[59] Not only was the AJC interested in using the Lees' book to refute Coughlin, but Miller hoped that the William C. Whitney Foundation might also support the project. Miller's efforts here were rewarded when the Whitney's board of directors voted on March 21 to supply the institute with a grant of $3,000.[60] Consistent with the IPA's view that covert support was a hallmark of propaganda, the September 1939 bulletin duly reported the receipt of the AJC grant along with monies received from the Good Will Fund and the Whitney Foundation.[61]

The institute's leaders discussed releasing the Lees' study as a special bulletin, but after consultation with various publishers, the organization secured a contract from Harcourt, Brace and Company to publish the manuscript as a book. By July, Elizabeth Lee was finishing work on the page proofs, and on September 1, 1939, the draft was published under the title *The Fine Art of Propaganda: A Study of Father Coughlin's Speeches*.[62] The exposé began with a treatment of how small-town, give-and-take discussions had been replaced by pressure-group politics. Here the Lees argued that radio priest Coughlin posed a special threat to intelligent public opinion because he used the orator's one-way microphone to spew name-calling and other dubious ploys in promotion of his so-called "democratic Corporate State." Observing that fascist Italy was the world's chief exemplar of the Corporate State, the Lees also pointed to an alliance between Coughlin's supporters and the proto-fascist German–American Bund. What was needed, they believed, was an "impartial scientific analysis of the techniques" used by such a master propagandist as Coughlin. The Lees then reprised and greatly augmented the definitional and orientation material about propaganda that had been given in the first three issues of *Propaganda Analysis.*

The bulk of the Lees' book was a one-by-one application of the seven propaganda devices to excerpts of Coughlin's radio addresses. To illustrate name-calling, for instance, they turned to the priest's intemperate references to "atheistic Jew," "Communist Jew," and other epithets tossed in without explanation or justification. Reinforcing Coughlin's name-calling were his various "virtue words," or glittering generalities, such as "patriotism" and "Americanism," which promoted a simplistic either–or kind of analysis. Closely related was Coughlin's effort to use the transfer device to link something prestigious (like the Roman Catholic Church) to his own controversial ideas of race, politics, and economics. Many of these connections were bolstered by Coughlin's tricky use of testimonials, some of which turned out to be faked or distorted attributions. For instance, the Lees discovered one case where Coughlin had attributed material to American and British governments that, actually, he had lifted word-for-word from a Nazi publication. Also objectionable was Coughlin's use of the plain-folks tactic whereby the radio priest gloried in being a simple man of the cloth. The Lees found Coughlin's ostensible modesty to be curious given his willingness to employ all manner of exaggerations to stack the cards against his opponents. Here radio's one-way voice enhanced Coughlin's power to stimulate a potential bandwagon reaction among his listeners, for instance, in favor of the rebel, pro-fascist armies of General Franco in Spain.

The release of the Lees' book caused a sensation for a brief period before American opinion leaders became preoccupied with the new European war. Initial sales were brisk, particularly since a number of organizations were promoting the book as an antidote for Coughlin's political clout. The Anti-Defamation League ordered 3,000 copies, and, nearer to Coughlin's home base, the Jewish Community Council of Detroit bought 1,750 copies.[63] The institute itself purchased some 12,000 copies for distribution either to subscribers or as premiums for new memberships. Harcourt, Brace sold an additional 8,000 copies by February 1940 before society's interest dramatically shifted from domestic radio controversialists to overseas conquerors.[64] Sales figures probably understate the impact of the book, which was much welcomed. Victor Riesel, writing in *The New Leader,* an anticommunist

Socialist Party organ, recommended the Lees' book as a useful "handbook for democracy" that exposed Coughlin's lies, tricks, and unsavory allies. *Public Opinion Quarterly,* a journal for academicians and practitioners, generally approved of the Lees' method and results. Moreover, its reviewer was intrigued with the pictographs that the Lees had developed for each propaganda device, which, when applied to Coughlin's sermons, caused the text to "take on an appearance reminiscent of a frieze of Egyptian hieroglyphics." Although the reviewer saw some wisdom in confining the study to the demagogic rhetoric itself, he longed for more effort to "illuminate the social scene that gives rise to the Hitlers and Coughlins."[65]

With so much of its energy devoted to spotlighting rightist propagandists during 1939 and 1940, the idea of balancing these critiques with an exposé of the Left naturally occurred to the progressives who headed the institute. Anxious to protect the IPA's reputation for evenhandedness, Miller had been interested as early as November 1938 in doing a study of the Communist Party of the USA (CPUSA), and many subscribers had been asking for such an exposé.[66] On the other hand, since the bulletin on the Communist Party amounted to one of the institute's earliest publications on domestic extremism, many in the IPA's inner circle questioned the timing of the project. Acknowledging that the "Institute's reputation demands such an analysis," Doob believed that muckraking the CPUSA would be "playing into the hands of the Dies committee and others who at this moment like to identify anything progressive or liberal with Communism."[67]

Despite Doob's objections, the IPA went ahead and released a bulletin on communist propaganda; however, the ironic tone and highly general content of the piece had the effect of muting the muckraker's sense of alarm that, in the previous month's issue, had been so dramatically conveyed by the Reverend Birkhead's pictures and clippings. To its credit, the IPA's exposé of the CPUSA correctly diagnosed the main lines of the party's strategy and accompanying propaganda. The institute observed that the party's purposes did not require a gigantic membership because the effort to infiltrate and capture labor unions and liberal organizations required only a modest number of active members backed by millions of sympathizers. CPUSA members eagerly accepted the "dozens of petty, burdensome jobs that nobody wants but which simply must be done." Where no suitable organizations existed, the CPUSA helped to launch the American League Against War and Fascism and other attractively titled groups that, although not working directly to further communism, gave communists a platform for propagandizing dissatisfied liberals. Specific propaganda tactics of the Communist Party included a promiscuous use of the term *democratic* to describe the CPUSA's programs and the term *fascism* as a catch-all devil term to tar any and all opponents. The IPA observed that several breakaway communist factions had accused the CPUSA of taking its orders directly from Moscow, but the bulletin did not pursue this matter.[68]

Miller recognized that the IPA's exposé of the American Communist Party had not penetrated much below the surface of the party's tactics and rhetoric and, in fact, earlier had pressed the Good Will Fund for "a special grant for research" to allow a deeper inquiry into domestic communism.[69] Further, the article's prominent point–counterpoint irony and its high level of generality muted any impression that Red extremism constituted an emergency. The bulletin contrasted the small membership and penurious circumstances of the formal communist organizations and publications to the extravagant charges of communist infiltration heard before the Dies committee. The IPA noted that the CPUSA was alternately boastful and reticent about its successes. Although the party faithful "think, act, talk, and vote as one," the CPUSA suffered an enormous turnover in membership. The bulletin acknowledged the CP's efforts to foment strikes and to influence a large number of liberal organizations, but the institute judged that the party's overall successes had been small.

Appearing relatively late in the IPA's investigation of extremism (January 15, 1940) was a bulletin focused specifically on the work of the Dies committee. The institute's interest in Dies dated back at least to 1938 when Paul Douglas, a liberal economist and later U.S. senator from Illinois, signed on as a member of the IPA advisory board and quickly asked Miller about issuing "a study of the smearing tactics of the Dies Committee and other groups." Somewhat more than one year later, the IPA responded by publishing "Mr. Dies Goes to Town," an exposé of the questionable purposes and disreputable tactics of hearings held by the House Committee on Un-American Activities. The IPA's irreverent appraisal began with the observation that Dies, the "boyish-looking towhead" from Texas, had succeeded in capturing front-page attention for accusers and their targets in an evocative drama in which "rarely does anyone bother to ask on what evidence the charges are based." Evidence needed to count for more, the institute maintained, because many barbs launched by HUAC's friendly witnesses smacked of a self-serving purpose as when Republicans from Minnesota blasted their chief political rival, the Farmer-Labor party, for being an allegedly communist-dominated organization. Of special concern to the IPA was the tendency of newspapers to print without editorial comment every sensational charge uttered before Dies even though a straw poll conducted by the *New York Daily News* showed that 19 of 21 reporters covering HUAC agreed that the hearings lacked basic fairness.[70]

Nearly half of the institute's bulletin on the Dies committee was devoted to a detailed analysis of charges by J. B. Matthews about communist infiltration of the consumers movement. Matthews, who had recanted his earlier socialist views, had taken up a close relationship with HUAC, first as a friendly witness and later as the committee's chief investigator. In the view of the IPA, Matthews's redbaiting of consumerists illustrated how resolving any one of the many blanket charges made before HUAC would require an extensive and careful sorting of evidence. The IPA's bulletin first explained that Matthews was an extremely biased witness because his major charges were against individuals who had broken away from his own consumer research organization to found the more successful Consumers Union (CU).[71] Further, Matthews provided only weak support for his argument that communists had founded the Consumers Union. One of the three founders mentioned by Matthews actually had had nothing to do with establishing CU; the "communist" connections of the other two persons cited by Matthews merely represented guilt by association. Similarly absurd was Matthews's effort to brand CU as communist because the organization had advertised in communist publications. Not only did the Consumers Union advertise far more in other organs but also many mainstream magazines and newspapers were at the time refusing CU's ads as a courtesy to sponsors who detested third-party product research.

A year after exposing "Mr. Dies," the IPA experienced Matthews's ire in the form of allegations and veiled threats issued in the name of the House Un-American Activities Committee. Matthews, as chief investigator for HUAC, announced on February 23, 1941, that the committee was seeking "to find out what this [IPA] organization really stands for." He pointed not only to the IPA's unflattering piece on HUAC but also to the "frankly left-wing" character of board members Eduard C. Lindeman and Kirtley Mather, who earlier had gone on record as opposing HUAC and supporting antifascist refugees from Spain. Obviously, Matthews's charges stemmed in part from a personal animus; however, the innuendo may have been triggered by an article about the institute's work that had appeared two days earlier on the front page of the *New York Times*. The text of the article drew upon an interview with the IPA's educational director, Violet Edwards, and gave a quite positive review of the institute's methods for helping students to probe the connection of conclusions to evidence. Unfortunately, the favorable content of the text was not matched by the accompanying ominous headline: "Propaganda Study Instills Skepticism in 1,000,000

Pupils." As Alfred and Elizabeth Lee recalled, "the negative headline echoed and re-echoed in the media and elsewhere," helping to coalesce accumulating anxieties about the IPA and possibly prompting Dies and Matthews to capitalize on the notoriety. Given that HUAC completely dropped its so-called investigation of the institute, the whole matter probably represented a headline-hunting put-up job that Dies and Matthews had initiated without participation of the full committee.[72] Yet the friction foreshadowed further attacks that came when the IPA's somewhat pacifistic political ethos became all too apparent.

Foreign Connections

Even before world crises culminated in World War II, the IPA had found it increasingly difficult to sustain its chosen focus on domestic propaganda. Although only one of the first fifteen issues of *Propaganda Analysis* had dealt with extrahemispheric sources of propaganda, the bulletin's second year featured articles on the Japanese invasion of China, the Spanish Civil War, the Munich Conference, and the effort of Britain to build solidarity with the USA. Clearly, the IPA was being influenced by the growing siege mentality under which progressives worried less about the cooptation of media channels by rightist elites and more that the nation was under attack from foreign propagandists (and their domestic henchmen).

Although the IPA responded to society's shift of attention from domestic to foreign affairs, the organization seemed to lack enthusiasm for the new enterprise. Where the IPA had waded into matters of education, labor relations, and journalism with gusto, the organization cultivated a bystanderish, somewhat squeamish position on foreign conflicts and their associated propagandas. Typical was Miller's affirmation that "increasing tension in world affairs following the Munich Pact" should evoke "a parallel realization of the need for cool-headed analysis of the propagandas assailing us." Leonard Doob, a specialist on the psychology of propaganda, agreed and recommended to Miller "a special bulletin on war propaganda" that would summarize "the known plans of this government for the next war" along with "a list of warnings to avoid the traps that may so shortly be set."[73] The IPA's carefully cultivated attitudes of coolheadedness and detachment were initially popular among progressives but later would bring condemnation when the institute's progressive supporters themselves began to opt for intervention against fascism.

One of the earliest of the IPA's articles on the foreign propaganda scene dealt with England's work to build links with America in the face of impending crisis. The bulletin pointed to speeches and ceremonies associated with the visit of King George and Queen Elizabeth as well as British exhibits at the New York World's Fair, which included a copy of the Magna Carta and a diagram of the English origins of George Washington. After publishing its detached scrutiny of Britain's solicitous posture of 1939, the institute got its first lesson in how coolheaded propaganda analysis might lose its luster when progressive opinion leaders preferred to take sides. The IPA's analogy between English propaganda of 1915–1917 and that of 1939 touched a sensitive nerve because revisionists long had condemned Britain for allegedly pulling America into the war by tugging on Liberty's heartstrings. IPA board member Grayson Kefauver agreed that criticism of the royal visit had "some merit" but complained to Miller that it placed the institute in the company of "a small number of small-calibre Congressmen in their effort to achieve headline publicity." While others on the advisory board granted the need to scrutinize Britain, Miller reported that several "were frank in saying they didn't like this bulletin because they believed in collective security." Miller did defend the controversial bulletin by informing Kefauver that it had served as a source for a "March of Time" news production.[74]

If the threat of war influenced the institute's publishing plans, the later actuality of it dominated the organization's editorial enterprise. During the year after Hitler invaded Poland, only four of twelve bulletins dealt with home-front America, and three of these concerned extremist "isms" having extrahemispheric connections. This shift in focus from domestic social competition to large-scale war gradually positioned the IPA less as the positive friend of tolerance and justice (as in earlier articles about education, media channels, and domestic extremism) and more the too-skeptical bystander who treated English and Hitlerite propaganda as equally dangerous. For instance, in "Who Started the War?" (December 1939), the IPA gave a skeptical review of official documents published by both Germany and Britain, noting that each power tried to foist war guilt on the other. Although the institute dismissed as "a caricature of the truth" German claims about peaceful diplomacy, the IPA also faulted the British Blue Book for putting too much stress on Prime Minister Chamberlain's earlier appeasement of Hitler. This tendency to find fault with both German and British propaganda continued in a succeeding bulletin (February 1940) where, in describing the two nations' short-wave broadcasting facilities, the IPA observed how both Germany and England quoted their adversaries for rhetorical effect. In a subsequent release (September 1940), the institute seemed unalarmed by Hitler's spectacular conquest of France and the

Benelux countries, preferring instead to register implied criticisms of England for having appeased Hitler and of Americans for widespread complacency.[75]

The IPA's conspicuous effort to hold a middle position appeared not only in coverage of the European scene but also when the bulletin treated America's own official communications as propaganda rather than straightforward self-defense. In the November 1939 release, for instance, the IPA analyzed Roosevelt's "propaganda for collective action with the democracies." The bulletin not only seemed to sympathize with isolationists' alarm about FDR's efforts to aid the Allies but also registered apparent surprise at the president's black-and-white contrasts between a totally evil Germany and a completely good Britain. Standing in the middle, the IPA advised the intelligent citizen to look behind the "slogans and propaganda devices" employed by those "propagandizing for or against Mr. Roosevelt's policies." In a later article on the wartime propaganda of religious organizations (April 1940), the IPA noted that all belligerents claimed the approval of God and reminded readers of those American clergymen who had climbed aboard the pro-war bandwagon in 1917. The institute then turned to the contemporary situation of British and French religious leaders (Protestant, Jewish, and Roman Catholic) working to convince their American co-religionists of the righteousness of the Allied cause.[76]

Because the IPA's bystanderish position was not entirely out of vogue during the Sitzkrieg period of inactivity on the Western Front, the IPA began in early 1940 its most ambitious foray into European war propaganda, not yet realizing the dangers of such a course. Eugene Davidson, director of the Yale University Press, contacted Harold Lavine about doing a book on "war propagandas in Europe today."[77] Agreement came quickly between the institute and Yale for a book to be written by Harold Lavine, the IPA's editorial director, and James Wechsler, a writer for *Nation*. By May 1940, members of the institute's board of advisers were reviewing galley proofs of the book, which appeared in late June. In deciding to mount a book-length analysis of war propaganda, the IPA's leadership clearly hoped to repeat the coup of the Lees' book, which had garnered good will, memberships, and grant-money income. However, where the criticism of Coughlin endeared the IPA to the pro-tolerance spirit of progressivism, the project to probe for propaganda on all sides of the Maginot line appealed little to the growing desire of progressives to take up for England and against Hitler.

Miller and IPA president Eduard Lindeman set the tone for Lavine and Wechsler's *War Propaganda and the United States* by acknowledging that the institute's general definition of propaganda (social influence directed toward "predetermined ends") cast the curtain of "propagandist" over everyone who took a position on participation in World War II. For their part, Lavine and Wechsler distinguished between contemporary Axis and Allied propaganda on the basis that the Allies at least tried to base their propaganda on kernels of truth (because "in a democracy lies can more readily be exposed") whereas Nazi propaganda was often contradictory and based on "staggering lies." Negating this oblique nod to the interventionist side, however, was the authors' description of President Franklin Roosevelt as the nation's "most active and significant propagandist." FDR's speeches favored the Allies, they pointed out, and the president strategically released information about German submarines sighted near the U.S. coast, probably to raise alarm. Lavine and Wechsler gave less prominent attention to the propaganda of isolationists.

In treating propagandas of the belligerents, Lavine and Wechsler pointed to Britain's efforts at intellectual and emotional bonding with America. More particularly, the British seemed to be targeting selected audiences as when Lord Lothian, British ambassador to the United States, told the American Jewish Congress that Jews had been the first victims of the enemy. The authors speculated that the Allies had hesitated to press their propaganda too aggressively for fear of raising renewed cries of "British propaganda." Turning to the other side, they described Germany's propaganda as largely wasted because Americans were "neutral against Germany." However, the authors rated the Germans as having a nourishable hope of tilting the balance away from intervention.

One might easily have inferred from Lavine and Wechsler's book that propaganda analysis stood as an enemy to interventionism. On the one hand, they explained that the era's rampant cynicism about propaganda created an obstacle to Allied wordsmiths while, on the other, they worried that Americans might become "too credulous, forgetful of the vast and cynical forces operating upon them, eager to reduce events to the vocabulary of moral simplicity." Lavine and Wechsler unintentionally documented the impending demise of their sponsoring IPA organization when they described how pro-intervention opinion leaders were beginning to speak out against propaganda analysis. For instance, they reported columnist Dorothy Thompson's lambasts against what she called the antipropaganda "hoax" whereby anyone claiming that important principles were involved in World War II became a suspected propagandist. For their part, Lavine and Wechsler seemed desirous to implement Lindeman and Miller's declaration that antipropaganda critics were "propagandists in behalf of reasonableness."[78]

Yale University Press was pleased with the "excellent press" that welcomed the appearance of *War Propaganda and the United States*. Newspaper reviews emphasized the volume's eye-opening factual character and relative lack of distracting editorial commentary.[79] Responses from the IPA's board, however, were more equivocal, varying from Frank Baker's praise for Lavine and Wechsler's "extremely illuminating and helpful" work to complaints by F. Ernest Johnson (who earlier had faulted the bulletin on "Britain Woos America") that the book's "facile" narration and "supercilious" tone toward Allied and pro-Ally communication brought into question the meaning and purpose not only of propaganda but also of propaganda analysis itself.[80] Lavine and Wechsler's book represented an ambiguous achievement for the IPA not only by focusing attention to the evaporation of the era's critical spirit of detachment but also by magnifying weaknesses in the institute's financial and staffing arrangements. The book had been intended to confirm the IPA's continued timeliness and to provide a tangible promotion to boost subscriptions. However, during a four-month absence from the office by Miller, the size of Lavine and Wechsler's book had been more than doubled (from 40,000 to over 100,000 words). This decision not only increased the institute's publishing costs but also drained so much of the organization's energy that the bulletins of May and June were not issued with a resulting rash of complaints and a falling off of subscriptions. The weight of the IPA's financial insolvency pressed heavily on Miller, who offered to resign as executive secretary.[81]

Theory versus Praxis

At the time of the IPA's chartering, the organization seemed poised to establish a critical praxis of progressivism that effectively linked social theory and social critique by marrying case-study research to useful educational frameworks in the context of hard-hitting progressive journalism. Those who directed the IPA eventually learned that a praxis that combined high-level scholarship with contemporary critique could not be sustained within the framework of pre–World War II American social science. Clyde Miller's early decision to present systematic schemas for scientific propaganda analysis showed his recognition of the limits of a popular debunking stance backed only by current-events journalism. However, if employment of the seven propaganda devices helped to distinguish the institute's bulletin from sundry liberal magazines, this analytic framework generated neither the quantitative data nor the sophisticated grand theory that, in the 1930s, served to legitimate social science. The seven devices were overlapping categories and therefore were unsuitable for systematic content analysis of the kind being developed by Harold Lasswell. Nor was the seven-devices format backed with any developed cultural or rhetorical perspectives that might have provided a rich theoretical grounding for application by academicians. As presented by Miller, the seven devices were an obvious patchwork conveyed as whole cloth. Miller introduced the devices in sections varying from 125 words (for the testimonial device) to 475 words (for name-calling and glittering generalities), with no indication of where they came from and with only the thinnest description that the seven were linked "because they appeal to our emotions rather than to our reason."[82]

Given a later disposition to unify theory and praxis, present-day commentators might be more willing than their predecessors to view the seven propaganda devices as arrayed in a useful middle position that permitted propaganda theory to tap into social practice.[83] However, from the standpoint of the 1930s, the combination of qualitative analysis and tepid theorizing placed the institute in a limbo region inhospitable to the aspirations of the social scientists who made up a crucial component of the organization's people power. To succeed as social scholarship, the IPA would have had to deepen its theoretical framework to the extent later attained by Alfred Lee and by Jacques Ellul.[84] However, efforts of this kind would have taken nourishment away from the IPA's practical case-study empiricism without guaranteeing a favorable reception in higher education. After all, Lazarsfeld eventually would throw up his hands at trying to marry Adorno's theoretically grounded criticism with radio-research surveys.

At the same time that the seven devices were being faulted for inferior theorizing and data-gathering powers, the IPA's definition of propaganda was becoming a focal point for further disputes about the organization's scientific and reform credentials. Although the institute's conception of propaganda was clear – even scientific – in statement, the definition placed the organization in a position of straddling two not-always-consistent tangents in propaganda critique, namely, the scrutiny of symbols and the scrutiny of social purpose. In the interest of authorizing the widest inquiries into efforts at social control through language and action, Miller had defined propaganda as *"expression of opinion or action by individuals or groups deliberately designed to influence opinions or actions of other individuals or groups with reference to predetermined ends."*[85] Here the IPA avoided the sanctimoniousness or cynicism of a debunking approach in which the critic raised alarm bells whenever efforts at social control were discovered. Further, the definition separated the idea of influencing people – something the IPA described as universal and inevitable in modern society – from an evaluation of the social desirability of those "predetermined ends" strategically pursued by the propagandist. Miller had provided a scientifically oriented definition that avoided setting up a pat case against certain propagandists and that supplied a construct around which more understanding of specific instances and general tendencies could be organized.

In actual practice, however, the IPA was not able to master the separation between the "expression of opinion or action," on the one hand, and the propagandist's "predetermined ends," on the other. Particularly when the nation's attention was riveted on the propagandas of war, the institute's scientific credentials teetered on a dilemma. To the extent that the organization treated some propagandas as socially distasteful (usually by taking what Johnson and Doob regarded as a cynical, supercilious, or sneering tone), it diverged from the scientific course marked out by its definition. Paradoxically, the IPA found that it could not preserve its scientific reputation by maintaining a relative neutrality of treatment when the opposed propagandas happened to be those of Britain versus Germany. In this case, equal treatment of propaganda rendered the IPA vulnerable to criticism that its approach was fundamentally defective for being unable to distinguish the relative moral qualities of democratic and fascist propaganda. Here evenhanded criticism worked to eviscerate the institute's reputation as a contributor to progressive praxis.

The IPA's Pyrrhic struggle to reconcile critique and science became even more painful in the context of efforts by leading grantors to sunder direct links between pure research and practical reform. Despite the liberal instincts of many grant administrators, foundations were a major force in articulating an increasingly hard-and-fast distinction between theoretical-scientific knowledge and critical-reformist understandings. The nature of the institute as a popular education group ultimately precluded funding from grantors such as Rockefeller's General Education Board and the Sloan Foundation. Although these two granting agencies supported social science research, they preferred to underwrite academic investigations that were crafted to minimize direct connection with ongoing social and political issues.

The IPA's overtures to the General Education Board, a Rockefeller endowment that operated between 1903 and 1964, began in August 1938 when Miller and Violet Edwards spoke with Robert J. Havighurst, the director, about funding for the institute's studies and educational materials. From the first, Havighurst saw "little likelihood of the Board's aiding the Institute," although he was willing to take a closer look at the question of "what do the best students in social psychology and sociology think of the approach that the Institute is making to the problem of propaganda?"[86] Given that Havighurst was willing to begin with reference to the opinions of Cantril, Lynd, Lindeman, and Speer – all members of the IPA's board – his pessimism seems somewhat inexplicable. Or perhaps not so, if the earliest unhappy political experiences of a sister institution, the Rockefeller Foundation, are recalled. Largest of the major endowments of the oil king, the Rockefeller Foundation in 1914 had engaged W. L. Mackenzie King to conduct a program of research in the area of industrial relations at the very time that Rockefeller's Colorado Fuel and Iron Company was engaged in a bitter and bloody struggle with striking miners. As a result of this connection, the U.S. Commission on Industrial Relations began an investigation of the role of the foundation in furthering the business interests of the family. "The Rockefeller trustees were given an unforgettable lesson about the hazards of becoming involved in social and economic issues," noted a later historian of the charitable foundations.

Chastened by experience, the Rockefeller Foundation turned to supporting high-level research of a kind that would provide the technical wherewithal for efficient social improvements without agitating for wholesale changes. This philanthropic bureau committed itself "to the proposition that science, especially medicine, offered the surest means of advancing civilization and the well-being of mankind." In 1924, when early grants in the social sciences by the Laura Spelman Rockefeller Memorial provoked new controversies about how the family's millions were distributed, "a committee of senior Rockefeller philanthropic advisers was promptly convened to lay down protective guidelines for its future work." This group drafted a memorandum recommending discretion in distributing Rockefeller largesse for social research such that support would not be given to projects directly connected to "social, economic, or political reforms." Paul Lazarsfeld's quantitative research as to how voting decisions were influenced by demography and information channels (press, radio, word of mouth) was the kind of social science that interested the foundation.[87]

Although the General Education Board (GEB) was constituted with the somewhat subversive (at the time) but firmly grounded objective of uplifting southern blacks through education, it is difficult to imagine that the board was not influenced by the general drift toward scientism and reticence about social controversy that affected the Rockefeller charities generally. Here it is worth noting that the institute's statement of objectives and methods, prepared for the GEB by Edwards and Lavine, took a somewhat defensive tone, opening with an acknowledgment that "The Institute for Propaganda Analysis does not attempt to serve the scholar." The document candidly accepted the label of popularizer by describing the monthly bulletins as "popularly written" for the lay reader. However, Edwards and Lavine declared that the IPA would like to conduct original research in the "vast, unexplored areas in the field of propaganda," but, lacking the funds to do so, the organization necessarily directed its attention to citizens and students. At the same time, the Edwards–Lavine document emphasized that the institute's experimental teaching materials were at work "in over 500 cooperating high school and college classrooms" and in "about 300 adult study groups."[88]

Some weeks after receiving the IPA's self-description, John Marshall, assistant director of the GEB, conveyed to Edwards the sad news that he and the director "cannot advise you to submit a request" for funding notwithstanding "the personal interest which Mr. Havighurst and I feel." Marshall recognized that the institute was "exerting every effort to make its analyses as valid as is now possible," but the crux of the matter was that "we should feel justified in recommending Board assistance only if the Institute's analyses were unassailably scientific." Marshall reminded Edwards that the IPA's own self-description suggested that unassailably scientific work was taxing if not impossible in the area of propaganda analysis.[89] It is difficult to imagine a more emphatic separation of scientific research and critical praxis than that given in Marshall's letter disposing of the institute's hopes for GEB funding.

Although the IPA had been tardy in picking up earlier clues from Havighurst and Marshall in the direction of "science now, practice later," Miller and his colleagues were loath to give up entirely the prospect of receiving much-needed checks from the board. Miller continued to ply Marshall with a variety of proposals including the probably useless idea of asking "two or three highly competent scientists to study both your projects and ours to evaluate methods and approach in terms of scientific validity." More promising but probably still too late was Miller's notion of setting up "an independent commission" that would "carry forward the more strictly scientific and educational phases of our work." In a subsequent remark that gave away Miller's unfashionably flexible notion of science, the IPA's founder was willing to have "matters of method" worked out by a joint committee of the GEB, the IPA, and the Progressive Education Association.[90] The executive committee later discussed how the institute might reorganize itself to become more attractive to Marshall and Havighurst. Since the bulletins were what seemed to put off the GEB, one idea was to separate the educational program, which carried neither the stigma of unmet scientific obligations nor the static of overt criticism, from the more controversial monthly newsletters. Also discussed was the possibility of constituting a committee to keep in touch with the GEB composed of "fairly innocuous people" who "would not be too closely identified with the Institute letters [i.e., bulletins]."[91]

Pressed from the first by the prospect that the Good Will Fund would vote to liquidate the IPA as part of settling the estate of the late Edward Filene, the institute actively approached a variety of potential grantors in addition to the General Education Board. None of the contacts, however, were to pan out, except for the small sums received from the American Jewish Committee and the Whitney Foundation to support the Lees' study of Father Coughlin. Just as the General Education Board was put off by the institute's popular studies of current disputes, the Sloan Foundation wished that IPA's academic credentials were more polished. Edgar Dale reported to Miller the results of a conversation with Harold Sloan, executive director of the Alfred P. Sloan Foundation. Dale got the impression that Sloan had a deep interest in the institute's work and described the grantsman as a "hot" prospect. However, according to Dale, Sloan expressed doubts about whether his foundation could support an organization that "wasn't connected organically with any University." Given the anti–New Deal economic convictions of Alfred Sloan, the long-time General Motors president who had endowed the foundation, the IPA's hopes here may have been somewhat exaggerated from the start.[92]

If the institute's ambiguous connection to the hypothesis-data-theory side of American social science posed problems for the organization's survival, so too did its particular brand of praxis. Ultimately, the IPA never fully worked out its connection to social reform in a time when theory and praxis were behaving like estranged lovers unexpectedly forced into proximity. True, the IPA stated and restated its commitment to democratic life even to the extent of acknowledging itself to be a propagandist for democracy.[93] Further, the institute's work unambiguously shone the light of progressivism upon such persuaders as the Associated Farmers, such channels as radio, and such professions as public relations. In the same way that Sinclair's *The Brass Check* muckraked journalism and encouraged George Seldes and other reporters to improve their profession, so too did the IPA's inquiries inspire progressives to demand standards of communication higher than those of efficient production, greater sales, and more polished images. Yet the institute never did fully work out whether it should act as a neutral referee in social competition or throw in with the reformers. The IPA sounded like a participant in progressive social action when it invited teachers to assess how democratic were their classrooms, schools, and communities. On the other hand, in articles on war propaganda and group medicine, the IPA's tone was less that of a participant and more that of a mercurial bystander who wished a plague on propagandists one and all in the belief that things somehow would work themselves out in the end.[94]

Ultimately, the problem of the IPA's praxis was not chiefly an internal one of coherence but rather was an external one of controversiality. Despite initial plaudits for the general idea of propaganda analysis, the IPA inevitably attracted a coterie of unhappy people and groups trailing in the wake of the bulletin's critical dragnet. Not even the institute's essentially evenhanded selection of topics would assuage the anger of conservatives who inevitably became the chief targets. George Sokolsky, confidant to businesspeople and a prominent newspaper columnist, objected that even members of the IPA's board such as Charles Beard and James Shotwell were prominent propagandists. A group called the Truth Society obtained some press attention for allegations about the institute's leftist leanings. Edward Bernays publicly corrected a minor error about his work for Western Union as described in the IPA's curriculum guidelines. Cantril conveyed to Miller a complaint by George Gallup that the IPA seemed to analyze only rightist propaganda. Although Cantril agreed with Miller that "this type of propaganda constitutes at least 90% of the total barrage we experience," the Princeton man wondered whether the IPA might not prepare "releases on New Deal propaganda, C.I.O. or Communist propaganda." He believed that such a wider choice of targets would convey impartiality and also that "a comparison of the goals of the propagandists would, in every case, work to the advantage of the side most obviously interested in the preservation of political democracy, and the establishment of an economic one."[95]

In candid moments, Miller recognized that his organization connected the officers and trustees of the Good Will Fund to embarrassing controversies.

> The chief objection of the Good Will Fund, as nearly as I can get it, is fear that the Institute may embarrass it with federal tax authorities by getting into the quick of certain conflicts which might involve the Institute's being charged with being a propagandizing agency.[96]

For his part, Miller claimed that he was "trying desperately to avoid" placing Filene's fund in peril of its tax exemption, and the IPA proudly pointed to its own tax-exempt status received on July 29, 1938. Doob, an insider, recognized that IPA tilted "slightly toward the left," but he believed that the organization "did not hesitate to dissect the left as well as the right." A friendly outsider, A. B. Hollingshead of Indiana University's Sociology Department, saw the IPA as somewhat more partisan. He credited the institute for providing a useful counterweight to the vast number of conservative newsletters but believed that Miller's bureau had been "too tender with the Left."[97]

Although early criticism of the Institute for Propaganda Analysis did not throw up any decisive aspersions on the group's choice of subjects or its critical method, Miller nevertheless had good reason to be concerned about the impact on the Good Will Fund of the accumulating font of outside ill feeling. Filene had thrust the institute upon the trustees of his fund somewhat abruptly, and Miller gained the impression that certain members of the fund's board never fully warmed up to issuing checks to the IPA.[98] To the Good Will Fund, Miller acknowledged that there had been "one or two biased articles about us" in the Hearst newspapers; but he emphasized that "respectable sources" from across the political spectrum – notably *Editor and Publisher* and the American Newspaper Guild – were supportive.[99] As the time for renewing the Good Will Fund's grant approached, Miller pursued this line, emphasizing that "most of our subscribers are pleased; some are enthusiastic; a few are adversely critical."[100] He similarly maintained that the sharp attacks by "reactionaries" were mitigated by the views of thoughtful conservatives, such as Willard Kiplinger, who "think very well of the Institute."[101]

Despite Miller's reassurances, the Good Will Fund inevitably grew increasingly unhappy about the controversiality of its charming but difficult financial ward as political criticism of the institute mounted. Objections raised by the New York State Economic Council were typical of how the bulletin managed to embroil the IPA in the polemicism of the age. The council's newsletter described the IPA as a "propaganda agency" with a "strongly leftist" orientation "for collectivizing the United States." Focusing on the institute's study of propaganda in the schools (February 25, 1941), the newsletter argued that the IPA showed itself to be blind to the explicit efforts of radical social studies teachers to indoctrinate disdain for America. The council asked how the IPA could claim to be impartial if Alfred Lee was branding the Dies committee a "disgrace" at the same time that Congress was reauthorizing the committee by a vote of 353 to 6? In a piece in *Harper's*, Bernard

DeVoto picked up on the tensions between the IPA's neutral definition of propaganda and its often feisty case studies, contending that the IPA's exposés by definition were a propaganda designed to influence events.[102]

Percy Brown expressed his concerns about the "repeated claims that the Institute itself is a propaganda agency."[103] Among the articles that concerned Brown was an unfavorable editorial review in the *New Leader* alleging that the IPA not only used innuendo against Britain but also gave out "the impression that Roosevelt is as big a liar as Hitler." Seeking to reassure Brown on this particular matter, Alfred Lee met with the publication's editor, William E. Bohn, and Lee assured Brown that the previously skeptical editor was now more favorable to the institute.[104] With carping reviews of the IPA's politics appearing here and there, the organization found that its own subscription solicitations began to generate a noticeable number of angry rejoinders. One respondent to a February–March 1941 promotional mailing added this penned note to the special subscription flyer: "You keep your propaganda out of the mails and it will help some." This respondent underlined the name of E. C. Lindeman claiming that this board member was both a "pink" and an "advocate of 'Defenseless America.' " Another recipient of the institute's promotional offer reacted with a claim that the IPA's board showed the "same broad streak of *yellow* down each back" that characterized Herbert Hoover and other opponents of participation in the war. Ironically, a third angry respondent blamed the institute for harboring "war mongers," asking "Are you on the British payroll?"

Defections

Directors of the Good Will Fund were not the only ones concerned about being connected to the embattled antipropaganda bureau. The IPA seemed to be offending just about everyone, upsetting conservatives with articles on education and putting off progressive interventionists by analyzing the machinations of the Allies. The organization was gaining a reputation of questionable political virtue notwithstanding the fact that it was difficult to point to significant examples of just where the institute had played an overt propagandizing role. In December 1940, treasurer Forrest Long reported that "the landlord may not allow us to remain since he suspects us of being a *radical* group."[105] That such a sentiment began to take hold among the IPA's moral landlords in 1940–1941 is clear from the onset of resignations by board members.

William Heard Kilpatrick, professor emeritus in Columbia's Teachers

College and one of the leading lights in progressive education, became one of the first in a stream of defections that were to plague the IPA's board during the last year of operation. Reflecting on his cordial relations with Miller and Edwards, Kilpatrick hoped that no one would be offended by his request to "quietly fade out of the picture" given that he was "too busy to give the proper attention to the work of the Institute." Kilpatrick also seems to have shared Doob's irritation with the bulletin's occasionally pungent phrases, reminding Miller that he had "for some time been troubled by what has seemed to be on the part of some of the Institute writers a disposition to discuss controversial matters not in a scientific manner and spirit, but with some apparent bias." Also resigning at this time was Gladys Murphy Graham, a professor of argumentation at UCLA, who earlier had warned that current propagandists seemed able to exploit the IPA as when one Los Angeles pro-Nazi managed "to get in more of his own Nazi propaganda under that protective coloration [the IPA's devices] than he did before!"[106]

Adding to the anxiety of board members were allegations about Clyde Beals, the new editorial director. In mid-January 1941, Alfred M. Bingham, social activist and editor of *Common Sense* magazine, conveyed his objections to Miller about the employment of Beals as editor of *Propaganda Analysis*. Bingham, who took pains to emphasize his own progressive credentials and his aversion to mindless redbaiting, nevertheless contended that Beals "is necessarily under suspicion of Communist sympathies because of his long connection with the *Guild Reporter*." Even liberals suspected the *Guild Reporter* of having followed the "[communist] party line," Bingham argued, "and those who edit it and control it are necessarily under suspicion of Communist connections." Believing that Beals would not want to open the guild to a searching inquiry as to its communist links, Bingham recommended that he be dismissed so that people could continue to have confidence in the impartiality of the bulletin.[107] In reply, Miller reassured Bingham that the board had reviewed Beals carefully but noted that he would look into the matter further. Bingham offered to withhold action until Miller had advised the Institute's board but noted that he felt urgency because his publication had steered many subscribers to the institute.[108]

In continuing the exchange of letters with his counterpart at *Common Sense*, the IPA's founder vouched for the integrity of Beals, explained the oversight authority of the editorial board, invited Bingham to provide specific evidence to support his charges, and promised that "the correspondence between yourself and myself with reference to Clyde Beals will be brought to the attention of members of the Board of the Institute."[109] At this point, Bingham enlarged the scope of his rather vaguely expressed discontents, informing Miller that a number of individuals he spoke with believed that "the Institute has acted as a Communist front organization for a long time, even before the appointment of Mr. Beals." Bingham needled Miller with a thinly veiled provocation to the effect that several local communists "share your own belief that it is more important to avoid any action that might be construed by the Communists as red-baiting than to eliminate Communist influence." Bingham also expressed regret that Miller's earlier letter had not arrived in time to be included alongside an editorial reference to the IPA that was to be published in the February *Common Sense*.[110]

Why Alfred Bingham would be so willing to paint the institute in broad hues of Red and Pink is puzzling in view of his many intellectual contacts with board members Beard, Lindeman, Lynd, and Douglas and in view of Bingham's own service on the board of the American Civil Liberties Union, an organization that invariably (and inaccurately) appeared on most short lists of communist front groups. Miller found Bingham's attitude quite exasperating and broke off correspondence with him in the belief that the editorial note about the IPA was not only "unjustified" but also "unfair" given that "you said you would take no action until I had a chance to bring before the board the issue you had raised concerning Mr. Beals."[111]

An explanation for Bingham's behavior perhaps may be found in his having rather recently converted from the position of ardent isolationist to committed interventionist. In 1936 and 1937, Bingham had been active as a speaker in the Emergency Peace Campaign, whose stated objective was "to help prevent the United States from going to war."[112] Also, between 1938 and 1939, Bingham and others had closely monitored the position of the Communist Party, which, in the words of Clarence Senior, executive secretary of the Keep America Out of War Committee, was then "continuing its propaganda for 'Collective Security.' "[113] Bingham's position at the time was that although the Keep America Out of War group had not articulated the need for an "adequate national defense," nevertheless this body was on target in urging "continued efforts for appeasement, disarmament and international cooperation."[114]

A campaigner for isolation in 1938, Bingham, as with many progressives of late 1940, was having a change of heart on how the United States should respond to the war situation. He asked to have his name removed from the stationary of the Keep America Out of War organization because "I am inclined to favor all out aid to Britain."[115] Given Bingham's own dramatic about-face, it is not difficult to understand how he might have assimilated the accumulated ire of interventionists

Spies and Lies

German agents are everywhere, eager to gather scraps of news about our men, our ships, our munitions. It is still possible to get such information through to Germany, where thousands of these fragments—often individually harmless—are patiently pieced together into a whole which spells death to American soldiers and danger to American homes.

But while the enemy is most industrious in trying to collect information, and his systems elaborate, he is not superhuman—indeed he is often very stupid, and would fail to get what he wants were it not deliberately handed to him by the carelessness of loyal Americans.

Do not discuss in public, or with strangers, any news or troop and transport movements, of bits of gossip as to our military preparations, which come into your possession.

Do not permit your friends in service to tell you—or write you—"inside" facts about where they are, what they are doing and seeing.

Do not become a tool of the Hun by passing on the malicious, disheartening rumors which he so eagerly sows. Remember he asks no better service than to have you spread his lies of disasters to our soldiers and sailors, gross scandals in the Red Cross, cruelties, neglect and wholesale executions in our camps, drunkenness and vice in the Expeditionary Force, and other tales certain to disturb American patriots and to bring anxiety and grief to American parents.

And do not wait until you catch someone putting a bomb under a factory. Report the man who spreads pessimistic stories, divulges—or seeks—confidential military information, cries for peace, or belittles our efforts to win the war.

Send the names of such persons, even if they are in uniform, to the Department of Justice, Washington. Give all the details you can, with names of witnesses if possible—show the Hun that we can beat him at his own game of collecting scattered information and putting it to work. The fact that you made the report will not become public.

You are in contact with the enemy today, just as truly as if you faced him across No Man's Land. In your hands are two powerful weapons with which to meet him—discretion and vigilance. Use them.

COMMITTEE ON PUBLIC INFORMATION
8 JACKSON PLACE, WASHINGTON, D. C.

George Creel, Chairman
The Secretary of State
The Secretary of War
The Secretary of the Navy

Contributed through Division of Advertising

United States Gov't Comm. on Public Information

This space contributed for the Winning of the War by

The Publisher of

"Spies and Lies," 1917–1918. Courtesy of the National Archives.

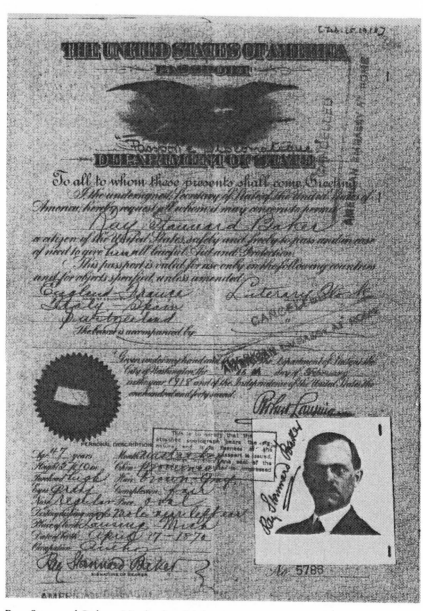

Ray Stannard Baker: Muckraker-Diplomat, 1918. Courtesy of the Library of Congress.

Harold D. Lasswell, c. 1930s. From the Harold Dwight Lasswell Papers, Manuscripts and Archives, Yale University Library.

The Goslings by Upton Sinclair, 1924. Collection of J. M. Sproule.

Alfred McClung Lee, c. 1950. Courtesy of Briant Hamor Lee.

Mrs. Miniver, lobby card, 1942. Courtesy of the Academy of Motion Picture Arts and Sciences.

In fact

An Antidote for Falsehood in the Daily Press

(No. 293)   Vol. XIII, No. 7   ← 412   May 20, 1946

George Seldes, *Editor*
Victor Weingarten, *Associate*

Re-entered as second class matter, March 12, 1941, at the post office at New York, N. Y., under the act of March 3, 1879.

Weekly newsletter, copyright 1946 in the United States of America by IN FACT, 280 Lafayette Street, New York 12, N. Y. Telephone: WOrth 4-6945. One Dollar (52 issues) a year. Canada $2.00 a year, Foreign $3.00 a year.

→ If Your Name Is Addressed in Red See Page 3

One Year of Peace Plans for New War

Annual Editorial

IN MAY the anti-fascist world celebrated the first anniversary of the ending of the war in Europe. IN FACT celebrated its sixth anniversary. The month was marked with the most alarming talk of a third World War.

The second World War was a real war against fascism, despite every effort to switch it. Hess flew to Britain to get his friends (Buchmanite leaders in Parliament and in the Cabinet itself) to change the character of the war. Fortunately Mr Churchill, despite the fact he had lauded Mussolini and Franco, hated Hitler (whom he saw as an eventual menace to the British Empire) and insisted on following Lincoln's dictum: "One war at a time, gentlemen."

Intrigue Began in 1942

In 1942, however, as Ralph Ingersoll and Capt Harry Butcher reveal in their new books, the Anglo-American pledge to open a Second Front in France and end the war quickly was broken for political reasons. Mr Churchill opposed it because he wanted to circumvent his own ally, Russia. Eisenhower said it was "the blackest day of the war." Many American boys are dead because of this political action which knocked out a military action.

The Allies pledged themselves at Potsdam "to destroy the vestiges of Naziism and fascism." However, every morning's paper reports Anglo-American business men interested in maintaining the Nazi industrial plant; the failure of the occupation to stop political Naziism; political intrigue aiding fascism.

Getting Ready for War III

Throughout the world preparations are obvious for a war, although UN speaks of peace. New blocs are being formed, most of them aimed to replace Hitler's notorious Anti-Komintern Pakt, the fascist Internationale, which conquered democracies, republics and monarchies as well, before it attacked the Soviets.

The big post bellum blocs today are:

1. The Anglo-American Bloc. This is of course the Churchill union of Britain and the United States, a new "racial" or Anglo-Saxon organization to take on the non-Nordic world, as outlined in the Fulton, Missouri, speech.

2. The Pan-American Bloc. The tip-off was Operation Musk Ox which, as exclusively revealed in this weekly, was instigated by the United States, and not by Canada, although the maneuver was conducted under Canadian auspices. It

PHONY "NEWS" FURNISHED FREE AS PROPAGANDA FLOODS NATION; "COLUMNISTS" SUPPLIED FOR 50¢

"Rural America" Poisoned by Pews' Press _____ p 4

DISGUISING THEIR WARES with fancy-sounding "news syndicate" titles, big business press agents are flooding the nation's "grass roots" newspapers with reams of craftily-concocted propaganda in a new attempt to steer the nation's thinking along reactionary NAM lines.

This new reactionary stream is supplemented by the political advertisements which the corporations use to pay off editors and publishers, and is followed by a barrage of anti-liberal pamphlets, newsletters, plain letters, speeches and reports sent to the homes of every man and woman who owns stock in a corporation.

Liberal Propaganda 1%, Reactionary 99%

More than 80% of the 1750 daily papers and the 10,000 weeklies in the U S are using some of this subsidized material, masquerading it as legitimate news. While the AFL, CIO, PAC also sends out press material, the combined liberal news releases does not amount to 1% of the great propaganda flood which is enveloping the country, poisoning the minds of many people.

The phony subsidized "syndicate" stuff is sufficient to enable an editor to put out his paper without paying one cent for news, features, columns, editorials, cartoons or photographs. It differs from regular news releases in that this material poses as "syndicate," is a permanent fixture in the papers; its propaganda never stops flowing.

Subsidized largely by the NAM, power trusts, corporations with special axes to grind, and scores of reactionary, pro-fascist outfits, the "syndicated" material is consistently anti-labor, anti-social legislation, pro-nationalist and pro-big business. Its most recent concentration has been against the OPA and the loan to Britain. It is always for labor-shackling laws, is always against unions, strikes, Russia.

Peck's Pap Printed by 3,000 Papers

Smoothest "free enterprise" nostrum on the market is Peck's packaged pap, ladled to 3000 "grass roots" newspapers each week. Second in size and influence only to the NAM's "Industrial Press Service" which supplies 5000 papers, the Peck syndicate, "The American Way," dishes out the subtlest anti-labor, anti-liberal, reactionary copy in the country.

Owned by George Peck, a garrulous individualist who warned IN FACT he'll sue for libel if he doesn't like what is said about him, it competes successfully with the dozens of phony press services whose stuff is available without charge.

Peck doesn't give his material away; he gets paid for it. He says that 2800 papers each pay him 50 cents a week, and that 400 others get the service without charge for six-month "trial" periods.

Peck's "Bad" Boys Labor for Love

The Peck "package" consists of a weekly column by himself, a roundup of editorial comment from various papers, by coincidence almost always anti-labor, anti-British, anti-Russian, and a column each week by one of four "associates," each of whom, strangely enough, has been accused of being pro-fascist. Peck says his "bad" boys are really wonderful fellows who don't ask for a penny of the $65,000 he gets for their work.

"They labor for love. They like this kind of thing," he said.

His unpaid "associates," all with other axes to grind are:

Rev Dr Norman Vincent Peale, pastor of NY's Marble Collegiate Church and former head of the Committee for Constitutional Govt, described in Congress as "America's No 1 fascist outfit."

In Fact (May 20, 1946). Collection of J. M. Sproule.

toward an institute that in 1941 was continuing to treat World War II as a two-sided subject for propaganda analysis. In a note to Lee, Bingham charged that the IPA's January 1941 bulletin ("Religious Propaganda Against the War") "is not an analysis of pacifist propaganda but is pacifist propaganda" of a kind that suggested a communist bias in the bulletin.[116] It is a matter of some interest that Bingham construed the IPA's thorough review of the religious pacifists as a piece as antiwar propaganda. If Bingham could so read an article that even made explicit reference to the pro-Nazi and pro-communist motives of some Christian propagandists, it is hardly surprising that he was able to take the matter one step further and link the essay to the American Communist Party's conversion to neutrality that came in the wake of the Hitler–Stalin pact.

Despite the vagueness of Bingham's charges about Beals and the institute, his missives prompted degrees of consternation among the organization's leadership when Miller distributed the correspondence. Ned Dearborn, education dean at New York University, is representative of those who were disposed to take the undocumented charges in stride. Dearborn considered the allegations against Beals to be "symptomatic of the times – nothing more" and advised supporting the IPA's editor unless it were clearly established that his politics had interfered with his duties.[117] Exhibiting somewhat more of a hand-wringing attitude were board members Malcolm MacLean of Hampton Institute and Grayson Kefauver of Stanford, who believed it would be inadvisable given rising social tensions to retain a man whose background could fuel further charges about the institute's allegedly radical character.[118]

The most extreme reaction to the burgeoning Beals affair was that of Paul Douglas, who on his own initiative (possibly after being contacted directly by Bingham) brought to Miller's attention both concerns and demands about Beals. Douglas believed that "the New York Guild and their organ, the *Guild Reporter,* were controlled by the C.P. and that hence Mr. Beals must, in a sense, have been under their direction." Douglas added that his informants told him that the *Guild Reporter* had adopted "the extraordinary about-face in policy which followed the infamous Stalin–Hitler pact." Given the "present emergency in this country," Douglas considered the appointment of Beals to be "an unwarrantable risk" despite whatever assurances the institute's editor had given the board of directors. "I can only say that if Mr. Beals still remains on the staff by March 15th, I wish my resignation as a member of the Board of Directors to be accepted and my name immediately removed from all stationery and literature issued by the Institute."[119] In reply, president Mather assured the economist that he had many of the facts wrong concerning Beals, notably that Beals's *Guild Reporter* was not the organ of the New York chapter but rather of the national guild.[120] Mather secured Douglas's agreement to hold his resignation in abeyance until the institute could mount an official inquiry.[121]

It fell to Alfred Lee, the IPA's treasurer and soon-to-be executive director, to investigate in specific the allegations brought by Bingham and pressed by Douglas. Between March 17 and April 3, Lee prepared a thirteen-page draft report exonerating Beals from the aspersions that were circulating about his work for the Newspaper Guild. Taking an approach suitable to the charge that Beals had towed the communist line, Lee compared stories in the *Guild Reporter* to the three turns in communist political machinations during the 1930s: (1) the anti–New Deal and anti–trade union phase (up to summer 1935); (2) the popular front period of alliances with liberals against fascism (late 1935– summer 1939); and (3) the pro-Axis phase (after the August 1939 Hitler–Stalin pact). Lee reported that he found no evidence to indicate that either the stories or the infrequent editorials in the *Guild Reporter* paralleled these expedient shifts in the Communist Party's line. His interpretation was that the guild variously supported or opposed the Roosevelt administration depending on specific issues that related to its own situation as a union of working journalists. Lee concluded that Beals's own statements in favor of liberal democracy were consistent with the conspicuous lack of internal evidence that he ever had been captive to an ideological line.[122]

On April 3, the IPA's board approved sending Lee's draft to Douglas for comments, and, on April 25, the group accepted the Lee report. Although Douglas probably did not concur in the institute's reaffirmation of Beals, neither his private letter of resignation to Miller (May 7, 1941) nor his public statement to the press made mention of the affair. Douglas emphasized to Miller that "I do not have the leisure to go over the publications and in these days of stress and strain, careful reading of the manuscripts is necessary." In his public statement, which expressed "great respect for most of the people in the institute," the Chicago professor reiterated the point about time and then highlighted his objection to being connected to treatments of the Roosevelt administration's defense policies that were more critical than were his own views.[123]

One sympathizes with the members of the IPA's board, many of whom were under fire for a variety of their intellectual and organizational commitments in addition to those created by the institute's monthly topical releases. For instance, a number of IPA board members – including Baker, Dale, Dearborn, Douglas, MacLean, and Miller – were on record as supporting the American Committee for

Democracy and Intellectual Freedom (ACDIF), which, among other things, had been actively opposing the efforts of Dies and others to mount political investigations of textbooks. Not surprisingly, the AC-DIF found itself being redbaited in New York by Senator Frederick Coudert's local HUAC-type operation.[124] In an atmosphere where intellectuals were shifting from isolation to intervention – and where many people were debating how such metamorphoses matched changes in the communist line – the institute's monthly releases began to seem less an expression of progressivism and more an extraneous social criticism.

However understandable were the defections from the board, they proved to be a disastrous kind of public relations for an organization whose budget for the year ending September 1941 relied heavily on the promised $20,000 grant from the Good Will Fund, a sum amounting to 50 percent of the total expected income.[125] Already the Good Will Fund had delayed payments of this grant for 1940–1941 because of concerns expressed by the institute's auditor about accounting changes.[126] It was reasonable to expect that the IPA's increasing controversiality would only further solidify the Filene fund's already very clear intention to make the 1941–1942 fiscal period the last year of support. Nevertheless, the institute had not entirely given up trying to polish its image in the eyes of the fund's directors. In what probably seemed to the Good Will Fund as an effort to compromise the prior decision to cut the institute adrift, the IPA's board requested that Percy Brown, executive director of the fund, "appoint a committee to make a critical appraisal of the Institute."[127] Brown proved cold to the proposition, believing that any such study would make the fund appear to be "seeking for a confirmation of its wise judgment in rather heavily subsidizing the Institute." Brown offered the less attractive option of entrusting such an investigation to a more unpredictable source – he suggested the American Society of Newspaper Editors – and the institute's board elected to drop the whole matter.[128]

Off to War

The timing of Paul Douglas's resignation (mid-1941) suggested that the Dies and Beals affairs were significant factors in loosening the hold of the institute on leading progressives. Far more important in the general picture, however, was the drumbeat of interventionism that had mounted after the collapse of France in June 1940 and again after the Germany–Italy–Japan alliance of September.[129] More than anything else, social pressures toward intervention were what imbued the Dies and Beals controversies with high tension. Public attacks and redbaiting did not bloody the ranks of the IPA's board until the time when liberals became inclined to see the institute's work as actually hindering the single most important progressive praxis of the day, namely, the world-wide contest against fascism. The sense that a gigantic military struggle was in the offing increased the yearnings of progressives for national unity, and propaganda analysis, which ever reminded people of society's divisions, seemed a clear barrier to the social consensus required for a liberal democracy to undertake the decisive act of war.

In the pressure-laden atmosphere of social crisis in early 1941, the IPA's board found itself accepting resignations from a relatively large group of its stalwarts including Charles A. Beard (in February) and E. C. Lindeman (in April).[130] Lindeman's abdication, announced in the same press articles that reported Douglas's defection, found Lindeman (a former anti-intervention stalwart) also expressing sentiments that he was "all-out for intervention" in contrast to the uncommitted tenor of *Propaganda Analysis*.[131] In May, Hadley Cantril asked to be released from service on the board since "I do not like to feel any responsibility when I cannot physically find time to assume the responsibility my connection should require." Since spring 1940, Cantril had been undertaking confidential work charting public opinion on the war for President Roosevelt, who used the information to help wean the nation from neutrality.[132] Ned Dearborn, who came out for the military draft in summer 1940, resigned in July 1941.[133] In addition, William H. Kilpatrick and Gladys Murphy Graham, both of whom had dropped out in fall 1940, were among those complaining, respectively, about the bulletin's attitude and the unreliability of the seven devices as an obstacle to current fascist propaganda.[134]

To be sure, not every board member who turned to intervention had lost faith in propaganda analysis; nor were all those who resigned committed to intervention. F. E. Johnson, who had described the Lavine–Wechsler book as "propaganda against war involvement," kept active until the organization itself suspended operations.[135] Leonard Doob and newcomer Peter Odegard continued with the IPA despite having taken official positions in Washington. For his part, Beard defected without having converted actively to interventionism. Nevertheless, it was the war that ultimately sundered the analytic and action dimensions of propaganda analysis. The institute had managed to keep theory and praxis in harmony on domestic matters by suggesting ways for progressives to make American institutions more democratic. Yet the organization was not willing to nudge its readers into any action regarding the war. To the contrary, the IPA's effort to promote coolheaded thinking seemed to many to impede the kind of steely determination required for intervention.

As with philosopher John Dewey, who convinced himself that progressives could transmute the Great War into a catalyst for social progress on the home front, America's interventionists of 1940–1941 were flocking to a number of organizational enterprises that allowed them to merge their adherence to democracy with active work against fascism. One such organization was the Committee for National Morale, which brought together various social scientists interested in how to avoid civilian demoralization during the projected struggle. Among those active in the committee were the IPA's erstwhile president, Hadley Cantril, and his friend, Gordon W. Allport, who had helped with the institute's first radio issue. Other propaganda critics attracted to the morale project included Lynd, who proposed a large-scale research effort to the committee, and Lindeman, who published ideas about the role of recreation in maintaining public esprit.

The Council for Democracy was another organization that permitted a merging of progressive social thought with action to defend freedom against the overseas fascists. Consisting of groups of academicians, publishers, industrialists, and others, the council sponsored meetings and issued reports both to build moral solidarity against Hitler and to support increased spending for defense. One council-sponsored radio program brought together prominent speakers from each of seven Nazi-occupied countries in Europe. A council memorandum advised Americans to be prepared for higher taxes for defense and also recommended ways to make sure that the burden of defense was shared fairly. At the same time that the council promoted spiritual and material preparedness, the organization's committees encouraged progressive reform as a vehicle of national security. For instance, one council pamphlet described racial discrimination in employment as a threat to the nation's unity by making the Negro community a "fertile ground for subversive propaganda, agitation and unrest."[136]

In contrast to programs of action by the progressive interventionist groups, the IPA's chief contribution to the war situation was its promotion of a coolheaded analysis of opposing propagandas coupled with a self-monitoring of one's thought processes. The IPA's aim to preserve democracy by keeping people from being swept up by propaganda was an intellectualized praxis far less satisfying in a time of national emergency than the alternatives offered by interventionists. The climate of 1940–1941 was one in which many people wanted to take sides and take action to preserve the democracies around the world. Given the steady advance of fascism abroad, propaganda analysis seemed to have become increasingly insensitive to the major social preoccupation of progressives. Conceding that propaganda analysis was by nature unsettling and anticonformist, Alfred Lee doubted whether it carried an intrinsic antiwar tendency given that some board members took an active role in the preparedness effort. Harold Lavine, the longtime IPA editor, similarly denied that propaganda analysis in any way precluded one from making a thoughtful decision for war, observing that analysis and reflection merely kept one from being stampeded into hasty action.[137] Still, as the *New York Times* headline (February 21, 1941) had proclaimed, the institute's approach was vulnerable to the charge that it created more of a destructive skepticism than an intelligent reflectiveness.

Allegations that the IPA promoted cynicism and skepticism had surfaced from time to time since the organization's inception, but until 1941, the institute had managed to keep such objections from undermining its program. In early 1940, for example, board member Robert Speer wondered whether the bulletin might be "too negative for children," adding that "teachers have complained that the Institute tears down but does not build up." In reply, Violet Edwards acknowledged that she was familiar with complaints of this type "from teachers who use the bulletins but who do not actually cooperate" in the IPA's study program.[138] In fact, the institute already had answered such a criticism in detail in the September 1939 *Propaganda Analysis*. Here the IPA conceded that early approaches to propaganda analysis had focused on detecting propaganda and becoming resistant to it; but the bulletin emphasized that the institute's study program now went far beyond having students shoot down the expressions of others. In this view, the IPA's total package encouraged students to build their own life philosophies as they participated in intelligent group discussion focused not on distant subjects but instead on topics of personal concern and about which they might do something.[139] In a later internal report on the education program, Violet Edwards similarly acknowledged that propaganda analysis might promote cynicism if instruction focused on a few detection devices or on analyzing one propagandist's message. She added that teachers could expect to find students passing through a stage where they overzealously labeled everything as propaganda. Gradually, however, as students participated in group discussions that encouraged mature habits of relating conclusions to information, they assimilated a model of democratic life.[140]

By 1941, the debate over whether propaganda analysis encouraged too acidic a skepticism was moving into the academic literature. Bruce

Smith, NYU social scientist, reported his experience that teaching the recognition of propaganda created a "destructive cynicism in students" who were initially excited about finding propaganda but who saw no solution to it except censorship. Smith advocated putting propaganda critique within a broader "Science of Democracy" focused on an empirical analysis of the social structure. In reply, Miller acknowledged that merely inducing a resistance to propaganda might create cynicism. But he argued that the institute's practice of coupling detection devices to the life-history technique taught students a broader understanding of how people formed goals or values in a society characterized by competition among pressure groups.[141]

Notwithstanding the efforts of the IPA to dampen the cynical debunking spirit with comprehensive study materials, the debate over propaganda analysis as destructive skepticism spread into newspapers and popular journals of opinion. As long as this objection had simmered in the educational community, the institute had been able to contain the criticism. The *New York Times,* in 1940, had not seen fit to seek an opposing view when Miller argued at some length that the IPA's program replaced undiluted cynicism with mature discrimination, for instance, helping students to replace a blanket distrust of newspapers with a capacity to recognize reasonable and fair reporting.[142] However, by 1940–1941, leading liberal interventionist commentators had picked up the cynicism charge thereby giving it both wide currency and political salience. Already by April 1940, Lewis Mumford was faulting liberals for a passivity induced by the effort to separate reason from emotion. Mumford added, in what was probably taken by many to be an indirect swipe at the institute, that many liberals were unable to go beyond emotional neutrality to defend civilization against fascist barbarism (after the war, Mumford amended the essay to name propaganda analysis explicitly as a culprit).[143]

Max Lerner was not so indirect in connecting propaganda analysis to the hesitation of progressives to embrace the crusade against fascism. Lerner characterized Lavine and Wechsler's *War Propaganda and the United States* as blind to the moral differences between German and British communications. In his estimation, the former had used secret methods to sow appeasement and fear, and the latter, merely overt promotions for an honest cause. Lerner further traced the IPA's alleged moral obtuseness to the organization's definition of propaganda (expressions influencing people to a predetermined end), which lumped together such incompatible bedfellows as a presidential message, a Coughlin broadcast, and a photo. Worse yet, the definition turned Americans into a "nation of amateur detectives looking for concealed propaganda in every effort to awaken America to the real nature of Nazi world strategy." The excessive fear of being tricked had led, Lerner argued, to a "collective indecision" and a "universal skepticism" that paralyzed the will to act and rendered the United States helpless against the ruthless Hitler. Although branding the institute's definition of propaganda as false, Lerner denied any wish to harm the organization since he otherwise shared much of its "social outlook."[144]

Privately, the IPA acknowledged that many of its cooperating teachers had been "sorely troubled" by Lerner's criticism and, in many cases, had found themselves unable to answer it.[145] The drift of opinion (that began in mid-1940) linking propaganda analysis to what Mumford soon was to call a "pathological resistance to rational persuasion" eventually took the form of an avalanche and, ultimately, became the final word on the IPA in the minds of many progressive intellectuals.[146] For its part, the IPA consistently maintained that there were good and bad propagandas, judged on the basis of their social purposes, and, later, emphasized its aim to promote a "democratic morale."[147] However, it was undeniable that the IPA's single most famous contribution to propaganda study – the seven devices – was in itself insensitive to such moral determinations. Unless one purchased the IPA's study materials, it was easy to lose sight of how the organization supplemented topical debunking and universally applicable propaganda devices with the life-history method and focused group discussion. Remembered for its neutral treatments of the war and its content-insensitive detection formulae, the IPA's style appeared vulnerable when compared to other methods for fostering wartime critical thinking among students. Detractors wrote off the IPA's approach as both pseudoscientific and as captive to a mechanical, message-centered analysis detached from wider social issues.[148]

There is irony in the somewhat contradictory criticisms leveled against the IPA's theory, method, and praxis. Dismissed as not neutral enough to be considered scientific, the institute's definition of propaganda and its antipropaganda devices were, from an interventionist political reading, stigmatized as overly detached. Indeed, it was not logic but progressive politics that cost the organization its friends and funds. From the time when Miller first put together his advisory board up through 1940, the institute had found progressive scholars and educators eager to join the antipropaganda enterprise. In 1938, for instance, five individuals were invited to serve on the board – Kilpatrick (Columbia), Kefauver (Stanford), Doob (Yale), MacLean (then of Minnesota), and Graham (UCLA) – and all accepted with pleasure. For his part, Doob "leapt at the opportunity" to join the board and, in fact, was somewhat miffed that he had not been considered until the IPA's second year.[149] As late as December 1940, the institute's acceptance rate was still 50 percent when Ralph D. Casey, director of the University of Minnesota's School of Journalism, accepted the call and John A. Bartky, president of Chicago Teachers College, declined.[150]

By summer 1941, the tide of resignations from the board was matched by a precipitous falloff in the number of persons accepting election to this body. At the director's meeting of May 21, a list of eight nominees was approved:

– Eleanor Carroll of Columbia's Journalism School
– Zechariah Chafee, Jr., of Harvard Law School
– Maurice R. Davie of Yale's Sociology Department
– Donald DuShane of the National Education Association
– Earl H. Hanson, superintendent, Rock Island, Illinois, schools
– Robert M. Hutchins, president of the University of Chicago
– Henry N. MacCracken, president of Vassar College
– Peter H. Odegard, Amherst College political scientist

In July, president Mather extended the board's offer of membership to all eight in a letter conveying his characteristic admonition that "if democracy is not to perish from the earth, the average citizen must learn how to think for himself and, above all, must require considerable skill in distinguishing the plausible but false from the astonishing but true."[151]

Notwithstanding the Harvard geologist's eloquence, only two of the eight luminaries were disposed to rearrange their schedules to take up the institute's mission. Allowing that "I value highly the work of the institute," Chafee begged off on the basis of other commitments. Although DuShane credited the IPA for "doing an important work," he regretted being unable to join the board in view of his having just accepted "a position at Washington D.C. which will demand all of my time." Owing to turbulent school conditions brought by new activity in the local arsenal, superintendent Hanson similarly declined appointment. President Hutchins expressed regret at having to decline but explained that he had found it necessary to "withdraw from everything but University work," a sentiment also expressed by Vassar's MacCracken. Despite considerable efforts to win over Professor Carroll, she persisted in her declination, and Miller similarly was unable to budge DuShane. Even with the spate of disappointments, the institute secured the participation of Lee's mentor, Maurice Davie, and Peter Odegard, who was "very happy indeed to accept" notwithstanding his current leave from Amherst to promote the Treasury Department's defense bonds.[152]

Not only was the institute finding it difficult to keep its board fully staffed in the summer of '41, but the organization now found publishers unwilling to embrace its material. Before the war cast a shadow, the IPA had found editors willing, even eager, to take on its major case studies. In conveying the contract to publish the Lees' study of Father Coughlin, the Harcourt Brace editor told Lavine "how very pleased we are to have the privilege of publishing this book." Yale University Press had initiated the approach to the IPA that culminated in Lavine and Wechsler's book on war propaganda. In addition to these two completed projects, the institute found itself with more publishing inquiries than it could accommodate, with offers from Silver Burdett, Harpers, and Modern Age.[153]

In the less receptive climate of 1941, Lee and Beals found publishers unsympathetic to their proposal for a new book under the imprimatur of the IPA. Lambert Davis reported the negative assessment of such a project by editors at Harcourt Brace:

> Our final conclusion is that this isn't a good time for any real commercial exploitation of such a book. As we see it, the whole drift of public opinion for the near future will be away from the critical examination of propaganda. Frankly, I think we are going to see an increase in the extent of the voluntary censorship that already prevails in a number of fields and a growling feeling that propaganda is not to be analyzed but is to be acted on in one way or another.[154]

Had the institute joined those individuals and groups who in 1941 were accommodating themselves to war preparedness, the Lend-Lease to Britain, and the attendant self-censorship, the organization might have found a place for a propaganda analysis focused on totalitarianism abroad and intolerance at home. By embracing what might have been called a "democratic propaganda analysis" predicated on intervention, the IPA might have preserved a good measure of its theory, method, and praxis – though at the loss of its detachment. In fact, just such an opportunity had been presented to the institute between spring and fall 1940. Percy Brown, the IPA's key financial guardian angel, was angling to have the institute join other groups that were forming the Council for Democracy, the progressive-interventionist consortium.

Although realizing that Brown was all-out for the council, the institute remained cool to the idea. The office staff conceded that the IPA did "propagandize for democracy" but still did not share Brown's belief that the council would "coordinate, intensify, and expand the work being done in defense of democracy in America." Acknowledging that Brown would probably raise a quarter of a million dollars for the council from foundations, Lavine questioned whether "propaganda for democracy is synonymous with propaganda for the Allies." Lavine further doubted that all the anti-Hitler groups coming aboard the council truly were committed to a democratic society. Furthermore, he complained, the constitution of the council would dilute the institute's influence by giving many insignificant organizations a voice equal to that of the IPA.[155] Not surprisingly, the IPA's directors found that "Mr. Brown's attitude toward the IPA changed after the formation of the 'Council for Democracy' " and that the Filene fund's chief had become increasingly noncommittal about continued support. Nor was Brown alone in his views. Harland Allen, a Chicago economist who had been one of the IPA's leading proponents on the Good Will Fund board, had moved to a preparedness position and now was entreating Miller to shift the institute's policy in this direction. Lavine and Edwards, who attended organizational meetings of the Council for Democracy, conveyed their impression that groups were joining the council chiefly "for the money they can get from it." In their estimation, Brown believed that the institute's reluctance to join was a sign that the IPA perhaps had outlived its usefulness.[156]

Through 1940, the Good Will Fund had been remarkably loyal to the institute, supporting the antipropaganda bureau despite financial uncertainties ensuing from the settlement of the late Filene's estate and despite trustees' concerns that opinions expressed in the bulletin might compromise the fund's tax-exempt status. For its part, the institute had justified the pains of its chief donor by working against anti-Semitism and domestic extremism. But now that issues of preparedness and intervention were uppermost in the minds of Filene's trustees and other progressives, the expensive and controversial institute must have appeared as a luxury that grantors no longer could afford. The Good Will Fund was deaf to continued overtures from the IPA, and the institute plied the American Jewish Committee to no avail with the IPA's progressive study materials used in Santa Barbara and Springfield (Massachusetts).[157] After the institute suspended operations in October 1941, Miller recalled how his unrequited fund-raising efforts of the previous year contrasted to the relatively easy money available from interventionist (or isolationist) groups. But Miller probably expressed a view common to members of the IPA's remaining board when he reflected that "the institute could neither solicit nor accept such money and still retain its integrity."[158]

In two meetings on October 29, 1941, held at the Advertising Club of New York, the institute's leadership decided to surrender to what increasingly seemed to be the inevitable. At 5:20 P.M., an executive-committee group consisting of Lee, Miller, Mather, Johnson, and Speer convened. Lee reminded those present that the IPA lacked a book for use in the fall promotional campaign unlike the situations of 1939 and 1940. To this Lee added his doubts that the institute's publications would be able to generate sufficient funds to offset the $10,000 cut in income brought by the Good Will Fund's reduced final grant that was available for 1941–1942. In view of the financial situation, the IPA's executives discussed creating a disposition committee that, by December 1, would review the institute's prospects for survival, but the group deferred action until the board meeting that was to follow immediately.

After dinner, the institute's leadership reconvened as the board of directors (with Long replacing Speer). President Mather reminded the group of the board's decision of February 27 to meet again in the event of war or the imminent onset of war. Mather expressed the opinion that Franklin Roosevelt's October 27 speech on conditions in the Atlantic "made it abundantly obvious that the United States is now involved in the war on a 'shooting basis.' " After extensive discussion, the group agreed to suspend publication of *Propaganda Analysis* and to liquidate the office.[159]

In the institute's press release of October 31, President Mather explained that in the present emergency "it is not practical to attempt dispassionate analysis of the steps being taken to impress the country with the seriousness of the crisis." Mather added that the institute could operate with integrity only in an atmosphere in which it would "be free to analyze all propaganda methods, whether good or bad." The *New York Herald Tribune* reprinted this release with the subheading "Institute Here Fears Its Work May Hurt Defense Effort." This caption anticipated the explanation later given in the February 1942 issue of *Propaganda Analysis* that the IPA recognized its "analyses could be misused for undesirable purposes by persons opposing the government's efforts."[160]

Miller was not happy that the IPA's public statements on suspension focused more on general wartime ideological self-restraint and less on the specific inability of the organization to raise funds in the changed social climate. Miller long had believed that the institute could play an important role during a wartime America, particularly in "immunizing young people and adults against propagandas calculated to incite racial and religious intolerance," and in fall 1940, a majority of the board had seemed to agree. Miller emphasized that his own vote to suspend had been based solely on reasons of funding, and he doubted whether the full board would have shelved the organization had money been available for continued operations.[161] As it was, only the willingness of *Common Sense* magazine to assume unexpired subscriptions and the decision of the Good Will Fund to extend additional monies permitted the IPA to meet its obligations to subscribers, staff, and creditors.[162]

From its inception, the Mather–Filene–Miller organization had served to institutionalize the antipropaganda movement of the 1920s and 1930s. The institute functioned as a perfectly natural union of several important vectors of the progressive movement's diffusion into social-action agencies after the Great War. Major participants in the institute's work also had significant ties to adult education (Kirtley Mather), the consumer movement (Robert Lynd), progressive journalism (Miller and Alfred Lee), progressive education (Miller, Edgar Dale, James Mendenhall), progressive social science scholarship (Charles Beard, Leonard Doob, James Shotwell), and critical social science (Lynd and Lee). As it became a focus for 1930s progressivism, the IPA also drew in educators who were interested in critical thinking (Edward Glaser) and in discussion and debate (Gladys Graham and Alan Nichols).

The IPA's great strength stemmed from its particular fusion of academic and practical progressivism into an organized antipropaganda critique that institutionalized the tradition of muckraking and also applied this characteristically American critical approach to the discontents of the Depression. Had not the war intervened, the institute might have weathered challenges from practitioners (the complaints of Gallup and Bernays), from polemicists (the Dies and Beals imbroglios), from grant-based communication science (the concerns of Cantril and the General Education Board), and from educators who found the IPA's definitions and devices variously too detached or too cynical to inculcate critical thinking in students properly. Ultimately, it was the muckraking critics themselves who exposed the essential weakness of their praxis of progressive propaganda analysis. When progressives rearranged their politics to favor the war, they projected in bold relief the annoying, self-reflexive character of propaganda analysis. It was not easy to be entirely happy with a critical apparatus that cast aspersions on the political commitments of its own operatives. Satisfaction was out of the question when those commitments anticipated a life-and-death struggle against democracy's fascist enemies.

CHAPTER 6

PROPAGANDA FOR DEMOCRACY

In the section on anthropology of the *Transactions of the New York Academy of Sciences* for fall 1943 appeared an article on radio and film propaganda contributed by Paul Lazarsfeld and his colleague in sociology at Columbia, Robert K. Merton. Although featuring data gathered by the authors as part of their wartime communication research, this collaborative treatise on contemporary symbolism functioned as a Pronunciamento.

> But it is long since time to halt discussions of propaganda in the large; discussions which have all the fascination of speculation uncontrolled by empirical inquiry. To bring certain problems of propaganda into clear focus, we must turn to propaganda in the particular, and develop definite procedures for testing our interpretations. It is not that general discussions of propaganda are necessarily invalid; it is only that they tend to outrun our funded knowledge. They are big with the bigness of vacuity.[1]

With the IPA safely interred alongside other early casualties of World War II, most of Lazarsfeld and Merton's readers would have recognized immediately that the progressive propaganda critics were the ones slated for replacement by new recruits mustering out of Columbia's Office of Radio Research. The Lazarsfeld–Merton piece suggested that the future belonged not to those who studied propaganda from a historical-cultural vantage point but rather to those who probed "the ascertainable effects of particular propaganda documents" for the purpose of "advising the writers and producers of this propaganda." In this view, society demanded research leading to "decision and action" in contrast to the old criticism's muddled and mottled "attitude of critical distrust."

This Is the Enemy

In their own public pronouncements up to 1941, progressive propaganda critics had managed to overlook what others construed as a spreading chasm between progressivism's commitment to democracy and its antipropaganda instrumentalities. To Edgar Dale it seemed obvious that, on the one hand, "to combat Fascism we must . . . teach the common man to detect and analyze propaganda," and on the other, that teachers must "realize that some types of propaganda are a valuable means of promoting desirable institutions such as health, economic security, and democracy itself."[2] The IPA's suspension, however, argued otherwise such that only the rural tangent of progressivism, reinforced by isolationist politics, held out against the rising tide of interventionist sentiment in fall 1941.

The last hurrah of progressivism's antipropaganda spirit took the form of a polemical rear-guard action led by Senator Gerald Nye who, just weeks before Pearl Harbor, held hearings on so-called pro-Ally propaganda in American films. Nye sat as an early witness before his own committee to charge that Hollywood's handful of powerful studio heads were using the silver screen to build up sentiment for joining Britain and France. What else could explain the recent appearance of such pictures as *Convoy, I Married a Nazi, Sergeant York, Confessions of a Nazi Spy,* and *The Great Dictator?* Nye repeated allegations that Harry Warner had circulated a petition begging FDR to give destroyers to Britain. Even granting that Americans did not like Hitler, Nye maintained, why did the movie industry have to make "hatred our fueling passion" such that the nation might forget its own interests?

For their part, the movie moguls of 1941 were no more willing to admit to a propagandistic purpose than William Randolph Hearst had been in 1927 when he faced the Senate's ire for publishing stories about Mexico's alleged bribery of members of Congress. Acknowledging that he supported FDR's foreign policy, Harry Warner of Warner Brothers held fast to the idea that sentiments were not the same as propaganda. "While I am opposed to nazi-ism, I deny that the pictures produced by my company are 'propaganda,' as has been alleged." *Confessions of a Nazi Spy,* for instance, reflected actual testimony heard in federal court. *Sergeant York* was merely a factual portrait of a hero from the Great War. Warner insisted that his studio's only guilt was "accurately recording on the screen the world as it is or as it has been." In the same vein, Darryl Zanuck wondered how Nye could even consider deterring studios from "dealing with subjects as timely, as vital, and as important as the current upheaval in the world."[3]

Nye's hearings amounted to the last gasp of the progressive antipropaganda spirit that, until the fall of France, had retained an enthusiastic following. The shift from neutralism to interventionism among progressive opinion leaders could be discerned from the number of former IPA officials who had arrived in Washington. Doob now served with the Coordinator of Inter-American Affairs (CIAA); Cantril with the Research Council, Inc.; Beals with the Office of War Information; Barrington Moore (briefly an IPA staff researcher) with the Justice Department; and Peter Odegard with the Treasury. Among progressive academicians who stayed home, a concern for national morale was replacing the former anxiety about propaganda.

"By way of a broad generalization we may say that from the fall of 1940 to the spring of 1942, social psychologists were pre-occupied with problems of civilian morale."[4] This comment by social psychologists Gordon Allport and Helene Veltfort headlined a 1943 report in which the authors summarized some 306 recent articles in social science journals that related to the conduct of the war. Even earlier, in summer 1941, bibliography had given testimony to the extent of social psychology's turn to topics of war when the Emergency Committee in Psychology took over the *Psychological Bulletin* for a special issue on "Military Psychology." As part of this compendium, Irvin Child reviewed some 98 articles or books treating matters of morale that had been published chiefly in 1939 and 1940. Child's categories included methods for assessing opinions and group climate, conditions that improved or worsened morale, and problems of social adjustment in industrial, family, cultural, and military groups.[5]

Providing further evidence of the new trend in public opinion scholarship were theme issues on morale that appeared in the fall 1941 issues of the *Journal of Educational Sociology* and the *American Journal of Sociology*. The former collection focused on problems of measuring and improving mental stamina on the home front during a time of crisis. Particularly interesting was a proposal for local morale managers contributed by Gregory Bateson and Margaret Mead. In their view, morale specialists and educators were natural allies because both favored "socially adaptive attitudes and values." Those who aimed to steady the civilian mind shared with teachers an awareness that it was important to avoid methods that would promote psychological conflicts. Bateson and Mead favored a localized social influence that would avoid propaganda's psychological disruptions, which, they believed, dulled a person's response to all symbols. They proposed the appointment of morale "wardens," close-at-hand opinion leaders, who would encourage local initiative and thereby avoid the odium attached to the national, top–down cajolery that had typified the work of the Creel committee.[6]

An even more comprehensive compendium about morale was to be found in the November 1941 number of the *American Journal of Sociology*. Psychiatrist Harry Stack Sullivan opened the discussion by making the connection between morale and efficiency. "Ineffectual persons anywhere in the social organization are a menace to the whole." The sixteen articles that followed Sullivan's fleshed out how communication channels and academic specialties could help to mobilize minds. James Angell of NBC described how radio contributed immediacy and psychological intimacy to mental mettle. Robert Park wrote of how public discussion combated social fragmentation. In the estimation of Walter Wanger, Hollywood producer, movies not only could inspire viewers about the principles of democracy but also could afford "individual relaxation from the urgent problems which crises impose." Edward Ames of the University of Chicago explained how religion helped people to identify and serve the key values of life. Eduard Lindeman, social-work expert and former IPA president, showed how recreation promoted sound bodies and minds, enabling people to "behave efficiently under pressure." Louis Wirth of the University of Chicago believed that if policy makers emphasized the common aspirations of Americans, the nation would be protected against Nazi efforts to sow dissatisfaction among minorities.[7]

Academicians recognized that the abrupt shift from propaganda critique to morale building raised the specter of manipulation. However, William Hocking of Harvard believed that contemporary social bolstering could escape association with the Great War's discredited persuasions if new-style morale building were grounded on reason, realism, and a willingness to acknowledge defects in America.[8] Yet service more than self-reflection was on the minds of leading academicians who now searched for ways to bring their work to the attention of defense agencies. In an effort to promote a liaison between academe and policy makers, the Division of Anthropology and Psychology of the National Research Council established an Emergency Committee in Psychology. This group mounted a major conference on "Psychological Factors in Morale" in November 1940. The Society for the Psychological Study of Social Issues formed a Committee on Morale and Leadership Research that metamorphosed into Gordon Allport's Committee on War Service and Research. Particularly active in this group were Kurt Lewin and Alvin Zander, leading researchers on group dynamics. In the realm of the public schools, teachers were recruited in the enterprise to bolster the national psyche through pamphlets distributed by the U.S. Office of Education that explained how to implement discussion forums in school and community.[9]

Among the most significant of academic social science's war apparatuses was the Committee for National Morale formed in July 1940 and affiliated with the Council for Democracy. The group's Subcommittee on Psychology included Gordon W. Allport, Hadley Cantril, Leonard Doob, Kurt Lewin, and Goodwin Watson. Active in the Subcommittee on Social Science were Gregory Bateson and Margaret Mead. Other social science luminaries flocking to the Morale Committee included Robert M. Yerkes of Yale, who had developed the Army's World War I intelligence tests. In this atmosphere, even Robert S. Lynd felt lured to the praxis of antifascist opinion engineering. Lynd had worked with the Agriculture Department's morale committee and, in fall 1940, proposed a project on public morale to the National Research Council that carried an anticipated cost of $250,000.[10]

Although important, morale was only one dimension of the nation's symbolic mobilization being investigated by academicians prior to the Day of Infamy. On November 26, 1939, representatives of the American Association for Applied Psychology met with deputies from the army, navy, and Department of Justice in a Round Table on Possible Psychological Contributions in a National Emergency. Discussants pursued a number of promising leads, not only reprising the intelligence-testing and personnel-selection work of the Great War but also considering how psychologists might aid in detecting spies and in maintaining morale and discipline among the troops. The relation of psychology to the home front also loomed large. For instance, Major Louis B. Hershey thought the profession of psychology might aid in establishing a favorable public attitude toward the draft. Also prominent on the agenda was the more general question of whether Gallup's psychological survey methods might be employed "for the adjustment of the home populations in the matter of war aims."[11]

The anxiousness of academicians to be of service was palpable, reflected not only in official liaisons between the academy and the military but also by the militarization of scholarship in the social science journals. Articles of the period dealt with how to probe the psyche of enemy populations, plant rumors, and rapidly promote in military rank those who measured up as I.Q. geniuses. Sociologist Stuart Queen offered that his profession might help by discovering "how propaganda works" and then by showing how the findings "may be put to practical use by government, industry, church, or any other social institution." For its part, Harvard University's Department of Psychology released periodic Worksheets in Morale. Speech teachers believed that they could boost civilian esprit by teaching the classics of American democracy and union. Education faculty looked for ways to help reverse the recent skepticism about war and propaganda.[12] Sadly, all such efforts to be useful could not completely militate feelings among academicians that they were outsiders to the important work going on in the Office of War Information (OWI) and Office of Strategic Services (OSS).[13]

Like the academicians, practitioners of the persuasive arts also felt the impulse to flock to the colors. Clyde Beals, who had replaced Lavine at the IPA, joined the OWI as one of the many journalists who took official service in the war agencies. A large number of advertising and marketing professionals similarly took appointments with the OWI. Still others, such as Edward Bernays, preferred to pitch suggestions from the sidelines. In *Speak Up for Democracy* (1940), the public relations guru and erstwhile CPI man offered ways to promote speakers, events, and forums as well as how to employ the press, public holidays, the schools, and educational associations. He emphasized the need to be on guard against various saboteurs of democracy including not only the Nazi appeasers but also the superpatriots and the antilabor and anti–civil-rights groups.[14]

Tools of Democracy

During the Great War, the contributions of journalism and advertising practitioners had far overshadowed those few initiatives undertaken by government servants drawn from faculty ranks. In World War II, however, the ivory-tower types more than held their own. Communication researchers were particularly poised to serve the war effort in ways that permanently raised the status of their incipient specialty. Wartime service gave this new paradigm of social influence an opportunity not only to find its social niche but also to diffuse widely its slant on symbolic inducement. Administrative-type propaganda analysis burgeoned as one avenue for intellectuals to monitor and modify opinion both national and international.

Some of the earliest war-related survey research was carried out on an informal and somewhat covert basis when Hadley Cantril first began to do polling work for the Roosevelt administration. Already by the mid-1930s, Cantril had made contact with Gallup, who, welcoming recognition of his new methods by an academic scholar, offered the Princeton man the full use of his facilities at cost. Later, in 1940, Cantril secured a Rockefeller Foundation grant to set up the Office of Public Opinion Research at Princeton. The objectives of this new institute included not only learning how to measure public opinion systematically and accurately but also understanding the psychology of public opinion, "how and why it changes, what motivates large segments of the public." Believing that the United States shortly would be joining

Britain, Cantril was particularly interested in monitoring the course of public opinion on intervention versus isolation. He also devoted much effort to probing the reliability of small samples in the belief that public opinion polling in wartime would require both rapid assessments of the American public and tightly organized clandestine polling in enemy territory.

Cantril's small-scale program at Princeton became more extensive in September 1940 when Nelson Rockefeller, FDR's Coordinator of Inter-American Affairs, asked the Princeton psychologist "to set up mechanisms which would gauge public opinion in Latin America." In cooperation with Gallup, and with funds from the Office of Emergency Management, Cantril established an ostensibly independent research organization, American Social Surveys. He recruited his friend Leonard Doob and another researcher, Lloyd Free, to analyze Nazi propaganda coming into Latin America. Through Rockefeller's office, the results of Cantril's program were brought to the attention of FDR. The president asked Cantril to monitor public sentiment on avoiding war versus aiding Britain. Cantril duly kept tabs on views about aiding England and on the public's willingness to change U.S. neutrality laws in favor of Britain.

Until Pearl Harbor, Cantril had been using the facilities of Gallup's American Institute of Public Opinion; but in late 1941, the Princeton psychologist accepted the offer of financier Gerald B. Lambert to underwrite a separate survey apparatus called Research Council, Inc. Cantril's Research Council conducted polls on demand from the White House and on contract from various wartime agencies. FDR was particularly interested in trends of opinion pointing to "the willingness of Americans to make peace with the German army, on the one hand, and Hitler on the other hand." Cantril also followed developments in Roosevelt's approval ratings and, on occasion, served up data on a short-order basis. In March 1944, Cantril's office conducted an overnight, small-sample poll for the White House on Protestant and Catholic opinion on bombing Rome. This snapshot of opinion provided needed reassurances two days before the Air Corps launched heavy attacks. Earlier, in 1942, data from Cantril had helped to convince the Allied leaders to place American troops in the vanguard of the invasion of North Africa on the basis of findings that the Vichy soldiers would resist more against the British. Cantril, drawing upon early experiments on clandestine polling, had helped the Psychological Warfare Branch of Military Intelligence to question unobtrusively French colonial officials about an Allied invasion.

However much Gallup had touted his survey techniques as socially neutral, his pupil Cantril proved that polling could be part and parcel of administrative strategizing. Cantril and Lambert endeavored to demonstrate that their data could help FDR to better manage his relations with Congress. After learning from Cantril that the public preferred a friendly approach to a scolding one, FDR softened the tone of a March 1944 address to Congress. After Cantril reported findings that the public would respond well to the president's admitting some errors, FDR told Congress that a certain number of mistakes were inevitable in so large an undertaking. In a noteworthy earlier episode, Roosevelt had released, verbatim, a text provided by Cantril and Lambert announcing General Douglas MacArthur's removal from the Philippines to head the Pacific campaign elsewhere. The Cantril–Lambert communiqúe was carefully worded to reflect findings that the public was equally split on whether MacArthur should fight or flee. Accordingly, FDR announced MacArthur's successful escape through Japanese lines, at the same time praising the general for his soldierly preference to fight to the finish with his forces in Manila Bay. In rendering his own perspective on administrative polling, Cantril lauded Roosevelt for not basing his policies on polls but rather using "such information to try to bring the public around more quickly or more effectively to the course of action he felt was best for the country."

In addition to the domestic polling operation mounted by Cantril, knowledgeable officials saw a need to monitor, transcribe, and analyze fascist propaganda systematically. This imperative had been one that underlaid the effort by Cantril, Doob, and Free to assess for Rockefeller's CIAA office the impact of various German and Italian propagandas on South America. So limited was the early American Social Surveys operation that, according to Doob, the address of the organization was none other than his own private residence in Hampton, Connecticut. In an effort to stimulate a broader administrative propaganda analysis, the Rockefeller Foundation had provided a grant in fall 1939 to establish what became known as the Princeton Listening Center. Directed by Harold Graves, the center monitored broadcasts emanating from Berlin, Moscow, London, Rome, and Paris with the objective of analyzing these materials "in order to understand better the psychology behind Nazi propaganda and possibly help predict Axis moves." The next spring, Graves and many of his staff moved to Washington to become part of a more extensive official government monitoring unit established by Lloyd Free under the Federal Communications Commission (FCC).[15]

Biweekly reports issued by the Princeton Listening Center presaged the quite extensive program of analysis undertaken by the Foreign Broadcast Intelligence Service (FBIS) of the FCC. The FBIS employed a large staff of "psychologists, sociologists, communication people, political scientists," many of whom would figure prominently in postwar communication research. Notable members of the FBIS team were John Marshall of the Rockefeller Foundation, Theodore Newcomb of Michigan, Otto Klineberg of Columbia, John Gardner of the Carnegie Corporation, Hans Speier, later chief of the RAND Corporation's division of social sciences, and Bernard Berelson, a junior colleague of Lazarsfeld and Douglas Waples and later director of the Ford Foundation's behavioral-science program. For a time, the chief analyst was Goodwin Watson of Columbia's Teachers College.[16]

Sifting through short-wave transcriptions to ascertain "the intentions, strategy, and calculations behind propaganda communications," the analysis group of the FBIS refined an administrative kind of propaganda scrutiny that predicted enemy initiatives. In some cases, the FBIS's analysts focused on the immediate content of Axis broadcasts, searching for the appearance of key symbols and noting also both the frequency of symbols and the ratio of relevant and irrelevant content. On other occasions, the social scientists of the FBIS pursued a more general approach that attempted to draw connections between the content of radio broadcasts and the habitual behavior of Germany's propaganda-producing elites. Knowing that Goebbels, the Nazi propaganda chief, also functioned as a key policy maker, analysts were alert to how Berlin seemed to use propaganda in advance of major actions. Analysts developed rules of thumb regarding the characteristic goals of German preparatory propaganda as well as the typical occasions of, audiences for, and communication channels used by such propaganda content. In one case, analysts predicted an imminent decision by Germany to initiate hostilities against Brazil on the basis that Radio Berlin had begun to issue threats of a kind to which "no nation in Latin America would bow." A later assessment by Alexander George, FBIS junior analyst, concluded that the predictions issued by the analysis section of the organization had been correct in between 81 and 85 percent of cases as corroborated by later historical evidence.[17]

With the outbreak of war, social scientists became involved in significant efforts to influence opinion as well as to measure it. One of the oldest programs that married survey research to policy making was Rensis Likert's survey operation in the Department of Agriculture. Likert's interviewers fanned out among America's farmers, memorizing carefully scheduled interview frameworks that, when administered to farmers, appeared to be open-ended conversations. Researchers later scored their interviews on five-point scales, also summarizing the conversations in narrative form. In some cases, two interviewers not only participated in a conversation but also independently rated it to allow for a check on data reliability. At Likert's central research bureau, the reports were analyzed "for types of arguments or thought-sequences." Frequency counts were made and cross-tabulated with a variety of economic and attitudinal data with the objective of finding out how farmers adjusted to new situations and policies.[18]

As the war approached, Likert's researchers also began to study the morale and bolster the attitudes of the farm population. Several months before Pearl Harbor, the Department of Agriculture was questioning local opinion leaders in dairy communities about what the United States should do about the war and about what factors might lead to increases in milk production. This information was gathered in preparation for a program whereby local farm committeemen were to contact their neighbors "to encourage farmers to raise more food of all kinds." The Department of Agriculture recommended that farm committee people explain to dairymen in their area that production goals were part of "a defense program." "The idea is to get enough food to take care of our own needs and help feed England."[19] Likert (who later organized an institute of social research at the University of Michigan) was widely recognized during the war for having put together a program that combined the most advanced survey research of the day (Lazarsfeld as a consultant) with cogent administrative propaganda analysis (Lasswell as a consultant). His program kept departmental propaganda appeals closely linked to research.[20]

However much social scientists such as Likert, Cantril, and the minions of the FBIS wanted to unite policy to social research, their efforts were not always completely successful. The earliest attempts to connect policy to polling were either somewhat out of the policy mainstream, as in the case of Likert's bureau, were somewhat informal and episodic, as was true of Cantril's independent survey research shop, or had no direct link to policy, as proved to be the situation in the FCC's radio-monitoring operation. The difficulty in bringing together research and policy into a comprehensive propaganda nexus sprang not only from Roosevelt's preference for competition among his advisers and advisory boards but also from memories of Creel's notorious juggernaut.

Wartime Washington ultimately saw a succession of somewhat overlapping propaganda shops rather than a Creel-style centralized propaganda enterprise. William J. Donovan, a Republican businessman and world traveler, won approval from FDR in July 1941 for his Office of the Coordinator of Information (COI), which, notwithstanding its bland title, was to be dedicated not only to intelligence gathering but also to military subversion. In August 1941, Robert Sherwood, playwright and speechwriter for FDR, established a Foreign Information Service (FIS) under the COI and brought on line a government radio propaganda station, the Voice of America (VOA), whose broadcasts began in February 1942. Another information agency, the Office of Facts and Figures (OFF), was established in October 1941 under poet Archibald MacLeish. OFF aspired to become a domestic information clearinghouse but ultimately was folded into a larger OWI in 1942. Tensions between Donovan and Sherwood in the COI office led to a split in June 1942 whereby the FIS became the Overseas Branch of the OWI. Donovan thereafter concentrated on covert activity in his OSS, which held a seat on the Joint Chiefs of Staff. Despite the administrative divorce, the OWI and OSS habitually contested the custody of overseas propaganda. Another competitor entering the fray after May 1943 was the Psychological Warfare Branch of the armed forces (reconstituted in 1944 as the Psychological Warfare Division of the Supreme Headquarters, Allied Expeditionary Forces).[21]

Out of the juggling of administrative titles and functions that characterized the wartime propaganda agencies, the OWI emerged as the closest thing to the CPI in title if not in function. On the domestic scene, the OWI went through a metamorphosis similar to that of the Creel committee, moving from an emphasis on coordinating news to a focus on conducting promotions to increase support for the war. The agency released pamphlets and documentaries and also established an office to advise the film industry on ways to build wartime morale. As had been the case with the CPI, the Domestic Branch of the OWI suffered from the suspicion of Congress that the organization aimed chiefly to boost the political standing of the president. Further, the progressive ideology expressed in the OWI publications and in movie liaison work drew fire from conservatives. During the war, Southern congressmen criticized the racial equality promoted by the OWI – for instance, in the agency's publication, *Negroes and the War*. After the war, when the nation's attention shifted to Russia, certain of the OWI's efforts to promote good feeling toward our Soviet ally would prove embarrassing.

The OWI quickly discovered that, even more than in 1917–1918, propaganda sponsored by a pluralistic government conjured up a variety of irrepressible conflicts. For their part, the OWI's idealistic writers favored a progressive reform agenda similar to that proclaimed by the CPI. Fearing that a focus on Pearl Harbor leant an excessively defensive cast to the war, OWI pamphleteers such as Arthur Schlesinger, Jr., and Malcolm Cowley preferred to recast the war as an antifascist crusade that harkened to a new era in international cooperation. When conservative members of Congress objected to defining the war in leftist ideological terms, the resulting notoriety alarmed OWI policy makers, who feared for the fate of the agency's appropriations. The senior staff of the Domestic Branch, headed by Gardner Cowles, Jr., Gallup's old mentor, attempted to rein in the writers, precipitating a rebellion within the OWI. A group of wordsmiths continued to press for their utopian program and against the tendency of administrators to favor the more contentless and sloganistic promotionalism of the War Advertising Council. Finding little support for their effort to frame the war in liberal terms, these writers resigned en masse, issuing an intemperate public statement charging that the OWI's domestic work was controlled by "high-pressure promoters who prefer slick salesmanship to honest information."[22]

The effort of the OWI's domestic division to infuse progressivism into wartime radio and movies represented a more indirect and ultimately more successful strategy for liberalizing the hostilities. Although authorized by the FCC to assume control of broadcasting, the OWI's Radio Program Bureau believed that it could avoid the odium of "government propaganda" by indirectly influencing programming. Accordingly, the bureau prepared Fact Sheets for radio stations that explained why a given message was important and that suggested ways that the government's plea could be incorporated into programming. For instance, the Fact Sheet of November 20, 1942, asked radio stations to spread the word: "DON'T TRAVEL AT XMAS." This OWI release emphasized that military travel required civilians to minimize unnecessary trips by train, bus, and auto. "The success of radio's selling hinges on creating a strong contrast between the *essential* and the *non-essential* trip." The OWI recommended playing on the consciences of the civilian whose selfish pleasure trip might make a soldier miss his Christmas visit home.[23]

The OWI's radio bureau sometimes went beyond the role of broadcast adviser to become the producer and distributor of announcements or programming. The agency prepared and distributed spot messages ready for broadcast. For instance, to promote good feelings toward America's allies, the agency arranged for radio commentators to record forty-three facts that the OWI believed would disprove certain misunderstandings and rumors about the United Nations (that OWI researchers had identified). The agency distributed these recorded messages to stations which agreed to play them six times in each of six weeks. The radio bureau also encouraged broadcast networks to modify existing programs in ways that better conveyed wartime themes. In some cases, the bureau executed and distributed its own series, such as "This Is War" and "This Is Our Enemy." OWI also helped to distribute programs sponsored by other federal agencies such as the "Treasury Star Parade." This latter program offered dramatic plays calculated to stir wartime emotions. One notable Treasury program was "Chicago, Germany" (spring 1942), which depicted starvation, forced Germanization, racial laws, and slave-labor camps imposed in the Windy City after the German conquest.[24]

Just as the OWI worked to promote strategic treatments of the war on radio, so too did the agency's movie-liaison office angle for film studios to supply the OWI with advance copies of scripts. The office had in mind more movies like *Mrs. Miniver* (1942), MGM's saga of a heroic English family bravely confronting the war's dangers and privations (produced before the OWI was up and running) and fewer of the kind that relied on anti-Japanese hatred and paranoia. First on the agency's list of seven guidelines for movie makers was the question "Will this picture help win the war?" Last was the cautionary question of whether the public later might "have reason to say they were misled by propaganda." In between these poles could be found the OWI's clearly expressed desire for Hollywood to tell the story of a people's total war pitting democracy against evil. Not desiring that film producers completely whitewash the nation's shortcomings, the OWI nevertheless advised emphasizing that the underprivileged were becoming less so.

The OWI's film monitors similarly favored an upbeat attitude toward the USSR in the belief that anti-Russian attitudes were an impediment to winning the war. So the agency applauded Warner Brothers' agreement to produce a film version of *Mission to Moscow,* the memoirs of Joseph E. Davies, Roosevelt's ambassador to the USSR between 1936 and 1938.[25] The film's opening scenes showed Davies traveling through the Red realm, impressed by how workers shared in the profits of their factories and collective farms. No dogmatic communism here: "Our methods are trial and error," explained Foreign Minister Vyacheslav Molotov. Davies observed Soviet officials dealing with curious instances of sabotage, allusions that lend plausibility to Stalin's purge trials, where opponents were executed for conspiracy and treason. Warner's movie suggested that Stalin's opponents were agents of the Germans and Japanese, and, to deny that confessions of the accused had been coerced and scripted, Davies was shown as "inclined to believe these confessions" based on twenty years' experience with trials. Later, Davies and other Western diplomats marveled about the Red Army on parade in Moscow. "At least one European nation is ready," the ambassador enthused, "and I say thank God for it." The kindly Stalin then took Davies aside to confide that he aimed to join "with the other democracies" (other?) against Hitler and begged Davies to pass the word to FDR. After Stalin offered that his regime never had reneged on a treaty obligation, Ambassador Davies put in that "your past record speaks well for the future."

In the immediate future, however, was the notorious Hitler–Stalin pact, which freed the Nazi dictator to invade Poland. To rationalize Stalin's complicity with Hitler, *Mission to Moscow* showed Davies and Winston Churchill speculating that Stalin might wisely undertake a "temporary" nonaggression pact to allow time for more preparation against the Nazis. When Germany later invaded Russia, Davies explained to FDR that the major obstacles to aiding Russia had been the domestic "fascist propagandists" who had poisoned the minds of Americans against the Soviet Union. A later scene showed U.S. businessmen anticipating lucrative trade with Hitler. The final portion of the film found Davies touring the United States to set the record straight on Russia. When a hostile questioner confronted the ambassador with Stalin's invasion of little Finland, Davies explained that the Finns had refused to swap land with the USSR and that this obstinacy threatened to prevent Stalin from preparing properly against the coming German horde. In a concluding voice-over narrative, Davies clarified that Russia's sacrifices had given the United States time to respond, with the result that Hitler's star now was fading. Continuing, in an epilogue delivered against the background of a shining city, Davies expounded on World War II as a "people's war" that would allow Americans to bring an end to war forever.

Even granting that the USSR in 1943 was bearing the brunt of the war against Hitler, the mission of *Mission to Moscow* was not universally welcomed at the time. Although the OWI and Jack Warner applauded the film for affirming Russia as a reliable ally, others bristled at suggestions that Stalin's blackened image was purely the product of domestic fascists or that prewar American isolationists were a small band of questionable irreconcilables. Liberals such as John Dewey blanched at the effort to dress up Stalin's purge trials in the garb of a progressive march toward collective security. William Randolph Hearst cabled Warner that his new picture perfectly presented "the communist side" of the case. After 1945, when the United States saw Soviet Russia as more competitor than ally, conservatives and reactionaries would gain a surer footing for driving home their own verdict on *Mission to Moscow* and other similar offerings of the war years.[26]

Just as the OWI's domestic wing reprised the CPI's tendency to oversell hostilities by wrapping them in a sometimes ill-fitting ideological raiment, the Overseas Branch of OWI resurrected conditions of the

Great War where academicians labored against odds to compete with communication practitioners. Leonard Doob, who served both as researcher and policy chief of the OWI's Overseas Branch, described the difficult situation faced by social scientists in an agency that paid "lip-service" to basing propaganda on facts and analysis but more often preferred a quick "hit-and-miss approach." In this intellectually permissive atmosphere, considerable weight was given not only to "risky and dogmatic inferences" by analysts who monitored foreign radio transmissions and newspapers but also to predictions by emigrés about how their compatriots might react to VOA broadcasts. Less frequently did social scientists "pool the available data and information of all experts in order to determine systematically – in terms of social science principles – how people might respond to propaganda."[27]

In neither domestic nor foreign fronts did the hurried, practical propaganda work of the OWI leave much room for academicians to draw from their strong suits of social science theorizing and in-depth quantification. Even if social scientists had reigned supreme in the OWI, however, such an enhanced status would not have guaranteed them direct access to the war's chief policy makers because their agency functioned as a propaganda retailer rather than wholesaler. Unlike Dr. Goebbels, whose Nazi propaganda shop directly advised Hitler, the OWI's key policy administrators took their instructions from higher up. OWI's policy people merely kept propaganda tied to what they knew to be official policy, what they assumed was policy, or what seemed appropriate given the nation's planned course of action.

Not only were the OWI's academicians limited to coordinating and distributing propaganda to expedite higher policy; their agency lacked an exclusive franchise in the key sphere of overseas communication. As had been the case with Creel's CPI, the OWI was unable to prevent the military from setting up its own somewhat-competing propaganda apparatus. Already in January 1942, the army was putting out the call to Heber Blankenhorn to help set up a program of psychological warfare. Unfortunately, as Blankenhorn reported, he was required to reprise the situation that he faced in 1917 when he had started from scratch against a background of army hostility or indifference, suffering further from "the same procession" of would-be civilian counselors.[28] Soon enough, however, it became clear that if there were to be an energetic wartime propaganda, the action would be practical and would take place in khaki.

In Psychological Warfare Division (PWD) parlance, all propaganda was divided into three parts. White propaganda was that directly identified as coming from Allied sources. Most familiar here, perhaps, were the safe-conduct passes that the Allies intended for soldiers of the Wehrmacht to keep in their possession for use when surrendering. These official-looking documents, bearing the facsimile signature of Dwight D. Eisenhower, Supreme Commander of the Allied Expeditionary Force, directed Allied troops to disarm, care for, and promptly remove from the battle area any surrendering German soldier or group of soldiers. The army's gray propaganda included those leaflets that bore no indication of their origin. A classic exemplar was *Nachrichten für die Truppe* [*News for the Troops*], prepared by the OSS and its British counterpart for the Psychological Warfare Division. Published in German, *Nachrichten* updated enemy soldiers on events back home about which German radio was saying little. Completing the army's threefold battery of paper bullets was the so-called black propaganda of overtly subversive leaflets and broadcasts purporting to originate from enemy sources. Notable was Radio "Annie," operated by the 12th Army which presented itself as a clandestine radio station of loyal but disillusioned Rhinelanders. Surveys taken among German POWs by army researchers suggested that somewhere between 65 and 90 percent of German soldiers saw PWD leaflets and that, in most cases, around 75 percent were influenced by them.[29]

Social Science and Promotional Democracy

Had social science's contributions to the war been limited to participation in the FBIS, OWI, and PWD, its record would have scarcely improved from that registered in World War I. However, the war years saw two particularly rarefied enterprises of social science take root in government service. First to emerge was Harold Lasswell's content-analysis shop bivouacked in the Library of Congress. Second was the army's Research Branch.

Since 1939, Lasswell had been participating in a round table on communication research organized by John Marshall of the Rockefeller Foundation's division of humanities. Others of the group included Paul Lazarsfeld, Hadley Cantril, Ralph Casey, Harwood Childs, and Douglas Waples. As the war approached, members of this informal consortium began to reflect over how studies in mass communication and public opinion might contribute to the national defense. Lasswell was invited to apply for a grant to further his work on methods for analyzing content and dissecting propaganda. He received a two-year stipend from the Rockefeller Foundation, later extended, to establish the Experimental Division for the Study of War-Time Communications, which, for reasons of convenience, was placed under the administrative direction of Archibald MacLeish at the Library of Congress. In addition to directing the experimental division, Lasswell also functioned as a "sort of roving consultant to public officials developing the government's various propaganda and intelligence programs."[30]

Foremost among the wartime projects of Lasswell's division was the World Attention Survey. Here Lasswell's coders kept track of some 120 newspapers, tabulating the occurrence of various key symbols. Items relevant to what Lasswell termed "the politically significant content of the press" included various "ideological symbols," such as "freedom," "democracy," "revolution," and "class," as well as the names of key persons, nations, agencies, groups, and policies. By recording the incidence of important expressions against the total number of words in a publication, Lasswell's content coders were able to prepare a relative measure of the attention paid around the world to important features of the wartime symbolic landscape. For instance, in the third quarter of 1939, favorable references to the United States could be found in no editorials appearing in the *Ta Kung Pao* of Hong Kong, a newspaper loyal to Chiang Kai-Shek. By way of contrast, positive attention to the United States could be discerned in 45 percent of editorials appearing during the period of June–July 1940.[31]

Lasswell's mission at the Library of Congress was to collect and synthesize basic communication content pertaining to the war, information of a kind that, in the case of the Great War, had been made available only years after the 1918 armistice. Lasswell believed that his systematic content-coding procedures allowed users of the resulting data to objectify the inferences that they made about communication and propaganda. Committed to the idea that only systematic methods of data gathering produced valid conclusions, Lasswell was wont to deprecate his own *Propaganda Technique in the World War* (1927) for having given a far too impressionistic rendering of the symbolic landscape of the late war. He faulted his early work for failing to show "that all the material studied by the author was examined with the same degree of care." Believing that his work at the Library of Congress would remedy the defects of his earlier historical-critical studies, Lasswell looked forward to creating a data base of communication content that would lay bare a society's organization and value system. He believed that his labors would bring about not only a better understanding of the intentions, strategy, and goals of society's agents but also a better awareness of the role of communication as a major social force.[32]

Lasswell's empirical quantification impressed leading social scientists, and his enterprise also won over leading administrative policy makers. The Rockefeller Foundation considered Lasswell to be a leading light of communication science and funded his proposed projects eagerly. The Justice Department turned to Lasswell in the belief that the aura of scientific certainty abiding in Lasswell's tabular approach could help the agency to muster evidence sufficient to convict pro-Nazi propagandists. Federal prosecutors reasoned that objective procedures would enable their witnesses to satisfy a jury that certain domestic American publications represented dangerous propaganda because they mimicked themes disseminated by overseas fascist media. In one case, Lasswell helped to secure a conviction under the Foreign Agents Registration Act when he demonstrated that the *Transocean* information service consistently presented German propaganda themes. In the case of William Dudley Pelley, who was tried for sedition, Lasswell and his team showed that this leader of the Silver Shirts consistently had varied his messages in tandem with Berlin.[33]

Not to say that all social scientists saw Lasswellian quantitative semantics as an ideal kind of social research. Barrington Moore, who served with the Justice Department as a propaganda analyst, thought Lasswell's methodologism somewhat inflated, representing a kind of "huge pretentious bubble." Lasswell's old mentor, Merriam, although a longtime evangelist for quantitative social science, harbored similar reservations. In a private review of publications stemming from Lasswell's wartime work, Merriam reported his impression that the high level of quantification represented "something in the nature of static – or perhaps the squeal that is put in the radio to prevent outsiders from understanding what is being said in code, even."[34]

It is worth observing that Lasswell designed his wartime project not merely to collect useful data but also to develop the science of communication as a foundation for more effective prosecution of the war. Unlike the army's intelligence testers of World War I, who found it necessary to minimize or hide their theoretical interests, Lasswell was quite open about his intention to conduct research in the basic theory and method of communication science. He informed MacLeish that "I am engaged in the preparation of a systematic treatise on the theory of communication, in addition to the preparation of comparative histories of public attention, opinion and propaganda in the present war." To be sure, Lasswell saw both his "re-formulation of basic theory in the field of communication" and his team's effort to "conduct special research work within the general field of communications" as consistent with pursuing "lines particularly desired by policy-makers in the Government." Lasswell touted the marriage of theory and practicality to be found in the content-analysis coding procedures developed by his team. Not only did he view content-analysis methodology as "an original contribution to the field of communication research," but Lasswell believed its administrative practicality had been proven conclusively when employed to detect propaganda for the Justice Department.[35]

Another way in which Lasswell integrated theory, method, and government service was his work to supply the OWI, OSS, PWD, and FBIS with social scientists trained in content-analysis methods. One of the objectives stated in Lasswell's Rockefeller grant was to "train technical personnel for agencies of the government that could be expected to become more actively involved in propaganda and intelligence activities." Among the young scientists who gained experience in Lasswell's shop were Morris Janowitz, Irving Janis, Edward A. Shils, Louis Nemzer, Nathan Leites, and Ithiel de Sola Pool.[36]

If Lasswell's experimental division allowed social scientists a secure bailiwick for their work plus a modest entree into the policy arena, the War Department's Research Branch marked an even greater triumph for academic social and communication science. The Research Branch was organized in October 1941 by Frederick H. Osborn, businessman, boyhood friend of FDR, and board member of the Carnegie Corporation, who had been commissioned as a general and given command of the Pentagon's Morale Division. Osborn's unit, eventually known as the Information and Education Division, took over the incipient Research Branch when a new officer in charge of the G-2 Intelligence section objected to the presence of so many "long-haired" fellows in his department. Charles Dollard, formerly assistant to President Keppel of Carnegie, became General Osborn's right-hand man and oversaw the administration of the branch. Under Dollard was Samuel Stouffer, who functioned as director of a professional staff that eventually consisted of around ten officers and thirty civilians. Included in this group were such important young academicians as Irving Janis, Nathan Maccoby, M. Brewster Smith, and several researchers from commercial survey organizations. The branch's professionals were divided into three sections: a survey section headed by Leonard S. Cottrell, an experimental section directed by Carl I. Hovland, and a smaller statistical wing.[37]

Evangelists of social science research found themselves initially at somewhat of a disadvantage in dealing with an officer corps that was blithely unaware of advances in the study of society and symbols. As had been the case with the army's intelligence testers and leaflet engineers of 1917–1918, Stouffer's social researchers quickly learned that their work carried no inherent weight in view of their academic reputations or self-promoting statements. In fact, the very nativity of the branch had been jeopardized by an earlier directive of the Secretary of War that prohibited administering anonymous polls to the troops. But by 1945, the army's social surveyors had dispensed more than 200 different questionnaires to a half-million soldiers stationed in all parts of the world. Throughout the war, the survey section had taken pains to make monthly and quarterly reports to the General Staff and to the army on attitudes of the troops; in fact, officers began to look forward to this exacting data on GI morale. By the end of the war, the army had come to have so high a regard for the work of the Research Branch that Osborn became a member of the General Staff, which at the time consisted of only twelve officers.[38]

During the war, Stouffer's corps of researchers sent more than 300 reports to army commanders treating a variety of subjects relevant to military effectiveness. In one study, researchers probed why soldiers in the South Pacific did not use atabrine, the antimalaria drug, as frequently as the army wanted. Other surveys varied from simple tallies of preferences regarding winter clothing to more complex studies of how soldiers in the India–Burma theater of operations viewed the Chinese people. In an innovative cooperative study with the Surgeon General's office, the staff of the Research Branch was able to postulate rough predictions of nonbattle injury rates on the basis of the expressed attitudes of troops toward combat. Stouffer's minions circulated within the army a useful publication called *What the Soldier Thinks*.[39]

The point system for discharging millions of GIs proved to be the survey section's pièce de résistance. Pentagon brass agonized over problems of morale and logistics inherent to demobilizing some 12 million servicemen. The staff of the Research Branch suggested the idea of a point system to determine the order of a soldier's discharge. Army social scientists surveyed the troops to find what the men regarded as the most significant and salient factors that should weigh in a soldier's order of release from military service. Researchers found that the troops regarded length of service, overseas duty, combat duty, and parenthood as most significant. The War Department and the White House eventually accepted a plan based on these considerations.[40]

The Research Branch was particularly proud of Carl Hovland's innovative section in which researchers employed controlled experimentation to determine the effectiveness of the army's lectures, filmstrips, motion pictures, and other modes of communication. In one study, army social scientists tested the hunch of broadcasting experts that documentary-type films would be more effective than filmed lectures in changing the attitude of the men. Although soldiers rated the documentary as more interesting, no statistically significant differences emerged when groups exposed to commentary and documentaries were polled as to their attitudes. In another set of comparisons, some groups of soldiers undergoing training with filmstrips were required to repeat out loud certain material projected on the screen. Researchers found that recitation significantly increased the amount of material recalled and that the highest level of retention occurred when GIs knew they were to be tested. The experimental section also made empirical assessments of various ways of implementing the army's directive to assemble materials that would prepare soldiers to expect a lengthy war against Japan. Here researchers found that presenting both sides of the question was significantly more persuasive in cases where men were skeptical of the position being advocated or where the audience consisted of highly educated troops. In converse conditions, a one-sided approach worked best.[41]

Most significant among Hovland's experimental programs was that developed to assess the effectiveness of the army's ideological orientation films, the "Why We Fight" series produced by Col. Frank Capra. General Osborn believed that the populist touch found in Capra's *Mr. Smith Goes to Washington* and other Hollywood hits could improve the motivation of the army's mass of conscripts. The Morale Division's chief accordingly arranged for the master of Capra-corn to be detached from the Signal Corps, although the Osborn–Capra alliance found itself constantly battling the jealousy of senior officers in the army's traditional film department who resented Capra's independent movie-production operation. Fortunately, Capra's friends in high places included Chief of Staff General George C. Marshall, who was personally promoting the idea of inspirational orientation films because of a concern that troops knew little of the history and politics of the years preceding World War II. Marshall felt that an offensive war required more than a defensive orientation that focused on Pearl Harbor and Hitler's declaration of war. He believed that if American troops understood how fascism plotted world conquest, both their willingness to serve and their fighting effectiveness would increase. Marshall challenged Capra to make documentaries that would "win the battle for men's minds."[42]

Surveys conducted by the Research Branch bore out Osborn and Marshall's sense that American boys lacked the gung-ho spirit of 1917, and the resulting data laid bare the magnitude of the task facing General Osborn's corps of morale builders. Fully agreeing that America's entry into the fray was "a matter of defensive necessity," American soldiers nevertheless exhibited considerable differences of opinion as to the wider purposes and meanings of World War II. In a finding that threw cold water on idealistic champions of the Four Freedoms and the Atlantic Charter, the Research Branch concluded that among the GIs "there was little support of attempts to give the war meaning in terms of principles and causes involved, and little apparent desire for such formulations."[43]

Army researchers strove to explain why only 13 percent of inductees could name three of Roosevelt's Four Freedoms and why only 15 percent of trainees "attempted to define the war for themselves in terms of the moral principles involved." Social scientists settled on an explanation that the rampant ideological lethargy and dissension flowed not only from the long debate on neutrality but also the "debunking process" that had followed the Great War. "The moral drawn from this was that people became converted to supporting causes by a kind of trickery – 'propaganda' – and that it was, therefore, wise to be on one's guard against being taken in by propaganda." Resulting from this withered capacity for inspiration, and concomitant distrust of abstract explanations, was an ideological paradox that disappointed those who found it easy to put the old progressive stamp on the new crusade. On the one hand, America's soldiery expressed a general satisfaction that the war was worth fighting; but on the other, soldiers were plagued with apprehensions that the conflict might have been avoided, that it entailed vast costs, and that a likely postwar battle with Russia might render the immediate struggle somewhat futile.[44]

Given that the army viewed prewar propaganda analysis as an impediment to be overcome, it is not surprising that Osborn's Morale Division sought to maximize what Bernays would soon call "the engineering of consent" through a marriage of Capra-style movies and Hovland-style empiricism. The stated objectives of the seven "Why We Fight" films centered on instilling a desire to join with the Allies in making a better world by defeating fascist aggressors. Hovland's researchers applied all the empirical creativity they could muster in assessing Capra's series by means of three measures of effectiveness. The three communication effects studied dealt with whether Capra's documentaries had the power to increase factual knowledge, to change how soldiers viewed various allies and enemies, and to build a greater willingness to serve.

Experimental investigations of *The Battle of Britain,* Capra's portrayal of the Royal Air Force triumphing over Hitler's air assault, illustrated the scale and sophistication of the Hovland group's effort to account for those media effects of interest to policy makers. Investigators of the Research Branch found that, while the film "produced relatively large effects" regarding Britain's performance in the air war of 1940, the documentary did not change opinions on "the war effort or integrity of the British." Not only did the film produce little of a general transfer effect, but *The Battle of Britain* (as with other films in the series) had no measurable impact on the willingness of soldiers to serve, what the Pentagon regarded as the principal objective of the ideological orientation program.

Hovland's researchers assiduously parsed their research data in an effort to explain, on both the practical and theoretical levels, how the "Why We Fight" films affected the knowledge, attitudes, and motivation of troops. A closer look at the audience revealed that soldiers were less influenced by *The Battle of Britain* if they connected it to such "propagandistic" or "manipulative" purposes as making the troops work harder or hate the enemy. Researchers also were intrigued by the statistical anomaly that the long-term effects on attitudes of *The Battle of Britain* sometimes were greater than the short-term ones. While experimenters were unable to find in their data any conclusive explanation for delayed opinion change – what they termed the *sleeper effect* -- researchers believed that part of the reason had to do with a predisposition to change on the part of the receiver.

Attached to the Research Branch as outside consultants, Lazarsfeld and Merton contributed some innovative approaches to unraveling the mysteries of wartime administrative persuasion. Notable was their employment of the Lazarsfeld–Stanton Program Analyzer to various army training and orientation films. Here researchers learned that GIs were more likely to press the "dislike" button when the camera focused on narrators or speakers giving their talks. The troops preferred the action sequences. Not that all kinetic content was equal, however. In *Back Home,* a film about a stateside machine shop, GIs expressed disdain over what they interpreted as the "pseudo-patriotism" of civilians who not only were escaping the "hardships of Army life" but also were being well compensated for their "patriotic" work as machinists.[45]

Given the strong impetus of social scientists to contribute to the nation's survival, the situation of Stouffer's Research-Branch experts seemed on the surface to represent the ideal opportunity for intellectuals to merge theory, research, and praxis. Here academic and business-oriented researchers sat at the same table with government policy makers. But the setup proved somewhat less than flawless from the point of view of academicians wanting to enhance the social station of social science. First, the army's rigid chain of command minimized the effectiveness of the research findings, which were distorted when transmitted up the hierarchy. More generally, Stouffer found himself ever torn between the demands of top brass and his research staff. A number of studies demanded by the Pentagon struck Stouffer's people as trivial – for instance, whether soldiers preferred Pepsi to Coke or whether they liked nuts in their candy bars. On the other hand, longer-range or more abstract inquiries laid Stouffer vulnerable to the charge of "trying to exploit our situation for social science." While the army took quite seriously the results of "factual studies," the brass placed little value on expert social science theorizing. Lacking the independence that Lasswell enjoyed in view of his Rockefeller grant, Stouffer was hampered in negotiating the rocky shoals between basic and applied research.[46]

However much the army preferred immediate data-based gratification, Stouffer's people saw themselves not only as opinion engineers for the army but also as scientists for humanity. Believing that their wartime work was important, the psychologists and sociologists of the Research Branch nevertheless felt a wider obligation "to report on their studies and thus to speed up the process of development of the science of man."[47] Charles Dollard, Osborn's overseer on leave from the Carnegie foundation, promised the army's young researchers, who were anxious about their postwar academic careers, that the American Soldier material would be published. Consistent with this commitment, *The American Soldier* volumes were produced by a special committee constituted by the Social Science Research Council and supported with a grant of around $100,000 to the SSRC by the Carnegie Corporation. A harbinger of later Rockefeller grants for work of this kind was the presence on this committee of Leland DeVinney, later an assistant director of the social science division at Rockefeller.[48]

The burgeoning alliance between policy makers, grantors, and quantitatively oriented researchers assured that the wartime work of leading social scientists would permanently influence both academy and society notwithstanding the interest of federal officers on the immediate results of social research. The direct connection between granting agencies and the Research Branch is shown not only in the Carnegie grant for the Stouffer–Hovland volumes but also in the support extended to this publishing project by the Social Science Research Council. The postwar SSRC was well peopled with Research-Branch alumni as evidenced by the presence of Donald Young, the SSRC's executive director, who had served as a civilian consultant to the branch, and by the appearance on the SSRC board of Osborn, Hovland, Kimbell Young, and Leonard S. Cottrell.[49]

The influence of *The American Soldier* series on American social science proceeded chiefly along vectors of methodology and administration. Most discussed at the time by leading lights of academe was the impact of the Stouffer–Hovland program in consummating and making manifest what previously had been the sporadic effort of the social studies to model themselves upon the natural sciences. A second significance, more discussed by the humanistic critics of quantified social science, was the tendency of *The American Soldier* volumes to increase the administrative orientation of postwar researchers.

In the years after 1945, methodology became key to the ethos of social science as science. Stouffer boasted of making every effort to establish his branch as a bastion against the older humanistic tradition of social inquiry, which he denigrated as too intuitive and grandiose. In Stouffer's hierarchy of research methods, even the "systematic and detailed" case study of a trained social science observer was accorded only a gentlemanly "C" because such research was "impressionistic" and prone to "erroneous generalizations." Better were the quantitative surveys based on "systematic questioning of representative samples of respondents." In Stouffer's estimation, however, only experimentation offered the best hope for reliable and valid social research. "The Research Branch, from its inception, held up the controlled experiment as our ideal . . . and we constantly tried to measure the inadequacies of mere panel studies, or worse, mere correlational studies, against the ideal of the controlled experiment." In one laboratory study, Stouffer's people found that soldiers (in experimental units) who earned the army's Expert Infantryman's Badge were more likely to become more favorable to the infantry than those (in control units) who did not take the test.[50]

The methodological Puritanism that took hold in the Research Branch added to the already considerable demands placed upon this organization. The effort to control up to six or seven variables went beyond anything treated in then-current textbooks of statistics and social research. Research-Branch operatives often found themselves improvising where no clear rules existed, and Stouffer encouraged the work of several methodological innovators, particularly Louis Guttman and Paul Lazarsfeld. Guttman labored on problems of attitude scale construction – for instance, how to maintain reliability while reducing the number of items in a questionnaire. Lazarsfeld contributed insights on attitude scales and also helped to solve general problems of obtaining accurate data from survey research. Regarding this latter problem, Lazarsfeld and his Columbia colleagues, who were serving as consultants to the Research Branch, experimented with interlocking questions to measure how much soldiers were evading or rationalizing their actual feelings. For instance, few soldiers cited the danger of infantry combat to explain why they preferred alternate assignments. Yet the Columbia team found that persons wanting to avoid infantry duty were more likely than others to agree with a question asking whether they worried about battle injury.[51]

In lionizing Stouffer's achievement, Daniel Lerner constructed what he termed a *nomenclatural sentence* that synopsized the notion of "modern method" coming out of the work of the Research Branch. Lerner believed that, henceforth, scientists of society would keep their eyes fixed on "the rigorous testing of explicit hypotheses on largely quantified data accumulated by structured observation in empirical situations approximating (with specified deviations) the model of con-trolled experiment." Lerner's review of immediate responses by leading scholars to *The American Soldier* series further demonstrated that the idea of "modern methods" loomed largest in American academe.[52] In the years that followed, methodologists continued to refer to *The American Soldier* volumes as models of thoroughly up-to-date social science. It is possible that publication of the Stouffer–Hovland volumes boosted the morale of social scientists even more than reports by the Research Branch had helped the army to improve the esprit of soldiers. Wartime work assisted scientists of society to define their unique social role of providing data certified by their mode of production.

Accompanying the methodological claims of the wartime social re-searchers were references to theoretical advances coming from government-sponsored attitude research. While admitting that their work was "dominated by practical rather than theoretical considera-tions," Hovland and his colleagues nevertheless maintained that they had chosen and manipulated variables in accordance with social science theory. Published retrospectives on the wartime research pointed to several cases where the minions of the Research Branch had added to theory. Although the army's sociologists studied individual soldiers, they claimed to have rediscovered the importance of the primary (infor-mal, face-to-face) group. Scholars of the Research Branch not only documented the influence of group membership on the behavior of soldiers but also identified factors that promoted or obstructed the formation of cohesive fighting groups. A major finding was that combat groups influenced their members to a far greater extent than either formal command structures or abstract devotion to patriotic ideals.[53]

In advancing another claim for the theoretical weight of the Stouffer program, Hans Speier pointed to the ability of *The American Soldier* researchers to connect demographic variables with expressions of opin-ion. As a result, Speier believed, army social scientists had helped to implement Karl Mannheim's speculations about the connection of ideol-ogy and social position. Specific findings that opinions were associated with race, rank, marital status, education, age, region, combat service, and branch of service pointed in the direction of a new era of more precise studies in the sociology of knowledge.[54]

Not that everybody was agreed as to the theoretical utopia implied by the efforts of the Research Branch. Alfred McClung Lee found the army's sociology merely bigger rather than better, arguing that the work of the Research Branch lacked "fresh observations of the sort that lead to the formulation of new theories or the basic modification of existing theories." Here Stouffer defended the theoretical significance of his group's work with the argument that critics such as Lee longed for "theory on the grand style" and did not recognize the benefits of more modest links between data and theory. In this connection, M. Brewster Smith, a minor contributor to the army research program, emphasized years later that the Stouffer group had turned up many findings that contradicted the prevailing wisdom of the period. For instance, against the assumption that Negroes lacked the initiative of whites, army researchers found that black soldiers were more eager than their white counterparts to become noncommissioned officers. Highlighting the innovativeness of the work, Princeton University Press promoted *The American Soldier* volumes with advertisements and dust-jacket notations that also emphasized an incipient methodological revolution.[55]

Not only was *The American Soldier* series crucial in consolidating the scientific and theoretical aspirations of social researchers, but the volumes announced to the academy that the species of administrative research foretold by Lazarsfeld in his prescient 1941 article had arrived. In this vein, the publicity announcement released by Princeton University Press mentioned how researchers skillfully had overcome the army's skepticism about using social science data for policy decisions. Nevertheless, the theme of administratively motivated research was treated in a relatively implicit fashion by Stouffer and his associates. Stouffer referred offhandedly to how the practical orientation of his army superiors caused his team to focus on "attitudes toward very specific things which might be manipulable." Lazarsfeld similarly did not give public weight to his private discovery that government grants were an easier source of funding than the commercial contracts on which his Bureau of Applied Social Research formerly had relied.[56]

The tendency of leading-edge social scientists to minimize the administrative thrust of the new-style social research undoubtedly flowed in part from a reluctance to raise the issue of "propaganda" or "manipulation." Some of the more cynical GIs surveyed by Stouffer's minions already had put on the record their suspicions about certain Machiavellian purposes that they discerned in the "Why We Fight" films. Clearly, the imprint of self-interested symbolic strategizing was the moral Achilles' heel of the Stouffer project. In a survey of reactions to the Stouffer–Hovland volumes, Daniel Lerner discovered that although the notion of "social engineering" was a decidedly secondary theme in reviews, certain commentators pursued this line of thought to such an extent that it became a troubling challenge.[57]

Lerner was referring chiefly to reviews prepared by the humanist sociologists Robert Lynd and Alfred Lee. Lynd acknowledged that the Stouffer volumes might induce the army to view the soldier in a more humane light, but he cautioned that the Research Branch exemplified "science being used with great skill to sort out and control men for purposes not of their own willing." Further, if the army program were to become the norm, sociology would find itself picking up mere crumbs for research on democracy's problems at the same time that researchers working for broadcasters and the army feasted at the funding table.[58] For his part, Lee agreed that the Stouffer–Hovland research showed both the strengths and weaknesses of "group or assembly-line research" that was "carried out with the value orientation characteristic of managerial technicians." Lee shared Lynd's apprehensions of the future of social science conducted along the lines that Stouffer seemed to be promoting.

> If managerial problems for industry and the military are to continue to dominate the research of leading social psychologists and sociologists, the value orientation of the managerial technician rather than the value orientation of the social science educator will dominate what evolves and is called social science. The emphasis can thus shift from service to citizens in democracy to service to those who temporarily control and who wish to control segments in our society.[59]

In a twenty-five-year retrospective on postwar critical sociology, Alfred and Elizabeth Lee concluded that Stouffer had indeed succeeded in helping to lead a movement whereby "propaganda analysis for consumers became largely replaced in sociological circles by a preoccupation with making mass communications more effective in the service of manipulators."[60]

If the democratic challenge to the social science of propaganda prompted occasional grudging nods from leading-edge social scientists, quantitative savants exhibited considerably more vigor and relish in dismissing or ridiculing other objections by humanists to *The American Soldier* series. Historians such as the young Arthur Schlesinger, and humanist social researchers such as Herbert Blumer and Nathan Glazer, remarked on what they saw as tendencies toward sterility, pretentiousness, and heavy-handedness in the mechanized social science pursued by the Stouffer and Hovland teams. Lerner dismissed Schlesinger as an "academic Miniver Cheevy" whose "anguished" and "petulant" cries belied his unwillingness "to descend from the mount on which historians through centuries have disputed pride of place only with poets and philosophers." Lerner similarly found the "vigorous negativism" of Blumer and Glazer easy to wave off on the basis that both these social scientists expressed little appreciation for quantitative, empirical research. Paul Lazarsfeld and his colleague (and later wife) Patricia Kendall similarly characterized the opposition to quantitative social science as a drama involving empirical insiders and critical outsiders.[61]

The wide attention and generally favorable notice paid to *The American Soldier* was not the only indication that wartime social research was modifying academic social science. Even during the war, Cantril had been busy publishing the fruits of his wartime polling for FDR and for various Washington agencies.[62] Lasswell and his people, too, soon were evangelizing about their work. At about the same time that Stouffer and Hovland were implementing their Carnegie grant for publication, the Rockefeller Foundation underwrote Lasswell's *Language of Politics,* a comprehensive report of his group's work at the Library of Congress and, earlier, at Chicago. Here Lasswell emphasized the scientific-process perspective on social influence by describing the key question of social semantics as that of "under what conditions do words affect power responses?" Even though he recently had discovered that the antique term of *rhetoric* called forth a historical debate about persuasion and manipulation, Lasswell was more interested in objective, process-oriented issues of how vested interests, reformers, and revolutionaries variously used symbols to gain advantage. Lasswell also emphasized the importance of quantitative research into language, citing the limitations of his earlier, somewhat-impressionistic study of Wilson-era propaganda.[63]

Supplementing Lasswell's own theoretical exegeses, *Language of Politics* also included chapters on content-analysis methodology contributed by his junior colleagues. These included chapters on validity in content analysis (Irving Janis), reliability considerations (Abraham Kaplan and Joseph Goldsen), coding techniques (Lasswell, Alan Grey, and David Kaplan), considerations of sampling (Alexander Mintz), and the "coefficient of imbalance," a formula to amalgamate favorable, unfavorable, neutral, and nonrelevant content (Janis and Raymond Fadner). Rounding out the exposition of the Library of Congress group's wartime theoretical and methodological work was a concluding chapter by Lasswell that reported the use of his content data in the prosecution of domestic fascist propagandists. Here Lasswell cited the eight tests that his group had developed for detecting when an advocate was functioning as a propagandist for a foreign government or movement.

The notion that social science – communication research, in particular – might benefit policy makers was indistinct and only tentatively
recognized in the years before World War II. Faint harbingers of such a
data-policy connection had come in the form of Lazarsfeld's gratifications research for CBS and Cantril's polling for FDR. Later, one of
Nelson Rockefeller's reasons for supporting Cantril's American Social
Surveys group was to demonstrate to official Washington the need for a
government radio to counter Axis propaganda in Latin America.[64] By
1945, however, the link between policy and data had been well established. From the War Department to the White House, Washington
policy makers understood that research data could facilitate policy
development and implementation and, at the same time, enhance public
acquiescence. True to the hopes of Stouffer (and to the fears of Lynd),
academicians began to accept that the best opportunities for social
science generally, and communication science particularly, lay in the
direction of alliances forged between researchers and policy makers.
Pleased by what they had contributed to the war effort, Lasswell,
Lazarsfeld, and other quantitative researchers felt confident that, by
serving policy makers, they could help to bring about a postwar society
that was not merely more efficient but also more humane and harmo-
nious.

The aim of communication scientists to help engineer reform from
the top, however, meant that the practitioner's view of a benign propaganda now had gained sway in academic social science. The term
propaganda analysis had undergone a subtle but quite revolutionary
transformation. Before 1941, this term meant exposing the objectives
of every self-interested persuader so that the public could consider this
information in making up its mind. The older meaning was not entirely
lost in administrative usage, as evidenced by Lasswell's pride in having
helped to alert the public to pro-fascist propaganda circulated in the
wartime United States. However, now that *propaganda analysis* had
become associated with enhancing efficient agency work, the term was
shedding its self-reflexive critical connotation.[65] The result was a notion
of propaganda *for* democracy in which leaders took firm reign and in
which intellectuals were given license to propagandize for the preservation of government "for" (if not "of" and "by") the people. Fewer
progressives now were inclined to challenge Bernays's assertion that
elites shouldered a responsibility to mold public opinion in the direction
of what leading lights considered to be proper democratic thought and
practice.[66]

In the mood of disappointment and regret that had reigned after the
Great War, only Charles Merriam and a few other social scientists active
in wartime service had preached the idea of propaganda for democracy.

In contrast, the practical and methodological triumphs of wartime social science – together with the new alliance of researchers, policy makers, and grantors – suggested that academicians would play an important role in planning for a better postwar world. The immediate emergence of Stalin as a specter to replace Hitler further contributed to the belief of academicians and policy makers that the greatest good would result if citizens were inclined to listen to their leaders.

Are We Losing the Propaganda War?

Warily and with real concern, polemicists, policy makers, and the public were posing this question by the late 1940s. Just as Depression-era skepticism and post–Pearl Harbor social solidarity set an agenda and methodological tone for social thought and social research, so too did the Cold War weigh in as an influence on both political expostulation and scholarship. Years of exposure to *Mission to Moscow* and other wartime folklore had temporarily boosted confidence that Russia could be trusted; such a view was endorsed by 55 percent of those polled in spring 1945 versus 39 percent in March 1942. After 1945, however, public sentiment returned to the notion of Hitler and Stalin as analogous enemies, an opinion that had been in vogue after the Nazi–Soviet pact of 1939. A curious process of symbolic transference was at work whereby symbols applied to Hitlerite Germany were projected onto the USSR on account of the dangerous "Red Fascism" promoted by Stalin.[67]

The sparsity of revisionist sentiment after 1945 reinforced the tendency simply to substitute Stalin and Red Russia for Hitler and Nazi Germany. Flushed with a difficult victory and faced with an uncertain peace, Americans were in no mood to meditate over such of their own moral vulnerabilities as mass civilian bombing or the internment of Japanese aliens and Americans of Japanese ancestry. Compared to the turnabout of sentiment on the Great War that had ensued between 1918 and 1920, one finds no major lines of revisionist rethinking chaining out within the general public after 1945. George Viereck, an early proponent of a rightist recasting of the war, complained that "it is next to impossible to get any leading publishing house or any serious newspaper or periodical to print anything which upsets the conventional fictions about the responsibility for the coming of war in September, 1939, and for our entry in December 1941." A few historians of revisionist bent, such as Harry Barnes and Charles Beard, questioned whether Roosevelt had been too eager to have the United States stand beside Britain. But most opinion leaders were inclined to view such retrospectives as mere sour grapes, and the disposition did not spread to the public at large.[68]

However much they abhorred the manic aspects of postwar anticommunism, the wartime communication elite of scholars and practitioners added their voices to what was becoming a general chorus of concern about whether the Red propaganda machine might defeat the propagandas of the democracies. Both in and out of government, the effort to promote pro-democracy propaganda seemed an unquestioned benefit based on the lesson of combating fascism with mass media and communication research. The question of whether the United States was losing the international propaganda war became so pressing that many intellectuals forgot their 1930s-era scrupulosity about the danger of scholarship becoming an adjunct of political and managerial initiative. Members of the communication elite played their part in setting out the merits of liberal democracy over communism not only by working as communication managers, researchers, and consultants but also by participating in research projects, conferences, and think tanks.

Early cautionary notes about a coming Cold War propaganda battle could be discerned amid the chorus of celebration about wartime "derring-do" in domestic and international propaganda. Wallace Carroll's postwar book, *Persuade or Perish,* chiefly reprised the deeds of OWI propaganda makers and reflected the postwar spirit of legitimate pride in a job trimly executed. Carroll, former director of the OWI's London office, began with how the agency broadcast information to discredit Pierre Laval, the French collaborationist leader. Carroll continued by explaining how comparisons of Hitler's Atlantic Wall to the ill-fated Maginot line had rattled the Germans and how his agency's broadcasts aroused in Germans the sentiment that defeat was the personal responsibility of the formerly sacrosanct Hitler. Yet Carroll's writing also revealed the ambivalence toward Russia growing among U.S. opinion leaders. Although Carroll reported with satisfaction how Goebbels had failed to break Allied unity by raising the Bolshevik Bogey of an iron-curtained, slave Europe, Carroll also pointed to a declaration by French communists that the wartime suspension of class warfare now was at an end.

Working from the popular analogy of Red fascism, Carroll accepted that communism's challenge required the United States to "convince . . . [allied] peoples and their governments that American aims were essentially the same as their own." Here Carroll feared that American actions, and neglect of pro-democracy propaganda during 1945 and 1946, had permitted the USSR to make great progress toward its objectives of sowing confusion mixed with envy of the United States. Policy lapses included the abrupt cancellation of the Lend-Lease to Britain, an obviously niggardly loan to England, the elimination of inflation controls which brought increased prices to nations dependent upon the United States, and the establishment of U.S. control over Japan's Pacific island chains. Further, because the United States had dismantled its information services abroad, the only propaganda emanating from the arsenal of democracy was that of The American Way of Life. In Carroll's estimation, such an unrealistic appeal by U.S. business and government to pure emulation sent an insulting message to the devastated Europeans that they "were poor because they were socialist."

Carroll contrasted America's propaganda of inadvertent arrogance to the Soviet propaganda offensive that had been built around a coordinated program of policy and symbols that conjured up both memories of common sacrifices during the war and a vision of benign socialism for the future. The Soviets also employed the rampant hunger and fear in Europe as levers to make rich America, with her nuclear monopoly and alleged aims of economic imperialism, seem the bully in her disputes with Russia. Although the Soviet propaganda was purely destructive, Carroll grudgingly admired its single-minded pursuit of a predetermined objective. Even more admirable, he believed, was America's belated discovery of how the wartime effort to coordinate intelligent policy with adroit propaganda might advance the cause of democracy. With the Marshall Plan of 1947, the United States finally "had produced an idea which caught the imagination of mankind." Moreover, Carroll hoped, America was coming to realize that, given the political warfare waged by the USSR, "we must persuade or perish." In Carroll's estimation, the best symbolic strategy of the Cold War was to eliminate any blemishes on the national honor, such as racial discrimination, and to make sure that generous acts were accompanied by "the right words," namely a "persuasion which binds the nations to us by ties of confidence and faith."[69]

Carroll's call for action was only one postwar manifesto in which propaganda was seen from the vantage point of the wartime managerial-scientific siege mentality. Edward Barrett, who directed America's world information services between 1950 and 1952, agreed with Carroll, his erstwhile OWI colleague, that "unless we Americans are bent on suicide, we have no wise choice but to master the techniques of international persuasion." As with Carroll, Barrett reprised certain high points of the OWI's work against Hitler; however, with five additional years of experience in Cold War propagandizing, Barrett provided a full-blown summary and assessment of the war of international persuasion waged between the United States and the USSR. Barrett recommended that Washington establish a "Persuader-in-Chief," who would be "at the President's elbow" and would oversee a Cold War information service characterized by on-the-scene control in the field. Further, Barrett enumerated a variety of self-defeating factors in America's Cold War propagandizing including jingoists in Congress who pressed for strident (but psychologically ineffective) propaganda broadcasts, excessive Congressional attention to discontented information-service employees, the binge–purge cycle of appropriations, and Joe McCarthy's carping about whether books critical of American society belonged in the U.S. Information Service's overseas libraries.[70]

As the reality of the Cold War became clear, academic savants from across the spectrum of the humanities and social sciences weighed in with efforts and ideas for helping to sell America and Americanism to a world now vulnerable to dangerous ideological liaisons. Humanist Everett Hunt, Dean of Swarthmore College, recommended looking back to the rhetorical heritage of Plato and Aristotle for weapons of an "anti-communist propaganda." "We shall need for our propaganda battles men with a broad knowledge of history, with a poetic imagination that can identify ourselves with others, with sympathy for the real needs of peoples very unlike ourselves, with something of Aristotle's hard, analytic intelligence, with Plato's lofty view of what the art of persuasion might be in the mind of a generous philosopher." Leo Lowenthal, a Frankfurt School emigré who had built up a social science–research staff of 150 during World War II, remained in the United States to direct the VOA's research staff between 1949 and 1956. His unit conducted systematic studies of audience "predispositions and prejudices" and assessed "the impact of a given communication" until it was abolished in one of the periodic reorganizations of the information services.[71]

The ability of Hunt and Lowenthal to reconcile classical studies and Frankfurt School critique with symbolic warfare amply revealed how the mood of social service ran strong on campuses of the 1950s. Reading the wrongs of American propaganda – and righting them – became a cottage industry in academic circles, and were reflected in many an ivory-tower think piece. A common concern was that American propaganda lacked a unifying principle other than national interest and that, therefore, America pursued a diplomacy of power without an effective recourse to ideals. A concatenation of general questions issued forth from this premise: Why did America permit Russia to present herself as the wave of the future? When would America learn to articulate (and, where necessary, improve) her own animating ideas and values of freedom, opportunity, and fellowship with diverse peoples? Why did America disburse economic aid in the assumption that dollars themselves talked? In specific, why was the U.S. Information Service in Italy diffusing a broad and bland message of individualism and spending so much time cultivating the not particularly popular conservative elite in that nation? In sum: "Are the Soviets Winning the Propaganda War?" asked George V. Allen, former U.S. Information Agency (USIA) director, who, departing from the idealists, concluded that meeting the material needs of the developing world would weigh more heavily than any symbolism.[72]

Treatments of "democracy through better propaganda" appeared not only in journals for academicians but also in current forums of intellectual opinion. Novelist John Schneider contributed to *Nation* a high-culture explanation of "Why We're Losing the Propaganda War." First, Washington was rife with too much bellicose talk about war preparations. Further, the United States exported too little of "such admirable artists as Marian Anderson and the *Porgy and Bess* company" and too much "rock 'n roll, ambulatory supermarkets, bodies beautiful, Cohn & Schine [McCarthy's traveling snoops], lush-living military officers, prizefighters, semi-literate and bad-mannered tourists, vacuous TV shows and Billy Graham." Operating from a different mindset, conservative commentary on American propaganda was more likely to complain about timidity and indecision in the U.S. Information Agency in Washington and the overly lush accommodations for its workers abroad.[73]

Illustrating how the Cold War propaganda controversy began to spill into the media was a forum of journalists and communication practitioners in *The Saturday Review*. This collection put into layperson's terms several of the dilemmas of effective world propaganda. Edward Bernays argued that America's current unpopularity was not inevitable if the public understood the need for international persuasion and if Congress would cooperate with the information services. George Gallup agreed that the "most *effective* way to deal with Russia is to *match* her efforts in ideological warfare." Gallup also believed that America's advantage over Russia lay in better communication research: "methods for pre-testing propaganda ideas and for measuring their success in use." Other suggestions, not always consistent, for effective Cold War propaganda in this symposium included: renaming the VOA as the Voices of America and broadcasting a diversity of expression; showing the great wealth of consumables produced by capitalism; encouraging foreign listeners to take pride in their various nations; making the VOA less strident; and developing tough policies to undergird a powerful propaganda – for instance, resolving to defeat the Reds in Vietnam.[74]

The Engineering of Consent

More than anything else, the emergence of the Cold War created the social context in which the administrative approach of detecting and defeating enemy propaganda – which earlier had animated the OWI, the Lasswell shop, and the Research Branch – continued to exert its hold over communication scientists and practitioners. Members of this communication elite felt a persisting impulse to operate on a war footing, to battle communist propaganda as they had contended against the fascists. Whether they remained in government service, returned to private life, or assumed an ivory-tower sinecure, academicians and practitioners of communication kept up their interest in selling liberal democracy.

In his phrase, "the engineering of consent," the redoubtable Edward L. Bernays most aptly captured the perspective taken on mass persuasion by high-level practitioners and scholars caught up in the Cold War mobilization of materiel and mind. Bernays believed that the remoteness of leaders from the masses created an imperative to extend and modernize the freedoms of speech and press with a "freedom to persuade." According to Bernays, "only by mastering the techniques of communication can leadership be exercised fruitfully in the vast complex that is modern democracy in the United States." In a democracy, results "do not just happen"; progress required the affirmative ministrations of ethical professionals serving responsible leaders.[75] With his customary energy and optimism, Bernays himself labored assiduously to reengineer America's overseas mass persuasion. In the mid-1950s, he founded the National Committee for an Adequate Overseas U.S. Information Program. He adroitly massaged the message of this group into the periodical press by means of conferences in which featured experts held forth on public opinion, communication, and international relations. Fifteen years later, Bernays was organizing a new Emergency Committee for Reappraisal of U.S. Overseas Information Policies and Programs. Here speakers such as Bernays, George Gallup, Jr., and Rep. Dante B. Fascell discussed how America had depleted her store of international good will and how the torpid "holding operations" of the USIA precluded goal-directed propaganda initiatives.[76]

Bernays was not the only communication practitioner who periodically waded in to clean up the chaotic conditions prevailing in America's Cold War propaganda program. In 1953–1954, Leo Bogart, a leading market-research professional, led a McCann–Erickson team that completed a five-volume study of the U.S. Information Agency based on interviews with agency personnel. Bogart's Herculean undertaking represented the research arm of a larger effort to improve the agency's performance then being coordinated by an industry–academy advisory panel, chaired by Wilbur Schramm, dean of the University of Illinois Division of Communication. Despite this official imprimatur, Bogart's study accomplished nothing more than Bernays's from-the-outside conferences. The Schramm committee soon was disbanded, and Bogart doubted whether either the USIA's director or associate director even had glanced at his report.[77]

The American "can-do" spirit notwithstanding, the program to engineer consent through overseas propaganda proceeded in fits and starts. Both the OWI and Nelson Rockefeller's CIAA operations both had been dissolved within weeks of Japan's surrender. The State Department maintained the Voice of America and established an Office of International Information and Cultural Affairs in 1946 (which became the Office of International Information and Educational Exchange in 1947). These relatively low-budget and ad hoc arrangements were legitimized and extended in the Smith–Mundt Act of 1948 (Public Law 402), which explicitly authorized what Leo Bogart termed "the first peacetime propaganda program in American history."[78] Sociologist Hans Speier of the New School for Social Research, later of the RAND Corporation, joined his social science colleagues in applauding the post-1947 resumption of international opinion engineering that had atrophied during the first two years after VJ Day. Speier, whose work during World War II included service as chief of the State Department's Division of Occupied Areas, also concurred with the emerging consensus of the time that, for the foreseeable future, America would need to keep herself primed for conducting strategic propaganda against enemies.[79] In this vein, a 1952 symposium found a number of leading lights of communication research working on problems of measuring the effectiveness of the Voice of America. Employing content analysis, researchers investigated references to the VOA in letters from five European countries and in Soviet newspapers and other official media.[80]

Hadley Cantril, who shared the common opinion that the postwar U.S. information program had shown itself to be dangerously ineffective, also searched for ways to leverage scientific technique to overseas persuasion. A firm believer in policy-oriented polling, Cantril prevailed upon the State Department in 1951 to underwrite some field experiments to test the persuasive power of appeals in favor of NATO and others designed to convert French communists. When the completed findings were presented to the new Secretary of State, John Foster Dulles, he dismissed Cantril's results on the basis that foreign opinion should be considered irrelevant in foreign-policy decision making.

Rebuffed by the government, and disgusted by McCarthy's self-serving and absurd intrusions into the USIA, Cantril and his old friend, Lloyd Free (of USIA), established the Institute for International Social Research. A million-dollar endowment for this venture was secured from the Rockefeller Brothers Fund, whose president, Nelson Rockefeller (serving at the time as special adviser to Eisenhower), had been Cantril's old mentor. The research institute conducted various policy-oriented surveys around the world – for instance, learning that Cubans would not rally against Castro. This information apparently was studied seriously by the Kennedy administration only after the Bay of Pigs fiasco. Cantril and Free also did polling in the Dominican Republic after the assassination of dictator Rafael Trujillo, and they duly passed along their findings to the White House during the 1965 Dominican crisis.[81]

Although officials such as Dulles sometimes failed to share the enthusiasm for administrative propaganda work felt by the academic types, collaborative efforts by the administrator–grantor–professor troika, which had begun with Marshall's Rockefeller Foundation communication seminars, became commonplace during the two decades before the Vietnam War. In 1948, the American Psychological Association appointed a liaison committee to pursue "matters of mutual concern" with the U.S. Army. Members of this group included Jerome S. Bruner of Harvard's Department of Social Relations, John W. Gardner of the Carnegie Corporation, Carl I. Hovland of Yale's Psychology Department, Rensis Likert of Michigan, and six others.[82] Unself-conscious manifestations of the government–grantor–professor axis continued throughout the 1950s. In June 1959, for example, the Social Science Research Council sponsored a conference on "The Social Sciences and National Security Policy," which was held at the U.S. Military Academy. Organized by the SSRC's Committee on National Security Policy Research, the gathering brought together many of the usual players in what was coming to be called "policy science." Harold Lasswell, one of the chief proponents of applying social science to policy, figured prominently in the program, as did such other academic luminaries as Pendleton Herring of the SSRC, Morris Janowitz of Michigan, Klaus Knorr of Princeton, Hans Speier, Harold Guetzkow of Northwestern, and Samuel P. Huntington of Columbia.[83]

Lasswellian policy science became an especially important line of thinking for those committed to the alliance of symbols, money, and action. Lasswell believed that policy decisions would be materially improved if social scientists of many specialties were permitted to integrate their findings and focus these data into a single beam that would illuminate the policy process. Unlike the prewar propaganda critics, who saw dangers in the alliance of researcher and administrator, Lasswell believed that democracy would not become a casualty of more efficient policy formulation and execution. To the contrary, he argued, well-intentioned policy administrators understood that solving domestic problems was inextricably bound up with attaining such strategic objectives as winning the Cold War. Lasswell's example in this connection was the arena of civil rights where the "future security of the country" was closely linked to "the realization of democratic aspirations." Lasswell's idealized policy scientist "accepts or rejects opportunities for research according to their relevance to *all* of his goal values"; only then did the scientist proceed with "maximum objectivity." Lasswell's colleagues Robert Merton and Daniel Lerner cautioned that clients sometimes wanted to exploit research findings "for propagandistic aims," by selectively or manipulatively deploying the data to immediate self-advantage. They emphasized that the scientist must vigilantly keep his own "freedom of choice" in selecting research projects and in conducting them so as not to become a "bureaucratic technician" bound to routinized service to a direction-giving organization or state.[84]

Business became a junior partner in the administrative turn of propaganda studies in the 1940s and 1950s. Carl Hovland explained to the American Psychological Association that the wartime research on communication might be applied with equal force to the problems of industry. Summarizing lessons learned in work for the U.S. Army, Hovland observed the importance of setting clear communication objectives, of carefully analyzing the attitudes of the target audience toward the subject to be presented, and of not expecting that mass communication could produce dramatic results. Although "mass communications are extremely effective in transmitting straight information," the wartime experiments showed "that attitudes are very resistant to change by mass media and that personal face to face communication is often required." Hovland emphasized, nevertheless, that the chief result of his wartime experimental program was to demonstrate "*how little we really know about transmission of factual information and methods of influencing opinion through communication.*"

Hovland invited industrialists to join in the "systematic attack on these problems by interdisciplinary research." Acknowledging that his call for carefully controlled experiments on persuasion "may sound too theoretical and not highly practical," Hovland reassured the businesspeople in his audience to the contrary:

> Our experience was that the studies which we did on problems in the Army paid off more in solving practical problems than those where we attempted to get immediate answers to empirical problems. We certainly verified the late Kurt Lewin's remark that "nothing is so practical as a good theory."

Hovland predicted that a ten-year project of "systematic research in the industrial setting" not only would "contribute greatly to our understanding of the communication process" but also would "shed light on the processes by which successes or failures are produced."[85]

From Propaganda to Communication

By extending a crisis atmosphere, the Cold War further suffused intellectuals with the service ethos whereby they functioned as staff assistants to organizational leaders whose intention to merge social progress and progressive democracy was assumed. Policy scientists such as Lasswell seemed equally at ease talking to fellow scholars, to foundation administrators, or to overseers of governmental policy. The transformation whereby *propaganda*'s meaning shifted from manipulation by domestic elites to defense of the realm through command decisions was reflected in the subjects chosen for study and in the terminologies employed. Beginning in 1941, *propaganda,* the muckraker's signifier, underwent a series of metamorphoses whereby the term first was replaced by *morale* and later by *psychological warfare.* By 1948, *persuasion, communication,* and *information* were the favored locutions for what formerly had been called *propaganda.*

Terminological transformations reflected a shift in attention from those being led to those who acted as leaders. By highlighting the question of whether the public good was served by institutional communication, the expression *propaganda* harkened to a consumerist approach to communication. In contrast, the center of action became the originator of symbols when the matter under inquiry was described as an achievement of persuasion, the process of communication, or the transmission of information. The years 1948–1949 marked the pivotal point at which the aggregate number of citations in *Psychological Abstracts* to "persuasion," "communication" and "information" regularly exceeded those relating to "propaganda." The shift resulted chiefly from the striking emergence of "communication" as the main marker for symbolic inducement; where this term registered but one citation in 1942, and four in 1946, a full 48 could be found in 1950. The almost-exponential trend continued such that the number of yearly references to "communication" increased to the 100–200 range in the 1960s, while annual citations to "propaganda" fell to single digits in the 1950s and disappeared entirely for a decade after 1966.[86]

By the Eisenhower years, the managerial research imperative, which had been boldly broached in Lazarsfeld and Merton's 1943 Pronunciamento on communication study, had become the standard for leading-edge work in symbolic inducement. In 1954, the Social Science Research Council sponsored a conference on "Research on Public Communication" to assess the progress of and to stimulate further inquiry in the emerging field of communication. Sociologist Bernard Berelson identified what he believed were the six essential strands of communication research. Three of the first four on Berelson's list encompassed work associated with the major wartime communication programs: "the *Lasswell* tradition"; "the *Lazarsfeld* tradition of empirical field studies and audience and effect studies, close to market research"; and "the *Hovland* psychological tradition of controlled experimental studies of communication effects." Filling out the top four slots, in Berelson's estimation, was "the tradition of *group dynamics and personal influence* of Lewin, Festinger, Bales, etc."

Included on Berelson's short list, but trailing noticeably behind, were the work of Robert Leigh on public policy (which Berelson may have included out of consideration for Leigh's preparation of the research summaries around which the SSRC conference was organized) and the clearly out-of-the-mainstream, macrohistorical studies of Harold Innis. In view of Berelson's position as director of the Behavioral Sciences grant program of the Ford Foundation (between 1951 and 1957), the parameters he established for communication research carried more than a little weight. Discussants, nevertheless, made mention of a number of additional lines of promising inquiry, including (1) the interpersonal communication research of Jurgen Ruesch and Gregory Bateson, (2) the information theory of Warren Weaver, Claude E. Shannon, and George A. Miller, (3) the quantitative psycholinguistics of Charles E. Osgood, and (4) role theory.

Despite Berelson's suggestion that some of the major lines of communication research might already be running their theoretical course "with little new to be expected from them," there is no question that attitude-effects research was nearly everyone's first choice as the cutting edge of the field.[87] Although the term *attitude* had been a perennial powerhouse in the *Psychological Abstracts* indexes since the 1930s, this line of work was now closely associated with Hovland's systematic program begun in the Research Branch and, after the war, continued with Rockefeller Foundation support at Yale University. Three premier volumes reporting the Yale persuasion studies appeared in 1953, 1957, and 1959, establishing a body of findings that Leonard Doob termed "the most significant trend of all" in the area of public opinion and propaganda. So successful was Hovland's research program in collecting an entourage that Paul Lazarsfeld later complained that researchers were overusing the attitude-questionnaire methodology. Among these

also-rans were researchers in the speech field who, despite two genera-
tions of work on rhetorical persuasion and stage fright, woke up with a
start to discover a tidal wave of statistical-empirical persuasion studies
that seemed on the verge of completely overlaying their own contributions.[88]

Extending Hovland's already impressive program for the U.S. Army,
the three Yale volumes laid out a panorama of statistically certified
findings on persuasive techniques. The first volume, *Communication
and Persuasion,* documented vicissitudes of communicator credibility,
fear-arousing appeals, the organization of arguments, factors associated
with resistance to persuasion, the relationship of behavior to attitude,
and the duration of opinion change. In one set of experiments, for
instance, groups of college students were given attitude questionnaires
and, later, booklets in which a message was attributed to different
sources. The results of many studies indicated that "reactions to a
communication are significantly affected by cues as to the communicator's intentions, expertness, and trustworthiness." In another group of
studies, the Yale researchers pursued the "sleeper effect" that had
turned up in the army studies. Why was it that a low-credible source
might, over time, produce an increasing amount of attitude change?
The answer seemed to be that, after time, people were less likely spontaneously to connect a communication to the source of that material
(although persons, when prompted, were able to reestablish the connection). As a result, whereas a low-credible source depressed persuasion
in the short term, over the long haul, the persuasion resulting from high-
and low-credible sources might be comparable.[89]

The second and third volumes of the Yale studies reported further
work on a variety of topics including the order of presentation of
arguments and the connection of demographic and personality factors
to susceptibility to persuasion. In the 1957 book, for instance, the
Hovland team researched whether the first or the last argument enjoyed
an edge, concluding that there was little evidence to support the so-
called Law of Primacy claimed previously by some researchers.[90] In
1959, the team reported findings on such questions as whether women
or men were more persuasible. Researchers found that high-school
females exposed to persuasive communications were significantly more
susceptible to influence by the message than the males, a result that
the researchers attributed to the differentiation of sex roles in then-
contemporary society. Further research suggested that personality factors were more influential in determining persuasibility in the case of
young men than when the responses of young women were studied.[91]

Closely vying with Hovland-style persuasion research was Paul Lazarsfeld's impressive research program of studies on voting, radio listening, and decision making. In the year following the Lazarsfeld–Merton announcement of a new quantitatively oriented, managerial approach to propaganda, Lazarsfeld and Frank Stanton brought out another volume of radio-research studies. In an effort to tie together an otherwise eclectic group of articles on program content, radio listening, audience psychology, historical changes in magazine biographies, and the panel and program-analyzer methodologies, Lazarsfeld and Stanton emphasized that "one broader discipline of communications research" was emerging from these various subjects and approaches.[92]

For the Lazarsfeld team, 1944 was a banner year not only in view of the new volume of radio studies but also because of the group's tour de force, *The People's Choice*, a quantitative panel study of the evolution of voting decisions. The Columbia researchers interviewed 2,400 voters in Erie County, Ohio, at least twice and contacted one panel of 600 subjects every month to probe their thinking about the 1940 presidential election. Great emphasis was placed on differentiating persons who stood by their initial voting preference and those who changed them. Results showed that voters who changed their minds were less interested in the election than those who did not change, and that preference changers experienced more demographic cross-pressures – for instance, being pulled toward the Democrats as a result of Catholic associates and toward the GOP by high-income associates. As to propaganda itself, researchers found that voters exposed themselves chiefly to propaganda with which they already agreed; hence, the role of propaganda mainly was to permit verbal expression of an existing predisposition. Further, the researchers learned that most people acquired the bulk of their political information from personal contacts with certain trusted associates. This latter finding, which surprised the researchers, served as the impetus for later work on the so-called "two-step flow of communication." In this conception, which the Bureau of Applied Social Research (BASR) at first offered tentatively, information moved from mass media directly to opinion leaders and then, indirectly, to the masses.[93]

BASR's media-research program proceeded apace well into the 1950s, at which time Lazarsfeld's interest in communication studies waned, and he turned more to matters of methodology. In 1948, Lazarsfeld and Patricia Kendall provided another comprehensive look at radio's audiences. In 1954, the BASR group, under the leadership of Bernard Berelson, offered a follow-up study of voting behavior. In 1955, Elihu Katz and Lazarsfeld attempted to lay out the relative weight of mass media and interpersonal communication in decisions to purchase products, to attend films, and to develop positions on public affairs.

This latter study was noteworthy because, in addition to confirming the general media/opinion-leader/non–opinion-leader configuration found in *The People's Choice,* the researchers added certain refinements regarding those characteristics of the opinion leader that contributed most heavily to her (all of those interviewed were women) personal influence. Life-cycle position (age plus marital status) weighed most heavily in all areas except public affairs, where gregariousness and social status figured more prominently. Katz and Lazarsfeld described their findings as part of a general rediscovery of the primary group (family or local associations), which the grander theories of mass society had forgotten.[94]

As reflected in the work of the Hovland and Lazarsfeld traditions, Berelson's favored lines of communication research were both highly quantitative and highly attuned to ways that data could be massaged into middle-range explanatory laws and theories. Hovland's research emphasized controlled conditions in which differences among experimental groups were evaluated with statistical tests of significance; Lazarsfeld's program emphasized survey data analyzed via the calculation and comparison of percentages. The Yale researchers focused their findings on such theoretical questions as the Law of Primacy in persuasion; the Columbia team employed data to test its process-oriented theory of propaganda versus personal influence.

Work by other researchers favored by the 1954 SSRC conferees displayed these favored characteristics in greater or lesser degrees. Although Kurt Lewin drew upon cultural study and psychoanalysis, his classic work on democratic versus authoritarian leadership styles was experimental, and his research was organized around an overall "field theory" (examining people as they were pushed or blocked by perceived forces in their social worlds or life spaces). For his part, Robert F. Bales followed the quantitative drift in developing measures of roles taken by members of task groups. The information theory of Claude Shannon and Warren Weaver was, even for those enamored by numbers, hypermathematical. Osgood's measurement-oriented study of meaning was based on advanced factor-analytic statistics applied to semantic differential scales (a series of continuua such as *clean/dirty, light/dark*). George Miller's famous dictum that humans typically could detect approximately seven gradations of quality ("plus or minus two") was based upon extracting information from experimental data. Although the works of Ruesch and Bateson, and those of Harold Innis, were hopelessly qualitative, these researches were based, respectively, on avant-garde psychoanalytic theory and probing macrohistorical empiricism.[95]

The direction of leading-edge communication research during the 1950s was unmistakably toward findings certified by their means of production on behalf of leaders whose mandates required precise data about audiences, messages, the process of social influence, and the chances of successful persuasion. If the producer-centered nature of this work was not obvious from its origination in wartime advice to command decision makers, from its sources of funding, from its research questions, or from its terminological constellations, then we may turn to congressional hearings of the mid-1960s, which reflected the consensus of the day that the behavioral sciences should be seen in the mode of Cold War strategizing. After taking testimony in the matter of Project Camelot, a social science enterprise on assessing revolutionary conditions in the Third World, a foreign-affairs subcommittee concluded in 1965 that the behavioral sciences had demonstrated their utility in the effective implementation of military assistance, army civic action work, and counterinsurgency. In 1967, the subcommittee recommended employing communication findings to construct culturally adroit messages for target countries and to help overcome such problems of developing nations as low motivation.[96]

Between Pearl Harbor and the Tet Offensive, communication science acted as the data-eliciting and data-organizing arm of hot-war and cold-war command decision making. Persuasion science represented a new mode of symbol study based on that tangent of progressivism that stressed production efficiency more than participatory democracy – thereby reversing the emphasis of the propaganda critics. Under the sway of World War and Cold War imperatives, Bernays's concept of "the engineering of consent" found favor not only among communication practitioners but also in the high-level scholarship and policy-science theorizing of Lasswell and his fellow academicians. Policy science, as with Bernaysian symbol engineering, relied upon the managed-democracy approach to American social governance. This new conception of social scholarship found scientists of society rendering service through fealty to America's legitimate, informed, and presumably well-intentioned leaders.

In the postwar period, under the influence of managed democracy's consent-engineering and policy-scientific strategizing, the notion of social competition had atrophied in communication theory. Acceptable models for this change were legion during the war against Germany and Japan, including Cantril's work for FDR, Likert's work for the Agriculture Department, Lasswell's help to the Justice Department, the FBIS's tips on enemy moves, and the Research Branch's reports to the Pentagon's General Staff. No wonder, therefore, that *propaganda* promptly was replaced on the domestic scene by the neutral-sounding expressions of *communication, information,* and *persuasion.* Only on the international front was one likely to find *propaganda* employed as a significant theoretical term, and even there as a decidedly secondary usage to *psychological warfare.*

Seen from the vantage point of war and international crisis, society required relatively little attention to protecting the discursive integrity of a locally active, Deweyesque public. More important was the project of helping trustworthy and well-intentioned administrators to solve their problems of persuasion. Backed by grants, communication scholars were on hand to help with powerful effects-discovering methodologies. The administrator–grantor–professor nexus, only loosely conceived of in the 1930s, had become closely welded during unremitting years of crisis. To in-the-know students of communication, the quantitative-research/policy-science axis seemed to include all that was necessary to understand democratic social influence.

CHAPTER 7

THE NEW COMMUNICATION – OR THE OLD PROPAGANDA?

The shift in parlance from *propaganda* (which carried connotations of communication's "role in social struggle"[1]) to *communication* (which cast no aspersions on the persuader's purposes) signified progressivism's failure to turn concerns about mass persuasion in the direction of a more alert and active citizenry. However, the hold of practitioners and communication scientists upon popular propaganda consciousness never was complete. The continued development of Big Communication, together with tensions in academe attending to methodological orthodoxy, provided referents for interest in the democratic ethics of communication. In addition, the renewed anti-Red purge of the 1940s and 1950s showed that polemicists yet were able to gain advantage from putting their own stamp on matters of propaganda.

A Paradigmatic Interlocking Directorate

The postwar impulse to channel propaganda consciousness was waged with greatest initial intensity in ivory-tower locales. There the replacement of propaganda analysis with communication research represented a clear case of what Thomas Kuhn would term a paradigmatic revolution in the construction of problems to be studied, the perceived future of the studies, the methods of inquiry viewed as appropriate, the exemplars memorialized by scholars, the professional allegiances of researchers, and the historical misperception of a discipline's past.[2]

The 1954 SSRC-sponsored conference on Research on Public Communication had thrown down the gauntlet regarding what were to be the proper parameters of postwar communication study. Half a decade later, Bernard Berelson, a key player at the 1954 conference, reiterated his position that, for leading-edge scholars, grantors, and policy makers, the most important avenues of communication study were those undertaken by Lasswell, Lazarsfeld, Hovland, and Lewin. In evaluating additional "minor approaches" of the era, Berelson severely applied criteria of empirical methods and quantification. By reference to these standards, the "reformist approach" of the Hutchins commission (Commission on Freedom of the Press), which had focused on "organization, structure, and control of the mass media," were "too value-ridden" to be scientific. Similarly, the "broad historical approach" of David Riesman and Harold Innis prompted the preemptory query: "Is it science?" Also questionable to Berelson was the "journalistic approach" of Ralph Casey and Wilbur Schramm, both of whom were concerned with "practical" topics including "control aspects of the media" and the "ethical responsibility in mass communication" – matters that Berelson deemed "valuable" but implicitly unscientific.[3]

When Berelson's favored lines were set against the secondary approaches, the most striking feature of his framework was the highly dualistic nature of new-style communication research. The Berelsonian paradigm strictly separated the favored approach of quantification from the less regarded tactic of analysis; empirical experimentation emerged as distinct from and superior to case-study inquiry; a studied fact–value split took shape, with a hearty nod to facts that might grow into theories.

Separating quantification from its ostensible opposite, analytic impressionism, was the dualism most directly related to the new paradigm's attractiveness to academic social scientists. In Doob's *Propaganda and Public Opinion,* so widely used that it "paid off the mortgage," the Yale psychologist and ex-IPA board member explained that the ability to reduce phenomena "to quantitative form characterizes any discipline that has reached a scientific stage." Daniel Lerner explained that "counting and computation" could do more to help people control their world than "guessing" which, according to Stouffer's Research-Branch team, started one down the slippery slope of "erroneous generalizations." Stouffer recalled that many a claim made by his researchers fell apart "when exposed to the white light of a statistical appraisal." Doob contrasted the IPA's insufficient interest in quantification to the newer content-analysis studies whose contributions, he believed, "will undoubtedly be more permanent."[4]

Communication researchers lauded the experimental method as uniquely positioned to provide generalizable empirical data without resorting to case-study methods that, earlier, had been the stock in trade both of propaganda critics and such early social science pioneers as Odegard and, to his embarrassment, Lasswell. Here quantitative communication researchers added a number of refinements to the definition of *empirical,* a term that in the philosophy of science generally had denoted knowledge gained through sense experience. Merton and Lazarsfeld described social science empiricism as the systematic collecting of data about a great number of persons in a social group rather than examining individual "anecdotal" cases. Leonard Doob contrasted the "snap judgment of the journalist" to the "verification" favored by the symbol scientist. Stouffer argued that only controlled and statistically analyzed manipulations would permit social scientists to advance "beyond the level of journalistic description" and, thereby, to situate their data in a context that permitted unambiguous theorizing and prediction. In Stouffer's view, social science theorization stood where medical theories had wallowed before instrumentation and experimentation became the norm and allowed for verification and prediction. After all, "the more mature sciences demand, where possible, evidence based on controlled experiment, before saying 'If you change X, then Y will change.'" Stouffer believed that experimentation lagged in social science because, on the one hand, researchers were ignorant of scientific method and inferential statistics and, on the other hand, they faced difficulties of costs, of obtaining human subjects, and of setting up variable-analytic treatments.[5]

A decided fact–value split emerged in American social research as a result of twentieth-century social science's self-conscious effort to distinguish itself from the humanities and to model itself on the natural sciences. Charles Merriam and other like-minded moderns had established the Social Science Research Council as a secure enclave from which a scientific brand of social inquiry might advance. Membership was studiously restricted to those disciplines, and to those disciplinary representatives, who demonstrated the proper interest in and fealty to those qualities of social research that legitimized the endeavor as science. Adherents to the SSRC were conscious in their desire to rid social science of its humanistic legacy of "speculative thought or normative judgment." In its effort to "eliminate values from the actual process of inquiry," SSRC-style research wrested matters of moral assessment from the collegial dimension of social science and relegated evaluation to the grayer, nebulous regions where scholars individually selected their subjects of study and where policy makers chose to (or chose not to) implement the findings.[6]

With the new paradigm of communication science moving toward quantification (and away from analysis), toward experiments (and away from case studies), and toward facts and theories (as severed from values), what role remained for issues of democratic communication ethics? Clearly, the new paradigm was not arranging itself to probe how communication might produce the untainted public opinion required by participatory democracy. In fact, some social scientists anxiously avoided anything that smacked of social ethics. Talcott Parsons of Harvard emphasized that sociology only recently had attained "maturity as a scientific discipline" of a kind clearly distinct from "the philosophical matrix." Keeping the discipline "pure" and free from "ideological contamination" was crucial, Parsons believed, and could be assured only if sociologists gave "unequivocal primacy" to their role of scientist (using the discipline to promote knowledge) over that of citizen (helping to bring knowledge to bear on society's practical problems). According to Hovland's team, the key to building scientific theory with data was to move in the direction of a sophisticated methodology of multivariable experiments such that microscopic studies would accumulate to build scientific theories of communication.[7]

Media effects ultimately supplied the mantra that permitted communication scholars to turn away from their field's historical interest in issues of propaganda and participatory democracy. Douglas Waples, a communication theorist in library science, explained that effects studies implemented "the long-range purpose of communications research . . . to learn how communications of different types affect different groups of people, and why." From such a pragmatic viewpoint, the old distinction between education and propaganda broke down because the two induced similar information-gain and attitude-change "effects." For this reason, Hovland and his associates rejected the approach to propaganda taken by the IPA because the institute's devices were shown, experimentally, not to reduce significantly the attitude-change "effects" of messages.[8]

Part of the allure of the effects orientation of communication research was its utility in refocusing the debate about mass communication from the matter of democratic social ethics to the question of what documented results could be discerned from one, or from a series of, persuasive messages. Not that the propaganda critics had rested their claims on a theory that individual messages worked massive effects. Their focus was on the larger sociocultural context of large persuaders constantly diffusing self-interested claims through major media, and the implications for democracy of this social condition. However, implicit to propaganda analysis was an assumption that, somehow and somewhere, society got moved when the media spoke. Clearly, the progressive critics, with their focus on manipulative intent expressed through media, were less adept at discerning the details of who listened and what reactions ensued.

By shifting attention from the democratic ethics of mass communication to the pragmatic measurement of media effects, the paradigm of communication research fit comfortably within the parameters of a newer notion of "science as method" that had grown up in the twentieth century. In the early nineteenth century, the term *science* generally was understood to denote a well-organized body of principles concerning an area of interest. Even when the expression became more associated with specific evidence and with careful observation, the works of historians and reformers were thought to contribute significantly to the scholarly conversation. The dramatic rise of the natural sciences in the later part of the century, however, helped to closely associate the term *science* with objectivity and the experimental method.

Leading social scientists who became committed to upgrading the status of their infant specialties embraced the era's restricted definition of science and, accordingly, redefined the scientific character of their enterprises.[9] As "scientists," communication scholars gravitated toward natural-science methods and, as they conceptualized how their work influenced the wider society, tended to view citizens as separate social atoms rather than members of a contentious community. In rediscovering the primary group, mass-communication researchers tended to forget the mass-movement potential in their audiences. Hovland's Distinguished Scientific Contribution Award from the American Psychological Association praised him for methodological innovations that helped him to discover how "an individual" dealt with "the complex informational output of a persuasive argument." Hovland's advice regarding establishment of the Ford Foundation's Behavioral Science Program similarly emphasized finding a "scientific solution" to "individual problems and afflictions." Berelson's Behavioral Sciences department at Ford proved strikingly unattuned to the collective-action dimension of social phenomena. After the Brown desegregation decision of 1954, Berelson and his associates discussed how his department might aid the civil rights movement. But they could find no lines of action that, at the same time, amounted to good behavioral science: "And I never could find anything . . . that the social sciences could usefully do to assist on the whole desegregation civil rights issue in the middle '50s."[10]

A study of the redbaiting phenomenon, published in 1949 by Joseph Klapper and Charles Glock of BASR, illustrated how, if the researcher were willing, scientific method could incapacitate the social conscience of communication research. "Trial by Newspaper" amounted to a statistical content analysis of how nine newspapers treated charges by the House Un-American Activities Committee against Edward U. Condon, the director of the National Bureau of Standards. Condon, although cleared by the Truman administration's departmental loyalty board, had come under fire from rightists in Congress such that, according to Klapper and Glock, "many citizens have become concerned about the affair as a striking example of what has sometimes been called trial by newspaper." Accepting a call from *Scientific American* to analyze the situation, BASR undertook a content study of certain daily papers in the New York area during a six-month period beginning March 1, 1948.

After examining 4,589 articles, the researchers constructed "a statistical measurement of the extent to which the newspapers treated him [Condon] favorably or unfavorably." For instance, Klapper and Glock discovered that the *New York Times* and *New York Herald Tribune* both had printed two statements favoring Condon for every one that was unfavorable to him. (Favorable information generally originated either from the Truman administration or from scientists; discrediting data normally originated in HUAC or the FBI.) In contrast, stories appearing in the *New York Journal-American* contained four unfavorable references to Condon for every favorable one. From their review, Klapper and Glock characterized the charges against Condon as "vague" and noted the tendency for background-type stories to be unhelpful to him. Further, they observed, "all the papers reported the Committee's [HUAC's] promise to give Dr. Condon a hearing far more often than they reported its failure to do so." However, the researchers emphasized, all of the foregoing were "objective findings" about which BASR was unable to offer any interpretation. "These are simply objective data revealed by the analysis. Whether they show that the New York press was fair or unfair in its coverage of the case is a matter of interpretation which is beyond the scope of this analysis. The interpretation will depend on the standards applied by the observer."[11]

From the viewpoint of progressive propaganda critique, the coquettish posture on evaluation taken by Klapper and Glock would have been seen either as overly fastidious posturing or as blatant critical blindness. However, the war had shifted the intellectual balance of forces away from the IPA and toward BASR in the debate over how society should treat propaganda. The effort to solidify the gains of wartime communication research ultimately produced a paradigmatic interlocking directorate centered in the granting foundations but also involving government, business, prestigious universities, research conferences, and research institutes. Wartime government work had brought together a critical mass of administrators, scholars, practitioners, and businesspeople committed to quantitative communication-effects data. Most of the leading postwar communication scientists had taken government service either as administrators, staff researchers, or regular consultants.[12] Further, the postwar Social Science Research Council, which served as a retailer for wholesale grants from major foundations, enjoyed the services of several alumni of the war-communication agencies including Frederick Osborn, Carl Hovland, Kimbell Young, and Leonard S. Cottrell (also, Donald Young, SSRC executive director, had served the Research Branch as a consultant).

Foundation grantors represented a particularly important link in the interlocking nexus that emerged after the war to promote persuasion science. Administrators and researchers from the wartime communication agencies played key roles in each of the three foundations most active in funding social science research. Leland DeVinney, who helped to put out *The American Soldier* volumes, was associate director of the social science grant program at Rockefeller; John Marshall, alumnus of the FBIS, served as associate director of Rockefeller's humanities grant program; Bernard Berelson of the FBIS was director of the behavioral-sciences program at Ford; psychologist John Gardner of OSS was a key social science grantsperson and, later, director of the Carnegie Corporation; Charles Dollard, Research Branch senior administrator, eventually served as president of the Carnegie Corporation. Furthermore, major communication research scholars served as consultants to the key foundations. In 1951, for instance, Berelson at Ford put out the call to Hovland, Lazarsfeld, Lasswell, Stouffer, Merton, and Leites for advice in setting up his grant operation.[13]

In contrast to the IPA's inability to secure reliable foundation support, communication science benefited greatly from the conscious effort of the major social science–oriented foundations to straddle the Left (pro-democracy) and Right (pro-efficiency) split within American progressivism. The reformist instincts of the foundation staff (who kept their eyes and ears attuned both to social conditions and to social commentary) blended with the pro-business inclinations of the foundation trustees (who were drawn from the higher echelons of capitalism) to produce social science grant programs that exhibited an ameliorative earnestness masked with safe conventionality. The orientation of communication science to abstract research hypotheses and to objectivist methodology rendered this arm of social science doubly attractive to representatives of Rockefeller, Carnegie, and Ford. On the one hand, the effort to apply natural-science approaches to social influence was clearly innovative and, therefore, fit with the urge of foundations to "be a little bit ahead of the wave of the future."[14] On the other hand, because communication research treated social influence abstractly, and with an administrative rather than a popular-action cast, few foundation trustees would associate this form of social science scholarship with socialism or perceive it as a direct threat to capitalism. Intellectual fence straddling of this kind was amplified by the Social Science Research Council, a group very much aware of its overwhelming dependence on the Rockefeller–Carnegie–Ford trio for funds.[15]

The effort to bestow capitalism's surplus in a way that bridged progressivism's reformist and efficiency-promoting tangents did not reflect simply the internal dynamics of the foundations. The impulse was rooted also in the relationship of rich foundations to the political world. Politicians were understandably anxious about the prospect that large privately controlled endowments might make unpredictable forays into the hustings. Therefore, the tax laws governing grantsmanship prohibited foundations from undertaking projects that could be construed as unleashing propaganda that could give rise to lobbying pressures on legislatures.[16] The late Institute for Propaganda Analysis, of course, had been dogged with the (not undeserved) aura of controversial progressive pleading, a characteristic that not only alarmed trustees of Filene's Good Will Fund but also put off Rockefeller's General Education Board.

The social science–granting foundations made their weight felt in communication scholarship through fellowships, sponsorship of conferences, and endowments to researchers and research institutes at major universities. Early in his career, Lasswell profited from a SSRC fellowship, and Lazarsfeld emigrated to America as a result of a similar Rockefeller program. Berelson was recruited into the field by Waples, who first steered a Rockefeller fellowship his way and later helped to bring the younger man into the FBIS.[17] Marshall's seminars were representative of the many sponsored conferences on communication science that took place during the 1940s and 1950s, as was the SSRC's 1954 confab where Berelson had outlined the field. Agency-originated conferences tended to be very select as to the people invited (around a dozen) and the approaches endorsed (quantitative or at least highly theoretical), such that proponents of historical-critical communication study either were excluded (e.g., Lynd and Alfred Lee) or conformed fully to the prevailing statistical-empirical norms (e.g., Harwood Childs in Marshall's January 18, 1941, conference or Ralph Casey in the 1954 SSRC gathering). Leading-edge conferences linked not only grantors and researchers but also government, as had been the case at Marshall's January 1941 meeting and at the SSRC's June 1959 seminar on the social sciences and national security.

Grantors not only supported individuals and short-term gatherings but also channeled their largesse into more permanent institutional arrangements. As explained by grants administrator Florence Anderson, the Carnegie Foundation operated in the "experimental, demonstration area" where, with limited money, the endowment sought to achieve a maximum national impact with each grant. Carnegie's grant officers believed that only top experts who enjoyed full administrative backing at leading schools were likely to produce the kind of blue-ribbon results that would catch attention and be emulated across the country. For instance, when John Gardner decided that there was a dearth of research on Russia, he helped to initiate the Russian Research Institute at Harvard to capitalize on that school's willingness to back an institute coupled with the fact that leading scholars already were on hand. Along these same lines, the Rockefeller grantspeople earlier had set up Yale's Institute of Human Relations and the Princeton Radio Project.[18]

The grant-supported research institute became an important link for keeping scholars in empirically oriented communication departments in touch with funding from foundations, government, and corporations. The postwar period saw the development of communication research institutes by Wilbur Schramm at Illinois and Stanford, by Likert at Michigan, and, of course, by Lazarsfeld at Columbia. Stouffer became head of Harvard's ongoing Laboratory of Social Relations, and Hovland pursued his persuasion program in cooperation with the existing social science research institute at Yale. As before, the model followed was that of funneling funds to projects undertaken by a select few scholars at a select few schools. During the postwar growth of the research-oriented university, colleges proved anxious for the prestige that came with cutting-edge work in social science, with highly regarded scholars who enjoyed access to major policy makers, and with the imprimatur of grant funding. Elite universities competed for superstars, as when Harvard lured Stouffer away from Chicago, and when Stanford won Schramm from Illinois; however, individuals counted only insofar as they contributed to keeping the directorate running smoothly. In advance of making major appointments, leading universities routinely sounded out the grant administrators to make sure "that they're not appointing someone who is *persona non grata* to the foundations."[19]

One finds little or no self-consciousness among leading academic members of the communication-research nexus about their work to set the direction and tone of scholarship on social influence. In fact, one of the objectives of the research institutes was to socialize novice investigators into the assumptions of the reigning paradigm, and to place them in university, governmental, and private sectors.[20] The aggrandizing and socializing work of leading departments and institutes was entirely fitting, according to Talcott Parsons, who argued that a field's "two fundamental functions" were "the advancement of its own discipline and the training of its core personnel." Parsons believed that the "apprenticeship in empirical investigations," which took place within institutes and/or under grant-supported research programs, was central to the coming of age of social science. Alfred Lee, in his 1976 presidential address to the American Sociological Association (ASA), gave a backhanded compliment to the statistical-empirical elite of his ASA, observing their success to date in having made clear to young sociologists "that lack of respect for the local orthodoxy leads inevitably to something called either 'the revolving door' or 'the tomb of the untenured teacher.' "[21]

The communication-science directorate promoted the paradigm not only within the academy, and within the foundation – industry – government entente, but also among the general reading public. Shortly after the war, Charles Dollard of Carnegie and Donald Young of the SSRC jointly approached Stuart Chase about preparing a book that would popularize quantified social science as his earlier *The Tyranny of Words* had brought semantics to the attention of America's opinion leaders. Finding Chase at first "a little cool to the idea," Dollard and Young "got him around to meet some of the people whose work we thought was important, and he got wildly excited about it." Thereupon, Dollard and Young helped to arrange interviews for Chase with leading social science researchers. These two, and others including Leonard Doob, also helped Chase to organize the book, digest the reviews, and revise the manuscript. The resulting product was Chase's *The Proper Study of Mankind*, which Alfred Lee remembered as being "useful to help legitimate 'scientific sociology,' to move social science away from its humanistic roots." Doob recalled Chase's effort as constituting "a public relations book written in simple language which people could understand" that, as a result, would help social science to accrue a greater share of postwar grant money.[22]

Chase's book brimmed with exclamation-pointed enthusiasm notwithstanding his studious and somewhat encyclopedic effort to review the nature of science, the scientific character of new-style social research, the important lines of social inquiry then under way, and the range and significance of the findings to date. Chase began with a treatment of science as an objective pursuit of hypotheses through experimentation and as assisted by the "powerful searchlight" of operational definitions and statistics. He invoked the customary cautions against overly general speculations that were unverified or unverifiable. Chase's own background and intellectual catholicism, however, found him interspersing favorable nods to the mixed-method work of the Lynds in Middletown and the reports of the IPA's Clyde Miller. Nevertheless, consistent with the objectives of the postwar SSRC, the lines of inquiry pursued in *The Proper Study of Mankind* typically were quantitative and occasionally experimental. Invoking postwar pragmatism, Chase emphasized instances where social research had helped to bring about social harmony and efficiency, as when studies of factory workers led to a greater understanding of teamwork in aircraft plants with resulting lesser levels of labor turnover and absenteeism. He reviewed how scientific polling by Likert had helped the Treasury Department to sell more bonds, and how Stouffer's research had helped to father the army's morale-maintaining point system for discharge.[23] By giving the statistical-empirical paradigm of social research a popular referent, Chase enhanced its claims of universality.

Magic Bullets and Administrative Reformers

A crucial marker of a paradigm shift is the tendency of spokespersons for the new framework to misremember the preceding research tradition and its contributions. As with the sophists of Athens, who are known chiefly through the works of Plato, their antagonist, the propaganda critics suffered the indignity of having their history related chiefly by their intellectual competitors. Not only that, but the new communication-science paradigm eventually claimed, somewhat self-consciously, that it delivered a better brand of democratic reform.

As narrated by the founders of communication research, the propaganda paradigm grew up in a time when, according to Katz and Lazarsfeld, newspapers and radio "were feared as powerful weapons able to rubber-stamp ideas upon the minds of defenseless readers and listeners." In this scenario, the propaganda critics erred by drinking too deeply of European theories of mass society and, accordingly, visualizing the audience as "an atomistic mass." According to Raymond and Alice Bauer, the approach of the IPA assumed "that there was almost a one-to-one relationship between the content of the media and their impact on the public." The Bauers believed that the propaganda critics gave too much credence to Creel's bragging and too little effort to assessing the audience; accordingly, these early critics supposedly assumed the kind of direct-effects model that Lazarsfeld and Hovland conclusively had disproved.[24] The work of the propaganda critics was variously characterized as the "magic bullet" or "hypodermic needle" theory of mass communication. Well into the 1980s, young persuasion scientists were told to be glad that their own teachers had broken ranks with the scientifically unsophisticated propaganda critics, who, because they imbibed an outmoded stimulus–response (S–R) psychology, drew the false inference that messages could be shot directly from one mind into another.[25]

For the most part, the evidence cited to support the "magic bullet" interpretation was indirect – for instance, the existence of S–R psychology in the early twentieth century, the influence of European mass-society theories on the Chicago School of social science, and the almost-universal belief that World War I propaganda had had an impact. Upon close examination, it is clear that progressive propaganda critics, in contrast to Chicago School social scientists, were little motivated by theoretical impulses and much activated by social ones relating to the wartime manipulations. This difference in critical motivation is what set Lasswell's 1927 book and article apart from contemporaneous muckraking studies of propaganda. Where Lasswell drew upon S–R psychology and mass-society theory, the propaganda critics grounded their work in the progressive mission to promote a participatory democracy characterized by free-flowing discourse.

The focus of propaganda critique on untheoretical case studies meant that the chief proof offered by communication scientists for the magic-bullet interpretation typically was that the propaganda critics said little about the specifics of how propaganda worked upon listeners; therefore, the argument went, they must have believed in direct effects. Here again, communication science assumed that the propaganda critics aimed to develop a theory of message perception. To the contrary, most critics pursued a reformist mission to expose instances of institutional manipulation so that the people, in their capacity as participants in democratic life, could make better choices both as citizens and as consumers. Unlike Hovland et al., propaganda critics did not conceive of audiences as a collection of individual perceivers (whose minds acted independently to make messages meaningful) but rather focused on a whole public participating in collective action. Critics were little concerned about who was more influenced than whom at a particular time by a particular message on a particular issue. Instead, media muckrakers emphasized the larger cultural landscape in which institutions monopolized information (as Lippmann demonstrated with regard to the Great War), in which professional persuaders orchestrated speakers and writers behind the scenes (as Ray Baker showed with reference to the railroads), and in which persuasion was disguised as education (in student contests), as information (in news), as entertainment (in sponsored films), or as religion (in preaching). Far from viewing the people as passive, the audience visualized by the IPA was supposed to act once it had been alerted.

If the magic-bullet formulation represented inaccurate history, this faulty memory of progressive propaganda critique nevertheless was rendered superficially plausible both by the postwar emphasis on measuring short-term media effects and by a postwar tendency to ignore the problem of manipulation in communication. Fully socialized into the communication-science paradigm, Leonard Doob recalled that, after the war, he "wouldn't have dreamed of" employing the seven propaganda devices in a theoretical description of social influence.[26] Many believed so confidently in the universal superiority of the communication-science paradigm that they touted their data-rich theories as actually delivering a superior kind of reform.

During the later 1940s, a number of communication researchers picked up Bernays's notion of producing the good society by instilling harmony between institutions and individuals. Nathan Glazer recalled the "great confidence in the power of the behavioral sciences to affect behavior and to create a better society" at this time. Although latter-day commentators have complained of the "anti-reformist consequences of the empirical tradition as it has evolved historically," it remains the case that such innovators of the paradigm as Lasswell, Lazarsfeld, Lewin, and Stouffer harbored meliorative inclinations. Those who promoted communication study believed that new-style social research was being deployed for better purposes than "solely to assist the status quo in government and the powers that be."[27]

Lasswell clearly saw vectors of reform radiating from the bonding of communication research to policy problems. As part of his desire to link research to action, Lasswell publicly proposed in 1941 a Council of Civil Education that would curtail antidemocratic propaganda by labeling it as such, and soliciting instant replies.[28] Throughout the 1940s, Lasswell sketched out ambitious plans for various organizations that would make manifest "the integration of morals, science, policy, and action." This work flowed from his belief that "morals, without science and policy, are helpless" and that "science and policy without morals threaten to destroy mankind."[29]

In June 1941, Lasswell prepared a memorandum regarding a proposed "American Policy Commission" to be located at the University of Chicago. Lasswell envisioned the commission working to "clarify the basic principles of a free society," to obtain information (through interviews) from opinion leaders, and to bring scientists and policy makers together. The result would be an addressing of "the pressing problems of the emergency and post-emergency period."[30] In mid-1942, Lasswell drafted a memorandum on establishing a college of government that, bringing together people from all walks of life, would train them as political leaders by providing them the widest possible education. In mid-1944, Lasswell was formulating ideas about postwar research institutes in Washington.[31] By January 1945, Lasswell had prepared a document, entitled "Remarks about a Proposed Method of Contributing to the Integration of Policy, Morals and Science," in which he laid out plans for yet another institute. Although Lasswell separated himself from those who were "contemptuous of the public," he believed it was important for scientists to give "guidance to public opinion." Hence, his proposal for an annual conference arrangement in which scientists of all kinds would meet to deliberate and "issue public recommendations" not only to policy makers but also to the widest possible audience. Lasswell envisioned approaching the Rockefeller Foundation for support of his plan.[32]

Lazarsfeld, too, was interested in how science could clarify from on high the contours of democratic life. Some of his intensity in keeping effects-oriented studies separate from politics flowed from Lazarsfeld's having assumed that documented communication effects, resonating in a democratic milieu, would lead to appropriate action. Lazarsfeld had not given up his hope that critical scholarship could inform administratively conducted research. Echoing his 1941 proposal to merge critical and administrative agendas, Lazarsfeld spoke in 1948 about "The Role of Criticism in the Management of Mass Media." Here BASR's director acknowledged that media managers reacted nervously to criticism and that "we academic people always have a certain sense of tight-rope walking: at what point will the commercial partners find some necessary conclusion too hard to take and at what point will they shut us off from the indispensable sources of funds and data?" The dilemma could be lessened, Lazarsfeld believed, if "criticism of the mass media," which was not yet "recognized as a formal and legitimate field of intellectual endeavor," were given greater standing. Citing such examples as A. J. Liebling's press-criticism articles in *The New Yorker,* Lazarsfeld proposed more attention to the "judgment of mass media." John Marshall of the Rockefeller Foundation invited Lazarsfeld to elaborate what kind of media criticism might be undertaken.[33]

Lazarsfeld's meditations on critical work always conflicted with his desire to separate data from theory and to keep research at arm's length from reform. His enigmatic position on criticism and reform was illustrated not only by his failure to integrate Theodor Adorno into the radio-research program but also by his later methodological and stylistic disagreements with C. Wright Mills, issues that prompted Lazarsfeld to sack Mills as field director of the survey program in Decatur, Illinois. Yet, for a time, Lazarsfeld directly advised the program of pro-tolerance research being spearheaded by the American Jewish Committee (AJC). Samuel Flowerman, head of the AJC's Department of Scientific Research, suggested in 1946 that opinion polls and other quantitative forms of audience analysis might provide useful lessons in the preparing of "mass protolerance propaganda." For instance, Flowerman believed that quantitative surveys might clarify the effect of salting spot announcements into programs and might illuminate how to change entrenched attitudes. Somewhat less sanguine, Lazarsfeld turned to the research data to enumerate a number of caveats about pro-tolerance propaganda. For instance, bigots misinterpreted cartoons that were designed to swat intolerance, and the audience for radio programs about ethnic groups chiefly consisted of members of the particular group. On the positive side, Lazarsfeld drew from BASR's study of 1940s voting to suggest that personal, face-to-face influence might be employed in grass-roots efforts to weaken prejudice, and that media could be used to keep the volunteers motivated.[34]

Lazarsfeld's remarks increased the saliency of the work of Lewin and his group as to how small-group decision making might reflect democracy's values. Continuing Lewin's early experimentation on the comparative results of democratic versus autocratic leadership in small groups, Ralph White and Ronald Lippitt identified apathy and over-conformity as significant obstacles to the effective working of democracy. They argued that the ability of some members of a small group to remain psychologically isolated from it boded ill, by extrapolation, for the larger society, which seemed remote to many citizens. Not only was democracy threatened by inability to bond with groups and with community, but conformity's pressures (in groups and in American culture) weakened people both as creative participants and as leaders. White and Lippitt's argument that participation promoted satisfaction had a progressive-reformist cast to it, even if some of their examples of participation were drawn from the world of industrial relations, where the intent seemed more in line with a managed-democracy approach.[35]

One finds even in the most harrowing years of the Haunted Fifties other examples of where the communication-science directorate undertook work oriented to top–down democratic action. In 1953, the Ford Foundation endowed the Fund for the Republic to conduct research in defense of civil liberties. Since the foundation undertook this initiative at the height of the McCarthy period, the Ford grantors suffered bitter attacks from leading pro-McCarthy columnists Westbrook Pegler and George Sokolsky. In one study released by the fund, Samuel Stouffer surveyed American attitudes toward communism and toward civil liberties, and he provided some mildly critical perspectives on the McCarthy-esque mood. Central to Stouffer's book were data about levels of tolerance for nonconformist speakers, including socialists, atheists, persons who were accused of (but denied) communist affiliation, and admitted communists. He labeled as exaggerated the extreme fear of a communist menace, and he challenged the media to report responsibly on the matter because most of what Americans knew (or thought they knew) about communist subversion did not originate in direct experience.[36]

Leading communication researchers were attracted to the idea of using research to bring important information to the public, to bring about more intelligent policies, to evaluate the effectiveness of media organizations, to combat prejudice better, to understand democracy better, and to safeguard civil liberties better. All of these initiatives by leading grantors and scholars, however, remained in the mode of the wartime democracy of data and theory-enriched decisions from the top as distinct from the participatory democracy of Dewey, Lynd, and the Institute for Propaganda Analysis. What Lasswell, Lazarsfeld, Marshall, Flowerman, Lewin, White, Lippitt, and Stouffer shared was an orientation away from popular action and toward theoretically informed data gathering and concomitant expert advice to society's designated leaders.

However much leading scholars of communication research wanted to bind action to scholarship, morals to science, and criticism to empiricism, the integrations that they proposed proved, for a variety of reasons, not entirely practicable given their research paradigm. For one thing, the limited-effects model of mass media that was gaining sway made the whole enterprise of administratively guided public action seem, as Glazer recalled, somewhat naive. Research by Lazarsfeld's bureau tended to throw cold water on the idea of pro-tolerance propaganda. Not only did the general tenor of BASR's voting studies suggest that media merely reinforced preexisting dispositions, but experimentation on pro-tolerance messages showed that receivers were able to misinterpret or ignore them. Furthermore, any interests in reform by communication researchers were dampened by the many dualisms inherent to the postwar social-research paradigm. For instance, in a time when reform was secondary to science, and criticism subordinate to empirical methods, it is not surprising that Lewin's circle devoted more energy to working out the processes of group dynamics and interpersonal communication than to touting the importance of democracy.[37] Finally, younger communication researchers were more narrowly trained and more administratively socialized (compared to Lasswell, Lazarsfeld, and Lewin); so the second-generation scientists had less motivation to articulate even the top–down reformism espoused by their old mentors.

If Lasswell favored intelligent social change, if Lazarsfeld and Marshall toyed with media criticism, if Lewin defended democracy, and if Stouffer hoped for responsible news reporting, it remained the case that active proponents of the critical slant on mass communication found themselves at a considerable disadvantage in leading-edge echelons of postwar social science. Alfred Lee experienced firsthand the tenuous position of critical work on communication when he served as a member of a committee charged by the Society for the Psychological Study of Social Issues to assemble a reader on public opinion and propaganda. Lee recalled that Daniel Katz, leader of the group, was reluctant to include certain critical essays suggested by Lee. Katz regarded this kind of work as "old stuff" that would detract from the cutting-edge material that he wanted for an advanced textbook in social science. Ultimately, the reader did include some few articles about agitators, about propaganda in institutional advertising, and about freedom of speech.[38] As will be seen hereafter, the colloquy between Katz and Lee on the parameters of postwar communication textbooks was a smaller version of a larger debate about the relative attention to be given to the study of social problems as opposed to social process.

With its strong emphasis on science and its satisfaction with top–down reform, communication research did its part in creating the intellectual context out of which grew Daniel Bell's thesis of a postwar end of ideology. Comparing the 1930s to the 1950s, Bell found less interest in a class-based analysis of society and social problems. In his view, the stresses of the preceding two decades had caused American intellectuals to come to a "rough consensus" such that the old battles between Marxism and liberalism were no longer helpful. Further, science seemed to provide a body of knowledge largely uncontaminated by ideological interests. To be sure, Bell was not unmindful of the manipulative element in industrial human-relations programs, nor did he ignore the populist discontents that manifested themselves in McCarthyism. Although Bell was not Pollyannaish about the Eisenhower era, he saw relatively little of the former all-or-nothing approach that had been rooted in deep ideological dissensus.[39]

However much society seemed more cohesive in the 1950s than in the 1930s, social science's dualisms became painfully apparent when researchers intruded into areas where Bell's "rough consensus" was absent. In the matter of civil rights for blacks, for instance, Berelson was learning that "on political grounds" Southern institutions were disinclined to sponsor any kind of work in the area. Similarly, when Muzafer Sherif was studying racial attitudes in a project with Hovland, he found administrators at one Texas college so worried about the "political dynamite" of a study on racial attitudes that the college's president hedged in participating.[40] If society's lack of consensus on race relations produced cautiousness at the top, what of the fissures produced by the postwar Red Scare? Lasswell and Lazarsfeld soon would learn that in the McCarthy period even work of an administrative-technical character might bring recriminations upon a researcher.

In sum, the reformist spirit in communication research was constantly at risk not only in view of the limited-effects model and the narrower training and dualistic socialization of young scholars, but also because of increasingly clear signals that social dissensus would keep communication research from moving against actual postwar social problems. The marriage of scientist and policy maker appeared to work when society's leaders were in agreement, as in the decision for all-out war against Germany and Japan. But when dissensus reigned, as it did in the postwar civil rights movement (and, as will be seen, in regards to the anti-Red purge), communication researchers discovered the practical limits to their assumption that intelligent ideas brought to the attention of administrators automatically brought forth social reform.

The Red Propaganda Menace

Communication practitioners and scientists, whose alliance burgeoned in the wartime agencies, proved able to displace propaganda critique from its formerly favored status in academe. At the same time, in the wider public sphere, polemicists also were undermining the work of progressive critics. As it turned out, members of the communication-science paradigmatic directorate would join the muckraking critics in suffering from rightist antipropaganda polemics.

Under fire in the academy for tepid theorizing and sentimental impressionism, progressive antipropaganda scholars found that their critical work also exposed them to public pillory. In 1942, Clyde Miller found himself branded as a communist in a letter to the *New York World-Telegram* written by Charles Yale Harrison. Harrison rehashed the same points made earlier against Beals and the IPA by Alfred Bingham, to wit, that the institute's analyses were biased against a strong national defense and, when directed against the communists, far too mild. Although reluctant to dignify Harrison's charges with direct comment, Miller did observe in a personal letter to the *World-Telegram*'s editor, Lee Wood, that "I had opposed our participation in World War II until Pearl Harbor (more heresy, to Communists!)."[41]

The case of Miller illustrates the two rich reservoirs of ideological ambiguity that sustained the redbaiting of progressives during the twenty years that followed Stalin's complex political maneuverings of 1935–1941. Progressive intellectuals and educators had associated themselves with communism either by attacking social conditions in

America (as did the Reds) or by calling for transformations that would render a competitive society more collective (as did the Reds). Also, during the time when Stalin courted liberals as potential allies against Hitler, many progressive-minded persons in America participated in meetings and joined groups in which communists had played key (although usually covert) roles. Robert S. Lynd became, in view of his published critical works, another easy target by the standards of red-baiting that were evolving during the 1940s. As a result of his *Knowledge for What?* (1939) and his participation in various progressive movements of the 1930s, the stigma of "radicalism" had attached itself firmly to the Columbia sociologist and former IPA board member. Since his days as a young divinity student preaching to oil-field workers, Lynd had harbored deep concerns about the impact of large business corporations on American life. Nevertheless, if Lynd hypothesized capitalism's decline and seemed to favor social planning over individualism, he remained a thoroughly academic and self-consciously tentative moralist. In the context of postwar fears of Russia, however, Lynd became so controversial that his stigma was projected even upon his wife and son, both of whom were investigated for radicalism during the 1950s and 1960s.[42]

If Lynd's oblique challenges to consumer capitalism and to corporate control of science offended against 100-percent Americanism, propaganda critic George Seldes had become one of the chief bugbears of the Right. Between 1940 and 1950, Seldes published his irritating *In Fact* newsletter, which showcased juicy scoops, suppressed or downplayed by the mainstream press, that were "sent in by volunteers, reporters, editors, foreign correspondents, Washington correspondents and free lancers." Seldes was particularly proud of his early series in *In Fact* that had brought to light a concerted effort by leading financiers and members of the National Association of Manufacturers to foist the ostensibly populist Wendell Willkie, an industrialist, on a GOP whose party workers preferred the intellectual and patrician Robert A. Taft.

Red hunters of the Dies committee had particularly good reason for animus against *In Fact,* a publication that proclaimed itself as "An Antidote for Falsehood in the Daily Press" and that enjoyed a circulation of over 100,000 due largely to blanket subscriptions purchased by many CIO union locals. In a startling and rare instance of propaganda-analysis praxis, the alliance between *In Fact* and the CIO helped to bring down Dies. HUAC's chairman, for all his power in Washington, was forced to withdraw for reelection in 1944 when faced with a constituency that contained large numbers of oil-field workers roused against him by *In Fact.*

A prolific writer, Seldes during the 1950s was caught up in the McCarthy dragnet when two of his books, found by committee operatives in overseas libraries of the U.S. Army and of the U.S. Information Agency, were branded pro-communist by Senator Joe McCarthy's aides. Seldes, as it turned out, proved a poor witness when, in an executive session of McCarthy's investigating committee, the writer defended his books as *anti*communist. Seldes reported his disgust with the lies and violence that the Communist Party used to gain and hold power, and he labeled himself an "Aiken Democrat," someone who split his franchise for George Aiken (R., Vt.) and FDR. Quickly losing interest in Seldes, McCarthy excused the writer from the public hearings and, a few minutes later, even invited Seldes to join him in the Senate elevator.[43]

As with Miller, Lynd, and Seldes, Kirtley Mather, the IPA's erstwhile president, had built up a record of political comment and action that made him vulnerable to attacks by those interested in branding progressives as Red propagandists. In 1937, Mather publicly refused to take the Massachusetts teachers' loyalty oath because, as he maintained, he already had pledged his loyalty to the Constitution when he took a captain's commission in the U.S. Army Reserves, joined the U.S. Geologic Survey, and served on the local school board. Later, Mather organized a fiesta to raise money for medical supplies to benefit Spanish loyalists fighting Franco, and he served as a member of the Massachusetts Committee to Abolish HUAC. *Life* magazine included Mather in a profile of America's leading communist "Dupes and Fellow Travelers" who were attending a Cultural and Scientific Conference for World Peace. Others pictured and profiled included scientist Albert Einstein, columnist Dorothy Parker, playwright Arthur Miller, novelist Norman Mailer, composer Leonard Bernstein, and additional notables including Thomas Mann, George Seldes, and Lillian Hellman. On the advice of counsel, Mather refrained from instituting a libel suit against *Life* since, according to attorney Arthur Garfield Hayes, the ambiguous wording of the "charges" against Mather and the others had been carefully structured to preclude a successful suit. By October 1950, Joe McCarthy was arguing that Mather's election as president of the American Association for the Advancement of Science exemplified the "Communist infiltration into the ranks of science." In 1953, Mather was summoned to appear before the Internal Security Subcommittee of the Senate Judiciary Committee, chaired by Senator William E. Jenner.[44]

Just as muckraking had exposed the propaganda critics to rightist polemical cudgels, so too did government service similarly make quantitatively oriented communication scholars vulnerable to political attack. Rightists in Congress had resented not only the New Deal's loud liberal promotionalism but also the stigmatizing of isolationists during World War II. One way for the Right to strike back was to associate social scientists serving in government with allegedly subversive propaganda. Goodwin Watson of Columbia, whom Hadley Cantril had tapped to head the analysis wing of the Foreign Broadcast Intelligence Service, became an early administrator–researcher casualty of the anti-Red polemical circus in Congress. Although the Dies committee was playing its cards relatively close to the vest in 1942–1943, its chairman rose up to demand that Congress delete Watson's salary from appropriations. Watson, never a communist, nonetheless was done in by his penchant for signing petitions and attending popular front meetings in the 1930s, actions that placed him in the vanguard of those who supported the loyalist cause in Spain, who praised certain innovations in the USSR, and who called for all manner of social transformations in the USA. Watson, as with others active in founding Consumers Union, also may have run afoul of HUAC because of committee-investigator J. B. Matthews's continuing animus toward his former competitors.

During a recess of an appropriations subcommittee hearing on his case, Watson reported approaching one member of the legislative panel to ask why so much attention was being paid to his minor position with the FBIS. The answer, as Watson recalled, was that the committee "wanted to get James Lawrence Fly, the head of the [Federal] Communications Commission, and one way they could beat him was to show up subversive employees." (Fly's FCC, it should be noted, had given out that none other than Martin Dies was the living American receiving the greatest number of favorable notices in Nazi propaganda broadcasts.) Later called before the Dies committee, Watson observed to his dismay how members "weren't interested in the explanation." "They were only interested in whether they could find some point, some place where they could get leverage to support their case." After Watson left Washington, Paul Lazarsfeld gave him work at the Bureau of Applied Social Research.[45]

Once redbaiting turned promiscuous, the stigma of subversive activities was apt to settle upon even the most politically cautious of the managerial scholars and foundation grantors who labored to establish the field of communication research. Some of the pioneer communication scientists were vulnerable because they could be called to account for youthful political association and expression. Thus, M. Brewster Smith, a junior member of the Research Branch, found himself called before HUAC as a result of his membership in the American Student Union, a popular-front organization. As with many of his generation, Smith had terminated his early flirtation with fellow traveling after the

Moscow purge trials and the Hitler–Stalin pact. Years later, Smith wrote of his deep shame at being forced to name others active in 1930s radicalism. Although a staff member of the prestigious SSRC, Smith secretly was placed on a number of blacklists that kept him off government peer-review boards for research grants.[46]

The vitae of Lasswell and Lazarsfeld, respectively liberal and socialist in their political orientations, carried fewer political loose ends than Smith, but the increasingly finely filtered machinery of redbaiting snagged the two, nevertheless. Lasswell's security investigation resulted more from bad luck than poor political prescience. Charged by the Army–Navy–Air Force Personnel Security Board with a long and sympathetic association with communism, Lasswell believed that the charges sprang from his early studies of communist propaganda in Chicago. Lasswell's source materials for this research briefly had become controversial when, during a move from the Windy City to Washington, Lasswell's van "overturned in a ditch along the way and burned." He recalled that "the discovery of charred fragments of communist books and pamphlets about the scene of the wreck caused a short-lived sensation in the nearby communities."

In an effort to retain his security clearance, Lasswell prepared an extensive dossier describing his research career, government service, impressive roster of references, and arm's-length connections with communism in his role as a scientist who studied the movement. In an accompanying cover letter, Lasswell reported that he was "deeply disturbed by the thought of the ignorance, carelessness, or malice that must have inspired the charges against me." As a citizen, Lasswell expressed his shock that "in light of my long and unambiguous record" he would suffer even a tentative denial of security access. This reading of McCarthyism proved far more passionate than Lasswell's earlier scholarly treatment of the subject in "Propaganda and Mass Insecurity." In this preceding nod at redbaiting, the Yale scholar of government dispassionately had discussed how, in a climate where loyalties were in doubt, "propaganda becomes increasingly a tool of tendencies which are made exempt from reality-testing."[47]

Paul Lazarsfeld also suffered from society's lapse of interest in careful "reality-testing" as regarded alleged communist propaganda activities. Investigated as part of a call to become a consultant to UNESCO, Lazarsfeld was required to answer a number of unreasonable and insulting charges about his loyalty. To the question of why he had attended a meeting of the American Writers Congress (a group cited by the Attorney General as a communist front), Lazarsfeld supplied some additional facts with the wryly understated recommendation that "I am sure that you will want to add the following information to your file." Lazarsfeld advised the security personnel that major studio heads and members of the armed forces also had been in attendance as was the president of the University of California who read a message of greeting from FDR. (Ironically, Lazarsfeld's talk at this "subversive" gathering was none other than the first draft of the managerial-administrative research Pronunciamento that he and Merton had published in 1943.) Responding to another charge against him, Lazarsfeld apologized for having failed to mention the alias, "Elias Smith," which he affixed to certain early radio-research articles in an effort to disguise what initially had been an almost one-man operation.[48]

If managerial-administrative scholarship might make one vulnerable to attack during the heyday of the Cold War anti-Red purge, it followed that the granting foundations that sponsored this seemingly inoffensive research also would suffer the shotgun style of inquiry that characterized the period. Because they favored support for leading researchers at prestigious universities, foundations ran afoul of the anti-elitist as well as the anticommunist strains of populism. Although the liberalism of major grantors was of an establishment kind, and although the foundations that funded social science grants favored theoretical treatises to reformist action, their largesse still was irritating to rightist ideologues whose favorite causes and supporters rarely obtained grants.

In 1952, a House committee, chaired by Rep. Eugene Cox, investigated alleged communist infiltration of the foundations. The Carnegie Corporation, which supported social science, found itself somewhat vulnerable according to the thinking of the day because Alger Hiss had been president of a separate Carnegie trust, the Endowment for International Peace. (Hiss, arguably the only real subversive that HUAC ever found, had been convicted for perjury after denying under oath that he passed secret documents to communists.) Corporation officials soon received questionnaires inquiring whether they had supported any "anti-American" people. Some eyebrows were raised about why Carnegie had supported Gunnar Myrdal, a Swedish socialist, in a study of the American Negro and of racial prejudice. Other typical questions included why the corporation had underwritten the National Council for the Social Studies, whose membership included many persons active in the causes of the 1930s.[49]

Although the Cox committee found little of substance to complain about, a later House investigating committee, chaired by Rep. Carroll Reece, took a more inflammatory line. For instance, Reece's investigators attacked Carnegie's support for the Citizenship Education Program

(CEP) designed to make school children better-informed citizens. Carnegie officials went to the extent of having an economist from the National Association of Manufacturers review the CEP's materials to tally them as "left," "right," and "center" in an effort to rebut Reece's charges of a leftist political tilt in the program. After experiencing two goings-over by Congress, the Carnegie Corporation became more sensitive to the political proclivities of its grant recipients and began to make inquiries along these lines to the scholars it supported.[50]

In responding to inquiries from the Reece committee, Dean Rusk, president of the Rockefeller Foundation and of the General Education Board, stoutly defended the practices of the two endowments in their 41,000 grants over a forty-year period. Rusk maintained that "there is no trace of Communist infiltration into either of these foundations." Responding to certain populist themes in the Reece committee's charges, Rusk denied that the Rockefeller family had established the trusts to evade taxation or that the foundations, for no good reason, had favored certain elite institutions. He dismissed the argument that the recent increase of governmental activities could be linked to social science research supported by the Rockefeller Foundation. Rusk emphasized, for instance, that his organization had "taken no position either for or against social security legislation." He explained that the Rockefeller Foundation tried to minimize the inevitable controversiality of work in social studies by "supporting objective studies which might illuminate such issues and reduce contention."

Rusk specifically defended the increasing proportion of awards for empirical studies as distinct from philosophical work in the social sciences. Stressing that his and other foundations had not worked to impose any kind of methodological uniformity on social research (an assertion that the IPA might have questioned), Rusk nevertheless praised recent empirical studies that had improved understanding of consumer behavior and of personnel selection. Rusk acknowledged that the two foundations he directed had made grants to twenty-nine individuals against whom allegations of communist affiliation had been made. However, Rusk underscored that many of the allegations were denied, that the grants were made before the controversies ensued, and that his foundations refused, as a matter of policy, to make grants to communists. Rusk denied that the Rockefeller foundations ever had violated their tax-exempt status by undertaking propaganda activities for a nationalized system of education or for a one-world system of government.[51]

During the 1950s, major communication researchers and their grant sponsors directly experienced society's lack of consensus on how to respond to communism and to social change. While foundations continued to support such critical social scientists as John Kenneth Galbraith and David Riesman, the populist-McCarthyite attack on the foundations only hurried social science's long march away from direct action that had been under way since the early part of the century.[52] Conditions of the 1950s may have helped to starve further the already poorly nourished instincts for reform of up-and-coming young social researchers.

Although communication critics, scientists, and grantors became frequent victims of the polemical style of ferreting out allegedly subversive propaganda, the Right gained bigger headlines with antipropaganda forays into America's major communication channels. In 1947, HUAC began a series of hearings on Red propaganda allegedly infiltrated into Hollywood films, setting in motion a blacklist mentality that reigned until the 1960s in the world of film and broadcasting. J. Parnell Thomas, HUAC chair in 1947, justified the committee's sojourn into Tinseltown on the basis that "what the citizen sees and hears in his neighborhood movie house carries a powerful impact on his thoughts and behavior." Thomas averred that communists had enjoyed "considerable success" in appropriating film as a vehicle for "boring from within." Jack Warner, Thomas's first witness, reminded the committee that *Mission to Moscow* had been produced "when our country was fighting for its existence, with Russia as one of our allies." "If making *Mission to Moscow* in 1942 was a subversive activity," he added, "then the American Liberty ships which carried food and guns to Russian allies and the American naval vessels which conveyed them were likewise engaged in subversive activities."[53]

Although initially outraged by HUAC's effort to exact revenge for certain wartime films, Hollywood's moguls abetted the committee's foray into filmmaking once it became clear that HUAC would refrain from attacking the studio production system and, instead, focus upon individual scapegoats taken from Hollywood's stable of leftist or procommunist writers. For its part, HUAC boasted of having identified wordsmiths responsible for infusing communism into films. Exaggerating what might reasonably have been inferred or projected from the Hollywood hearings, the committee expressed the hope that its "investigation of Hollywood will have a far-reaching effect and prevent a large-scale future Communist infiltration of the television industry."[54] Hollywood thereupon dutifully churned out such anticommunist films as *The Red Menace,* atoning for the now-out-of-fashion ideological service given in films such as *Mission to Moscow.*

Survival on the Periphery

Disparaged in the academy as nonscientific and on the hustings as subversive, progressive propaganda analysis nevertheless abided on the intellectual periphery during the 1940s and 1950s. Also, because both scientism and McCarthyism contained self-serving elements of special pleading, these two antimuckraking trends paradoxically nurtured propaganda critique during its period of hibernation.

No one was more active in keeping progressive propaganda analysis alive during the postwar period than Alfred McClung Lee, who some years after his stint with the IPA had joined the faculty of sociology at Brooklyn College. As he continued to refine his critical and praxical work as a humanist social scientist, Lee developed a concept of "clinical" sociology, that is, the observation of particular cases with a view toward taking action. As applied to mass persuasion, Lee's clinical view emphasized the at-the-time neglected tension between public service and manipulation in communication. In understanding mass media in society, Lee explained, one had to distinguish between a "societal" view (i.e., how propaganda figured in the competition between particular groups) and a "social-psychological" view that focused on how audiences responded to appeals. Lee was at work on a theory of propaganda that would make it possible to diagnose when propaganda operated variously as a social boon or social problem.[55]

As he pursued his lonesome, rear-guard defense of progressive-critical propaganda study, Lee completed in 1952 a book-length exposition of his multifaceted, clinical approach to propaganda analysis. In *How to Understand Propaganda,* Lee treated his topic from a consumerist perspective, arguing that mass persuasion could be comprehended, and its harmful effects combatted, if alert citizens would pay heed to propaganda's characteristic techniques, its chief purveyors, its favorite media, its typical organizations and front groups, and its motivational savvy. With reassurances that "a consumer does not need to be highly skilled" to break free of propaganda's hold, Lee contended that, through propaganda analysis, people in a mass society could do much to maintain the "town-meeting spirit" by which citizens controlled their destiny.[56]

Despite Lee's confidence that propaganda analysis fit squarely with American common sense, the publisher of his 1952 opus harbored some reservations about releasing a study of top–down manipulation at the height of McCarthy's reign. Not only did the title word of "propaganda" raise a red flag, but the book's questioning spirit and irreverent treatment of the era's "pall of orthodoxy" were unsettling in a time when intellectual loose ends were prone to become caught in the fly-wheel of redbaiting. As things turned out, however, the book created very little in the way of controversy such that neither McCarthy nor the conservative president of Lee's Brooklyn College paid any attention to it. If the book remained at the margins of the era's politics, it was relegated to the sidelines of academe as well. One reviewer dismissed the work because it failed to include "the analytical methods of Likert, Doob, Childs and Whitton, Guttman, Lazarsfeld, and others." This commentator probably was too close to the struggle between humanistic and quantified social science to recognize that these omissions were part and parcel of Lee's consumerist, clinical approach to mass persuasion.[57]

Yet there were others who agreed with Lee that the turn toward experimentation, quantification, and managerially organized research were subverting the critical-reformist mission of the American Sociological Society (later the ASA or American Sociological Association). In 1950–1951, Lee and his wife, anthropologist Elizabeth B. Lee, spearheaded a movement to combat what they believed were trends in the ASA toward elitism, the engineering model of research, and an overarching "scientism" that worshiped the methodological trappings of social inquiry. From their service on the ASA's Press Relations Committee (as a result of which they received advance copies of convention papers and journal articles), the Lees observed "how that society's gatekeepers limited access to convention programs and to the one periodical it then published, the *American Sociological Review*." The Lees believed that the ASA's "austere image" of scientific propriety and theoretical sophistication was a self-absorbed pretense that ignored pressing national and world problems.[58]

After toying with various alternatives, the Lees decided that the reforms they favored required establishment of a new autonomous organization sufficiently flexible and democratic that it could coordinate a response by reform-oriented social scientists to pressing issues. Given the tenor of the times, "McCarthyism was one of the challenges we wished to meet," the Lees recalled. Alfred Lee recruited a number of prestigious older sociologists, notably Ernest Burgess and Arnold Rose, to help build momentum toward establishing the Society for the Study of Social Problems (SSSP). After an initial organizational meeting of the SSSP in fall 1951, the first convention of the organization took place in September 1952 concurrently with the ASA meeting. Soon the SSSP brought out its own journal, *Social Problems,* and entered into an affiliate relationship with the larger ASA. In the decades that followed, problems of identity plagued the SSSP as the organization struggled to decide whether its role would be collaborative or provocative vis-à-vis the ASA and whether articles would be descriptive or critical. Nevertheless, as a result of the SSSP and its journal, the sociological curriculum became more attentive to social problems as distinct from social theory.[59]

If McCarthyism helped to prompt the Lees in their work to reinvigorate a muckraking praxis of social inquiry, this phenomenon also alerted scholars of speech to the value in giving critical attention to contemporary persuaders and communicative events. Where newfangled communication science impeded the Lees' effort to bring muckraking propaganda critique into academic sociology, the older humanistic tradition had a similar retarding effect upon contemporary criticism among scholars affiliated with the Speech Association of America (later the Speech Communication Association or SCA). The speech communication field found itself, as with other social studies disciplines, straddling somewhat uncomfortably the widening canyons that separated quantitative studies, humanistic inquiry, and performance studies. As each group of specialists within the speech field searched for intellectual anchor points, those devoted to social influence tended to settle upon the classical heritage of Graeco-Roman writings on rhetoric. Although this theoretical model accorded well with the field's roots in public speaking and debate, the forum model of social inducement predisposed speech scholars to study single orators and individual addresses. Moreover, since the chief models for rhetorical study were literary criticism and historical biography, the earliest rhetorical-critical studies tended to focus on yesterday's oratorical giants, such as Daniel Webster, or epic encounters, such as the Lincoln–Douglas debates. Happily applying their critical tools to the oratorical persuasions that unfolded in the small-town America of yesteryear, rhetoricians played almost no part in the propaganda analysis movement of the 1930s.[60]

During the 1950s, however, rhetorical critics took note of how their analytic tools might usefully dissect such contemporary matters of concern as McCarthy's propaganda of projecting communism onto everything progressive, liberal, or otherwise contentious. Given the era's loyalty oaths and HUAC investigations, rhetorician Lee Hultzen believed that speech courses had a "function beyond exercise of the oratorical musculature." Hultzen recommended giving students practice in arguing the battles between democracy and totalitarianism rather than carrying on with the forms of speech training as if all were well in the political world. Two years later, the SCA approved a resolution condemning the employment of "loose charges of guilt by association" as pressures "to intimidate free expression of convictions."[61]

Analyzing contemporary persuasion and non-oratorical settings went against the grain of postwar rhetorical scholarship; however, Frederick Haberman, the associate editor for rhetoric of the SCA's *Quarterly Journal of Speech*, put together a symposium on the thirty-six–day Army–McCarthy hearings of spring 1954. In the view of theater director Jonathan W. Curvin, the hearings were a drama whose plot unfolded "like a stone tossed in a pool." Beginning with charges and counter-charges about how the army treated McCarthy's aide, draftee G. David Schine, the dramatic action diffused in ever-widening circles to include a view of contemporary politics and of McCarthyism itself. In his review of the sundry concentricities of action, the rhetorician on the *QJS* panel, Orville Hitchcock, discussed McCarthy's tactics for handling the matter of Schine and for censuring the army's alleged interference with anticommunist investigations. While contending that the two sides fought to a "stalemate," Hitchcock believed that McCarthy was the chief loser because his loud and vituperative performance had been pitched not to the average viewer but to the senator's diehard supporters. The essayist from NBC focused not only on the impact of TV's immediacy and huge audience but also on broadcasters' new "responsibility to decide" which Congressional investigations deserved expensive air time.[62]

Attention to the Army–McCarthy hearings was but one sign of the increasing disposition of rhetorical scholars in speech communication to deploy their concepts for analyzing contemporary speakers, current disputes, and mass audiences. Other harbingers included analyses of the quadrennial presidential campaigns (beginning with the 1948 contest), attention to General Douglas MacArthur's dramatic speech to a joint session of Congress, and the formation in 1961 of the Freedom of Speech interest group of the SCA by a group of signatories that included Leo Lowenthal, the Frankfurt School media critic. A number of these petitioners earlier had called upon the SCA to follow through on its expressed support for free speech by providing more "scholarly research and publication" in the area.[63]

During the time when propaganda analysis had fallen out of favor in academe, sociology's SSSP and the SCA's small Free Speech division clearly provided a haven for criticizing the media–McCarthy alliance and other top–down trends injurious to the formation of democratic public opinion. Two further intellectual centers, critical thinking and German critical theory, also provided resources – albeit somewhat ambiguously – for a renewal of muckraking propaganda critique.

To be sure, in the postwar period, some work in critical thinking did remain sympathetic to the aims and methods of IPA-style progressive propaganda critique. This generalization applies to a number of pedagogies circulating in the fields of English, speech, semantics, and education.[64] Nevertheless, it bears noting that the procedurally oriented approach to critical thinking (that had supplanted IPA-style propaganda critique by the early 1940s) chiefly dominated the field. Most notably embodied in the popular Watson–Glaser tests, many prominent postwar models of critical thinking emphasized the application of formal reasoning or cognitive processes to hypothetical, apolitical problems or cases. Max Black's book, with its focus on deduction, the scientific method, and the need to flee from fallacies and slogans, became a standard reference. An influential framework for critical thinking outlined by Robert Ennis emphasized logic, criteria for judgment, and contextual background in an effort to steer postwar teachers away from the "indiscriminate condemnation" found in propaganda analysis and toward a deeper understanding of thinking than that offered by Dewey's reflective pattern. Another familiar approach was the practical logic of philosopher Monroe Beardsley, which, although focused on deduction, validity, and hypothesis, did at least suggest that students might transfer what they learned from the book's argument forms (and sample excerpts) to the torrent of media messages.[65]

The tendency for critical thinking pedagogies to emphasize hypothetical examples and apolitical theory continued through the 1980s. A great number of higher education's programs of critical thinking were oriented either to models of formal analysis or to kindred pedagogies of formal scientific process in which observation, classification, and cause–effect relationships were applied to hypothetical or physical-science problems. Still other programs called for students to generate strategies for dealing with hypothetical problems or to develop points of view relevant to such a question as "Should children be allowed to leave school as soon as they have learned to read and write?" Some programs approached critical thinking from the vantage point of teaching good writing or teaching various types and structures of argument, as in the Toulmin system of claim, grounds, warrant, backing, qualifier, and rebuttal.[66]

If education in critical thinking tended to miss the mark in alerting students to issues of democratic public opinion, the Frankfurt School also provided less rationale than might have been anticipated for validating the muckraking impulse to probe communication's democratic ethics. The Frankfurt emigrés gave lectures and seminars at Columbia University beginning in 1936 in which they pursued a number of issues proximate to propaganda analysis. As part of their exploration of instrumental reason, reified scientific methods, mechanical thought, and knowledge pursued for purposes of domination, Max Horkheimer and Theodor Adorno explored what they called the Culture Industry. In their view, radio's endless repetition and pseudo-authoritative voice helped to complete the domination of the no longer independent middle class by making all participants into bystanders, on the one hand, and into sorted-and-classified targets for advertising, on the other. Because popular films left nothing for the imagination, the cinema figured prominently as a "propaganda for the culture" in a process by which art was transformed into a vehicle for consumption and by which independent thinking atrophied in favor of a passive acceptance induced through cheap gratifications.[67]

Although Frankfurt School works seemed poised to nurture America's antipropaganda critique during its time of relative quiescence, a number of factors reduced the power of German critical theory to sustain muckraking. First, Horkheimer and Adorno's dialectical admonishment of the Culture Industry remained unpublished in English until the 1970s. More generally, Frankfurt School works came across, variously, as abstract (Adorno's analysis of the fetishization of music) and/ or remote (Franz Neumann's treatment of German fascism as the ultimate expression of the will to dominance unleashed by the Enlightenment). German critical theory tended to frame issues in terms removed from American experience such that it did not provoke the soul searching that Lee and Lynd had evoked in their critical reviews of *The American Soldier* series. In fact, because of the theoretical depth of Frankfurt School work (mass-society theory mixed with a cultural Marxism linked to Freudian psychology), many social scientists interpreted this body of work as yet another resource for building quantitative empirical theories. At the same time that Doob rejected propaganda critique's claim to academic legitimacy (because of its plain-spoken progressive assumptions and terminology), he accepted Marxist critique as "a great contribution to social science" because, grounded on a deeper conceptual substructure, it could enrich, if not confirm, social science theory.[68]

Frankfurt School studies indulged the speculative fancy of American social science without directly threatening the alliance of communication researchers, broadcasters, grantors, and government. For this reason, propaganda critics often were less enthusiastic about Frankfurt work than were quantitative scholars. Alfred Lee recalled being not particularly impressed with the "academic glitter" of the Frankfurt School seminars given by Adorno and others at Columbia. Especially grating was their effort to appear as "unique missionaries . . . bringing enlightenment to the colonies." Only in the 1960s did German critical theory begin to offer a substantial stimulus to reinvigorate American muckraking. Herbert Marcuse's *One-Dimensional Man* became popular for its exploration of the rational irrationality of the totally mobilized society. Marcuse, more pessimistic about modernism than the propaganda critics, wrote about a society in which opposition not only was neutralized by the preconditioning power of technological efficiency but also was purged from the popular arts by the reproduction of dominant social views in radio, film, and other media.[69]

However much trends in academe maximally or minimally nurtured propaganda critique, American journalists, acting both collectively and individually, contributed a number of influential critical forays into the propaganda phenomena during the postwar years. Within the profession, the Commission on Freedom of the Press opened up certain lines of critical thought on mass media by asking whether channels of news were playing a constructive role in bringing about the kind of society that people wanted. Between 1944 and 1946, under the direction of Robert M. Hutchins, president of the University of Chicago, such luminaries as Harold Lasswell, Zechariah Chafee, Reinhold Niebuhr, and Archibald MacLeish assessed the respective merits of external control versus media self-regulation. The Hutchins commission (financed by media mogul Henry Luce) gave prominence to certain moral obligations attending to media and their managers. Under Lasswell's guidance, the commission expressed the belief that, in the context of some kind of citizens' agency, the outputs of the press could be evaluated and improved.[70]

The commission's vision of a more responsible press became a centerpiece of *Four Theories of the Press,* a widely used survey published in 1956. Here Theodore Peterson's essay on "The Social Responsibility Theory of the Press" rooted the accountability approach to mass communication in the increasing ubiquitousness of media, the concentration of ownership and control, and the professionalization of journalists. Citing Will Irwin as the grandfather of the "contemporary criticism of the newspaper," Peterson reviewed various standard lines of radio–TV and film criticism, to wit, the lack of public affairs programming, the overly conservative commentators on radio–TV, and the excessive sex and violence in the movies. However, the narrowness of Peterson's critical parameters was clear since he cited the rulings of the Federal Communications Commission, as well as ethical codes in the publishing and broadcasting professions, as exemplars of the move toward media responsibility. Correspondingly, Peterson was unsympathetic to the critiques of advertising offered by Upton Sinclair and George Seldes. On the other hand, by affirming that the press should not simply report statements and charges, but instead should put them in a meaningful context, Peterson seemed to express the guilty conscience of McCarthy-era journalism.[71] Many reporters feared that their focus on objectively reporting official statements, and their corresponding failure to dissect the charges and tactics of the Wisconsin senator, had rendered them accomplices in spreading the anti-Red paranoias.

A number of individual working journalists kept up interest in the propaganda analysis of news during the 1950s. Although redbaiting had brought down George Seldes's *In Fact* (1940–1950) by scaring off subscribers to this journal of press criticism, others continued the muckraking, pro-democratic exploration of journalism's foibles. With advice from Seldes, I. F. Stone launched in 1953 his own independent newsletter of media and political criticism, *I. F. Stone's Weekly*. Until 1971, Stone's journal of exposé and commentary specialized in taking a close look at official massaging of fact. For instance, Stone exposed the effort to hide from the public the government's ability to detect Soviet underground nuclear tests, part of Washington's effort to minimize demands for a nuclear test ban treaty. Stone explored Lyndon Johnson's endeavor to exaggerate evidence of a second attack on U.S. ships by North Vietnam, part of the administration's effort to stampede public opinion about the Gulf of Tonkin resolution.[72]

Just as I. F. Stone's exegeses of official posturing undermined the saintly image of policy savants, so too did A. J. Liebling's press criticism for the *New Yorker* help to keep alive the idea of elite manipulation during the period before Vietnam-era revisionism became rampant. Liebling's treatments of the press lords varied from cogent assessments of how these millionaires were out of touch with post–Adam Smith economics to wry reflections on the atomic-bomb-proof building and war-surplus B-17 bomber of Col. Robert McCormick of the *Chicago Tribune* (George Seldes's old boss). Liebling humorously reported entering the Tribune Tower to find that, despite the colonel's assurances that reprints of his public speeches were available to all inquirers, a request for them "elicits a certain amount of astonishment." For more than twenty-five years, Liebling contended with a host of journalism's darker tendencies including declining press competition, congenitally inadequate foreign coverage, and biased treatments of labor affairs. In the process, Liebling contributed his share and more to journalism's store of aphorisms including "freedom of the press is guaranteed only to those who own one," and his rule of thumb that reporters rarely learned more than half of what was available to be known – and only occasionally transmitted more than half of what they learned. Spencer Klaw, longtime editor of the *Columbia Journalism Review*, described Liebling as "kind of a father of press criticism" and credited the emergence of press reviews in the 1960s partly to Liebling's sharp and clever writings.[73]

Two postwar popular studies of mass-mediated social influence added substance to the somewhat sub rosa journalistic resources available to sustain antipropanganda critique. Gilbert Seldes, media critic and educator, typically had been optimistic about America's communication channels (unlike his muckraker brother, George); however, the younger Seldes's optimism flagged (briefly) when he meditated over transformations that the communication industry was working on the popular arts. In *The Great Audience* (1950), Seldes questioned whether mass-mediated popular pleasures worked in the public's interest inasmuch as radio and film catered to but a series of minorities and inasmuch as the entertainment industries were profiting by recycling endlessly the same showy but designed-to-be-forgotten product in which unauthentic characters rarely evidenced real emotions. Seldes saw mass media as refashioning people by creating "the climate of feeling in which all of us live." In an indictment reminiscent of the Frankfurt School, Seldes complained that "commercial radio creates an atmosphere of acceptance" in which the critical was banished from programs lest it rebound against the simple assertions of advertising. Similarly, the TV industry calculated its fare to be suitable as a vehicle for advertising. Seldes believed that the public welfare was at stake when media managers employed programming research to create audiences for commercial purposes. By aiming to bring audiences down to a common level, Seldes argued, the radio–TV–film industry seemed "committed to the destruction of democracy."

It should be noted that Seldes soon apologized for the ominous tone of *The Great Audience*. In *The Public Arts*, Seldes returned to his prior practice of basing his analysis on a review of individual cases, such as Jackie Gleason's "Honeymooners" and Edward Murrow's challenges to McCarthyism on "See It Now." These and other instances of quality and courage in the communication industry bucked up Seldes's optimism that the future of the popular arts was not necessarily in the direction of irresponsible institutions pushing manipulative, formula-for-profit programming.[74]

If the muckraking spirit of the younger Seldes was compromised by his appreciation for moments of genius and responsibility in the communication arts, journalist Vance Packard's bombshell treatment of engineered persuasion conjured up memories of Upton Sinclair. In *The Hidden Persuaders*, Packard questioned what it meant "for the national morality" when "so many powerfully influential people" felt free to take "a manipulative attitude toward our society." Packard's pantheon of deceptive persuasion included the market-research polling of Likert and Stouffer, the "engineering of consent" pursued by Bernays, and the in-depth motivational studies of Ernest Dichter. Packard's book focused heavily on Dichter's Institute for Motivational Research, an organization that interviewed consumers in detail to find which of their anxieties and psychological needs were – or might be – linked to purchasing behaviors. Illustrative of this "playing upon hidden weaknesses and frailties" was Dichter's work to brief executives in Detroit about how men regarded a convertible as "a possible symbolic mistress," and his counseling of California prune growers about the image problems of their wrinkled, murky-colored fruit. In politics, Dichter preached a doctrine that issues counted for little and that the "emotional pull" of the candidates was crucial. What proved most evocative in Packard's popular best-seller, however, was his very brief treatment of subliminal sales messages that he believed were being flashed onto the screen during films shown in an unnamed New Jersey movie theater.[75]

In sum, although the administrator–grantor–researcher entente clearly dominated thinking about communication in the postwar period, a number of trends kept academicians and opinion leaders from falling entirely under the spell of quantified communication research, apolitical pedagogies of critical thinking, McCarthyesque polemical diatribes, and ultra-abstract cultural explorations. Developments as diverse as the Hutchins commission, the SSSP, the SCA's Free Speech interest group, Gilbert Seldes's warnings about mechanized entertainment, Vance Packard's exposé of technologized manipulation, I. F. Stone's weekly, and A. J. Liebling's columns, all acted together to render America more poised for the return of propaganda critique than one might otherwise have surmised.

It further proved to be the case that the paradigmatic pretensions of social science's engineering model created the very conditions that began to erode this producer-centered perspective on social action and social influence. Given the claims of universality brashly advanced by representatives of quantified social and communication research, it is not surprising that, by the later 1950s, this dominant quantitative-experimental paradigm was undergoing challenge. For instance, in connection with his thesis that modern people needed to resist being enveloped by organizations, William Whyte anathematized "scientism," which, for him, meant the notion that everything important about humans could be learned through the quantitative, physical approaches of the natural sciences. Whyte labeled scientism as one of the major social conditions supporting the contemporary orthodoxy that society's first principle should be that of implementing institutionally determined objectives. Sociologist William Albig echoed this complaint with curmudgeonly reflections on what he believed was the "crude empiricism" and amoral perspective increasingly adopted by the younger people of communication research.[76]

Pitirim A. Sorokin, Stouffer's colleague at Harvard, and C. Wright Mills, Lazarsfeld's nemesis at Columbia, proved to be the two most colorful of the early critics of the move to pursue social and communication research in the model of the natural sciences. In a shotgun polemic, Sorokin railed against social science's jargon, narrow training and reading, formulaic routines, "testomania," "quantophrenia," false precision, myopic operationalism, sham objectivity, preoccupation with prediction, amnesia about relevant scholarly precursors, and general overemphasis on cognitive assumptions. Lazarsfeld, one of Sorokin's prominent targets for the critique of hyper-quantification, complained that the Harvard man was unfair to use as evidence against the idea of prediction the very works that he and Stouffer had undertaken to improve predictability.[77]

Lazarsfeld was no less perturbed by the critique of social science offered by his associate, Mills. Although the younger Columbia man provided less of a scattershot treatment than Sorokin, Mills deftly parodied the abstractions of Talcott Parsons and, more to the point, critiqued Stouffer and Lazarsfeld's measurement ethos in a sufficiently spirited manner as to violate the academic norm that departmental colleagues should temper their public debates. Mills characterized both the voting studies of his Columbia associate and the army-related research of Stouffer as variously overcelebrated, pridefully contemptuous of past or differing work, and flawed in a number of important ways. For instance, Mills believed that by making public opinion synonymous with the results of polls, quantified studies of voting had reified its referent. The result was to tear opinion from the surrounding context of history, interest-group expression, and public debate. Mills subtly punctured the apologetical posturing of social scientists that, but for the temporary accidents of time and money, their specific applications of "The Method" would revolutionize the world.[78]

By 1963, Irving Horowitz had enlarged the critique of social science's scientism by describing the quantitative paradigm's tenets less as an inevitable triumph and more as "an ideology." Why had Establishment Sociology "retained its preeminence in the face of challenges from all quarters?" wondered Horowitz. His answer took the form of an exegesis of social science's interlocking institutional arrangements that included selective recruitment practices, a striving to emulate the prestigious natural sciences, a strategic selection of research problems to ingratiate scholars with the prevailing powers, and pecuniary benefits in the form of research grants from business and government. As a result of the foregoing, the "value-free," professional orientation had become "not simply a sociological methodology, but a social ideology."[79]

The competition between quantitative policy research and anti-establishmentarian rejoinders took on a public cast in May 1965, when, in the context of a controversy over the army's so-called Project Camelot, empirical research for purposes of counterinsurgency began to take on a bad name. Project Camelot sprang up in the army's Special Operations Research Office in 1964 as "the largest single grant ever provided for a social science project." Its aim was nothing less than production of "a general social systems model which would make it possible to predict and influence politically significant aspects of social change in the developing nations of the world." Although somewhat uncomfortable with military sponsorship, the scientists of Project Camelot did not see themselves as "spying for the United States government" but rather as enlightening the army and preventing new revolutionary holocausts. Unfortunately for the army and its multimillion-dollar stable of scholars, details of the project were made available to leftist elements of the Chilean press, and the ensuing controversy over the project's arguably imperialistic purposes reverberated among the intelligentsia of two continents. Eventually, the army terminated Project Camelot, and President Lyndon Johnson weighed in with a ruling that Washington should not sponsor any overseas research project that would, in the judgment of the Secretary of State, "adversely affect United States foreign relations."[80]

The predominant reaction in Congress to Project Camelot, however, was one of cautious support for using empirical research to improve America's position vis-à-vis world opinion. At the same time, as acknowledged by a House subcommittee, the late project had demonstrated that some research might "provoke extremely unfavorable reactions abroad not only from the Communists and their sympathizers but also from academic and political groups that are generally friendly to the United States."[81]

Communication research was heavily implicated in the growing inclination to rethink whether Cold War imperatives provided a universal justification for administratively organized social research conducted abroad. Persuasion science became a target for such reevaluation because of its centrality in the movement both to study and to encourage the move in the Third World away from traditional practices and toward modern social organization. Contributors to the communication-

and-development literature regarded mass media as particularly important in the process by which Western cognitive patterns and efficient secularization seemed to be spreading almost irresistibly, not just within elite echelons but also among the masses of the developing nations. The unself-conscious tendency of international communication research to take the perspective of the West, and to side with native elites in preference to the masses, helped to make this brand of scholarship vulnerable to anti-establishmentarian trends that swept American society and social science during the later 1960s.[82]

By the mid-1960s, therefore, intellectual outrage with the excesses of McCarthyism and rising doubts about the sanctity of scientific research had created the basis for an uprising against the dominant paradigm of managed democracy, policy studies, and administrative communication research. It began to seem possible that issues of antidemocratic propaganda might resurface to compete with questions of efficient communication. All that was lacking was a socio-intellectual crisis more visceral than Project Camelot and more encompassing than second thoughts about imposing modernism on the Third World. The Johnson administration's post-1964 escalation of the Vietnam War provided just such a climate of national urgency.

CHAPTER 8

EPILOGUE: REDISCOVERING PROPAGANDA

A reemergence of the critical spirit, both in society and in academe, continues unabated in the post-Vietnam and post-Watergate U.S.A. The role of progressive propaganda critique in this still recent transformation is worth some exploration if only to clarify the contours of what some would call today's "culture of complaint" or "culture wars."[1]

In the context of the post-sixties resurgence of interest in elite manipulation, it bears remembering that, for a time, the Johnson administration enjoyed support for its war policies. American reporters and news organizations – with the notable exception of I. F. Stone – generally went along with the official line that the Vietnam War was a logical extension of anticommunism, that American forces promoted democracy, and that the fighting was proceeding, inexorably, toward victory. Only when the war proved more lengthy, most costly, and less inspiring than anticipated, did cracks begin to appear in the facade of popular support for carrying on Johnson's, and later Nixon's, war.[2]

As with the calls to arms put out in 1918 by the Wilson administration and in 1941 under the auspices of FDR, the Johnson administration's case for intervention in Vietnam included all manner of claims that, if motive and opportunity obtained, might be critically dissected by intellectuals and commentators. Early antiwar books, such as *The Bitter Heritage,* by historian Arthur Schlesinger, *The United States in Vietnam,* by Cornell professors George Kahin and John Lewis, focused on high-level politics and/or the details of the Vietnam situation. Soon, however, the floodgates opened for oppositional perspectives on every facet of the war – notably including issues of elite manipulation of public opinion on the war. For instance, had the North Vietnamese actually launched the second attack on U.S. ships in the Tonkin Gulf that President Johnson cited to justify America's first direct military action against the Hanoi regime?[3]

The revisionist spirit that imbued most antiwar books was quintessentially progressive. The accounts were highly factual, contrasted official statements to demonstrable evidence, focused on the manipulation of a confused public, and called for (or implied) citizen action to bring about changes in policy. The revisionist line on the war contained considerable doses of the antipropaganda approach prevalent after World War I (and virtually absent after World War II). Antipropaganda thinking on the Vietnam War began to precipitate into the general public on the strength of news coverage of the Vietnam Teach-ins and, later, the war protest movement.

The Nixon administration's Watergate scandal provided another focal point for propaganda critique along progressive lines. Not only did the hearings of the Senate Watergate committee provide a behind-the-scenes view of manipulations by the White House, but the published Oval Office transcripts seemingly confirmed a cynical view that politicians were outwardly sanctimonious but inwardly debased. The Watergate period of 1973–1974 also produced calls for more investigative journalism on the basis of the popular (if not disputable) belief that reporting by the *Washington Post*'s Carl Bernstein and Bob Woodward had been the key in bringing down the Nixon-era abuses of power. Watergate brought into bold relief journalistic trends of the preceding fifty years toward "interpretation analysis," "inside dope," and assessing the "why" of a story. All this reinforced the post-1960s tendency for the media themselves to "become a big story," reported not only in journalism reviews but also by the "full-time media reporters" of major media outlets.[4]

Whether or not the Watergate affair stimulated investigative journalism, or simply enhanced its presumed status, the drawn-out scandal made academicians, who were already agitated by Vietnam, more disposed to comment on current controversy. By 1971–1972, the National Council of Teachers of English (NCTE) had established a Committee on Public Doublespeak as a response to "the manipulation of language by the government and the military in the Vietnam war." The Doublespeak committee devoted one of its significant early publications to the semantic chicanery associated with Watergate. Arguing that Watergate was a master symbol for the era's "propaganda blitz unequaled in human history," the Doublespeak group offered its series of studies as a resource for teachers to help counter "commercial and political propaganda." Essays focused on bureaucratic language and evasive circumlocutions designed to finesse institutional and individual responsibility and guilt, as when a Watergate fib was labeled "inoperative."[5]

As with the popular antiwar books, the NCTE's energetic entry into the hustings grew from the remembered legacy of post–World War I propaganda analysis. For all its enthusiasm for illuminating shadows of propaganda cast by the Watergate's dramatis personae, however, the NCTE's Doublespeak committee clearly was searching widely and somewhat desperately for theoretical models and applied frameworks to undergird its assault on mass manipulation. The literary orientation of the English field predisposed these writers to turn to sources such as George Orwell or James Thurber as well as to leading semanticists such as Chase and Hayakawa. However, the anti-doublespeak writers cast their net widely to include works on the mass media (e.g., Joe McGinniss's *The Selling of the President 1968* and Fred Friendly's *Due to Circumstances Beyond Our Control*), treatments of manipulative institutions and professions (e.g., J. William Fulbright's *The Pentagon Propaganda Machine* and Vance Packard's *The Hidden Persuaders*), publications of the late Institute for Propaganda Analysis, and rhetorical theorists such as Aristotle. The NCTE group also showed an interest in importing a number of more theoretical approaches to the subject, as reflected, for instance, in Jacques Ellul's comprehensive sociology of propaganda.

Both the references cited (and not cited) and the brief history of propaganda analysis given by Hugh Rank (the Doublespeak committee's editor) showed that academicians had forgotten much about propaganda critique in the thirty years since the closure of the IPA's New York office. Yet the earnestness of the NCTE's Doublespeak committee also highlighted the great interest among academicians of the early 1970s in reactivating the old progressive approach to mass communication's role in social conflict and competition. As with the muckrakers of 1900–1910 and the propaganda critics of 1920–1940, these teacher–scholars were animated less by grand theoretical projects and more by critical incidents and the discovery of the extent to which whole professions had grown up with the object of managing and guiding democracy. Accordingly, anti-doublespeak teachers turned instinctively to the native American strain of muckraking and progressive propaganda critique. A predictable result of this turn was that the Doublespeak committee, as with the IPA, prompted some complaints that its exposés neglected the "semantic tyranny" of the Left.[6]

The confluence of the Vietnam and Watergate imbroglios proved powerful in stimulating a popular and academic literature that frequently was indistinguishable from 1930s propaganda analysis. On the best-seller side of the ledger were works such as *The Politics of Lying* by David Wise, with its focus on official deception and media-based manipulation, and *The First Casualty,* by Phillip Knightley, which explored how battlefield correspondents had figured in the great propagandas of war. On the academic side of the post-Vietnam, post-

Watergate bibliography could be found Herbert Schiller's *The Mind Managers,* a readable exposé of "packaged consciousness" promoted by elites in government, the military, entertainment, and polling. Schiller's book, like Stuart Ewen's *Captains of Consciousness,* seemed one in spirit and approach with Upton Sinclair who, for an earlier generation, had mixed the vocabularies of class manipulation (socialist theory) and participatory democracy (progressive theory) in books about education, journalism, and the arts. The increasing interest in mass-mediated propaganda widened the audience for Marshall McLuhan's otherwise abstruse and literary treatment of how media determined popular consciousness and social organization.

The increased attention to situations and problems of manipulative propaganda not only opened the door to a renewed progressive critique but also provided fuel for a new polemical literature on the subject. As exemplified by the Overman, Fish, and Dies committees, the polemical tangent of propaganda criticism could devolve into relatively flimsy guilt by association. In contrast, a large number of post-1960s antipropaganda polemics were contributed by intellectuals of the Left and Right who, although closely connected to their respective partisans, pursued an analysis having intellectual credibility. The premier antipropaganda polemicists of the Left were Noam Chomsky and his frequent co-author, Edward S. Herman; from the Right emerged a large bibliography of works articulating a theory of "liberal bias" in the media.

The signature opening of Chomsky's antipropaganda campaign was *American Power and the New Mandarins,* where the MIT linguist attacked Schlesinger's *Bitter Heritage* for giving only a tepid opposition to the Vietnam War that rested upon fundamental errors of contemporary liberal ideology. Chomsky argued that liberalism had assimilated the imperialist ethos as regarded Cuba, China, and Vietnam, and he censured Schlesinger for a merely tactical opposition to Vietnam policy. Enlarging his critique to include the status-quo liberalism of the American professorate, Chomsky launched a broadside against warrior intellectuals such as Herman Kahn, the sociologist of thermonuclear war, and against objectivity-minded scholars in general for their inactivity as regarded Vietnam and its associated assumptions of Pax Americana. In *At War With Asia,* Chomsky expanded his critique to include how policy makers had built up "the ideology of anti-Communism" not only to mobilize public support for military intervention but also to prevent independent economic development in the Third World and to sustain public subsidies for a war-oriented American economy.[7]

Beginning with Vietnam-era critiques of domination abetted by liberal academicians, Chomsky and Edward Herman muckraked American interventions in Cambodia, the Dominican Republic, El Salvador, and elsewhere. In the process, they refined a theory of "state propaganda" whereby democratic intellectuals became bound to prevailing policies due to background propagandas embedded in news. By the 1980s, they had outlined a "propaganda model" in which intellectuals and large media companies were coopted by prevailing power elites and thereby transformed into mere resources for selectively mobilizing the public. Chomsky's forte was politically engaged scholarship, undiluted by academic pretensions, in which, à la Upton Sinclair, he pursued theory and analysis to a political purpose.[8]

As counterpoint to the reasoned antipropaganda radicalism of Chomsky and Herman, William F. Buckley, Jr., helped to set in motion a conservative antipropaganda polemicism. In *God and Man at Yale* (1951), Buckley called for alumni to take up arms against the agnostical and collectivist ideology being imparted to Yalesmen by the faculty. Buckley faulted Leonard Doob for giving religion the "silent treatment" in his course on Social Psychology, and he railed against various economists for assuming that a managed economy was the wave of the future.[9] Buckley's ability to initiate a credible literature of conservative antipropaganda criticism marked an almost inevitable response to the post-1930s gains of progressivism in journalism, in education, and in many social-action agencies of government.

News reporting quickly became the greatest front in the polemical war waged by conservatives against progressive propaganda. By the early 1970s, several critical or quantitative studies were available for those who believed that media channels, with one hand, were giving verbal aid and comfort to America's international foes, and, with the other, were stigmatizing at-home conservatives. The most prominent of these critiques was that by Edith Efron, who offered quantitative data to argue that Left-leaning aims governed how political figures were presented on TV. The "liberal bias" theory of journalism espoused by Efron et al. was not immune to counterargument; notably, Efron's content analyses garnered rebuttals from academicians. However, this conservative version of political-action scholarship contributed insights more credible than those ever attained or intended by HUAC, and the approach became institutionalized with the Accuracy in Media organization of conservative commentator Reed Irvine.[10]

By the mid-1980s, concern for institutional manipulation had returned to such an extent that, as Garth Jowett explained to readers of the *Journal of Communication*, the venerable verbalism of *propaganda* had reemerged as a significant theoretical term. Headlining the newly available academic literature about propaganda was Terence Qualter's comprehensive review of how the public in liberal democracies lived under a system of hierarchical information management and concentrated control of media, both of which acted to define as normal what already existed. Paralleling the new academic studies of propaganda were new curricula and books suitable for use in undergraduate classrooms. In 1986, Garth Jowett and Victoria O'Donnell broke a generation's silence on comprehensive antipropaganda education with the first edition of their book, *Propaganda and Persuasion,* the likes of which had not been seen since Alfred Lee's 1952 book. By the mid-1990s, three similarly intentioned books also were available for those who wished to implement a course focusing on the propaganda problem in American social influence. In *Age of Propaganda,* social psychologists Anthony Pratkanis and Elliot Aronson looked at propaganda in advertising and politics with an emphasis on building intelligent resistance through understanding. In *The New Propaganda,* social scientists James Combs and Dan Nimmo similarly complemented their case studies of palaver (beguiling talk) with methods for improving critical thinking. In my own *Channels of Propaganda,* the emphasis was on developing an electronic form of participatory democracy to defuse propagandas hidden in news, education, entertainment, research, religion, and government agency action.[11]

The reinvigoration of propaganda studies was motivated chiefly by characteristically progressive concerns for such critical incidents as Vietnam and Watergate and, more generally, for the ever-expanding scope of the professions dedicated to opinion engineering. Most of the works took the muckraking tack of examining where and how participatory democracy was negated by particular manipulators located strategically in key institutions and channels of public expression. But however much propaganda studies enjoyed a revival in both popular and academic venues, much of the impetus and energy in American social criticism after the 1970s seemed to emerge from vectors of fragmentation and radicalism that drew sustenance from roots other than the muckraking tradition.

Just as vocabularies of class-oriented criticism could be found during the 1920s and 1930s alongside the dominant progressive parlance, so too did radical theoretical and practical movements grow up in the post-Watergate period to challenge the muckraker's assumption that overcoming specific propagandists and particular propagandas was the key to democracy in a mass-mediated society. The theoretical challenge to antipropaganda critique came chiefly from literary studies influenced variously by Marxism and postmodernism. In the academy, the Western Marxism of the Frankfurt School metamorphosed into an alternative to progressivism's take on propaganda and democracy. The Frankfurt School gained renewed prominence in the USA not only because of Martin Jay's definitive biography of the Institute for Social Research but also because of the circulation of translated works by Horkheimer and Adorno and by the neo-Frankfurtian, Jürgen Habermas.[12]

Perhaps the most powerful impetus to tread beyond progressivism's critical boundaries, however, came with the wave of French and British critical works that swept onto the American scene beginning in the 1970s. Most notable was Michel Foucault, who offered an intriguing alternative to the arguably nostalgic town-meeting ethos of progressive critique. His preference for treating institutions and society as expressions of power relations permitted academic criticism to support a challenge more fundamental to existing social structures and norms than that sanctioned by progressivism. French criticism raised the troubling question of how participatory democracy might function in a milieu in which people were oppressed by the very language needed to articulate change. For its part, British cultural studies entered the picture to underscore the importance of class-oriented thinking in social critique. John Fiske and his associates, for example, explicated the visual grammar of television and critiqued media outputs from the standpoint of the class-tinged nature of their production and consumption.[13]

Given the untheoretical tendencies of Americans, noted since the time of de Tocqueville, it might have seemed surprising that abstruse European deconstructions of society would resonate deeply enough in two decades to challenge the old, practical, muckraking strain of American reform and critique. Post-1960s cultural conditions, however, increased the interest of both intellectuals and the general public in treating language itself as the vehicle of oppression and in characterizing domination as a class-based phenomenon rather than as resulting from the misdeeds of individual actors and particular institutions. By the early 1970s, the American Left had begun to fragment into separatist streams of social thought and social action. Black nationalists, feminists, Chicano radicals, Native Americans, gay activists – all became increasingly disinterested in the coalition-type approach that had prevailed in the Left's earlier civil rights (à la Martin Luther King, Jr.), Free Speech (à la Berkeley), and antiwar movements. The gradual shift on campus from free speech and free love to speech codes and sexual harassment created an intellectual market for European critical theories that accommodated the new impulse to form into separate classes, each fine-combing the various languages of oppression. America's so-called "Culture Wars" have come about as the familiar progress-oriented view of history, politics, and social influence undergoes assault along lines of language and class. Searching for a moniker for the general tenor of leftist critical strands in the 1990s, Paul Berman coined the term *race/class/gender-ism*. Berman's neologism suggested that the critical ethos prevailing in America at the Second Millennium might turn out to be a fusion of race/gender polemicism and class-oriented theoretical thinking in which language itself transmitted inequity and oppression.[14]

It is certainly possible that the synthesis represented by American separatism and European class- and language-based critique may permanently replace progressive propaganda analysis as the critical hook for reining in communication practitioners and polemicists, on the one hand, and for adding social relevance to critical thinking pedagogies and empirical communication science, on the other. In this connection, however, it bears noting that, in the 1990s, race/class/gender-ism itself underwent critique from the standpoint of progressive propaganda scrutiny. For instance, Daphne Patai and Noretta Koertge faulted feminist education for creating academic centers dominated by discourse practices of self-serving exaggeration and indoctrination. The result, they feared, was intellectual and social incapacitation of students exposed to Women's Studies. Dinesh D'Souza leveled a similar charge against Afrocentrism, arguing that many of its promoters purveyed historical speculations and outright distortions for the purpose of advancing their own pet cause of black nationalism. Todd Gitlin argued that leftist hyper-separatism in general had undermined not just sensible discussion but also hopes for democratic life itself. The broad political spectrum of these critiques – the first by feminists, the second by a rightist, and the third by a New Left stalwart – suggested that the old muckraker's nose for self-serving posturing will remain acute in American social thought, even in a postmodern environment.[15]

The nearly hundred-year survey given in this book suggests that progressive critique continues to be valuable as a tool for monitoring the relationship of propaganda and democracy. This typically American kind of muckraking has emerged whenever elites seemed too aggressive in their prerogatives or too arrogant in their methods. Society's muckrakers never will permit citizens to forget that the communication media play a role in furthering competition among self-serving institutions and that a steady diet of top–down communication can starve participatory democracy. Implementing the democratic tangent of progressivism, propaganda analysis emphasizes the recognition of social influence for what it is: an attempt by leaders, educators, and media types to modify democracy's rank and file, who, because they are citizens, deserve a say in the change.

For all the virtues of propaganda analysis – popular and academic – the American experience of the last century also suggests that progressive critics do not tell the full story of propaganda's relation to democracy. Communication practitioners, on their part, usefully remind Americans that societal cohesion or consensus can have social value, as shown by campaigns against fascism, and that top–down reform can offer benefits in mitigating intolerance. Practitioners also add perspective to the debate about propaganda by pointing to the limited power of elites and to the considerable stubbornness of Americans. From a practitioner point of view, it may be true that the techniques of propaganda are neither universally evil nor overwhelmingly powerful. At the same time that practitioners fill in certain gaps left by antipropaganda criticism, the scientific perspective alerts us to the importance of closely examining phenomena under investigation (even if communication scientists sometimes forget that many of the hard questions about propaganda are not answerable by measurement and that the tools of scientific social influence are not necessarily available to all in equal measure). Clearly, communication researchers have added to our understanding of democracy's propaganda problem by explaining how communication may be deployed to rally the public to socially productive ends (the war against fascism) or against destructive ones (McCarthyism).

The polemical view of propaganda – despite its proven attraction to political fanatics and extremist crackpots – brings to the fore the useful question of whether, when, and how much intellectuals should act on their convictions that symbolic manipulation is dampening democracy. If the polemicists are correct, then reforms stemming from the progressive movement may not be enough to make democracy prevail against manipulations by ideologues ensconced in society's institutions. The polemical line of thought includes all forms of politically engaged and committed scholarship and, therefore, exists as an important corrective to overly detached, ivory-tower thinking.

Finally, the critical-thinking school of thought on propaganda, with its focus on evidence, proof, and reasoning, may be the most concentrated antidote not only to orchestrated persuasion but also to polemical posturing. While critical thinking arguably neglects the passion and praxis necessary for a properly seasoned application of intelligence to society, the straight thinkers, nevertheless, remind America that, to be useful, passion must be guided by reason. Given that each generation of students must grow to maturity as citizens, it seems helpful to give them specific occasion to investigate, to compare, and to base decisions on intelligent, thorough analysis. If the history of propaganda's many connections to democracy proves anything, it is that neither progressive critique, communication research, practitioner expertise, polemical fulminations, nor critical thinking provide a complete solution to democracy's discursive dilemma. None of these schools of thought on social influence fully explains how a society aspiring to democracy may balance the right to persuade with the right of the public to free choice. If all schools are incomplete, all nonetheless provide elements of the answer; taken together, they constitute a quintessentially American colloquy about self-serving communication in a large-scale, relatively open society.

NOTES

Chapter 1. Prologue: Discovering Propaganda

1 Oswald G. Villard, *Fighting Years* (New York: Harcourt, Brace, 1939), 247–249.

2 Quotations, *Cleveland Plain Dealer*, 17 June 1918, 1–2. See also McAlister Coleman, *Eugene V. Debs* (New York: Greenberg, 1930), 275–288; Nick Salvatore, *Eugene V. Debs* (Urbana, IL: University of Illinois Press, 1982), 290–295.

3 *Cleveland Plain Dealer*, 21 June 1918, 14; 30 June 1918, 8; 18 June 1918, 9; and 16 June 1918, unpaged insert.

4 Clyde R. Miller, "Propaganda in the Authoritarian State and in the Democratic State," typescript, Papers of the Institute for Propaganda Analysis, privately held by Alfred McClung Lee (later deposited in New York Public Library), hereafter cited as IPAP; Miller, *How to Detect and Analyze Propaganda* (New York: Town Hall, 1939), 5–13; Miller, "The Man I Sent to Jail," *Say* (Winter 1954): 7–11.

5 Miller, "Authoritarian State," IPAP.

6 *Cleveland Plain Dealer*, 1 July 1918, 1; 12 September 1918, 1.

7 *Cleveland Plain Dealer*, 10 September 1918, 1, 6; 11 September 1918, 1, 5; Coleman 1930: 275–277.

8 Zechariah Chafee, Jr., *Free Speech in the United States* (Cambridge, MA: Harvard University Press, 1941), 72–73, 84–86; *Cleveland Plain Dealer*, 13 September 1918, 1; 15 September 1918, 1–2; *United States Reports*, 294: 211–217.

9 Miller 1939: 10.

10 H. Schuyler Foster, Jr., "How America Became Belligerent," *American Journal of Sociology* 40 (1935): 464–475; Foster, "Charting America's News of the World War," *Foreign Affairs* 15 (1937): 311–319.

11 Gilbert Parker, "The United States and the War," *Harper's Monthly Magazine* 136 (March 1918): 522; M. L. Sanders and Philip M. Taylor, *British Propaganda During the First World War, 1914–1918* (London: Macmillan, 1982); James D. Squires, *British Propaganda at Home and in the United States from 1914 to 1917* (Cambridge, MA: Harvard University Press, 1935), 17–60; Ivor Nicholson, "An Aspect of British Official Wartime Propaganda," *Cornhill Magazine* 70 [New Series] (January–June

1931): 593–606; T. L. Gilmour, "The Government and Propaganda," *The Nineteenth Century and After* 85 (January 1919): 148–158; George Aston, "Propaganda – And the Father of It," *Cornhill Magazine* 48 [New Series], No. 284 (February 1920): 233–241.

12 Great Britain, Committee on Alleged German Outrages, *Report of the Committee on Alleged German Outrages* (New York: Macmillan, 1915).

13 Will Irwin, "Let's Not Be Suckers Again," typescript, box 1, Papers of Will Irwin, Hoover Institution Archives. Also Frederick Palmer, *Newton D. Baker*, 2 vols. (New York: Dodd, Mead, 1931), 1:38; H. C. Peterson, *Propaganda for War* (Norman, OK: University of Oklahoma Press, 1939), 53; James M. Read, *Atrocity Propaganda: 1914–1919* (New Haven, CT: Yale University Press, 1941), 201–208.

14 George S. Viereck, *Spreading Germs of Hate* (New York: Liveright, 1930), 115–116. Also Johann Bernstorff, *My Three Years in America* (London: Skeffington, 1920), 47.

15 Emanuel Voska and Will Irwin, *Spy and Counterspy* (New York: Doubleday, 1940); William G. McAdoo, *Crowded Years* (Boston: Houghton Mifflin, 1931), 324–330; *World*, 15 August 1915, 1–3; Franz Von Papen, *Memoirs*, trans., Brian Connell (London: Andre Deutsch, 1952), 48–50.

16 *The Reminiscences of James T. Shotwell* (1964): 65–66, in The Oral History Collection of Columbia University, cited with permission of the Trustees of Columbia University in the City of New York; Ronald Steel, *Walter Lippmann and the American Century* (Boston: Little, Brown, 1980); Eric Goldman, *Rendezvous with Destiny* (New York: Knopf, 1952); Carol S. Gruber, *Mars and Minerva* (Baton Rouge, LA: Louisiana State University Press, 1975), ch. 2.

17 Lillian Schlissel, ed., *The World of Randolph Bourne* (New York: Dutton, 1965), xxxi–xxxviii.

18 George Creel, *How We Advertised America* (New York: Arno Press, 1972 [1920]); Creel, *Rebel at Large* (New York: G. P. Putnam's Sons, 1947); Stephen Vaughn, *Holding Fast the Inner Lines* (Chapel Hill, NC: University of North Carolina Press, 1980); James R. Mock and Cedric Larson, *Words that Won the War* (Princeton, NJ: Princeton University Press, 1939); Shotwell, *The Autobiography of James T. Shotwell* (Indianapolis, IN: Bobbs-Merrill, 1961); *Shotwell Reminiscences* (1964), 61.

19 Creel 1972/1920: 56, 104; Creel, "Propaganda and Morale," *American Journal of Sociology* 47 (1941): 340–351; *The Reminiscences of Guy Stanton Ford* (1955), 383, 387–388, in The Oral History Collection of Columbia University, cited with permission of the Trustees of Columbia University in the City of New York; James T. Shotwell, *Heritage of Freedom* (New York: Charles Scribner's Sons, 1934), 36; Shotwell to George S. Viereck, 6 December 1937, box 1, Viereck Papers, University of Iowa (hereafter, GVPI); *Conquest and Kultur*, comp. Wallace Notestein and Elmer E. Stoll, January 1918.

20 Stanford Museum Collection; Mock and Larson 1939: 65, 102; Vaughn 1980: 150, 163; *Ford Reminiscences* (1955), 383.

21 Villard 1939: 327; Newell D. Hillis, *German Atrocities* (New York: Revell, 1918), 8–34; Wilson to Creel, 14 November 1917, Container 1, Creel Papers, Library of Congress (hereafter, GCPLOC); Creel 1947: 6.

22 Lillian Gish, *The Movies, Mr. Griffith and Me* (Englewood Cliffs, NJ: Prentice-Hall, 1969), 188–201; Laemmle to Viereck, 8 May 1930, box 1, GVPI; *New York Times*, 10 March 1918, 18.

23 Creel 1972/1920; *Bulletin* No. 1 (22 May 1917); *Bulletin* No. 31 (27 May 1918); Clark in Vaughn 1980: 129.

24 Gruber 1975.

25 Box 2, Papers of the U.S. War Department, Committee on Education and Special Training, Hoover Institution Archives.

26 Vaughn 1980: 36; Upton Sinclair, *The Brass Check* (Pasadena, CA: Author, 1919), 207–208; Sinclair, *The Autobiography of Upton Sinclair* (New York: Harcourt, Brace, World, 1962), 220; Granville Hicks, "The Parsons and the War," *American Mercury* 10 (1927); Newell D. Hillis, *Murder Most Foul!* (London: Field and Queen, 19[18?]); Ray H. Abrams, *Preachers Present Arms* (New York: Round Table, 1933).

27 Creel 1972/1920: 70–76.

28 "The Daily German Lie," CPI 1–C1, Records of the Committee on Public Information, National Archives (hereafter, CPIR).

29 Songsheets in box 2, World War I Collection, Yale University Library.

30 Irvin S. Cobb, *Paths of Glory,* revised ed. (New York: Grosset and Dunlap, 1918), 78–79, 142; Heywood Broun, *The A.E.F.* (New York: Appleton, 1918), 273, 282–283; George Seldes, interview with author, Hartland-4-Corners, Vermont, 12–13 May 1984.

31 George H. Mead, *The Conscientious Objector* (n.p.: National Security League, n.d.).

32 Villard 1939: 313, 328–329; Beard in Schlissel 1965: 78–84; *Ford Reminiscences* (1955), 396–397; *Humanities Exchange* [OSU] 4, No. 1 (1988); Edward H. Doan, *The La Follettes and the Wisconsin Idea* (New York: Rinehart, 1947), 78–91.

33 Creel 1972/1920: 181–182; Ford[?] to Creel, 24 August 1918, CPI 3–A2, CPIR; Wilson to Creel, 28 February 1918, container 1, GCPLOC; Abrams 1933: 96–99, 182–184; Scott Nearing, *The Making of a Radical* (New York: Harper and Row, 1972), 96–97, 114–117.

34 Will Irwin, *Propaganda and the News* (New York: Whittlesey House, 1936), 211–212; Senate Res. 436, 4 February 1919, Senate Subcommittee of the Judiciary Committee, *Brewing and Liquor Interests and German and Bolshevik Propaganda*, Hearings, 66th Congress, 1st Session, 3 vols., 1919, 1:xxix.

35 Philip Gibbs, *More That Must Be Told* (New York and London: Harper, 1921), 344; Ernest M. Hopkins, "The Heyday of Propaganda," *Nation's Business* 11, No. 1 (January 1923): 37; Alfred McC. Lee, *How to Understand Propaganda* (New York: Rinehart, 1952), 22.

36 George Seldes, *The Facts Are* (New York: In Fact, 1942), 99–103; Seldes,

You Can't Print That! (Garden City, NY: Garden City, 1929), 435–445; Seldes interview (1984); cf. "Behind the Scenes at Constantinople," *Nation* 107 (28 December 1918): 807 and "More Revelations from Russia," *Nation* 109 (23 August 1919): 235–236.

37 Sidney B. Fay, "New Light on the Origins of the World War, I, "*American Historical Review* 25 (1920): 616–639; Fay, "New Light on the Origins of the World War, II," *AHR* 26 (1920): 37–53. Cf. Philip Gibbs, *The Soul of the War* (London: William Heinemann, 1915) and Gibbs, *Now It Can Be Told* (London: Harper, 1920).

38 Creel 1972/1920: 4; Charles E. Merriam, "American Publicity in Italy," *American Political Science Review* 13 (1919): 541–555.

39 William C. D'Arcy, "The Achievements of Advertising in a Year," *Printer's Ink* 104 (11 July 1918): 17; Edward L. Bernays, interview with author, 19 May 1984, Cambridge, MA; cf. Bernays, *Propaganda* (New York: Liveright, 1928a).

40 *The Reminiscences of Heber Blankenhorn* (1956), 60–123, in The Oral History Collection of Columbia University, cited with permission of the Trustees of Columbia University in the City of New York; Blankenhorn, *Adventures in Propaganda* (Boston: Houghton Mifflin, 1919).

41 Daniel J. Kevles, "Testing the Army's Intelligence," *Journal of American History* 55 (1968): 565–581; J. McKeen Cattell, "The Psychological Corporation," *Annals of the American Academy of Political and Social Science* 110 (November 1923): 165–171.

42 Lippmann, unattributed clipping, 3 July 1920, container 26, GCPLOC.

43 Walter Lippmann, "The Basic Problem of Democracy, I," *Atlantic Monthly* 124 (November 1919a): 616–627; Lippmann, "Liberty and the News," *Atlantic Monthly* 124 (December 1919b): 779–787; cf. Lippmann, *Liberty and the News* (New York: Harcourt, Brace, 1920).

44 Will Irwin, "An Age of Lies," *Sunset* 43 (December 1919).

45 John Dewey, "The New Paternalism," *New Republic* 17 (21 December 1918): 216–217; Charles A. Beard, "Propaganda in Schools," *The Dial* 66 (14 June 1919): 598–599.

46 Robert Herrick, "The Paper War," *The Dial* 66 (8 February 1919): 113–114; Frank Crane, "Propaganda Overdone," *Current Opinion* 69 (November 1920): 609–610; Edward G. Lowry, "The Special Interests – New Style," *Saturday Evening Post* 192 (31 January 1920): 5, 58, 61.

47 Walter Lippmann and Charles Merz, "A Test of the News," supplement to the *New Republic* 23 (4 August 1920): 1–42; *Blankenhorn Reminiscences* (1956), 134–174; Commission of Inquiry of the Interchurch World Movement, *Report on the Steel Strike of 1919* (New York: Harcourt, Brace and Howe, 1920), 248; Commission, *Public Opinion and the Steel Strike* (New York: Harcourt, Brace, 1921).

48 Raymond Dodge, "The Psychology of Propaganda," *Religious Education* 15 (October 1920): 241–252; Everett D. Martin, *The Behavior of Crowds* (New York: Harper and Brothers, 1920), 101, 282.

Chapter 2. The Progressive Propaganda Critics

1   Edward L. Bernays, "The Engineering of Consent," *Annals of the American Academy of Political and Social Science* 250 (March 1947): 113–120.

2   Ray S. Baker, "How Railroads Make Public Opinion," *McClure's Magazine* 26, No. 5 (March 1906): 535–549.

3   George J. Nathan, "Press Agents of Royalty," *Harper's Weekly* 53 (11 December 1909): 27; "Confessions of a Literary Press Agent," *Bookman* 24 (1906): 335–339; "Autobiography of a Theatrical Press-Agent," *American Magazine* 69 (April 1913): 67–70; (May 1913): 78–87; and (June 1913): 70–77.

4   Will Irwin, *The American Newspaper* (Ames, IA: Iowa State University Press, 1969 [1911]), quotation, 52; Robert E. Park, "The Natural History of the Newspaper," *American Journal of Sociology* 29 (1923): 285.

5   Will Irwin, *The Making of a Reporter* (New York: G. P. Putnam's Sons, 1942), 167–168; Irwin 1969/1911: 73–74.

6   George Creel, "How 'Tainted' Money Taints," *Pearson's Magazine*, March 1915, 289–297; Walter Lippmann, "The Campaign Against Sweating," *New Republic* 2, No. 21 [Part 2] (27 March 1915): 1–8.

7   *Congressional Record* 51, pt. 8 (5 May 1914), Senate, 63rd Cong. 2nd sess., 7728–7729, 7999.

8   James Bryce, *The American Commonwealth*, 3rd ed., 2 vols. (New York: Macmillan, 1894), quotations, 2:322, 368.

9   Donald Hayworth, "The Development of the Training of Public Speakers in America," *Quarterly Journal of Speech* 14 (1928): 489–502; Ota Thomas, "The Teaching of Rhetoric in the United States During the Classical Period of Education," in *A History and Criticism of American Public Address*, 2 vols., ed. William N. Brigance (New York: Russell and Russell, 1943), 1:193–210; Helen F. Roach, *History of Speech Education at Columbia College, 1754–1940* (New York: Teachers College, 1950); Marie Hochmuth and Richard Murphy, "Rhetorical and Elocutionary Training in Nineteenth-Century Colleges," in *A History of Speech Education in America*, ed. Karl A. Wallace (New York: Appleton-Century-Crofts, 1954), 153–177; Ronald F. Reid, "The Boylston Professorship of Rhetoric and Oratory, 1806–1904," *QJS* 45 (1959): 239–257; William Gering, "David Starr Jordan on 'Flavorless Foolishness,' " *QJS* 52 (1966): 16–22; Daniel J. Boorstin, *The Americans: The Democratic Experience* (New York: Random House, 1973), 465ff.

10 Nan Johnson, *Nineteenth-Century Rhetoric in North America* (Carbondale, IL: Southern Illinois University Press, 1991).

11 S. Michael Halloran, "Rhetoric in the American College Curriculum," *Pretext* 3 (1982): 245–269; James A. Berlin, *Writing Instruction in Nineteenth-Century American Colleges* (Carbondale, IL: Southern Illinois University Press, 1984), 58–76.

12 Joseph W. Wenzel, "Rhetoric and Anti-Rhetoric in Early American Scientific Societies," *Quarterly Journal of Speech* 60 (1974): 328–336.

13 Richard Whately, *Elements of Rhetoric* (Carbondale, IL: Southern Illinois University Press, 1963 [1846]); Adams S. Hill, *The Principles of Rhetoric*, 2nd ed. (New York: Harper, 1895).

14 William Albig, *Public Opinion* (New York: McGraw-Hill, 1939).

15 Gustave Le Bon, *The Crowd* (New York: Viking, 1960 [1895]), quotations, 3, 24.

16 Charles H. Cooley, *Social Organization* (New York: Charles Scribner's Sons, 1909), quotation, 138; Robert E. Park, *The Crowd and the Public and Other Essays*, ed. Henry Elsner, Jr., trans. Charlotte Elsner (Chicago: University of Chicago Press, 1972 [1904]), 57.

17 Walter Lippmann, "Trotter and Freud," *New Republic Fall Literary Review*, 18 November 1916, 16, 18; Graham Wallas, *Human Nature in Politics* (London: Constable, 1948 [1920 ed.]), 18.

18 William McDougall, *The Group Mind* (New York: G. P. Putnam's, 1920); Martin 1920: 87; Norman Angell, *The Public Mind* (New York: Dutton, 1927); Charles Merriam, *A History of American Political Theories* (New York: Macmillan, 1928); Albig 1939; Max Lerner, *Ideas Are Weapons* (New York: Viking, 1939).

19 James Bryce, *Modern Democracies*, 2 vols. (New York: Macmillan, 1921), quotations, 1:155, 2:483.

20 Albert A. Sutton, *Education for Journalism in the United States from Its Beginning to 1940* (Evanston, IL: Northwestern University, 1941); Michael Schudson, *Discovering the News* (New York: Basic Books, 1978), 151–159; Herman Cohen, *The History of Speech Communication* (Annandale, VA: Speech Communication Association, 1994); Edwin Puls, "Speech Training for Business Men," *Quarterly Journal of Public Speaking* 3 (1917): 332–335; Giles W. Gray, "How Much Are We Dependent on the Ancient Greeks and Romans?" *Quarterly Journal of Speech Education* 9 (1923): 258–280; Everett M. Rogers, *A History of Communication Study* (New York: Free Press, 1994); J. Michael Sproule, "The New Managerial Rhetoric and the Old Criticism," *Quarterly Journal of Speech* 74 (1988): 468–486.

21 Llewellyn White, "The Growth of American Radio," in *Mass Communications*, 2nd ed., ed. Wilbur Schramm (Urbana, IL: University of Illinois Press, 1960); Herman S. Hettinger, *A Decade of Radio Advertising* (New York: Arno, 1971 [1933]), 42; Walter D. Scott, *The Theory of Advertising* (Boston: Small, Maynard, 1903).

22 Archibald M. Crossley, "Early Days of Public Opinion Research," *Public Opinion Quarterly* 21 (1957): 160; Elmo Roper, "The Client Over the Years," *POQ* 21 (1957): 28–32; Rensis Likert, "A Method for Measuring the Sales Influence of a Radio Program," *Journal of Applied Psychology* 20 (1936): 175–182; Paul F. Lazarsfeld, "The Psychological Aspect of Market Research," *Harvard Business Review* 13 (1934): 54–71.

23 Crossley 1957: 160–161; J. Fred MacDonald, *Don't Touch that Dial!* (Chicago: Nelson–Hall, 1979), 33; Donald L. Hurwitz, *Broadcast "Ratings,"* Ph.D. diss., University of Illinois, 1983; Daniel J. Czitrom, *Media*

and the American Mind (Chapel Hill, NC: University of North Carolina Press, 1982), 126–129.

24 Paul F. Lazarsfeld, "Radio Research and Applied Psychology," *Journal of Applied Psychology* 23 (1939): 1–7; Lazarsfeld, ed., "Progress in Radio Research," Special Issue, *JAP* 24 (1940b): 661–859; Lazarsfeld and Frank N. Stanton, eds., *Radio Research: 1942–1943* (New York: Duell, Sloan and Pearce, 1944).

25 Edward L. Bernays, *Public Relations* (Norman, OK: University of Oklahoma Press, 1952), 74; Bernays interview (1984).

26 Edward L. Bernays, *Propaganda* (New York: Liveright, 1928a), 53–56; Bernays interview (1984). Also Bernays, *Crystallizing Public Opinion* (New York: Boni and Liveright, 1923), 15–16; Bernays, "Molding Public Opinion," *Annals of the American Academy of Political and Social Science* 179 (May 1935): 83–87; Bernays 1952; Bernays, *Biography of an Idea* (New York: Simon and Schuster, 1965).

27 Garth Jowett and James M. Linton, *Movies as Mass Communication*, 2nd ed. (Newbury Park, CA: Sage, 1989).

28 Edgar Dale, *The Content of Motion Pictures* (New York: Macmillan, 1935); Darwin Teilhet, "Propaganda Stealing the Movies," *Outlook and Independent* 158, No. 4 (27 May 1931): 112–113, 126; *The Reminiscences of George Gallup* (1972), 138–155, in The Oral History Collection of Columbia University, cited with permission of the Trustees of Columbia University in the City of New York.

29 Barnet Baskerville, *The People's Voice* (Lexington, KY: University Press of Kentucky), 154–158; Herbert N. Craig, *Distinctive Features of Radio-TV in the 1952 Presidential Campaign*, Master's thesis, State University of Iowa, 1954; Boorstin 1973: 467–469; Terry Hynes, "Media Manipulation and Political Campaigns," *Journalism History* 4, No. 3 (1977): 96.

30 Graham Wallas, *The Great Society* (New York: Macmillan, 1914).

31 Walter Lippmann, *Public Opinion* (New York: Macmillan, 1922), quotations, 15, 47, 248, 270, 289, 396.

32 Irwin 1936.

33 Seldes interview (1984); Seldes 1929; Seldes, *Freedom of the Press* (Indianapolis, IN: Bobbs-Merrill, 1935), quotations, xi, 349; Seldes, *Lords of the Press* (New York: Julian Messner, 1938), quotation, 237.

34 "The Confessions of a Shirt Stuffer," *New Republic* 46 (3 March 1926): 35–38; Duncan Cassidy, "Editing in Iowa," *New Republic* 57 (28 November 1928): 36–38; Willard Cooper, "Journalistic Poison," *The Independent* 116 (20 March 1926): 329, 339; Stanley Walker, "Men of Vision," *American Mercury* 10 (January 1927): 89–93; John T. Flynn, "Edward L. Bernays," *Atlantic Monthly* 149 (May 1932): 562–571.

35 George J. Nathan, "The Tabloids," *American Mercury* 7 (1926): 363–364; Samuel Tenenbaum, "The Camera Learns to Lie," *Nation* 124 (8 June 1927): 633–634.

36 Charles Angoff, "The Higher Learning Goes to War," *American Mercury*

11 (June 1927): 177–191; C. Hartley Grattan, "The Historians Cut Loose," *AM* 11 (August 1927): 414–430.

37 H. S. Rauschenbush and Harry W. Laidler, *Power Control* (New York: New Republic, 1928); Ernest Gruening, *The Public Pays* (New York: Vanguard, 1931a); Gruening, "Power and Propaganda," *The American Economic Review* (supplement) 22 (1931b): 202–241; Edwin R. A. Seligman, "Propaganda by Public Utility Corporations," *Bulletin of the American Association of University Professors* 16 (1930): 349–368.

38 National Education Association, *Report of the Committee on Propaganda in the Schools* (NEA, July 1929); William McAndrew, "French Wine-Growers and American School Children," *School and Society* 32 (19 July 1930): 96–97; "Prize Contests of the League of Nations Association," *SS* 31 (1930): 111–112; "Educational News and Editorial Comment" *Elementary School Journal* 31 (May 1931): 642–644.

39 Teilhet 1931: 112–113, 126; Harold A. Larrabee, "The Formation of Public Opinion Through Motion Pictures," *Religious Education* 15 (1920): 144–154; Mark Fackler, "Moral Guardians of the Movies and Social Responsibility of the Press," in *Mass Media Between the Wars*, ed. Catherine L. Covert and John D. Stevens (Syracuse, NY: Syracuse University Press, 1984), 181–197; Czitrom 1982: 30–59; Garth S. Jowett, "Social Science as a Weapon," *Communication* 13 (1992): 211–225; Shearon Lowery and Melvin L. De Fleur, *Milestones in Mass Communication Research* (New York: Longman, 1983), 31–57; Dale 1935: 185.

40 Hicks 1927; Abrams 1933; Commission 1920; Commission 1921.

41 Jean de Pierrefeu, "Building the National Lie," *Nation* 118 (9 January 1924): 28–30; "La Follette's Foreign Policy," *Nation* 119 (29 October 1924): 476–478; "Professors and Propaganda," *Nation* 131 (30 July 1930): 114; H. C. Engelbrecht, "How War Propaganda Won," *The World Tomorrow* 10 (April 1927): 159–162; Walter Millis, "The President," *Atlantic Monthly* 149 (March 1932): 265–278.

42 Charles A. Beard, "Our Confusion over National Defense" *Harper's Magazine* 164 (February 1932): 257–267; George Seldes, "The New Propaganda for War," *HM* 169 (1934): 540–554; Robert Wohlforth, "Catch 'Em Young – Teach 'Em Rough," *New Republic* 64 (22 October 1930): 257–258.

43 Walter Millis, *Road to War* (Boston: Houghton, Mifflin, 1935), quotations, 64, 202.

44 Zechariah Chafee, Jr., "The Conscription of Public Opinion," in *The Next War* (Cambridge, MA: Harvard Alumni Bulletin Press, 1925), 41–66; Quincy Howe, *England Expects Every American to Do His Duty* (New York: Simon and Schuster, 1937); Gerald P. Nye, "Propaganda in the Next War," *Congressional Record,* 25 April 1939, offprint. Also "Fooling the Americans Again," *Nation* 115 (20 December 1922): 680; John Gunther, "Funneling the European News," *Harper's Magazine* 160 (April 1930): 635–647; "Japan's 'Official' Propaganda," *Literary Digest* 71 (5 November 1921): 16; Ellis Freeman, *Conquering the Man in the Street* (New

York: Vanguard, 1940); Dorothy Thompson, "Stopping Propaganda," *Vital Speeches* 5 (1 June 1939): 494–495.

45 H. C. Engelbrecht and F. C. Hanighen, *Merchants of Death* (New York: Dodd, Mead, 1934); "Arms and the Men," *Fortune* 9 (March 1934): 52–57, 113–126.

46 George H. Gallup, ed., *The Gallup Poll*, 3 vols. (New York: Random House, 1972), 1:192–193.

47 For instance: Norman Hapgood, *Professional Patriots* (New York: Albert and Charles Boni, 1927); James Rorty, *American Medicine Mobilizes* (New York: W. W. Norton, 1939); Frederick E. Johnson, "Prohibition Without Propaganda," *Atlantic Monthly* 137 (February 1926): 158–167; Howard E. Jensen, "Propaganda and the Anti-Prohibition Movement," *South Atlantic Quarterly* 32 (1933): 254–265; Charles Merz, "The Propaganda Against Mexico," *The World Tomorrow* 10 (April 1927): 152–155.

48 F. H. Hodder, "Propaganda as a Source of American History," *Mississippi Valley Historical Review* 9, No. 1 (June 1922): 1–18.

49 For instance, George G. Bruntz, "Propaganda as an Instrument of War," *Current History* 32 (1930): 743–747; James M. Read, "Atrocity Propaganda and the Irish Rebellion," *Public Opinion Quarterly* 2 (1938): 229–244; Read 1941; Mock and Larson 1939; Peterson 1939.

50 J. Fred Rippy, "Pan-Hispanic Propaganda in Hispanic America," *Political Science Quarterly* 37 (1922): 389–414; Harold W. Stoke, "Executive Leadership and the Growth of Propaganda," *American Political Science Review* 35 (1941): 490–500. Also, Peter H. Odegard, *Pressure Politics* (New York: Columbia University Press, 1928).

51 Peter Odegard, *The American Public Mind* (New York: Columbia University Press, 1930); Harwood L. Childs, *A Reference Guide to the Study of Public Opinion* (Princeton, NJ: Princeton University Press, 1934); Childs, ed., *Propaganda and Dictatorship* (Princeton, NJ: Princeton University Press, 1936); [Childs and Edward L. Bernays] "Propaganda – Asset or Liability in a Democracy?" *America's Town Meeting of the Air* [Series 2] No. 22 (15 April 1937).

52 Harold D. Lasswell, *Propaganda Technique in World War I* (Cambridge, MA: MIT Press, 1971 [1927]); Lasswell, "The Theory of Political Propaganda," *American Political Science Review* 21 (1927): 627–631.

53 Leonard W. Doob, interview with author, 20–21 May 1982, New Haven, CT; Doob, *Propaganda* (New York: Henry Holt, 1935).

54 Frederick E. Lumley, *Principles of Sociology* (New York: McGraw-Hill, 1928); Albig 1939: 282–333; Lumley, "The Nature of Propaganda," *Sociology and Social Research* 13 (1929): 315–324; Lumley, "The Essential Aspects of Propaganda," *SSR* 16 (1932): 517–526; Richard T. LaPiere, "Propaganda and Education," *SSR* 20 (1935): 18–26; James E. Foster, "Censorship as a Medium of Propaganda," *SSR* 22 (1937a): 57–65; J. E. Foster, "The Group in Terms of Propaganda," *American Sociological Review* 2 (1937b): 247–252; H. S. Foster 1935; H. S. Foster 1937.

55 Frederick E. Lumley, *The Propaganda Menace* (New York: Century, 1933), quotations, 44, 94; cf. Doob 1935: 9, 100.

56 Abrams 1933: quotation, 243; Alfred McC. Lee, *The Daily Newspaper in America* (New York: Octagon, 1973 [1937]).

57 Herbert M. Bratter, "The Committee for the Nation," *Journal of Political Economy* 49 (1941): 531–553; Wilford J. Eiteman, "The Rise and Decline of Orthodox Tariff Propaganda," *Quarterly Journal of Economics* 45 (1930): 22–39; Chafee 1941: 517–555; Harold D. Lasswell, Ralph D. Casey, and Bruce L. Smith, eds., *Propaganda and Promotional Activities* (Minneapolis, MN: University of Minnesota Press, 1935); John Higham, "The Schism in American Scholarship," *American Historical Review* 72 (1966): 1–21.

58 Ralph D. Casey, "The National Publicity Bureau and British Party Propaganda," *Public Opinion Quarterly* 3 (1939): 623–634; O. W. Riegel, *Mobilizing for Chaos* (New Haven, CT: Yale University Press, 1934); Sutton 1941: 80–81; Alma Johnson, "Propaganda Analysis and Public Speaking," *Southern Speech Bulletin* 4, No. 3 (1939): 12–15; Harold F. Graves, "Public Speaking in Propaganda," *Quarterly Journal of Speech* 27 (1941): 29–38; Elsa A. Schilling, "Why the Debate Student Should Be Able to Recognize Propaganda," *SSB* 7 (1941): 15–17; S. I. Hayakawa, "General Semantics and Propaganda," *POQ* 3 (1939): 197–208; Arno Jewett, "Detecting and Analyzing Propaganda," *English Journal* 29 (1940): 105–115.

Chapter 3. Different Lessons I: Managed Democracy

1 Eric F. Goldman, *Two-Way Street* (Boston: Bellman, 1948), 8.

2 Ivy L. Lee, *Publicity* (New York: Industries Publishing, 1925).

3 Ivy Lee, *The Problem of International Propaganda* (n.p., [1934]).

4 House Special Committee on Un-American Activities, *Investigation of Nazi Propaganda Activities and Investigation of Certain Other Propaganda Activities,* Hearings, 73rd Cong., 2nd sess., 5–7 June 1934, 175–193; Ray E. Hiebert, *Courtier to the Crowd* (Ames, IA: Iowa State University Press, 1966), 286–291, 310.

5 Flynn 1932: 566.

6 Bernays 1928a; Bernays, "Manipulating Public Opinion," *American Journal of Sociology* 33 (1928b): 958–971; Bernays interview (1984); Bernays 1965: 294.

7 Bernays 1923: quotations, 14, 56, 212, 214, 216–217.

8 Bernays, 1928a: quotations, 11, 109.

9 "Does Propaganda Menace Democracy?" *Forum* 99 (June 1938); *America's Town Meeting of the Air* [Series 2] No. 22 (15 April 1937); Bernays, "The Minority Rules," *Bookman* 65 (April 1927): 150–155; Bernays 1928b; Bernays 1935.

10 Cattell 1923; Forrest R. Kingsbury, "Applying Psychology to Business," *Annals of the American Academy of Political and Social Science* 110

(November 1923): 2–12; Harry D. Kitson, "Understanding the Consumer's Mind," *Annals*, 131–138.

11   *Gallup Reminiscences* (1972).

12   George Gallup and Saul F. Rae, *The Pulse of Democracy* (New York: Simon and Schuster, 1940): quotations, 6, 12, 13, 26, 146, 214, 218–220, 270.

13   George Gallup, *A Guide to Public Opinion Polls* (Princeton, NJ: Princeton University Press, 1944), quotations, 9, 40.

14   Gallup and Rae 1940: 289.

15   Floyd H. Allport and D. A. Hartman, "The Measurement and Motivation of Atypical Opinion in a Certain Group," *American Political Science Review* 19 (1925): 735–760; Louis L. Thurstone and E. J. Chave, *The Measurement of Attitude* (Chicago: University of Chicago Press, 1929), 7; Erwin Esper, *A History of Psychology* (Philadelphia, PA: W. B. Saunders, 1964), 273; William W. Biddle, *Propaganda and Education*, Teachers College Contributions to Education, No. 531 (New York: Teachers College, Columbia University, 1932); Thurstone, "Influence of Motion Pictures on Children's Attitudes," *Journal of Social Psychology* 2 (1931): 299; William K. C. Chen, "Retention of the Effect of Oral Propaganda," *JSP* 7 (1936): 479–483; Henry J. Wegrocki, "The Effect of Prestige Suggestibility on Emotional Attitudes," *JSP* 5 (1934): 384–394; Douglas Waples, Bernard Berelson, and Franklyn R. Bradshaw, *What Reading Does to People* (Chicago: University of Chicago Press, 1940).

16   Frank N. Stanton, "The Outlook for Listener Research," typescript, c. 1937, box 3b (series I), Papers of Paul F. Lazarsfeld, Columbia University (hereafter, PLPC); Stanton, "Psychological Research in the Field of Radio Listening," in *Educational Broadcasting 1936*, ed. C. S. Marsh (Chicago: University of Chicago Press, 1937), 365–377.

17   Paul F. Lazarsfeld, "An Episode in the History of Social Research," in *The Intellectual Migration*, ed. Donald Fleming and Bernard Bailyn (Cambridge, MA: Harvard University Press, 1969); Lazarsfeld 1939; Lazarsfeld 1940b.

18   Paul F. Lazarsfeld, *Radio and the Printed Page* (New York: Duell, Sloan, Pearce, 1940a); Lazarsfeld 1969.

19   Paul F. Lazarsfeld, "The Prognosis for International Communications Research," *Public Opinion Quarterly* 16 (1952): 482.

20   *The Reminiscences of Paul F. Lazarsfeld* (1973), 34–35, 70, 88, in The Oral History Collection of Columbia University, cited with permission of Robert K. Lazarsfeld.

21   Paul F. Lazarsfeld, Bernard Berelson, and Hazel Gaudet, *The People's Choice*, 3rd ed. (New York: Columbia University Press, 1968 [1944]); William Albig, "Two Decades of Opinion Study: 1938–1956," *Public Opinion Quarterly* 21 (1957): 21.

22   Charles E. Merriam, *New Aspects of Politics*, 3rd ed. (Chicago: University of Chicago Press, 1970 [1925]), quotations, 76, 300.

23   Charles E. Merriam, *The Making of Citizens* (Chicago: University of

Chicago Press, 1931), quotations, 333, 349; Merriam, "Government and Society," in President's Research Committee on Social Trends, *Recent Social Trends in the United States,* 3 vols. (New York: McGraw-Hill, 1933), 3:lxxiv, 1513–1514.

24 Harold D. Lasswell, "Autobiographical Affidavit," 23 October 1951, Papers of Harold D. Lasswell, Yale University Library (hereafter, HLPY); Lasswell 1971/1927: x–xiii, 9; Lasswell 1927: 627.

25 Martin Bulmer, *The Chicago School of Sociology* (Chicago: University of Chicago Press, 1984), 125–126; Lasswell 1971/1927: 191, 222. Also Lasswell 1927: 631.

26 Lasswell 1971/1927: quotations, 4, 5, 222.

27 Harold D. Lasswell, "Propaganda," *Encyclopaedia of the Social Sciences,* ed. Edwin R. A. Seligman (New York: Macmillan, 1933), 12:521–527; Lasswell and Dorothy Blumenstock, *World Revolutionary Propaganda* (New York: Alfred A. Knopf, 1939), 20–21. Also Lasswell, "A Provisional Classification of Symbol Data," *Psychiatry* 1 (1938): 197–204.

28 Lasswell and Blumenstock 1939: quotations, 230, 248.

29 Harold D. Lasswell, *Psychopathology and Politics* (Chicago: University of Chicago Press, 1977 [1930]), quotations, 31, 153, 173, 194, 197.

30 Fritz J. Roethlisberger, *The Elusive Phenomena* (Cambridge, MA: Harvard University Press, 1977), 32–54; Roethlisberger and William J. Dickson, *Management and the Worker* (Cambridge, MA: Harvard University Press, 1939), 500–522.

31 Kurt Lewin, Ronald Lippitt, and Ralph White, "Patterns of Aggressive Behavior in Experimentally Created 'Social Climates,' " *Journal of Social Psychology* 10 (1939): 271–299; Dorwin Cartwright and Alvin Zander, "Origins of Group Dynamics," in Cartwright and Zander, eds., *Group Dynamics,* 2nd ed. (New York: Harper and Row, 1960), 3–32.

32 Muzafer Sherif, *The Psychology of Social Norms* (New York: Octagon Books, 1965 [1936]), 90–106.

33 Nathan Glazer, interview with author, Cambridge, MA, 14 May 1984; Roethlisberger 1977: 305–306.

34 *Lazarsfeld Reminiscences* (1973), 3, 29, 55; Roethlisberger 1977: 21–23; Dorothy C. Adkins, "Louis Leon Thurstone," in *Contributions to Mathematical Psychology,* ed. Norman Fredericksen and Harold Gulliksen (New York: Holt, Rinehart and Winston, 1964), 5–6; Roethlisberger 1977: 21, 344.

35 Cantril to Clyde Miller, 1 February 1938, IPAP.

36 Martin Bulmer, "Support for Sociology in the 1920s," *American Sociologist* 17 (1982): 185–192; Rogers 1994: 142–145, 358–359; *Reminiscences of Florence Anderson* (1969), 20–30, in The Oral History Collection of Columbia University, cited with permission of the Trustees of Columbia University in the City of New York.

37 *The Reminiscences of Bernard Berelson* (1967), 4, in The Oral History Collection of Columbia University, cited with permission of the Trustees of Columbia University in the City of New York; Lasswell to MacLeish,

25 August 1941, HLPY; Memorandum on Communication Conference, 18 January 1941, HLPY.

38 Marshall in Memorandum on Communication Conference, 18 January 1941, HLPY; *Lazarsfeld Reminiscences* (1973), 4, 15–16; *The Reminiscences of Charles Dollard* (1969), 10, in The Oral History Collection of Columbia University, cited with permission of the Trustees of Columbia University in the City of New York.

39 *Dollard Reminiscences* (1969), 10; *Anderson Reminiscences* (1969), 256–257, 283–284.

40 *Anderson Reminiscences* (1969), 70, 284; Waldemar A. Nielsen, *The Big Foundations* (New York: Columbia University Press, 1972), 53–54; Raymond Fosdick, *The Story of the Rockefeller Foundation* (New York: Harper and Brothers, 1952), quotations, 201; Bulmer 1982: 190.

41 Report of the Institute of Human Relations, 1 December 1934, box 4 (series I), Institute of Human Relations Papers, Record Group 37–U, Yale University Library. Also Edward H. Berman, *The Influence of the Carnegie, Ford, and Rockefeller Foundations on American Foreign Policy* (Albany, NY: State University of New York Press, 1983), 105–111; Rogers 1994: 358–361.

42 Merriam 1970/1925: 184–219; Bulmer 1984: 154–189; Dorothy Ross, "The Development of the Social Sciences," in *The Organization of Knowledge in Modern America, 1860–1920*, ed. Alexandra Oleson and John Voss (Baltimore, MD: Johns Hopkins University Press, 1979), 127–129; Laurence R. Veysey, *The Emergence of the American University* (Chicago: University of Chicago Press, 1965), 126–127, 140–142; *Lazarsfeld Reminiscences* (1973), 55, 150.

43 Abraham A. Roback, *History of American Psychology* (New York: Library Publishers, 1952), 122–127; Ross 1979; Veysey 1965: 125, 133–140; Shotwell to Newton D. Baker, 14 October 1931, container 211, Papers of Newton D. Baker, Library of Congress (hereafter, NBPLOC).

44 Higham 1966.

45 George H. Mead, *Mind, Self and Society* (Chicago: University of Chicago Press, 1934); Talcott Parsons, *The Structure of Social Action*, 2nd ed. (Glencoe, IL: Free Press, 1949 [1937]); Barrington Moore, Jr., interview with author, Cambridge, MA, 16 May 1984.

46 Theodor W. Adorno, "A Social Critique of Radio Music," *Kenyon Review* 7 (1945): 208–217; Adorno, "Scientific Experiences of a European Scholar in America," in Fleming and Bailyn 1969: 340–355; Martin Jay, *The Dialectical Imagination* (Boston: Little, Brown, 1973), 191, 222–223; Lazarsfeld 1969.

47 Paul F. Lazarsfeld, "Remarks on Administrative and Critical Communications Research," *Studies in Philosophy and Social Science* 9 (1941): 2–16; Leo Lowenthal, "Biographies in Popular Magazines," in Lazarsfeld and Stanton 1944: 507–548.

48 Alfred McC. Lee, letters to author, 18 March 1985 and 2 April 1985; Lee, interview with author, Madison, NJ, 13 June 1987.

49 John Dewey, "Practical Democracy," *New Republic* 45 (2 December 1925): 52.

50 John Dewey, *The Public and Its Problems* (Chicago: Swallow, 1954 [1927]), quotations, 131, 147, 167, 205, 208; James H. Robinson, *The Mind in the Making* (New York: Harper and Brothers, 1921); Plato, *Protagoras*, 321–322; I. F. Stone, *The Trial of Socrates* (Boston: Little Brown, 1988), 40–48. Also Dewey, *Individualism Old and New* (New York: Minton, Balch, 1930), 122–133.

51 Robert E. Park, "The City," in Park, Ernest W. Burgess, and Roderick D. McKenzie, *The City* (Chicago: University of Chicago Press, 1967 [1925]), quotations, 2, 17, 21, 22, 35, 37. Also Park 1923: 273–289; Park, "News as a Form of Knowledge," *American Journal of Sociology* 45 (1940): 669–686; Park, "News and the Power of the Press," *AJS* 47 (1941): 1–11.

52 Robert S. Lynd and Helen M. Lynd, *Middletown* (New York: Harcourt, Brace, 1929).

53 Park, "Community Organization and Juvenile Delinquency," in Park, Burgess, McKenzie 1967/1925: 99–112; Bulmer 1984: 68, 76; *The Reminiscences of Helen Lynd* (1973), 250, in The Oral History Collection of Columbia University, cited with permission of the Trustees of Columbia University in the City of New York; Alfred McC. Lee, *Toward Humanist Sociology* (Englewood Cliffs, NJ: Prentice–Hall, 1973), 127.

54 Robert S. Lynd, *Knowledge for What?* (Princeton, NJ: Princeton University Press, 1939), quotations, 1, 119, 120, 129, 164n, 218, 219.

55 Lazarsfeld 1940a: xiv–xv; *Lazarsfeld Reminiscences* (1973), 35, 127–128, 323–324; Lazarsfeld 1969: 328–329. Also Lewis A. Coser, "Introduction," in Lynd, *Knowledge for What?* (Middletown, CT: Wesleyan University Press, 1967), xi–xii.

56 *Lazarsfeld Reminiscences* (1973), 127–128; Lynd to Lazarsfeld, 20 August 1951[?], box 2b (series I), PLPC; Patricia Kendall Lazarsfeld, interview with author, New York City, 9 June 1987.

57 Jowett 1992: 211–225; W. W. Charters, *Motion Pictures and Youth* (New York: Macmillan, 1933), 55; Herbert Blumer, *Movies and Conduct* (New York: Arno, 1970 [1933]); Dale 1935: 186; Herbert Blumer, letter to author, 15 June 1985; Samuel Stouffer, "A Sociologist Looks at Communications Research," in Douglas Waples, ed., *Print, Radio, and Film in a Democracy* (Chicago: University of Chicago Press, 1942), 144. Also Lowery and De Fleur 1983: 32–57.

58 Lee 1973/1937; Lumley 1933; Doob 1935; Odegard 1930; Albig 1939. Cf. Lee 1952; Jacques Ellul, *Propaganda* (New York: Vintage, 1965); Terence H. Qualter, *Opinion Control in the Democracies* (New York: St. Martin's, 1985).

59 Lasswell, Casey, and Smith 1935; Smith, Lasswell, and Casey, *Propaganda, Communication, and Public Opinion* (Princeton, NJ: Princeton University Press, 1946), 32, 145; Lasswell and Nathan Leites, *Language of Politics* (Cambridge, MA: MIT Press, 1965 [1949]), 3–5.

60 Consult issues of the *Quarterly Journal of Speech*.

61 Irving L. Janis, "Meaning and the Study of Symbolic Behavior," type-script, May 1943, HLPY.

Chapter 4. Different Lessons II: Protecting the Public

1 Steel 1980: 23–44; D. Steven Blum, *Walter Lippmann* (Ithaca, NY: Cornell University Press, 1984), 29–39; Lippmann, *A Preface to Politics* (New York: Mitchell Kennerley, 1913); Lippmann, *Drift and Mastery* (Madison, WI: University of Wisconsin Press, 1985 [1914]), 15–16.

2 Lippmann 1920; Lippmann and Merz 1920.

3 Lippmann 1922; Lippmann, *The Phantom Public* (New York: Harcourt, Brace, 1925), quotation, 70–71.

4 Lippmann 1925; Lippmann, *The Good Society* (Boston: Little, Brown, 1937).

5 Robert B. Westbrook, *John Dewey and American Democracy* (Ithaca, NY: Cornell University Press, 1991).

6 John Dewey, *Studies in Logical Theory* (Chicago: University of Chicago Press, 1903), x.

7 Morris R. Cohen and Ernest Nagel, *An Introduction to Logic and Scientific Method* (New York: Harcourt, Brace, 1934), iv.

8 John Dewey, *Essays in Experimental Logic* (New York: Dover, 1953 [1916]).

9 John Dewey, *Logic* (New York: Henry Holt, 1938), v.

10 Dewey 1938; also Dewey, *Democracy and Education* (New York: Macmillan, 1916).

11 John Dewey, *How We Think* (Boston: D. C. Heath, 1910), quotations, 72, 203, 204. Also Dewey 1916.

12 Lumley 1933: vii, 31.

13 James W. Carey, "The Mass Media and Critical Theory," *Communication Yearbook 6*, ed. Michael Burgoon (Beverly Hills, CA: Sage, 1982), 18–33; John D. Peters, "Democracy and American Mass Communication Theory," *Communication* 11 (1989): 199–220.

14 Henry Hazlitt, *Thinking as a Science* (New York: Dutton, 1916); Daniel S. Robinson, *The Principles of Reasoning* (New York: Appleton, 1924).

15 Edwin L. Clarke, *The Art of Straight Thinking* (New York: Appleton, 1929), vii.

16 Robert H. Thouless, *Straight and Crooked Thinking* (New York: Simon and Schuster, 1932), 219.

17 Goodwin B. Watson, *The Measurement of Fair-Mindedness*, Teachers College Contributions to Education, No. 176 (New York: Columbia University, 1925), quotations, 8, 43.

18 Edward M. Glaser, *An Experiment in the Development of Critical Thinking*, Teachers College Contributions to Education, No. 843 (New York: Columbia University, 1941).

19 Elmer Ellis, ed., *Education Against Propaganda*, 7th Yearbook (n.p.: National Council for the Social Studies, 1937), quotation, iii.

20 Howard R. Anderson, ed., *Teaching Critical Thinking in the Social Stud-*

ies, 13th Yearbook (Washington, DC: National Council for the Social Studies, 1942).

21 Dewey 1916: 272–273; Dewey 1953/1916: 186; Richard M. Weaver, *The Ethics of Rhetoric* (Chicago: Henry Regnery, 1953).

22 C. K. Ogden and I. A. Richards, *The Meaning of Meaning* (New York: Harcourt Brace Jovanovich, 1923); Richards, *The Philosophy of Rhetoric* (New York: Oxford University Press, 1965 [1936]).

23 Alfred Korzybski, *Science and Sanity,* 4th ed. (Lakeville, CT: International Non-Aristotelian Library, 1958) [1st ed., 1933]; S. I. Hayakawa, *Language in Action* (New York: Harcourt, Brace, 1941), quotations, xii–xiii, 76–79.

24 Thurman W. Arnold, *The Symbols of Government* (New Haven, CT: Yale University Press, 1935), quotations, 8, 22, 111, 233, 269.

25 Stuart Chase, *The Tyranny of Words* (New York: Harcourt Brace Jovanovich, 1966 [1938]), quotation, 22. Also Chase to Ogden, 23 September 1936, 8 June 1937, 11 August 1937 and Chase to Korzybski, 23 September 1936, box 7, Papers of Stuart Chase, Library of Congress (hereafter, SCPLOC).

26 Thurman W. Arnold, *The Folklore of Capitalism* (New Haven, CT: Yale University Press, 1937), quotations, 40, 42, 118, 268.

27 Sinclair 1919: quotations, 42, 329.

28 Quotation in Seldes 1935: 173. Also Edwin Emery, *The Press and America,* 3rd ed. (Englewood Cliffs, NJ: Prentice-Hall, 1972), 699; George Seldes, *Can These Things Be!* (Garden City, NY: Garden City, 1931), 200; Seldes interview (1984); Judson Grenier, "Upton Sinclair and the Press," *Journalism Quarterly* 49 (1972): 427–436.

29 Published in Pasadena, CA, by Upton Sinclair: *The Profits of Religion* (1918); *100 Percent* (1920); *The Goose-Step* (1923); *The Goslings* (1924); *Mammonart* (1925). Sinclair, *Money Writes!* (New York: Albert and Charles Boni, 1927).

30 James Rorty, *Our Master's Voice* (New York: John Day, 1934), quotations, 16, 78, 100, 188, 266.

31 Norman D. Katz, *Consumers Union,* Ph.D. diss., Rutgers University, 1977, 4–25; Stuart Chase and F. J. Schlink, *Your Money's Worth* (New York: Macmillan, 1927); Arthur Kallet and F. J. Schlink, *100,000,000 Guinea Pigs* (New York: Vanguard, 1933); Arthur Kallet, *Counterfeit* (New York: Vanguard, 1935), quotation, 94; J. B. Matthews and R. E. Shallcross, *Partners in Plunder* (New York: Covici, Friede, 1935), quotation, 3; J. B. Matthews, *Guinea Pigs No More* (New York: Covici, Friede, 1936), quotation, 16.

32 Lawrence A. Cremin, *The Transformation of the School* (New York: Knopf, 1961); *Progressive Education* 2, No. 1 (1925), opposite title page; "Progressive Education," *PE* 18 (1941): 32–page supplement between 248 and 249; Jesse H. Newlon, "Democracy and Education in Our Time," *PE* 14 (1937): 589–594; Harold Rugg, *Culture and Education in America* (New York: Harcourt, Brace, 1931), quotations, 352, 355.

33 Cremin 1961: 259–264; *The Reminiscences of Goodwin Watson* (1963),

56–64, 180–181, in The Oral History Collection of Columbia University, cited with permission of the Trustees of Columbia University in the City of New York.

34 Container 170, NBPLOC; box 1, Papers of Consumers' League of Connecticut, Collection B-17, Schlesinger Library, Radcliffe College; box 1, Papers of Consumers' League of Massachusetts, Collection B-24, Schlesinger Library.

35 Katz 1977: 53–139.

36 Container 218, NBPLOC; *New York Times,* 3 January 1939, 49, and 31 March 1941, sec. 3, p. 7.

37 *Arlington News* (MA), 18 February 1938, and Boston *Advertiser,* 9 January 1938, Scrap Book No. 10, Papers of Kirtley F. Mather, Denison University Archives (hereafter, KMPD); "Fact Sheet on Paul Douglas," uncatalogued box ("Press Releases March 1950–June 1951"), Papers of Paul Douglas, Chicago Historical Society; [Douglas], "The Place of the Consumer in the New Industrial Set Up," 26 June 1934, uncatalogued box ("Speeches 1932–41; 1946–49?"), Douglas Papers; [Douglas], "The Real Advantages of Consumer Cooperation," MS 1936, uncatalogued box ("Articles by Paul H. Douglas 1932–1951"), Douglas Papers; Katz 1977: 3–6.

38 Eduard C. Lindeman, *The Meaning of Adult Education* (New York: New Republic, 1926); Charles A. Beard, "The Electric Fire of Thought," *Journal of Adult Education* 2 (1930): 5–7; C. Hartley Grattan, *In Quest of Knowledge* (New York: Association Press, 1955); "Boston Center for Adult Education, June 1936," mimeograph, and "Boston Center for Adult Education, Spring 1936," booklet, box HUG 4559.500.5.2, Papers of Kirtley F. Mather, Harvard University Archives (hereafter, KMPH); Dorothy Hewitt and Mather, *Adult Education* (New York: Appleton-Century, 1937); *The Reminiscences of Lyman L. Bryson* (1951), 71–84, in The Oral History Collection of Columbia University, cited with permission of the Trustees of Columbia University in the City of New York; *Journal of the American Association for Adult Education* 2, No. 1 (15 December 1927): 1–4.

39 Cantril to Mather, 28 November 1933 and Mather to Cantril, 29 November 1933, box HUG 4559.500.2, KMPH; Boston *Traveller,* 26 September 1935, Scrap Book No. 6, KMPD; *Bryson Reminiscences* (1951), 98–103.

40 *Bryson Reminiscences* (1951), 117–134; Harry A. Overstreet and Bonaro W. Overstreet, *Town Meeting Comes to Town* (New York: Harpers, 1938), 3–8.

41 Leo C. Rosten, *The Washington Correspondents* (New York: Harcourt, Brace, 1937); Irwin 1936; George Seldes, *Never Tire of Protesting* (New York: Lyle Stuart, 1968); Richard O'Connor, *Heywood Broun* (New York: G. P. Putnam's Sons, 1975).

42 Mark Schorer, *Sinclair Lewis* (New York: McGraw–Hill, 1961); Tony Buttitta and Barry Witham, *Uncle Sam Presents* (Philadelphia, PA: University of Pennsylvania Press, 1982); Hallie Flanagan, *Arena* (New York:

Limelight, 1969 [1940]); Lewis, *It Can't Happen Here* (New York: Dramatists Play Service, 1938).

43 Erich M. Remarque, *All Quiet on the Western Front*, trans. A. W. Wheen (Boston: Little, Brown, 1929); Laemmle to Viereck, 8 May 1930, box 1, GVPI.

44 *Bryson Reminiscences* (1951), 153.

45 Charles G. Miller, *The Poisoned Loving-Cup* (Chicago: National Historical Society, 1928); Elisha Hanson, "Official Propaganda and the New Deal," *Annals of the American Academy of Political and Social Science* 179 (May 1935): 176–186; George Michael, *Handout* (New York: G. P. Putnam's Sons, 1935).

46 S. H. Walker and Paul Sklar, *Business Finds Its Voice* (New York: Harper, 1938); Edward L. Bernays, "Recent Trends in Public Relations Activities," *Public Opinion Quarterly* 1 (1937): 147–151; Bernays 1952: quotation, 105.

47 Otis Pease, *The Responsibilities of American Advertising* (New Haven, CT: Yale University Press, 1958); "Propaganda Purge," *Time*, 10 July 1939, 42.

48 B. G. Portwell, "Mumbo Jumbo in Education," *American Mercury* 50 (1940): 429–432; Augustin G. Rudd, "Our 'Reconstructed' Education System," *Nation's Business*, April 1940, 27–28, 93–94.

49 "NAM Textbook Survey Arouses Storm," *Publishers' Weekly* 139 (1 March 1941): 1023–1024; W. A. MacDonald, "Viewpoint on Education," *New York Times*, 23 February 1941, sec. 2, p. 6; Max Lerner, *Ideas for the Ice Age* (New York: Viking, 1941), 358–361; Boston *Herald*, 29 November 1937, Scrap Book No. 9, KMPD.

50 Grattan 1955; *Bryson Reminiscences* (1951), 91–93; Katz 1977.

51 Quotations in Seldes 1968: 13, and Seldes, *Witness to a Century* (New York: Ballantine, 1987), 240. Also Seldes 1929; Seldes 1942.

52 Senate Special Committee to Investigate Propaganda or Money Alleged to Have Been Used by Foreign Governments to Influence United States Senators, *Alleged Payments by the Mexican Government to United States Senators,* Hearings, 70th Cong., 1st sess., 5 parts, December 1927–January 1928.

53 John E. Wiltz, "The Nye Committee Revisited," *The Historian* 23 (1961): 211–233; Senate Subcommittee of the Committee on Education and Labor, *Violations of Free Speech and Rights of Labor,* Hearings, 76th Cong., 3rd sess., Part 54, January 1940, 20212–20234.

54 House Subcommittee of the Committee on Interstate and Foreign Commerce, *Motion-Picture Films,* Hearings, 74th Cong., 2nd sess., 9–11, 16–17, 25–26 March 1936, 8–35, 521.

55 Senate, *German and Bolshevik Propaganda* (1919 Hearings), quotations, 1:iii, xxix; House Committee on the Judiciary, *Sedition, Syndicalism, Sabotage, and Anarchy,* Hearings, 66th Cong., 2nd sess., 11 and 16 December 1919 (Serial 10); Villard 1939: 462; Will Irwin, "Patriotism that Pays," *Nation* 119 (12 November 1924): 513–516; Irwin 1936.

56 House Special Committee to Investigate Communist Activities in the United States, *Investigation of Communist Propaganda,* Hearings, 71st Cong., 2nd sess., June–December 1930. Quotations: pt. 1, vol. 3 (18 and 19 June), 14; pt. 1, vol. 4 (10, 24–25 November, 5 Demember), 406; pt. 3, vol. 4 (26–27 September), 39.

57 House Committee on Rules, *Investigation Into the Activities of Communists in the United States,* Hearings, 71st Cong., 1st sess., 17 April 1930, 6–8; Will Irwin, "How Red Is America?" *World Tomorrow* 10 (April 1927): 158; McGregor cited in Gruening 1931b: 226.

58 House, *Nazi Propaganda* (1934 Hearings), 5–7 June, 9–12 July 1934, 7 August, 17–18 December, 29 December.

59 Richard L. Stokes, "Dies' Hunt for Un–Americanism – A Circus with a Purpose," *St. Louis Post-Dispatch,* 29 October 1939, ed. sec., pp. 1, 4; August R. Ogden, *The Dies Committee* (Washington, DC: Catholic University of America Press, 1945); Walter Goodman, *The Committee* (New York: Farrar, Straus and Giroux, 1968); Kenneth O'Reilly, *Hoover and the Un-Americans* (Philadelphia, PA: Temple University Press, 1983).

60 Dies and Thomas in Ogden 1945: 48; House Special Committee on Un-American Activities, *Investigation of Un-American Propaganda Activities in the United States,* Hearings, 75th Cong., 3rd sess., vol. 1 (12, 13, 15–20, 22, 23 August 1938).

61 House, *Propaganda* (1938 hearings), vol. 4 (19, 22, 23, 28 November, 1, 5, 6–9, 14 December), 2843–2858.

Chapter 5. Propaganda Analysis, Incorporated

1 Kennard B. Bork, "Kirtley Fletcher Mather's Life in Science and Society," *Ohio Journal of Science* 82 (1982): 74–95; *Herald Tribune,* 5 August 1937, Scrap Book No. 9, KMPD; Bernays 1965: 443.

2 Bernays 1965: 443–444; Mather to Roy F. Bergengren, 16 December 1941, IPAP; Miller to Mather, 18 March 1937, IPAP; Miller to Mendenhall, 5 April 1937, IPAP; Miller to Robert Szold, 19 March 1938, IPAP.

3 Mather to Miller, 19 August 1937, IPAP; Lynd to Miller, 19 August 1937, IPAP; Baker to Miller, 26 July 1937, IPAP.

4 "Minutes of First Meeting of Incorporators" and "Minutes of the First Meeting of the Board of Directors," IPAP.

5 Lynd to Miller, c. August 1937, IPAP.

6 Lynd to Miller, 19 August 1937, IPAP.

7 Miller to Good Will Fund board, 28 October 1937, IPAP.

8 Miller to William Leiserson, late October 1937, IPAP.

9 Miller to Good Will Fund board, 28 October 1937, IPAP.

10 "Announcement," *Propaganda Analysis* 1, No. 1 (October 1937): 1–4.

11 "Propaganda Study is Aim of Institute," *New York Times,* 10 October 1937, sec. 2, p. 1; "Propaganda Probe," *Time,* 11 October 1937, 59; Baker to Miller, 1 November 1937, IPAP.

12 Miller to Lynd, 16 October 1937, IPAP.

13 Miller to Dale, 14 October 1937, IPAP.
14 Miller to Good Will Fund board, 28 October 1937, IPAP.
15 Report, Myron Lyons, 19 April 1938, IPAP.
16 Miller to Szold, 12 November 1938, IPAP.
17 "The Institute Mailbag," typescript, 31 October 1937, IPAP; Leiserson to Lynd, 16 October 1937, IPAP.
18 Harold Lavine and Violet Edwards Lavine, interview with author, Phoenix, AZ, 11–12 December 1982; Doob interview (1982); Clyde R. Miller and Fred Charles, *Publicity and the Public School* (Boston: Houghton Mifflin, 1924); *Time,* 11 October 1937, 59.
19 Invoice S-5667, Columbia University Press, 17 November 1937, IPAP.
20 Box 9, and diary book MC-273/39v (1937), box 2, Papers of Lillian Schoedler, Schlesinger Library, Radcliffe College.
21 "How to Detect Propaganda," *Propaganda Analysis* 1 (November 1937): 5–7; Clyde R. Miller and Violet Edwards, "The Intelligent Teacher's Guide Through Campaign Propaganda," *The Clearing House* 11, No. 2 (October 1936): 69–77; V. E. Lavine interview (1982); Miller to Edward Glaser, 24 July 1941, IPAP; Miller to Lee, 6 December 1946 and 13 March 1947, IPAP. Also Miller, "Some Comments on Propaganda Analysis and the Science of Democracy," *Public Opinion Quarterly* 5 (1941): 660; [Miller], "The Nature of Public Opinion" (ch. 11), in *The Improvement of Education,* 15th Yearbook, American Association of School Administrators (Washington, DC: Dept. of Superintendence of the National Education Association, 1937), 152–163.
22 E.g., *New York Times,* 31 October 1937, sec. 2, p. 1 and *Science News Letter* 32 (25 December 1937): 410; Dale to Miller, 1 November 1937, IPAP; Dale to author, 16 April 1982.
23 H. Lavine interview (1982); Lynd to Miller (plus attached note), c. November 1937, IPAP.
24 "Some ABC's of Propaganda Analysis," *Propaganda Analysis* 1, No. 3 (December 1937): 9–12. Cf. Miller and Edwards 1936: 70; Miller, "A Guide to the Study of the Life History" ("Education s306K," Su. 1939) and Miller, "Education 200E," c. 1939/1940, IPAP.
25 "How to Analyze Newspapers," *Propaganda Analysis* 1 (January 1938): 12–15; "Newspaper Analysis," 1 (February 1938): 16–18.
26 Callender, 11 February 1938, IPAP; Cantril to Miller, 14 February 1938 and Miller to Cantril, 16 February 1938, IPAP.
27 Seidle to Doskow, 7 December 1937, IPAP.
28 Miller to Lindeman et al., 26 September 1940 and Miller to Brown, 7 March 1938, IPAP.
29 Miller to Cantril, 17 September 1937, IPAP.
30 Miller to Dale, 14 October 1937 and Miller to Speer, 25 October 1937, IPAP.
31 Miller to Cantril, 14 February 1938, IPAP.
32 Miller to Good Will Fund board, 28 October 1937, IPAP.
33 Miller to Dale, 8 November 1937, IPAP.

34 "The Movies and Propaganda," *Propaganda Analysis* 1 (March 1938): 29–32; Miller to Dale, 8 November 1937, IPAP; Dale to Miller, 24 January 1938, IPAP; Miller to Dale, 26 January 1938, IPAP.

35 Miller to Cantril, 16 February 1938, IPAP.

36 Miller to Baker, 26 January 1938, IPAP; Miller to Cantril, 14 February 1938, IPAP; "Office Salaries and Additional Assistance," c. 1940, IPAP.

37 Miller to Dale, 8 November 1937, IPAP; Cantril to Miller, 9 November 1937, IPAP; Cantril to Seidle, 6 December 1937, IPAP.

38 Cantril to Miller, 1 February 1938 and 11 February 1938, IPAP.

39 Lazarsfeld 1941.

40 Cantril to Miller, 22 October 1937 and 1 February 1938, IPAP.

41 "The Public Relations Counsel and Propaganda," *Propaganda Analysis* 1 (August 1938): 61–65; Lynd to Miller, 19 August 1937, IPAP; Doskow to Miller, 28 July 1938, IPAP. Regarding authorship, Miller to Cantril, 2 February 1938 and "Office Salaries and Additional Assistance," c. 1940, IPAP.

42 "The A & P Campaign," *Propaganda Analysis* 2 (1 December 1938): 7–12; H. Lavine interview (1982).

43 "Propaganda in the News," *Propaganda Analysis* 2 (1 April 1939): 47–52.

44 Miller to Brown, 23 August 1939 and "Financial Reports to Dr. Dearborn," IPAP.

45 "The Associated Farmers," *Propaganda Analysis* 2 (1 August 1939): 89–104.

46 Kefauver to Miller, 7 November 1939 and Lavine to Kefauver, 17 November 1939, IPAP. "Correction" in *Propaganda Analysis* 3 (15 December 1939): 10.

47 In IPAP: Miller to Brown, 23 August 1939; "Office Salaries and Additional Assistance," c. fall 1940; "Financial Reports to Dr. Dearborn"; checkbook of June 1940.

48 In IPAP: Miller to Brown, 23 August 1939; Baker to Miller, 18 May 1939; Doob to Miller, 15 May 1939.

49 Miller to Mather, 5 December 1938, IPAP.

50 Edwards and Lavine, "Memorandum" to Miller, 13 December 1938, IPAP.

51 "The Attack on Democracy," *Propaganda Analysis* 2 (1 January 1939): 13–28.

52 Lee to author, 18 July 1989.

53 Alan Brinkley, *Voices of Protest* (New York: Knopf, 1982); Charles E. Coughlin, *"Am I an Anti-Semite?"* (Detroit, MI: Author, 1939).

54 Lee to author, 18 July 1989; A. McC. Lee and Elizabeth Briant Lee, interview with author, Short Hills, NJ, 17–18 May, 1982; "Office Salaries and Additional Assistance," c. 1940, and Lavine to Miller, 11 January 1939, IPAP.

55 Lavine to Miller, 11 January 1939, IPAP.

56 Doob to Miller, 27 February 1939, IPAP.

57 In IPAP: Rothschild to Miller, 8 February 1939; [H. Lavine] to A. Lee, 27 February 1939; Lavine to Miller, c. 8 February 1939; Miller to Baker, 10 February 1939.

58 Lehman to Miller, 23 March 1939 and Miller to Lehman, 29 March 1939, IPAP.

59 Trager to Miller, 27 March 1939, IPAP; Lee and Lee interview (1982).

60 Miller to Baker, 10 February 1939 and Anna Bogue to Miller, 29 March 1939, IPAP.

61 "Let's Talk About Ourselves," *Propaganda Analysis,* 2 (1 September 1939): 107.

62 Alfred McC. Lee and Elizabeth B. Lee, *The Fine Art of Propaganda* (San Francisco, CA: International Society for General Semantics, 1979 [1939]). Regarding publication, in IPAP: Miller to Baker, 10 February 1939; "Agreement" IPA and Harcourt, Brace, 2 May 1939; Charles A. Pearce to Lavine, 14 April 1939; Donald Brace to Miller, 10 July 1939. Also Lee to author, 18 July 1989.

63 Brace to Miller, 10 July and 18 July 1939, IPAP.

64 Miller to Brace, 13 July 1939 and minutes of executive board meeting, 10 February 1940, IPAP.

65 Clippings in IPAP: Riesel, *The New Leader,* 6 January 1940; George B. Vetters, *Public Opinion Quarterly,* March 1940.

66 Miller to Szold, 12 November 1938, IPAP.

67 Doob to Miller, 27 February 1939, IPAP.

68 "Communist Propaganda, U.S.A., 1939 Model," *Propaganda Analysis* 2 (1 March 1939): 35–46.

69 Miller to Szold, 12 November 1938, IPAP.

70 Douglas to Miller, 30 November 1938, IPAP; "Mr. Dies Goes to Town," *Propaganda Analysis* 3 (15 January 1940): 1–10.

71 Also Katz 1977.

72 "Dies Scrutinizes Propaganda Study," *New York Times,* 23 February 1941, 1; Katz 1977: 67–84, 174–200; Benjamin Fine, "Propaganda Study Instills Skepticism in 1,000,000 Pupils," *New York Times,* 21 February 1941; Elizabeth B. Lee and Alfred McC. Lee, "The Fine Art of Propaganda Analysis – Then and Now," *ETC.* 36 (1979): 121; A. Lee and E. Lee, "An Influential Ghost," *Propaganda Review* No. 3 (Winter 1988): 13; Goodman 1968: 125–126.

73 Miller to Szold, 12 November 1938 and Doob to Miller, 16 September 1938, IPAP.

74 "Britain Woos America," *Propaganda Analysis* 2 (10 June 1939): 73–80; Kefauver to Miller, 12 June 1939 and Miller to Kefauver, 6 July 1939, IPAP.

75 "Who Started the War?" *Propaganda Analysis* 3 (15 December 1939): 1–7; "Propaganda via Short-wave," 3 (26 February 1940): 1–4; "Where England Stands," 3 (1 September 1940): 1–4.

76 "Mr. Roosevelt's Foreign Policy," *Propaganda Analysis* 3 (15 November 1939): 1–10; "Soldiers of the Lord," 3 (1 April 1940): 1–10.

77 Minutes of executive committee meeting, 10 February 1940, IPAP.
78 Harold Lavine and James Wechsler, *War Propaganda and the United States* (New Haven, CT: Yale University Press, 1940), quotations, vii, viii, 37, 47, 352.
79 Norman Donaldson to Miller, 7 August 1940 and Davidson to Lavine, 3 October 1940, IPAP.
80 Baker to Miller, 29 May 1940 and Johnson to Miller, 26 July 1940, IPAP.
81 Minutes of executive board, 24 September 1940 and Miller to Lindeman et al., 26 September 1940, IPAP.
82 *Propaganda Analysis* 1 (November 1937): 5–7.
83 E.g., Leo Lowenthal and Norbert Guterman, *Prophets of Deceit*, 2nd ed. (Palo Alto, CA: Pacific Books, 1970 [1949]), xv.
84 Lee 1952; Ellul 1965.
85 *Propaganda Analysis* 1 (October 1937): 1.
86 Havighurst to Miller, 15 September 1938, IPAP.
87 Nielsen 1972: quotations, 54, 55, 57; Lazarsfeld, Berelson, and Gaudet 1968/1944: xlii, acknowledged the Rockefeller Foundation's support.
88 [Edwards and Lavine], "Brief Statement of Objectives and Methods of the Institute for Propaganda Analysis, Prepared at the request of the General Education Board," typescript, c. April 1939, IPAP.
89 Marshall to Edwards, 15 May 1939, IPAP.
90 Miller to Marshall, 22 May 1939, IPAP.
91 Minutes of executive committee, 25 May 1939, IPAP.
92 Dale to Miller, c. April 1938, IPAP; Nielsen 1972: 192–195.
93 Miller to Bernard DeVoto, 27 May 1938, IPAP.
94 Cf. "Propaganda Over the Schools," *Propaganda Analysis* 4 (25 February 1941) to *PA* 4 (26 September 1941) and 4 (27 March 1941).
95 Seldes 1938: 325; Dale to Miller, 31 October 1938, IPAP; cf. [Violet Edwards], *Propaganda* (New York: IPA, 1938), 76–77 and Bernays in *Time*, 24 January 1938, 26; Cantril to Miller, 2 February 1939, IPAP.
96 Miller to Dale, 14 March 1938, IPAP.
97 Leonard Doob, *Public Opinion and Propaganda* (New York: Henry Holt, 1948), 285; Hollingshead in Stanley Walker, Report No. 13, 5 March 1940, IPAP.
98 Miller to Brown, 12 December 1938 ("proposed letter," presumably never sent), IPAP.
99 Miller to Brown, 7 March 1938, IPAP.
100 Miller to Szold, 12 November 1938, IPAP.
101 Miller to Brown, 17 October 1938, IPAP.
102 New York State Economic Council, *Economic Council Letter No. 91*, 1 March 1941; Miller to DeVoto, 27 May 1938, IPAP.
103 Brown to Mather, 7 April 1941, HUG 4559.500.5.2, KMPH.
104 Lee to Bohn, 11 June 1941 and Lee to Mather, 10 June 1941, HUG 4559.500.5.2, KMPH.
105 Long to Lindeman, 8 December 1940, IPAP.

106 In IPAP: Kilpatrick to Miller, 9 October 1940; Graham to Miller, 7 January 1940; minutes of board, 22 October 1940.

107 Bingham to Miller, 11 January 1941, box 23, Papers of Alfred Bingham, Yale University Library (hereafter, ABPY).

108 Miller to Bingham, 13 January 1941 and Bingham to Miller, 18 January 1941, box 23, ABPY.

109 Miller to Bingham, 22 January 1941, box 23, ABPY.

110 Bingham to Miller, 25 January 1941, box 23, ABPY.

111 Miller to Bingham, 5 February 1941, box 23, ABPY.

112 Kirby Page to Bingham, 20 February 1936 and Kenneth J. Brooks to Bingham, 20 April 1936, box 4 (Series I), ABPY.

113 Senior to Bingham, 9 May 1938, box 5, ABPY.

114 Bingham to Norman Thomas, 28 March 1938, box 5, ABPY.

115 Bingham to John T. Flynn, 10 February 1941, box 5, ABPY.

116 Bingham to Lee, 10 February 1941, box 21, ABPY.

117 Dearborn to Miller, 14 March 1941, IPAP.

118 Kefauver to Miller, 26 February 1941 and MacLean to Miller, 14 March 1941, IPAP.

119 Douglas to Miller, 27 February 1941, HUG 4559.500.5.2, KMPH.

120 Mather to Douglas, 11 March 1941, HUG 4559.500.5.2, KMPH.

121 Mather to Lee, 17 March 1941, IPAP.

122 Lee to board members, 3 April 1941 and minutes of board, 25 April 1941, IPAP; Moore interview (1984); Miller to Mather, 9 March 1941, HUG 4559.500.5.2, KMPH.

123 Douglas to Miller, 7 May 1941 and Miller to Kefauver, 14 May 1941, IPAP; *New York Times*, 31 May 1941, reported Douglas's and Lindeman's resignations; Alfred Lee interview with author, Madison, NJ, 10 May 1983; Miller to Mather, 2 December 1942, HUG 4559.500.5.2, KMPH.

124 Miller to Mather, 9 March 1941, HUG 4559.500.5.2, KMPH.

125 Minutes of executive committee, 16 December 1940, IPAP.

126 Miller to executive committee, Dearborn and Long, 22 January 1941, IPAP.

127 Minutes of board of directors, 3 April 1941, IPAP.

128 Brown to Mather, 18 April 1941 and minutes of board of directors, 25 April 1941, IPAP.

129 Hadley Cantril, "America Faces the War," *Public Opinion Quarterly* 4 (1940a): 387–407; Cantril, "America Faces the War," *POQ* 4 (1940b): 651–656.

130 Minutes of board of directors, 27 February 1941 and 25 April 1941, IPAP.

131 *New York Times*, 31 May 1941, 13; cf. Page to Bingham, 20 February 1936, box 4 (series I), ABPY.

132 Cantril to Lee, 30 May 1941, IPAP; Cantril, *The Human Dimension* (New Brunswick, NJ: Rutgers University Press, 1967), 35–38.

133 Miller to Speer, 19 August 1940 and Mather to Lee, 19 July 1941, IPAP.
134 Kilpatrick to Miller, 9 October 1940 and Graham to Miller, 7 January 1940, IPAP.
135 Johnson to Miller, 26 July 1940, IPAP.
136 *New York Times:* 14 April 1941, 22; 6 June 1941, 24; 12 June 1941, 20.
137 A. Lee interview (1982); H. Lavine interview (1982).
138 Minutes, special meeting, 10 February 1940, IPAP.
139 "The Institute's Study Program," *Propaganda Analysis* 2 (1 September 1939): 108–109.
140 Violet Edwards, "Propaganda Analysis: Three Years, October 1937–October 1940," IPAP.
141 Bruce L. Smith, "Propaganda Analysis and the Science of Democracy," *Public Opinion Quarterly* 5 (1941): 250–259; Miller 1941.
142 *New York Times,* 4 August 1940, sec. 2, p. 4.
143 Lewis Mumford, "The Corruption of Liberalism," *New Republic* 102, No. 18 (29 April 1940): 568–573; cf. Mumford, *Values for Survival* (New York: Harcourt, Brace, 1946), 39n.
144 Lerner 1941: 185–188.
145 Violet Edwards [?], "The Speakers Bureau," c. fall 1940, IPAP.
146 Mumford 1946: 39n. Also William Garber, "Propaganda Analysis – To What Ends?" *American Journal of Sociology* 48 (1942): 240–245; Curtis D. MacDougall, *Understanding Public Opinion* (New York: Macmillan, 1952), 96–97; Roger Brown, *Words and Things* (Glencoe, IL: Free Press, 1958), 301–306.
147 *Propaganda Analysis:* 1 (October 1937): 1; 4 (24 June 1941): 6–7; 4 (9 January 1942): 4–5; 4 (24 June 1941): 8. Also Lee and Lee 1979/1939: 4, 14–15, 22–25; Miller to Mather, 15 April 1941, HUG 4559.500.5.2, KMPH.
148 Garber 1942: 240–245; Lester Thonssen and A. Craig Baird, *Speech Criticism* (New York: Ronald, 1948), 282; T. R. Vallance, "Methodology in Propaganda Research," *Psychological Bulletin* 48 (1951): 35–37; Brown 1958: 301–306, 339; Marvin Bressler, "Mass Persuasion and the Analysis of Language," *Journal of Educational Sociology* 33 (1959): 17–27; Thomas M. Steinfatt, "Evaluating Approaches to Propaganda Analysis," *ETC.* 36 (1979): 161–164; Suzanne C. Schick, "Propaganda Analysis," *ETC.* 42 (1985): 63–71.
149 Minutes of board of directors, 25 October 1938, IPAP; Doob interview (1982).
150 In IPAP: minutes (preliminary copy) of board of directors, 26 December 1940; minutes of the board, 27 February 1941; minutes of the board, 3 April 1941.
151 In IPAP: minutes of board of directors, 21 May 1941 and 30 June 1941; Mather to the eight nominees, 2 July 1941.
152 In IPAP; Chafee to Mather, 11 July 1941; DuShane to Mather, 31 August 1941; Hanson to Mather, 8 August 1941; Hutchins to Mather, 7 July

1941; MacCracken to Mather, 8 July 1941; Mather to Lee, 19 July 1941; Miller to DuShane, 25 July 1941; Odegard to Mather, 11 July 1941.

153 Charles A. Pearce to Lavine, 14 April 1939, IPAP; minutes of special meeting, 10 February 1940, IPAP.

154 Davis to Beals, 19 June 1941, IPAP.

155 Lavine to Speer, 11 June 1940, IPAP.

156 Minutes of executive directors, 24 September 1940, IPAP.

157 Miller to Dale, 15 July 1941, IPAP.

158 Miller to Beals, 19 November 1941, HUG 4559.500.5.2, KMPH.

159 Minutes of executive committee and of board of directors, 29 October 1941, IPAP.

160 Lee and Beals, press release, 31 October 1941 and Mather to Lee, 6 November 1941, IPAP; *New York Herald Tribune*, 31 October 1941; *Propaganda Analysis* 4 (9 January 1942): 1.

161 Miller to Beals, 19 November 1941, HUG 4559.500.5.2, KMPH. Also Miller to Lee, 14 November 1945 and 24 February 1958, IPAP. Minutes of board, 22 October 1940 and minutes of executive committee, 5 August 1941, IPAP.

162 In IPAP: Catherine Royer to Lee, 17 November 1941; Selden Rodman memorandum, 2 January 1942; Mather to Bergengren, 16 December 1941. Also Lee to Mather, 10 January 1942, HUG 4559.500.5.2, KMPH.

Chapter 6. Propaganda for Democracy

1 Paul F. Lazarsfeld and Robert K. Merton, "Studies in Radio and Film Propaganda," *Transactions of the New York Academy of Sciences* 6 (1943): 58–79.

2 Edgar Dale and Norma Vernon, "Introduction," *Propaganda Analysis* (Columbus, OH: Bureau of Educational Research, May 1940), i. Cf. Dale "Notes on Propaganda," *The News Letter* 5, No. 2 (December 1939): 2.

3 Senate Subcommittee of the Committee on Interstate Commerce, *Propaganda in Motion Pictures*, Hearings, 77th Cong., 1st sess., 9–26 September 1941, 22–56, 338–346, 411.

4 Gordon W. Allport and Helene R. Veltfort, "Social Psychology and the Civilian War Effort," *Journal of Social Psychology* 18 (1943): 214.

5 Irvin L. Child, "Morale," *Psychological Bulletin* 38 (1941): 393–420.

6 Gregory Bateson and Margaret Mead, "Principles of Morale Building," *Journal of Educational Sociology* 15 (1941): 206–220.

7 *American Journal of Sociology* 47 (1941): Harry S. Sullivan, "Psychiatric Aspects of Morale," 277–301; James R. Angell, "Radio and National Morale," 352–359; Robert E. Park, "Morale and the News," 360–377; Walter Wanger, "The Role of Movies in Morale," 378–383; Edward S. Ames, "Morale and Religion," 384–393; Eduard C. Lindeman, "Recre-

ation and Morale," 394–405; Louis Wirth, "Morale and Minority Groups," 415–433.

8 William E. Hocking, "The Nature of Morale," *American Journal of Sociology,* 47 (1941), 302–320.

9 Gordon W. Allport and Gertrude R. Schmeidler, "Morale Research and Its Clearing," *Psychological Bulletin* 40 (1943): 65–68; Allport and Veltfort 1943.

10 Rensis Likert to Robert Lynd, 8 November 1940, reel 1, Robert S. and Helen M. Lynd Papers, Library of Congress.

11 *Round Table XXV, American Association for Applied Psychology, Possible Psychological Contributions in a National Emergency,* 26 November 1939, Ts Psychology A512 S476, Hoover Institution Archives.

12 John G. Watkins, "Offensive Psychological Warfare," *Journal of Consulting Psychology* 6 (1942): 117–122; Watkins, "Further Opportunities for Applied Psychologists in Offensive Warfare," *JCP* 7 (1943): 135–141; Stuart A. Queen, "Sociologists in the Present Crisis," *Social Forces* 20 (1941): 1–7, rpt. Edward A. Tiryakian, ed., *The Phenomenon of Sociology* (New York: Appleton-Century-Crofts, 1971), 210–218; Alfred Westfall, "What Speech Teachers May Do to Help Win the War," *Quarterly Journal of Speech* 29 (1943): 5–9; Francis J. Brown, "Editorial," *Journal of Educational Sociology* 15 (1942): 317–319.

13 Allport and Veltfort 1943: 195.

14 Edward L. Bernays, *Speak Up for Democracy* (New York: Viking Press, 1940).

15 Cantril 1967: quotations, 24, 28, 31, 42, 51; Doob interview (1982).

16 *Berelson Reminiscences* (1967), 4–8; *Watson Reminiscences* (1963), 64–66; Alexander L. George, *Propaganda Analysis* (Evanston, IL: Row, Peterson, 1959).

17 George 1959: quotations, vii, 151.

18 Edward A. Shils, "A Note on Governmental Research on Attitudes and Morale," *American Journal of Sociology* 47 (1941): 474–475.

19 "Committeemen Interview: Form I, Wisconsin Dairy Study, September 19, 1941" and "The Wisconsin Production Goals Campaign in Action," 27 October 1941, box 2b (series I), PLPC.

20 *Watson Reminiscences* (1963), 176; [Harold Lasswell], Memorandum, 19 March 1942, HLPY.

21 Holly C. Schulman, *The Voice of America* (Madison, WI: University of Wisconsin Press, 1990); Allan M. Winkler, *The Politics of Propaganda* (New Haven, CT: Yale University Press, 1978).

22 Sydney Weinberg, "What To Tell America," *Journal of American History* 55 (1968): 73–89.

23 Charles A. Siepmann, "American Radio in Wartime," in Lazarsfeld and Stanton 1944: 121–122, 564–565.

24 Ibid.; J. Fred MacDonald, "Government Propaganda in Commercial Radio," in *Rhetorical Dimensions in Media,* ed. Martin J. Medhurst and Thomas W. Benson (Dubuque, IA: Kendall/Hunt, 1984), 157–159.

25 Clayton R. Koppes and Gregory D. Black, *Hollywood Goes to War* (New York: Free Press, 1987), quotations, 66–67.

26 Ibid., quotation, 206.

27 Leonard W. Doob, "The Utilization of Social Scientists in the Overseas Branch of the Office of War Information," *American Political Science Review* 41 (1947): 652–653.

28 "Heber Blankenhorn, Psychological Warfare Report," (Ms) D810 P7 U5 B6, Papers of Heber Blankenhorn, Hoover Institution Archives.

29 Winkler 1978: 128; "Leaflet Operations, Western European Theatre, Supreme Headquarters Allied Expeditionary Force, Psychological Warfare Division, 415 (Lft-R), 2 July 1945," box 3, World War 2 Allied Propaganda Collection, Hoover Institution Archives.

30 Harold D. Lasswell, Affidavit, 23 October 1951, HLPY. Also Rogers 1994: 224–228.

31 Lasswell to MacLeish, 25 August 1941, HLPY; Lasswell, Paul Lewis, Joseph W. Martin, and Joseph Goldsen, "The Politically Significant Content of the Press," *Journalism Quarterly* 19 (1942): 12–23.

32 Lasswell to MacLeish, 25 August 1941, HLPY; Morris Janowitz, "Harold D. Lasswell's Contribution to Content Analysis," *Public Opinion Quarterly* 32 (1968): 646–653; Lasswell and Leites 1965/1949: 40–47.

33 Lasswell and Leites 1965/1949: 48–49, 173–178.

34 Moore interview (1984); Merriam to Lasswell, 6 February 1946, HLPY.

35 Lasswell to MacLeish, 25 August 1941, HLPY.

36 Lasswell, Affidavit, 23 October 1951 and Lasswell to MacLeish, 25 August 1941, HLPY; Allport and Veltfort 1943: 192.

37 Samuel A. Stouffer, Edward A. Suchman, Leland C. DeVinney, Shirley A. Star, and Robin M. Williams, Jr., *The American Soldier,* 2 vols. (Princeton, NJ: Princeton University Press, 1949), 1:13, 19, 22–23, 38; *The Reminiscences of Frederick Osborn* (1967), 1, 38, 49, 51, 75–77, 117, in The Oral History Collection of Columbia University, cited with permission of the Trustees of Columbia University in the City of New York.

38 *Osborn Reminiscences* (1967), 77, 118; Stouffer et al. 1949: 1:12.

39 Stouffer et al. 1949: 1:6–10.

40 Ibid., 1:6–7; *Osborn Reminiscences* (1967), 75–78.

41 Carl I. Hovland, Arthur A. Lumsdaine, and Fred D. Sheffield, *Experiments on Mass Communication* (Princeton, NJ: Princeton University Press, 1949).

42 Frank Capra, *The Name Above the Title* (New York: Vintage, 1971), 316–349; *Osborn Reminiscences* (1967), 99–100.

43 Stouffer et al. 1949: 1:431–434.

44 Ibid., 1:435–444.

45 Hovland, Lumsdaine, and Sheffield 1949: quotations, 53, 100–101, 113.

46 Stouffer et al. 1949: 1:viii–ix, 11–12, 201; Stouffer, "Some Afterthoughts of a Contributor to 'The American Soldier,' " in *Continuities in Social Research,* ed. Robert K. Merton and Paul F. Lazarsfeld (Glencoe, IL: Free Press, 1950), 200–201.

47 Stouffer et al. 1949: 1:5.

48 *The Reminiscences of Charles Dollard* (1969), 139, in The Oral History
    Collection of Columbia University, cited with permission of the Trustees
    of Columbia University in the City of New York; *Osborn Reminiscences*
    (1967), 79, 119; Stouffer et al. 1949: 1:28.

49 Stouffer et al. 1949: 1:26; Carolyn E. Allen to Hovland, 23 July 1947, box
    11 (series III), Papers of Carl I. Hovland, Yale Library (hereafter, CHPY).

50 Stouffer et al. 1949: 1:37, 39, 309–311; Stouffer 1950: 204.

51 Stouffer 1950: 209; Stouffer et al. 1949: 1:43; Patricia Kendall and Paul F.
    Lazarsfeld, "Problems of Survey Analysis," in Merton and Lazarsfeld
    1950: 171–173.

52 Daniel Lerner, "*The American Soldier* and the Public," in Merton and
    Lazarsfeld 1950: 220, 236; John Madge, *The Tools of Social Science*
    (Garden City, NY: Doubleday, 1953), 64–69, 74.

53 Hovland, Lumsdaine, and Sheffield 1949: 15, 179; Edward A. Shils, "Pri-
    mary Groups in the American Army," in Merton and Lazarsfeld 1950:
    17–23.

54 Hans Speier, "*The American Soldier* and the Sociology of Military Organi-
    zation," in Merton and Lazarsfeld 1950: 120–121.

55 Lee 1952: 38; Stouffer 1950: 202–203; M. Brewster Smith, "*The Ameri-
    can Soldier* and Its Critics," *Social Psychological Quarterly* 47 (1984):
    193–194; Lerner 1950: 216–217.

56 Stouffer et al., 1949: 1:37; *Lazarsfeld Reminiscences* (1973), 110, 114.

57 Lerner 1950: 221–222, 244–247.

58 Robert S. Lynd, "The Science of Inhuman Relations," *New Republic* 121,
    No. 9 (29 August 1949): 22–25.

59 Alfred McC. Lee, review, *Annals of the American Academy of Political
    and Social Science* 265 (September 1949): 173–175.

60 Elizabeth B. Lee and Alfred McC. Lee, "The Society for the Study of Social
    Problems," *Social Problems* 24 (1976): 5.

61 Lerner 1950: 219–220, 227; Kendall and Lazarsfeld 1950: 168–169.

62 Hadley Cantril, *Gauging Public Opinion* (Princeton, NJ: Princeton Uni-
    versity Press, 1944).

63 Lasswell and Leites 1949: quotation, 18.

64 Doob interview (1982).

65 Ruth Strang, "Methodology in the Study of Propaganda and Attitudes
    Relating to War," *School and Society* 54 (1941): 334–336; Queen 1971/
    1941: 215; Shils 1941: 477; Allport and Veltfort 1943: 192; Marjorie Fisk
    and Leo Lowenthal, "Some Problems in the Administration of Interna-
    tional Communications Research," *Public Opinion Quarterly* 16 (1952):
    153–156; George 1959: vii–ix.

66 Bernays 1940: ix.

67 "The Quarter's Polls," *Public Opinion Quarterly* 9 (1945): 103; Les K.
    Adler and Thomas G. Paterson, "Red Fascism," *American Historical Re-
    view* 75 (1970): 1046–1064.

68 Arthur Schlesinger, Jr., interview with author, New York City, 26 April 1984; Louis Filler, *Progressivism and Muckraking* (New York: R. R. Bowker, 1976), 99–100; George S. Viereck and H. K. Thompson, Jr., "Three Times Invaded," typescript, box 2, Papers of George S. Viereck, Hoover Institution Archives; Charles A. Beard, *President Roosevelt and the Coming of the War 1941* (New Haven, CT: Yale University Press, 1948).

69 Wallace Carroll, *Persuade or Perish* (Boston: Houghton Mifflin, 1948), quotations, 373, 380, 387, 389, 391.

70 Edward W. Barrett, *Truth is Our Weapon* (New York: Funk and Wagnalls, 1953), quotations, 6, 245.

71 Everett Hunt, "Ancient Rhetoric and Modern Propaganda," *Quarterly Journal of Speech* 37 (1951): 157–160; Fisk and Lowenthal 1952: 149–159.

72 Edward H. Carr, "Propaganda and Power," *Yale Review* 42 (1952): 1–9; H. M. Spitzer, "Presenting America in American Propaganda," *Public Opinion Quarterly* 11 (1947): 213–221; Paul M. A. Linebarger, "The Struggle for the Mind of Asia," *Annals of the American Academy of Political and Social Science* 278 (November 1951): 32–37; George Catlin, "Propaganda and the Cold War," *Yale Review* 43 (1953): 103–116; J. A. Raffaele, "United States Propaganda Abroad," *Social Research* 27 (1960): 277–294; George V. Allen, "Are the Soviets Winning the Propaganda War?" *Annals* 336 (July 1961): 1–11.

73 John G. Schneider, "Why We're Losing the Propaganda War," *Nation* 186 (1958): 182–184; Eugene W. Castle, *Billions, Blunders and Baloney* (New York: Devin-Adair, 1955).

74 "What Do We Say to the World?" *The Saturday Review,* 17 September 1955, quotation, 14.

75 Bernays 1947. Also Bernays, ed., *The Engineering of Consent* (Norman, OK: University of Oklahoma Press, 1955).

76 Edward L. Bernays and Burnet Hershey, eds., *The Case for Reappraisal of U.S. Overseas Information Policies and Programs* (New York: Praeger, 1970).

77 Leo Bogart, *Premises for Propaganda* (New York: Free Press, 1976).

78 Ibid., x–xi. Also Ralph Block, "Propaganda and the Free Society," *Public Opinion Quarterly* 12 (1948): 677–686.

79 Hans Speier, "The Future of Psychological Warfare," *Public Opinion Quarterly* 12 (1948): 5–18.

80 "Content Analysis for the Voice of America," *Public Opinion Quarterly* 16 (1952): 605–642.

81 Cantril 1967; Cantril to Chase, 10 August 1952 and 4 May 1956, box 12, SCPLOC.

82 Memorandum to Board of Directors, American Psychological Association, 4 June 1948, box 5, CHPY.

83 Committee on National Security Policy Research, Conference on The

Social Sciences and National Security Policy, 17–19 June 1959 (Preliminary Program), HLPY.

84 Harold D. Lasswell, "The Policy Orientation," 10, 11; Robert K. Merton and Daniel Lerner, "Social Scientists and Research Policy," 299, 306 in Lerner and Lasswell, eds., *The Policy Sciences* (Stanford, CA: Stanford University Press, 1951).

85 Carl I. Hovland, "Some Implications for Industry of War-Time Research on Communication," typescript, (series II), box 6, CHPY.

86 Cf. Albig 1957: 14–22.

87 Conference on Research on Public Communication, 31 May–1 June 1954, box 8, CHPY.

88 Leonard W. Doob, *Public Opinion and Propaganda,* 2nd ed. (Hamden, CT: Archon, 1966), vii; *Lazarsfeld Reminiscences* (1973), 71; Herman Cohen, "The Development of Research in Speech Communication," in *Speech Communication in the 20th Century,* ed. Thomas W. Benson (Carbondale, IL: Southern Illinois University Press, 1985), 294.

89 Carl I. Hovland, Irving L. Janis, and Harold H. Kelley, *Communication and Persuasion* (New Haven, CT: Yale University Press, 1953), 35, 254–259.

90 Carl I. Hovland and Wallace Mandell, *The Order of Presentation in Persuasion* (New Haven, CT: Yale University Press, 1957), 13–22.

91 Irving L. Janis and Carl I. Hovland, *Personality and Persuasibility* (New Haven, CT: Yale University Press, 1959), 55–68.

92 Lazarsfeld and Stanton 1944: vii.

93 Lazarsfeld, Berelson, and Gaudet 1968/1944.

94 Paul F. Lazarsfeld and Patricia L. Kendall, *Radio Listening in America* (New York: Prentice-Hall, 1948); Bernard R. Berelson, Lazarsfeld, and William N. McPhee, *Voting* (Chicago: University of Chicago Press, 1954); Elihu Katz and Lazarsfeld, *Personal Influence* (Glencoe, IL: Free Press, 1955).

95 Kurt Lewin, *Resolving Social Conflicts* (New York: Harper, 1948); Robert F. Bales, *Interaction Process Analysis* (Reading, MA: Addison-Wesley, 1950); Claude E. Shannon and Warren Weaver, *The Mathematical Theory of Communication* (Urbana, IL: University of Illinois Press, 1949); Charles E. Osgood, George J. Suci, and Percy H. Tannenbaum, *The Measurement of Meaning* (Urbana, IL: University of Illinois Press, 1957); George Miller, "The Magical Number Seven, Plus or Minus Two," *Psychological Review* 63 (1956): 81–97; Jurgen Ruesch and Gregory Bateson, *Communication* (New York: W. W. Norton, 1951); Harold A. Innis, *The Bias of Communication* (Toronto: University of Toronto Press, 1951).

96 House Subcommittee on International Organizations and Movements of the Committee on Foreign Affairs, *Behavioral Sciences and the National Security,* Committee Print, 89th Cong., 1st sess., 6 December 1965; House Subcommittee on International Organizations and Movements of the Committee on Foreign Affairs, *Modern Communications and Foreign Policy,* Committee Print, 90th Cong., 1st sess., 1967.

Chapter 7. The New Communication – Or the Old Propaganda?

1 Lee 1973: 141.
2 Thomas S. Kuhn, *The Structure of Scientific Revolutions*, 2nd ed. (Chicago: University of Chicago Press, 1970).
3 Bernard Berelson, "The State of Communication Research," *Public Opinion Quarterly* 23, No. 1 (1959): 1–17.
4 Doob interview (1982); Doob 1948: 90, 285–289; Lerner 1950: 246; Stouffer 1950: 206; Stouffer et al. 1949: 1:39.
5 "Empiricism," in *Dictionary of Philosophy*, ed. Dagobert D. Runes (Ames, IA: Littlefield, Adams, 1959), 89–90; Merton and Lazarsfeld 1950: 9–10; Doob 1947: 655; Stouffer 1942: 133–141; Stouffer et al. 1949: 1:51, 461.
6 Higham 1966: 14–17.
7 Talcott Parsons, "Some Problems Confronting Sociology as a Profession," *American Sociological Review* 24 (1959), rpt. in Edward A. Tiryakian, *The Phenomenon of Sociology* (New York: Appleton-Century-Crofts, 1971), 326, 332; Hovland, Lumsdaine, and Sheffield 1949: 8; Hovland to DeVinney, c. 1953, box 1, CHPY.
8 Waples 1942: vi–x; Lloyd Morrisett, c. 1954, box 3, CHPY. Also Allport and Veltfort 1943: 190; Rex M. Collier, "The Effect of Propaganda upon Attitude Following a Critical Examination of the Propaganda Itself," *Journal of Social Psychology* 20 (1944): 3–17.
9 Veysey 1965: 125–139, 173–175; Ross 1979.
10 American Psychological Association, Distinguished Scientific Contribution Award, 1957, box 5, CHPY; Proposed Plan for the Development of the Behavioral Sciences Program, November 1951, box 13 (series IV), CHPY; *Berelson Reminiscences* (1967), 21.
11 Joseph T. Klapper and Charles Y. Glock, "Trial by Newspaper," in Daniel Katz, Dorwin Cartwright, Samuel Eldersveld, and Alfred McC. Lee, eds., *Public Opinion and Propaganda* (New York: Dryden, 1954), 105–112 (originally published 1949).
12 Not only senior scholars Stouffer, Lasswell, Lazarsfeld, Hovland, Likert, Cantril, Doob, Odegard, Merton, Speier, and Waples but also second-generation researchers Bernard Berelson, Alexander George, Daniel Katz, Daniel Lerner, Irving Janis, Nathan Maccoby, M. Brewster Smith, Louis Guttman, Joseph Goldsen, Theodore Newcomb, Nathan Leites, Edward Shils, Ralph White, Ithiel de Sola Pool, Joseph Klapper, and Morris Janowitz.
13 Telegram, Berelson to Lazarsfeld, [8 November (?)] 1951, box 1a (series I), PLPC.
14 *Anderson Reminiscences* (1969), 40.
15 Ibid., 256–259, 283–284; *Berelson Reminiscences* (1967), 20; Berman 1983: 107.
16 *Anderson Reminiscences* (1969), 70.
17 Harold D. Lasswell, "Affidavit," 23 October 1951, HLPY; *Lazarsfeld Reminiscences* (1973), 4; *Berelson Reminiscences* (1967), 7–8.

18 *Anderson Reminiscences* (1969), 28–30, 74–77.

19 *Berelson Reminiscences* (1967), 95.

20 Wilbur Schramm, "The Beginnings of Communication Study in the United States," in *Communication Yearbook 4,* ed. Dan Nimmo (New Brunswick, NJ: Transaction, 1980), 81–82; Schramm, "The Unique Perspective of Communication," *Journal of Communication* 33, No. 3 (1983): 10–12; Morris Janowitz, "Professionalization of Sociology," in *Varieties of Political Expression in Sociology* (Chicago: University of Chicago Press, 1972), 121; Lazarsfeld 1969.

21 Parsons 1971/1959: 334; Alfred McC. Lee, "Presidential Address," *American Sociological Review* 41 (1976): 927.

22 *Dollard Reminiscences* (1969), 217–218; Doob interview (1982); Lee to author, 2 April 1985.

23 Stuart Chase, *The Proper Study of Mankind* (New York: Harper and Brothers, 1948), quotation, 22.

24 Katz and Lazarsfeld 1955: 15–17; Raymond A. Bauer and Alice H. Bauer, "America, Mass Society and Mass Media," *Journal of Social Issues* 16, No. 3 (1960): 6–11.

25 Melvin L. DeFleur and Sandra Ball-Rokeach, *Theories of Mass Communication,* 4th ed. (New York: Longman, 1982), 144–165; Wilbur Schramm, "The Nature of Communication Between Humans," in Schramm and Donald F. Roberts, eds., *The Process and Effects of Mass Communication* (Urbana, IL: University of Illinois Press, 1971), 3–12; Everett M. Rogers, *Diffusion of Innovations,* 3rd ed. (New York: Free Press, 1983 [1962]), 272–273; Schramm 1983: 14. Cf. Jeffery L. Bineham, "A Historical Account of the Hypodermic Model in Mass Communication," *Communication Monographs* 55 (1988): 230–246; J. Michael Sproule, "Progressive Propaganda Critics and the Magic Bullet Myth," *Critical Studies in Mass Communication* 6 (1989): 225–246.

26 Doob interview (1982).

27 Glazer interview (1984); Steven H. Chaffee, "Differentiating the Hypodermic Model from Empirical Research," *Communication Monographs* 55 (1988): 247.

28 Harold D. Lasswell, *Democracy Through Public Opinion* (n.p.: George Banta, 1941), 107–110.

29 Harold D. Lasswell, "The Dictionary of Social Change," typescript, c. 1941, HLPY.

30 Lasswell, memorandum, 3 June 1941, HLPY.

31 Memorandum on proposed college of government, 18 May 1942 and "The Library of Congress and the Future of National Institutes of Research in Washington," 15 May 1944, HLPY.

32 Harold D. Lasswell, "Remarks about a Proposed Method of Contributing to the Integration of Policy, Morals and Science," 30 January 1945, HLPY.

33 Paul F. Lazarsfeld, "The Role of Criticism in the Management of Mass Media," *Journalism Quarterly* 25 (1948): 115–126; Marshall to Lazars-

feld, 29 September 1948 and 27 October 1948, box 2b (series I), PLPC. Also Glazer interview (1984).

34 *Lazarsfeld Reminisences* (1973), 355–361, 372; Samuel H. Flowerman and Marie Jahoda, "Can We Fight Prejudice Scientifically?" *Commentary* 2 (December 1946): 583–587; Flowerman, "Mass Propaganda in the War Against Bigotry," *Journal of Abnormal and Social Psychology* 42 (1947): 429–439; Paul F. Lazarsfeld, "Some Remarks on the Role of Mass Media in So-called Tolerance Propaganda," *Journal of Social Issues* 3, No. 3 (Summer 1947): 17–25.

35 Ralph K. White and Ronald Lippitt, *Autocracy and Democracy* (New York: Harper and Brothers, 1960), 246–262.

36 Nielsen 1972: 84–85, 353; Press release, 5 January 1955, box 28 (series I), PLPC; Samuel A. Stouffer, *Communism, Conformity, and Civil Liberties* (Garden City, NY: Doubleday, 1955).

37 Glazer interview (1984); Lazarsfeld 1947; Eunice Cooper and Marie Jahoda, "The Evasion of Propaganda" [1947], in Schramm and Roberts 1971: 287–299; Cartwright and Zander 1960; Bales 1950; Robert F. Bales, *Personality and Interpersonal Behavior* (New York: Holt, Rinehart and Winston, 1970).

38 A. Lee interview (1987); Katz, Cartwright, Eldersveld, and Lee 1954.

39 Daniel Bell, *The End of Ideology*, revised ed. (New York: Collier, 1962), quotation, 402.

40 *Berelson Reminiscences* (1967), 22; Daniel Brown to Sherif, 28 February 1951, box 3, CHPY.

41 *New York World-Telegram*, 23 November 1942, HUG 4559.500.5.2 and Miller to Wood, 3 December 1942, KMPH.

42 *H. Lynd Reminiscences* (1973), 87, 182–195, 260–261; Lynd 1939: 202–250.

43 Seldes 1968: 21–44, 189–196; Seldes interview (1984).

44 Clippings, KMPD: *Boston Herald*, 3 October 1935; *Waltham Tribune*, 19 November 1937; *Boston Advertiser*, 26 June 1938; *Life*, 4 April 1949; *Harvard Crimson*, 24 October 1950. Mather to Dorothy Sterling, 6 September 1950, KMPD.

45 *Watson Reminiscences* (1963): 49–89.

46 M. Brewster Smith, "McCarthyism," *Journal of Social Issues* 42, No. 4 (1986): 73–77.

47 Harold Lasswell, Affidavit, 23 October 1951, HLPY; Lasswell, "Propaganda and Mass Insecurity," *Psychiatry* 13 (1950): 291.

48 Paul Lazarsfeld, memorandum [c. 1954], (series I), box 2b, PLPC.

49 *Anderson Reminiscences* (1969), 266–268. Also Gunnar Myrdal, Richard Sterner, and Arnold Rose, *An American Dilemma* (New York: Harper and Brothers, 1944).

50 *Anderson Reminiscences* (1969), 269–278.

51 Report of the Rockefeller Foundation and General Education Board to the Special Committee to Investigate Tax Exempt Foundations, August 1954, box 14, CHPY.

52 Veysey 1965: 133–149; Barry Skura, "Constraints on a Reform Movement," *Social Problems* 24 (1976): 15–36; Leon Bramson, *The Political Context of Sociology* (Princeton, NJ: Princeton University Press, 1961), 73–95; Glazer interview (1984); Schlesinger interview (1984); *The Reminiscences of David Riesman* (1969), 78, in The Oral History Collection of Columbia University, cited with permission of the Trustees of Columbia University in the City of New York.

53 House Committee on Un-American Activities, *Hearings Regarding Communist Infiltration of the Motion Picture Industry*, 80th Cong., 1st sess., 20–24, 27–30 October 1947, 2, 10.

54 House Committee on Un-American Activities, *Report of the Committee on Un-American Activities*, Committee Print, 80th Cong., 2nd sess., 31 December 1948, 9; House Committee on Un-American Activities, *Annual Report of the Committee on Un-American Activities for the Year 1951*, Committee Print, 17 February 1952, 7; Goodman 1968: 218–237; Larry Ceplair and Steven Englund, *The Inquisition in Hollywood* (Berkeley, CA: University of California Press, 1983), 279–360.

55 Alfred McC. Lee, "The Analysis of Propaganda," *American Journal of Sociology* 51 (1945): 126–135. Also Lee, *Multivalent Man* (New York: George Braziller, 1966), 327–341.

56 Lee 1952: quotations, 26, 268.

57 A. Lee and E. Lee interview (1987); Glen E. Mills, review, *Quarterly Journal of Speech* 39 (1953): 109.

58 Lee and Lee 1976.

59 Ibid., 7 (quotation); Alfred McC. Lee to author, 12 December 1983; Skura 1976; "SSSP as the Organization of a Social Movement," *Social Problems* 24 (1976): 37–53; "*Social Problems* as the Journal of a Social Movement," *SP* 24 (1976): 76–90.

60 Sproule 1988.

61 Lee S. Hultzen, "Rhetor in Democracy," *Quarterly Journal of Speech* 36 (1950): 533–536; "Freedom and Security," *QJS* 39 (1953): 94.

62 Frederick W. Haberman, "Views on the Army–McCarthy Hearings," *Quarterly Journal of Speech* 41 (1955): 1–18.

63 Frederick W. Haberman, "General MacArthur's Speech," *Quarterly Journal of Speech* 37 (1951): 321–331; "New Interest Group," *QJS* 47 (1961): 303; "Free Speech and the Speech Association," *QJS* 47 (1961): 188–189.

64 William Hummel and Keith Huntress, *The Analysis of Propaganda* (New York: William Sloane, 1949); Archibald W. Anderson, "Protecting the Right to Teach Social Issues," *Progressive Education* 26 (1948–1949): 24; Robert G. Gunderson, "Teaching Critical Thinking," *Speech Teacher* 10 (1961): 100–104; S. I. Hayakawa, "General Semantics and the Cold War Mentality," *ETC.* 21 (1964): 417–424.

65 Max Black, *Critical Thinking*, 2nd ed. (New York: Prentice-Hall, 1952); Robert H. Ennis, "A Concept of *Critical Thinking*," *Harvard Educational Review* 32 (1962): 81–111; Monroe C. Beardsley, *Practical Logic* (New York: Prentice-Hall, 1950).

66 Raymond S. Nickerson, David N. Perkins, and Edward E. Smith, *The Teaching of Thinking* (Hillsdale, NJ: Lawrence Erlbaum, 1985), quotation, 217.

67 Max Horkheimer and Theodor W. Adorno, *Dialectic of Enlightenment*, trans. John Cumming (New York: Continuum, 1972 [1944]), quotation, 156.

68 Jay 1973: 255; Franz Neumann, *Behemoth* (New York: Oxford University Press, 1944); Erich Fromm, *Escape from Freedom* (New York: Holt, Rinehart and Winston, 1941); Doob interview (1982).

69 Alfred McC. Lee to author, 18 March 1985 and 2 April 1985; Herbert Marcuse, *One-Dimensional Man* (Boston: Beacon Press, 1964).

70 Commission on Freedom of the Press, *A Free and Responsible Press* (Chicago: University of Chicago Press, 1947); Jerilyn S. McIntyre, "The Hutchins Commission's Search for a Moral Framework," *Journalism History* 6, No. 2 (1979): 54–57, 63; McIntyre, "Repositioning a Landmark," *Critical Studies in Mass Communication* 4 (1987): 136–160.

71 Fred S. Siebert, Theodore Peterson, and Wilbur Schramm, *Four Theories of the Press* (Urbana, IL: University of Illinois Press, 1956), 73–103.

72 Seldes 1968: 50–57, 274; I. F. Stone, *In a Time of Torment* (Boston: Little, Brown, 1967), xvii–xx, 195–203.

73 A. J. Liebling, *The Press* (New York: Pantheon, 1975), quotations, 32, 227; Spencer Klaw, interview with author, New York City, 25 April 1984.

74 Gilbert Seldes, *The Great Audience* (Westport, CT: Greenwood, 1950), quotations, 4, 137, 232; Seldes, *The Public Arts* (New York: Simon and Schuster, 1956).

75 Vance Packard, *The Hidden Persuaders* (New York: David McKay, 1957), quotations, 87, 183, 216, 255, 258.

76 William H. Whyte, Jr., *The Organization Man* (New York: Doubleday, Anchor, 1956); Albig 1957: 18.

77 Pitirim A. Sorokin, *Fads and Foibles in Modern Sociology and Related Sciences* (Chicago: Henry Regnery, 1956); *Lazarsfeld Reminiscences* (1973), 74–75.

78 C. Wright Mills, *The Sociological Imagination* (New York: Oxford University Press, 1959), 50–75; Irving L. Horowitz, *C. Wright Mills* (New York: Free Press, 1983), 95–99.

79 Irving L. Horowitz, "Establishment Sociology," *Inquiry* 6 (1963): 129–140.

80 Irving L. Horowitz, *The Rise and Fall of Project Camelot* (Cambridge, MA: MIT Press, 1967), quotations, 4–5, 8, 17.

81 House, *Behavioral Sciences* (1965), 5R.

82 Daniel Lerner and Lucille W. Pevsner, *The Passing of Traditional Society* (Glencoe, IL: Free Press, 1958), 43–110, 398–412; Lucian W. Pye, ed., *Communication and Political Development* (Princeton, NJ: Princeton University Press, 1963); Rogers 1983/1962; Everett M. Rogers, "Communication and Development," *Communication Research* 3 (1976): 213–240.

Chapter 8. Epilogue: Rediscovering Propaganda

1 Robert Hughes, *Culture of Complaint* (New York: Warner Books, 1993); James D. Hunter, *Culture Wars* (New York: Basic Books, 1991); Todd Gitlin, *The Twilight of Common Dreams* (New York: Metropolitan Books, 1995).

2 John E. Mueller, "Trends in Popular Support for the Wars in Korea and Vietnam," *American Political Science Review* 65 (1971): 357–375; Edward J. Epstein, *Between Fact and Fiction* (New York: Vintage, 1975), 210–232; Daniel C. Hallin, *The "Uncensored War"* (New York: Oxford University Press, 1986).

3 Arthur M. Schlesinger, Jr., *The Bitter Heritage* (New York: Fawcett Crest, 1967); George McT. Kahin and John W. Lewis, *The United States in Vietnam* (New York: Delta, 1967); Joseph C. Goulden, *Truth Is the First Casualty* (Chicago: Rand McNally, 1969); J. Michael Sproule, *The Case for a Wider War*, Ph.D. diss., Ohio State University, 1973.

4 Epstein 1975; Klaw interview (1984).

5 Hugh Rank, ed., *Language and Public Policy* (Urbana, IL: National Council of Teachers of English, 1974), xii–xv, 241.

6 Christine L. Nystrom, "Not By *Any* Means," *ETC.* 36 (1979): 257–260.

7 Noam Chomsky, *American Power and the New Mandarins* (New York: Pantheon, 1969); Chomsky, *At War with Asia* (New York: Pantheon, 1970), 8.

8 Noam Chomsky and Edward S. Herman, *The Washington Connection and Third World Fascism* (Boston: South End Press, 1979); Herman, *The Real Terror Network* (Boston: South End Press, 1982); Herman and Frank Brodhead, *Demonstration Elections* (Boston: South End Press, 1984); Herman and Chomsky, *Manufacturing Consent* (New York: Pantheon, 1988); Chomsky, interview (by telephone) with author, Cambridge, MA, 18 May 1984.

9 William F. Buckley, Jr., *God and Man at Yale* (Chicago: Regnery, 1951).

10 E.g., Joseph Keeley, *The Left-Leaning Antenna* (New Rochelle, NY: Arlington House, 1971); Ernest W. Lefever, *TV and National Defense* (Boston, VA: American Strategy Press, 1974). Cf. Edith Efron, *The News Twisters* (Los Angeles, CA: Nash, 1971) and Robert L. Sevenson et al., "Untwisting *The News Twisters*," *Journalism Quarterly* 50 (1973), 211–219.

11 Garth S. Jowett, "Propaganda and Communication," *Journal of Communication* 37, No. 1 (1987): 97–114; Qualter 1985; Jowett and Victoria O'Donnell, *Propaganda and Persuasion* (Newbury Park, CA: Sage, 1986); Anthony Pratkanis and Elliot Aronson, *Age of Propaganda* (New York: W. H. Freeman, 1991); James E. Combs and Dan Nimmo, *The New Propaganda* (New York: Longman, 1993); J. Michael Sproule, *Channels of Propaganda* (Bloomington, IN: ERIC/EDINFO, 1994).

12 Jay 1973; Horkheimer and Adorno 1972/1944; e.g., Jürgen Habermas, *Communication and the Evolution of Society*, trans. Thomas McCarthy (Boston: Beacon Press, 1979).

13 Michel Foucault, *The Archaeology of Knowledge and the Discourse on Language,* trans. A. M. Sheridan Smith (New York: Pantheon, 1972); Steven Best and Douglas Kellner, *Postmodern Theory* (New York: Guilford, 1991); John Fiske and John Hartley, *Reading Television* (London: Methuen, 1978); Fiske, *Television Culture* (London: Methuen, 1987).

14 Gitlin 1995; Paul Berman, ed., *Debating P.C.* (New York: Dell, 1992), 1–26.

15 Daphne Patai and Noretta Koertge, *Professing Feminism* (New York: Basic Books, 1994); Dinesh D'Souza, *The End of Racism* (New York: Free Press, 1995); Gitlin 1995.

NAME INDEX

Abrams, Ray H., 44, 50
Adams, Samuel H., 12
Addams, Jane, 112
Adler, Alfred, 130
Adorno, Theodor W., 79, 80, 155, 237, 254, 268
Aiken, George, 243
Albig, William, 32, 49, 66, 89, 259
Alfonso XIII, 24
Allen, George V., 212
Allen, Harland, 175
Allport, Floyd H., 62–63
Allport, Gordon W., 133, 139, 169, 180, 181–182
Ames, Edward S., 181
Anderson, Florence, 75–76, 231
Anderson, Marian, 212
Angell, James R., 181
Angell, Norman, 31
Angoff, Charles, 42
Aristotle, 28, 89, 211, 264
Arnold, Thurman W., 70, 102–103, 105–106
Aronson, Elliot, 267
Avila, Miguel, 121

Bachmann, Carl G., 123
Baker, Frank E., 130–131, 154, 166
Baker, Newton D., 6, 112, 113
Baker, Ray S., 22–24, 26, 235
Baldwin, Roger, 115, 124
Bales, Robert F., 218, 221
Barnes, Harry E., 133, 208
Barrett, Edward W., 210–211
Bartky, John A., 173
Barton, Bruce, 36–37
Bateson, Gregory, 180, 182, 218, 221
Bauer, Alice H., 234
Bauer, Raymond A., 234

Beale, Howard K., 100
Beals, Clyde, 163–167, 174, 177, 180, 183, 241
Beard, Charles A., 14, 15, 17, 19, 21, 37, 45, 121, 131, 160, 164, 168, 177, 208
Beardsley, Monroe C., 253
Becker, Carl, 17
Bell, Daniel, 240
Berelson, Bernard R., 186, 218, 220–221, 224–225, 228, 230, 231, 240
Berlin, Irving, 13
Berman, Paul, 269
Bernays, Edward L., 17–18, 22, 35, 41, 48, 49, 52, 56–59, 62, 74, 118, 130, 131, 139, 140, 160, 177, 183, 199, 207, 212–214, 222, 236, 258
Bernstein, Carl, 263
Bernstein, Leonard, 243
Biddle, William W., 63
Bingham, Alfred M., 163–166, 241
Birkhead, Leon M., 143, 147
Black, Max, 253
Blankenhorn, Heber, 18, 20, 44, 192
Blumenstock, Dorothy, 70
Blumer, Herbert, 44, 87–88, 205–206
Bogart, Leo, 213–214
Bohn, William E., 162
Borah, William E., 121
Bourne, Randolph, 9
Brady, Robert A., 138–139
Broun, Heywood, 13, 41
Browder, Earl, 115
Brown, Percy S., 113, 130, 131, 134, 162, 167, 174–175
Bruner, Jerome S., 215
Bryce, James, 7, 27, 30, 32
Bryson, Lyman L., 114, 117, 130
Buckley, William F., Jr., 266
Burgess, Ernest, 77, 250

SUBJECT INDEX

Printed in the United Kingdom
by Lightning Source UK Ltd.
107488UKS00001B/146